Theater and Film

Theater and Film

A Comparative Anthology

Edited by Robert Knopf

Yale University Press

New Haven and London

Published with assistance from the Louis Stern Memorial Fund.

Set in Adobe Garamond type by The Composing Room of Michigan, Inc.
Printed in the United States of America by Vail Ballou Press, Binghamton,
New York.

Library of Congress Cataloging-in-Publication Data
Knopf, Robert, 1961–
    Theater and film : a comparative anthology / edited by Robert Knopf.
        p. cm.
    Includes filmography.
    Includes bibliographical references and index.
    ISBN 0-300-10336-0 (pbk.: alk. paper)
    1. Motion pictures and theater.   I. Title.
    PN1995.25.K58 2004
    791.43'6—dc22

                                                        2004042046

A catalogue record for this book is available from the British Library.

The paper in this book meets the guidelines for permanence and durability
of the Committee on Production Guidelines for Book Longevity of the Council
on Library Resources.

10 9 8 7 6 5 4 3 2 1

For my children, Ally and Lara, who know a good performance
when they see one

Contents

Acknowledgments

I would like to thank the R. F. Johnson Fund and the Hodgkins Fund for providing the funds for the film stills that illustrate this book. I would also like to acknowledge the support of the ConnSharp Fund for Faculty-Student Research Partnerships. My research assistants, Mary Ellen Osborne, Kristin Knapp, and Jeremy Make were invaluable in helping me locate potential essays for this volume and organize the massive amount of bibliographic as well as filmographic data. Cara Gabriel, Anthony Cantrell, and Vanessa Luke contributed greatly to the organization and preparation of the manuscript. My editors, Lauren Shapiro and Harry Haskell, and my copyeditor, Joyce Ippolito, provided invaluable editorial assistance and support throughout the process. James Welsh's suggestions and support helped me broaden the appeal and comprehensiveness of this volume. And my wife, Elizabeth Pascal, was unbelievably patient in reading drafts of the introduction more times than any one reasonable person would or should.

Last, my thanks to my parents, Richard and Florence Knopf, for always letting me stay up late to watch the end of the movie.

Introduction

Robert Knopf

For as long as film has existed, comparisons have been made between the ancient mother, theater, and her youthful offspring, film. The two media have a lot in common, not the least of which is that their predominant end has been storytelling. Yet the two differ in many ways as well, most of which have been noted by the critics and theorists found in this book, who have carried on a scholarly debate that extends over the greater part of the twentieth century. At base, we can probably all agree that theater is live and exists in the moment, whereas film consists of a performance or story preserved, indeed most would say *constructed,* on celluloid.

Traditionally, the study of most theater-and-film courses has centered on the adaptation of dramatic texts to film, and it is precisely this focus that *Theater and Film: A Comparative Anthology* aims to challenge. For the adaptation of plays to film is a small, albeit significant, portion of artists' and scholars' investigation of the relationship between theater and film—a relationship that begins with the birth of film in 1895, when the earliest showings were exhibited in theatrical houses and, a short while later, as "acts" within vaudeville bills.[1] The

1

time has come to broaden the scope of this inquiry by expanding the "lens" through which we view theater and film. For this reason, the essays in this volume focus less on adaptation and more on the economic, aesthetic, cultural, and technological relationships between theater and film. To examine theater and film in this context, we must therefore look beyond the products—the theatrical performance and the cinematic screening—toward the interweaving of influence and differentiation between the two media, to borrow the terminology (first used by A. Nicholas Vardac) that had its roots in the days of pre-film and early cinema.[2] Only by doing so can we see the complexity of this relationship, which extends far beyond the initial question of how to transfer a story from one medium to another.

Vardac was the first, or at least the most prominent, scholar to note that cinema's precursor may be detected in the spectacle theater of the nineteenth century. As he states in this volume, there was a cultural push toward a realist-romantic aesthetic that first developed in melodrama and spectacle theater. A growing cultural desire to see the world in precise detail, to locate the audience as closely as possible to both the spectacular and the everyday, created, in a sense, the appetite for the invention of film. For despite all of the advances of the nineteenth-century stage—seen most clearly in the stage spectacles and melodramas of Steele MacKaye, Henry Irving, and David Belasco—film could bring audiences to places they could not travel and position them closer to events than might otherwise be safe in person.

The historical section of this anthology therefore sets up the give-and-take between the two media and seeks to help students and scholars of theater and film chart the course of the technological, aesthetic, and economic interaction between the two media. Film was initially, and in many cases still is, considered the more visual medium. Yet how much of this bias comes from the simple fact that the first films were silent? Not truly silent, for music, either recorded or live, accompanied most "silent" films, and words were relegated to intertitles, literally detaching the dialogue from the characters. Conversely, how much of the bias toward seeing theater as the more verbal medium stems from the fact that the first twenty-five hundred years of Western theatrical production disappeared into thin air, not preserved by the camera and leaving predominantly one concrete trace of its existence—the script?[3] So, even though early Greek tragedy and comedy were frequently filled with the spectacle of masks and a dancing chorus, as well as the sound of music (now lost to the ages), and even though silent theater predates the more language-based theater of Aeschylus,

Sophocles, Euripides, and their brethren,[4] theater is often categorized as the more verbal, or text-based medium.

Yet the assumption seems to linger that film is primarily a visual medium and theater primarily a verbal one. Certainly this need not be the case. We need look no further than Julie Taymor's productions—for example, *The Lion King* (1997) and *The Green Bird* (2000)—for a predominantly visual theater and Neil LaBute's films—such as *In the Company of Men* (1997) and *Your Friends and Neighbors* (1998)—for a predominantly verbal cinema. Both these artists, moreover, have shown themselves able to switch media and emphasis with ease. So where does this initial and enduring visual-verbal assumption come from? Most scholars have accepted the notion that these qualities are inherent in the media, but I prefer to categorize their view as just one "lens"—a particular way of looking at the issue that shapes the conclusions one may draw. Instead, I would like to propose a historical explanation for the widespread belief that film is inherently visual and theater is inherently verbal. First, let us examine the assumption that theater is a verbal medium.

Although many contemporary theater historians suggest precursors to theater in shamanism, Egyptian rituals, and other "primitive" performances, for just as many the ancient Greek theater remains the first truly significant one that we can fully imagine. Why? Because it is the first theater with a significant number of extant scripts. Greek theater also claims the first significant drama critic and theorist: Aristotle. Both the preservation of scripts and Aristotle's *Poetics* (ca. 335–323 B.C.) lead us to think of the "great" contributions of theater as words, scripts, plots, and characters. The scripts can be revived, retranslated, and reimagined. And Aristotle, in ranking his six elements of theater, put text-based elements of theater (plot, character, thought, and language) in the top positions and visual and sensual elements (music, spectacle) in the bottom two spots. Aristotle's relative rankings of dramatic and theatrical elements may be explained, in part, by the fact that he was writing approximately one hundred years after the great Greek tragedians had written and produced their plays. Many scholars have pointed out that the quality of theatrical production in Aristotle's time had declined, and for this reason among others he preferred scripts to productions. The time has come to put aside these useful, though perhaps outdated, assumptions and examine the relationship between theater and film afresh.

Even if we look at each medium and examine its supposed strengths and weaknesses, the medium does not irrevocably determine the form of any par-

Fig. 1. Buster Keaton in *Sherlock, Jr.* (1924). Keaton drew his influences from vaudeville magicians, combining their magic acts with new cinematic techniques that he and his cameraman invented to create new screen magic. Courtesy of BFI Stills, Posters and Designs.

ticular film or play. Whereas it is true that many playwrights and screenwriters write with the medium, and often particular actors, theaters, and production companies, in mind—the most famous example being none other than William Shakespeare, who wrote his plays with the Lord Chamberlain's Men and the Globe in mind—it may be most useful and liberating for artists, scholars, critics, and students to see conditions of production as a challenge rather than a limitation. Whenever something appears to be impossible in theater or film, someone invents a way to make it happen anyhow. And it is through productions that creatively cross the border between what was considered impossible, and what is then found to be realizable, that both media grow and change.

Film may offer greater visual possibilities, but that does not prevent theater professor-turned-film director Neil LaBute from writing screenplays that are as highly verbal as his plays.[5] At the same time, it would be difficult if not impossible to categorize some of the most exciting and popular theater in New York as verbal. What of Bill Irwin's "new vaudeville" pieces, *Largely New York* (1989) and *Fool Moon* (1993), productions that are virtually silent? What of experiential and nearly nonverbal productions such as Blue Man Group's *Tubes* (1991) and De La Guarda's *Villa Villa* (1998), both still running as of 2003 to sold-out houses? These productions do not happen to be successful in spite of their neglect of the supposed strengths of their chosen medium. It is, to my mind, precisely by choosing to overcome the limitations of their medium that these artists achieve success, for what greater thrill can there be than to see either art form transcend the boundaries that we have become accustomed to assigning to it?

In her seminal essay "Film and Theater," Susan Sontag concludes that most scholars and critics see theater and film as either inherently separate or inherently interchangeable. Thus, for most scholars and critics, film is film and theater is theater, or film can be theatrical and theater can be cinematic, points of view that are problematic only to the extent that any one individual makes claims to "truth" and fails to recognize that the relative balance between the verbal and the visual is a matter of choice, regardless of medium. By comparison, Sontag calls for a new notion of the relationship between film and theater without proposing one, thereby provocatively challenging us: "We need a new idea. It will probably be a very simple one. Will we be able to recognize it?"[6] What might this new idea be, and how might we go about discovering it? This anthology is structured on the premise that a new notion of the relationship between theater and film must be based not only on the history and theory of the two media but also on the contributions of the artists who have been most influential in them; that the inherent differences in the media provide different options but do not predetermine what kind of film or theater can be created; and that there is no single "idea" that can answer Sontag's bold challenge. Rather, there is a multiplicity of answers, and the scholar's or artist's journey toward a particular answer will ultimately be personal, depending upon the "lens" through which he or she views the two media.

To the above, I would add one more observation: both media are constantly changing in terms of technology, style, economics, and their influence on each other. For example, one of the most-quoted, though probably apocryphal, tales of early cinema concerns the first Parisian audience's viewing of film footage of a train coming into a station in the Lumière brothers' *Arrival of the Paris Express* (1895). As the story goes, audience members screamed when the train appeared to come toward them, temporarily unable to distinguish palpable reality from cinematic imagery. In those early days of film, its novelty as technological in-novation was its principal draw. Yet film does not have a monopoly on new technology; theater has been swayed by its own flirtation with technology and special effects. The first audiences who saw *Miss Saigon* had a sensation similar to the Lumières' audience when a helicopter appeared to land on a Broadway stage.[7] For this reason, all claims to the inherent discreteness of theater and film as media are spurious and subject to the yet-to-be-seen influences of future technological innovation on both these art forms.

In 1917, when Hugo Münsterberg observed that theater is bound by causal-ity whereas film is not, the use of simultaneous action and non-causal action on the avant-garde stage had just begun. By 2003, the computerized light boards of contemporary theater, which allow easy cross-fades from one location to an-other, have changed the nature of theater as a medium and continue to revolu-tionize it, so that Münsterberg's observation becomes less and less accurate with time.[8] And with today's generation of young playwrights having been raised on film, plays are no longer being written predominantly in the "well-made-play" form. Episodic theater, jumping from place to place and time to time, is on the rise—though anticipated by medieval mystery plays by a mere five hundred years or so. And with the Internet encouraging contemporary artists to see time and place as non-linear, I believe we can expect further experimentation with shifts of time and place in new drama and film.[9]

If there is an inherent quality of theater that I would isolate at this point, it is the fact that theater performance, by virtue of its "live-ness," disappears as soon as it is spoken, leaving texts (scripts) as the primary record and most widely consumed "artifact" of the theatrical event. Film performance, by nature of its preservation on celluloid and now videotape and DVD, is kept "alive" in a way that theater performance, even in the best-taped performances or in written documentation, cannot be.[10] The cinematic artifact, therefore, is the film itself, whereas the theatrical artifact is the script.

Yet the theatrical artifact (the text), though subject to exhaustive and (occa-sionally exhausting) scholarly debate, should not be confused with the theatri-cal product, whereas the cinematic artifact *is* the product. Plays and films are made to be seen, and therefore the focus on the dramatic text shines the spot-light on the words to a degree that is not always commensurate with their sig-nificance in production.[11] With the possible exception of the plays of Shake-speare, Oscar Wilde, and perhaps George Bernard Shaw, theater audiences by and large remember fully realized, staged moments of a play with greater fre-quency than lines from the text. All of which begs the question, why is theater considered the more verbal form and, even if it is, does this change the theater's capacity in any significant way?

I believe that the answer lies in the way that plays and screenplays develop into production and films. For the dramatic text leaves open a multitude of interpretations during its artistic life, and these interpretations can be realized in production without rewriting a word of the script. Films, however, are sometimes remade, and this process rarely, if ever, has been based word-for-word on the original screenplay—a fact indicating that play texts are viewed, at least by a significant minority, as sacrosanct, whereas screenplays are not. Yet this need not be the case, and the overall validity of this generalization tells us more about the power of producers, directors, and writers in each medium. A theater director like the late Jerzy Grotowski, who used to adapt or radically reinterpret other playwrights' texts, is labeled "experimental" (among other adjectives), whereas a filmmaker such as Martin Scorsese can completely rewrite a movie like *Cape Fear,* and his "remake" has its own legitimacy as a separate work of art. Whether a cinematic remake has any more independent validity as a work of art than an experimental theater production can be examined only on a case-by-case basis, however. I would observe, moreover, that theater produces a greater number and range of interpretations of its most esteemed scripts than film does of any of its screenplays.

One dominant quality to which both film and theater have often aspired is life-likeness—what often comes under the terms "realism," "naturalism," or simply representationalism. Indeed, it has often been said that theater's ability to mimic reality has been surpassed by film, because films can capture behavior in actual environments to an extent nearly impossible in theater. Whereas theater enthusiasts could point to the sensory appeal of theater—its ability to communicate to all five senses of the audience—as evidence of its greater life-likeness, film lovers will counter with film's capacity to bring the audience closer to the actors' behavior, in circumstances that are "real" and not "staged." Yet theater and film have always tried to claim, and still do claim, representationalism or life-likeness as their own special province. From the earliest days of film, we clearly see *theatrical* innovators such as André Antoine, Konstantin Stanislavsky, and Duke of Saxe-Meiningen experimenting with numerous ways of making the theater more lifelike. Antoine put carcasses of beef on stage in *The Butchers* (1888), Stanislavsky incorporated extensive environmental sound in his productions of Anton Chekhov's plays at the Moscow Art Theater, and as early as the mid-nineteenth century the Duke of Saxe-Meiningen used real trees, rocks, and foliage on many of his sets.

At the same time, film's first significant achievements occur both in the realm of representationalism (in the Lumière brothers' short, slice-of-life films, such as *Arrival of the Paris Express* and *Passengers Descending from the Brooklyn Bridge* [1896]) and in the realm of fantasy (in the magical films of George Méliès, such as *A Trip to the Moon* [1902]). And while early film artists were exploring these two possible directions for cinematic art, theatrical realism was being challenged by the non-realistic experiments of the avant-garde, seen first in the Symbolist theater of the 1890s and then in the bizarre antics of Alfred Jarry's character King Ubu, who first appeared on the professional stage in 1896. So, from the beginning, both media displayed the capability of achieving realism or non-realism. And because some of the earliest exhibitions of films occurred in vaudeville houses, interspersed between live variety acts, we can see that either medium was able to contribute "variety" to vaudeville's already wide range of styles. The economic competition and technological developments of the two media thus result in their being polarized at times, drawn together at others, like two magnets whose ends either meet or repel.

For example, the greater economic pressure on film, caused by film's larger audiences, led Hollywood to adopt a more realistic and cost-effective norm, as Bordwell, Staiger, and Thompson have convincingly argued.[12] Theater is bound less by such economic factors, as the audience for any production is much smaller and therefore so are the budgets and financial risks. Avant-garde theater, which tends to be lower budget, can take greater chances, whereas Broadway and the West End productions are confined by the financial risks of their larger budgets. Only a project with a guaranteed audience, like *The Lion King,* finally brought the work of the experimental director Julie Taymor to Broadway and West End audiences. Artistically, the two media influence each other, then, while economically they push each other further apart in an effort to carve out their own niche and audience.

Technological innovations (at the time, some would have called them "changes," but not truly innovations) like the introduction of spoken words to films, which becomes the dominant practice between 1926 and 1929, change the relationship of these two media or magnets, as I have referred to them above.[13] Once sound recordings of dialogue became the norm in film, Hollywood needed scripts with extensive dialogue—not merely because Hollywood wished to take advantage of sound's capabilities but also because the earliest sound equipment required indoor studio sets and nearly static camera work to preserve the quality of the recording. Combined with audiences' interest in seeing actors speak, the static camera thus impelled studios toward dialogue-driven films in an effort to meet audience demand for "talkies" while keeping movies at least verbally dynamic. As the technological innovations in sound created a market for dialogue, Hollywood began to raid every easily accessible source for dialogue-focused narrative and drama, including the theater's troves of plays. And as Hollywood looked to theater for scripts, theater needed to compete directly with film studios for dramas and comedies that primarily depended upon dialogue while also searching for other forms and additional qualities it could call its own. Thus the attraction-repulsion between theater and film continued, with their supposed strengths temporarily reversed— while theater explored the visual and the spectacular, film (at least in the early 1930s) found its "voice" in its first extensive use of dialogue.

Several of the essays in this anthology try to come to grips with the long-standing tensions between spectacle and narrative (be it silent or spoken) that emerged during the early period of competition between theater and film. Whereas Vardac explores the roots of cinema in theater, Tom Gunning looks at the earliest cinema, from 1895 to 1906–08—sometimes called "primitive cinema"—and traces its aesthetic backward to the theatrical "montage of attractions" (a phrase first coined by Vsevold Meyerhold and the theater-turned-film director Sergei Eisenstein) and forward to the avant-gardes of the 1910s and 1920s. The "attractions" of the cinema of attractions are moments of spectacle that break free from narrative—an impulse that, by 1906–07, "goes underground" into the cinematic avant-garde, as well as into certain genres of film like musicals, which "contain" them within safer narrative confines.[14] Gunning also connects the "primitive" cinema to the vaudeville aesthetic of early sound films as well as the cinema of Busby Berkeley and Buster Keaton, suggesting the path for future work by Henry Jenkins, Martin Rubin, and myself.[15] Gunning is very adept, too, at linking early cinema's interest in sensation to both Eisenstein's and F. T. Marinetti's interest in the aesthetics of shock, comparing the sensational spectacle of "primitive" film to the more aggressive interaction between the performers and the audience found in early avant-garde theater.

Rubin takes up the argument about the tension between narrative and spectacle started by Gunning and relates it to film musicals. Rubin connects the "aggregate forms" popularized by P. T. Barnum's dime museum and three-ring circus, as well as by minstrel shows and vaudeville, to the Berkleyesque movie musical, and we might go further in connecting these forms to contemporary theatrical "experiences" such as Blue Man Group, Cirque du Soleil, and De La Guarda, which place a premium on spectacle and experience over narrative values. There is almost no narrative involved in the work of these three groups; instead, the audience's shifting experience from moment to moment creates a shape or an arc that substitutes for story. Or, to put the matter another way, the experience of the audience *is* the story. Thus, when the Blue Men in *Tubes* drive audience members into a frenzy through their mounting interaction with them, a non-narrative climax occurs through experience alone—an experience that has been built throughout the performance by the Group's continually topping each event or attraction (as Eisenstein and Meyerhold would term it) with something even more physically, visually, or musically aggressive or spectacular. And this type of structure owes much to all the following: "primitive" cinema, the early theatrical and cinematic avant-gardes, and slapstick cinema.

My own essay deals with the ways in which Buster Keaton, Harold Lloyd, and Charlie Chaplin blended slapstick with traditional narrative to navigate the transition from short- to feature-length slapstick comedy. I examine how their theatrical backgrounds and the types of work they did on the vaudeville and music hall stages formed each artist's approach to this transition. Such a dynamic can still be found in the films of such contemporary stand-up comics as Jim Carrey, Chris Rock, and Roseanne, martial artists like Jackie Chan, multimedia superstars like Madonna, and such athletes as Shaquille O'Neill, Dennis Rodman, and in decades past, O. J. Simpson(!), where the celebrity of the actor and his or her original field of expertise bring a material self-referentiality to the celluloid performance that disrupts the narrative by the weight they exert on our consciousness.[16]

Whereas the historical relationship between theater and film, established in the earliest days of cinema, exerted a strong influence on the development of each medium through aesthetic cross-fertilization and differentiation, economic competition, and the establishment of classical Hollywood cinema production norms in imitation of their equivalents in realistic theater, an equally important relationship was occurring between acting for the camera and acting on the stage. Many scholars have noted, for example, that amateur actors can turn in successful performances on film, whereas this is rarely the case on stage in a featured role. Several reasons for this are apparent. Unlike film, the stage requires the actor to display vocal power and performance stamina. A theater actor must "fill the house," whereas the same performance on film can be smaller yet still be captured by the intimate intrusion of the camera. A theater actor must sustain a character over an entire performance, night after night, whereas the same performance on film can be captured in bits, over several takes, until the director has found the exact movement and intonation desired. And a theater actor must find an arc to a role that the process of filming, in which scenes are often shot out of order, almost completely impedes. Filming nonsequentially breaks up the performance and reduces the actor's ability to find a character arc. But who says it needs to be this way? Historical practice is just that: practice. It is not set in stone. To the contrary, the minute practice becomes set, someone usually comes along to unsettle it, lest habit cause art to die and the blood in its veins to dry up.

The claim is often made that film uncovers a deeper character psychology for its audience by its use of the close-up and the tracking of an individual's point of view throughout a film. Münsterberg, for example, argued that screenplays create a harmony that reflects the "inner movement of the mind" through detail, cross-cuts, and flashbacks.[17] Yet these techniques can be found as far back as Elizabethan England in the plays of Shakespeare and his contemporaries, who achieved the same "movement" through much more modest means: shifting place and time by "cross-fading" from one scene to another on stage; displaying the "inner mind" through the use of soliloquy; and moving backward in time through the "flashback" of a history play. Once again we see that although one medium may have an easier time achieving a style or effect, little is beyond the reach of the other; in fact, theater and film anticipate each other's techniques, suggest them, perhaps even create a hunger in each other to match or exceed its rival through different means. In writing this, I come to the verge of attributing an anthropomorphic presence to the two media, as if they were living creatures growing with age. Perhaps they are, for theater and film begin to take on lives of their own, the old interwoven with the new, influencing each other through their collective development and innovation, grafting techniques onto their "bodies" so as to find out what will grow and what will die. If one wishes to remain essentialist, one may argue for the inherent strengths of a medium, but the fact remains that the only absolute limitation on the aesthetics of film and theater lies in as yet unrealized advances of technology and the boundaries of the individual artist's imagination.

When we debate whether drama or cinema achieves a particular effect, style, or characterization more effectively than its rival, we thus reveal more of our own preferences—the "lens" through which we frame and view these two media—than we uncover essential, immutable truths about theater and film. For example, we tend to think of cinema as a director's medium, yet must it be? I would argue that there are ways to temper the film director's artistic control. To wit: when the filming of *Smoke* (1995) was complete, the company still had eight days left of shooting budget and film stock, so several of the actors stayed on to improvise the "sequel," *Blue in the Face* (1995), joined by friends of the cast and the directors. Although the sequel is very loosely constructed by Hollywood standards, there is an incredible freshness (though some might see this as a fault) to seeing actors improvise and create before the camera in the same way that some of the earliest silent filmmakers did. Keaton was fond of saying that he didn't really need a complete script—just give him a beginning and an ending and he would find the middle as he filmed. This is the type of filmmaking to which *Blue in the Face* harkens back, and the freedom that it provides allows none other than Michael J. Fox, as down-and-out fast talker Pete Maloney, to create an extraordinary monologue recorded with an almost completely static camera and few or no cuts. Perhaps even more strikingly, Harvey Keitel's improvised work in *Blue in the Face* is virtually indistinguishable from his performance in *Smoke,* as the same character, the owner of a Brooklyn cigar shop—which makes one of the most accomplished American actors of the stage and screen an *auteur* in his own right.

Smoke is a deceptively simple film about storytelling, plot, and character—Aristotle's old favorites—and the camera by and large remains content "merely" to capture the actors' work, in the same way that Keitel, as the central figure, takes a snapshot of his corner cigar shop every day for years, merely trying to record its daily image without comment. Is his own performance psychologically deeper due to its recording on film and its construction in the cutting room? I don't think so. Would it have the same power and depth on stage? I believe so. Would Keitel modulate the size of his performance if he were to transfer it to the stage? Almost certainly, depending upon the size of the theater. So we are left with the paradox that an extraordinary performance might work in similar ways in either medium, should the actor and director choose to approach it the same way in each.

Allardyce Nicoll argues that, counter to what he assumes we would at first think, stage acting is more typified and less "real" than film acting—not because of the style of acting, but because the audience remains aware of the fact that the actors are performing in a theater. Therefore, watching an actor in the theater, we see "imaginative illusion" rather than an illusion of reality.[18] And, of course, this raises the very real issue of realism on the stage: can the stage ever achieve as effective an illusion of reality as the cinema? Perhaps not, but this depends upon how we define the illusion of reality and what elements of reality are most important to a successful illusion for a particular viewer.[19] In terms of its three-dimensionality, theater achieves life-likeness that film cannot approach, even in 3D IMAX. So the essential paradox of "realism/life-likeness" remains an issue for both media: whereas theater is inherently more lifelike because it occurs live and in three dimensions, the presence of three-dimensional actors in a theater—a "non-real" space—may undercut the production's resemblance to life at the same time that the actors increase its "liveness." Yet both media have responded to the challenge to "be real." While film experimented with three dimensions through the use of multicolored eyeglasses, experimental theater groups such as the Living Theater, the Open Theater, Grotowski's Polish Laboratory Theater, and the Performance Group created environmental theater, which tried to overcome theater's spatial limitations by using an existing environment that was as close to reality as possible, or by designing such an environment—one that envelops the audience, thereby erasing the distinction between viewing space and playing area.[20]

Expanding his argument on the limitations of theater in relation to film, Nicoll puts forward the idea that theater cannot be as psychologically "deep" as the cinema, due to film's ability to express a subjective point of view. But I think theater reaches a similar depth in a different way: through dialogue, direct address and soliloquies, and the physical presence of the actor. Is Nicoll privileging visual subjectivity as an indicator of psychological depth? And why is film's subjective, visual point of view necessarily superior in psychological depth to the theater's use of language?[21] Nicoll proceeds to propose that the "rediscovery of convention" will save theater, contrasting convention with naturalism, which he views as the death of theater. I agree that the rediscovery of convention can be a valuable contribution to new theater, but Nicoll overstates his case and neglects the importance of "artistic quality" in this formulation.[22] He holds up Greek and Elizabethan theater as exemplary models of convention-conscious theater, emphasizing their acknowledgment of the audience—though surely the quality of this work is not based solely on this element—but he neglects to acknowledge the powerful appeal of cinematic voyeurism and of future, related voyeurisms that he could not have anticipated.

As I write this in late 2003, we live in an age of "virtual" voyeurism: Internet chat, video and DVD, large, widescreen televisions in our own homes with surround-sound systems that compete with the best movie palaces. And theater provides a purer form of this voyeurism, which is one of the reasons that theater has come under attack through the centuries. I say "purer" because in theater things are what they are—relative to other new media, at the very least. If we consider the by now oft-told, turn-of-the-millennium Internet joke, "On the Internet, no one knows that you're a dog," I think it is fair to say that on the stage, to deliberately misquote Gertrude Stein, a dog is a dog is a dog, even if it is representing a person. This statement holds a good deal of practical truth, because audience members may interpret the dead goat at the end of Edward Albee's *The Goat or Who Is Sylvia?* (2002) as a stand-in for a gay lover (if one is looking for such symbolism, or reading it into the play on the basis of Albee's life) at the same time that they see what appears to be a real (albeit dead) goat on the stage. Alternatively, when Sarah Jessica Parker played a dog in the New York production of A. R. Gurney's *Sylvia* in 1995 (why are both animals named Sylvia, I wonder?), the audience accepted her as a stand-in for a dog, while always acutely aware that the actress was human. This argument, along with the Internet joke I have used as a jumping-off point, will date with new technological innovations, but that's precisely the point: new technologies will force us constantly to revise our appraisal of the relationship between film and theater.

For André Bazin, absolute identification of the cinema audience with characters produces a mass mentality within the audience, whereas the live presence of the actor in theater keeps identification to a minimum. Therefore, he sees theater as more moral and the theater spectator as more active. In the process, Bazin appears to argue that psychological depth and the audience's identification with a character are one and the same. Yet such depth may come at the cost of the audience's critical sense and active participation in the creation of an imaginary world. I would note that, though Bazin sees these as the dominant tendencies in the two media—cinematic empathy versus theatrical distance— he understands that these tendencies can be overcome or compensated for in a particular theatrical production or film.

Sontag inquires whether the two arts are in "opposition" and notes that many scholar-critics see the history of cinema "as the history of its emancipation from theatrical models," first from frontality, second from exaggerated acting, and third from theatrical furnishings—thus, a move toward "naturalness" or "fluidity."[23] She sees television as capable of making film into "another performing art to be transcribed, miniaturized on film."[24] But by 2003, Sontag's view of television has already been rendered obsolete by the advent of large-screen HDTV, "home theaters," and DVDs. The creative endeavors pouring out of HBO, including original movies, theatrical adaptations like *Wit* (2001), *The Laramie Project* (2002), and *Angels in America* (2003), as well as "cinematic" television programs—by which I mean television that is virtually indistinguishable from film in terms of style, image, and sound quality, like *The Sopranos, Sex and the City,* and *Six Feet Under*—meanwhile further blur the line between television and film.[25]

So why is it that we equate the static camera with theater? Theater is staged—with the exception of environmental staging—for a static audience because it must be or because convention demands it, but the camera need not be static. If theater spectators had their choice, would they choose to remain static? And why, if the camera may free itself of stasis, must the static camera be deemed "theatrical"? I could make the claim that film is a derivative of theater and, in some ways, an advance on it. In fact, classical Hollywood cinema derived many of its structural techniques from the well-made play, and the theatrical avant-garde pre-dates the cinematic avant-garde and indeed the invention of film by several years. So why should we view film as a completely separate, opposed, and unique art when the history of its interaction with theater suggests that film does not consistently function or exist in this way?

Sontag is quite right in observing that most scholar-critics who favor the strict division between theater and film define cinema, on the basis of its silent roots, as image with sound added (essentially a visual medium) and theater as "plays," language-strong and plot-heavy, perhaps because we tend to think of theater as language—or scripts with visuals. But either definition is descriptive of the majority practice in each medium, not of the inherent qualities of each. For what is film but celluloid that can, but need not, capture image and sound? Or, to quote Buster Keaton, "There's nothing wrong with talkies that a little silence couldn't fix." And what is theater but a space that audience and actors inhabit together for a period of time, to share an event?

It seems to me that reductive notions of film and theater tend to inhibit our realization of the influence of the two on each other, whereas expansive notions increase our realization of that mutual influence. And the simple truth is that today's theater artists all watch films, so there's no fighting the influence of film on theater, except as a choice by an individual artist who avoids this influence like Thoreau in the wild. Not all of today's film artists see theater, alas, but they should—not to raid the theater of its most promising artists, as television and film have been doing for years, but to appropriate the creative techniques that theater constantly invents so as to overcome the limitations of its medium.

Perhaps when all is said and done, the influence of theater and film on each other may be best seen as the intermingling of high art and popular art, the trading of elements and stylistic conventions back and forth over the decades, tempered (or tempted) by technological innovation. I am partial to Stanley Kauffmann's comparison, at the end of his essay, between drama and cinema: "The crucial historical difference between theater and film is this: the theater began as a sacred event and eventually included the profane. The film began as a profane event and eventually included the sacred."[26] And perhaps the different limitations of each medium recast its potential approaches to the same dramatic material, be it sacred or profane. Yes, there may be stories that are better told by film or by theater—at least by a particular artist in either medium—but the best artists merely see the qualities of each medium as a challenge to find its other strengths, potential styles, and possible techniques. Instead of seeing these qualities as limitations, many theater and film artists both use and overcome the supposedly "inherent" qualities of the medium within which they choose to work. It is precisely this ability to think "beyond the box," or in this case beyond the screen or space, that frequently defines the most innovative and influential work in either medium.

I would note as well that whereas realism finds its ultimate form with the invention of cinema in 1895, the avant-garde in theater begins in earnest between 1890 (with Symbolism) and 1896, with the premiere of *Ubu the King*. It may be that avant-garde theater was one reaction to the usurping of realism by film. Moreover, just as classical Hollywood cinema came together as an economic system and aesthetic style in the 1920s, the dramatic avant-garde reached the height of its popularity (if you can call it that) with the flowering of Futurism, Dada, and Surrealism. Thus, the chaos of destruction visited upon the world in the First World War may have shifted film toward wishful systems of order (classical Hollywood cinema), while theater experimented with purposeful disorder (the avant-garde). And certainly economics plays a part in this polarization as well: the costlier the medium and more institutionalized the industry, the less experimental and politically subversive the range of creative output. Yet the two media never totally diverge.

Griffith goes furthest in formally separating film from theater. In his essay "Some Prophecies," he anticipates computers and CD-ROMs as learning devices and storehouses of information, with their emphasis on seeing things rather than reading them. In making such a strong case for the independence of filmmaking as an art, is Griffith right? Or was this essay written at a moment of historical necessity, when filmmakers needed to stand up for filmmaking as an art, independent of its competing, older stepsisters, the novel and the drama?

And yet, despite his stated preference for film, Griffith emerges as an important figure in the interaction between theater and film, and as an apt "prophet" of the technological advances to come, which I predict will continue to push apart and pull together these two media in relationship to one another. The montage techniques made famous by Soviet filmmakers, for instance, were presaged by Eisenstein and Meyerhold's use of similar techniques on the stage. The fluidity the camera can produce by moving through space can be seen as creating an increased interest in non-proscenium stage configurations in theater, beginning with a return to the earliest stage configuration, theater-in-the-round or arena staging, in the mid-twentieth century and followed by the more frequent use of thrust staging and even environmental theater from the 1960s on.

These days theater audiences can see Sam Mendes's long-running production of *Cabaret* (which began as fiction, then was transformed into a "straight" play, a musical one, and finally a film version) performed in a cabaret theater setting in New York's former Studio 54. They can watch actors perform above the audience and even lift them high in the air in De La Guarda's *Villa Villa.* In the cinematic world, films like *Run Lola Run* (1999) offer alternative endings, effectively demonstrating to the audience that film, like life, can turn out in different ways depending on a single choice at a particular moment in time. At the same time, film's special effects have become so lifelike that in a reversal of what purportedly occurred at the first screening of the Lumières' *Arrival of the Paris Express,* when the first footage of the attack on the World Trade Center was shown on television—captured from a myriad of angles by hundreds of personal video cameras—it was virtually indistinguishable from what Hollywood studios could have manufactured for a picture such as *Armageddon* (1998). When film becomes this close to life, is it therefore lifelike, or has reality started to resemble a film? When video games of mass annihilation are found in the bedrooms of children who have donned ski masks and shot their schoolmates, as two teenagers did at Colorado's Columbine High School, is there an uncomfortable moment when we realize that some of our children (and perhaps some adults) can no longer tell the difference between created images and reality?

All of this leads me to think about what the cinematic as well as theatrical future may hold. For as Løvborg says in Ibsen's *Hedda Gabler* (1890), though it may be hard to imagine what the future holds, "There may be one or two things worth saying about it anyhow."[27] I believe that technology will continue to have the greatest influence on how films are made, and that theater and cinema will continue to absorb, reject, and react to each other's innovations. When I look ahead and imagine thousands of homes with large, widescreen televisions and surround-sound, I wonder who will go to the multiplexes of today, which themselves made obsolete the movie palaces and drive-ins of yesteryear. I believe that in a short time most films will be viewed at home and that the multiplex will become the nearly exclusive province of families and teenagers (this trend has started already).

If I am right, and films become a predominantly private experience, shared by small groups in living rooms, what might then become of theater? Will the experimental theater groups of the future perform in our living rooms, or will the desire for human contact and community drive us back to more traditional theaters? Or will 3D IMAX be replaced by holographic film, creating three-dimensional worlds that we can walk into, until we eventually "holographize" old films (just as we colorize them now) and offer audience members the chance to sit down with Rick in *Casablanca* (1942), have a drink, and say, "Play it again, Sam." We learn from the past as we imagine a future that cannot accurately be predicted, because technology, culture, economic pressures, and the events of the world are beyond the power of any one person to control. But that shouldn't stop us from making art and creating living stories, for the power of theater and film to help us make sense of the world, or sometimes simply to escape from it, will remain potent no matter what form these media take.

NOTES

1. Charles Musser, *The Emergence of Cinema: The American Screen to 1907* (New York: Charles Scribner's Sons, 1990), 273.
2. *Stage to Screen: Theatrical Method from Garrick to Griffith* (Cambridge, Mass.: Harvard University Press, 1949).
3. In point of fact, our understanding of Greek theater scripts is skewed by the vagaries of historical preservation, since even our possession of these artifacts of Greek performance is a matter of chance, having more to do with which scripts survived the ages than anything else.
4. The earliest Greek theater was actually performed without dialogue by Doric mimes in the sixth century B.C., a full century prior to the plays of Aeschylus. See *History of the Theater*, by Oscar G. Brockett with Franklin J. Hildy, 8th ed. (Boston: Allyn and Bacon, 1999), 21.
5. See *bash: Latterday Plays* (Faber & Faber, 2001) and *The Shape of Things* (Faber & Faber, 2001) for the plays of Neil LaBute. The screenplay of *In the Company of Men* (1997) is unpublished, whereas the script of *Your Friends and Neighbors* (1998) was published by Faber and Faber in 1999.
6. See page 151 in this volume.
7. The stage helicopter weighed 8,700 pounds and was 75 percent of the size of the actual helicopter used in Viet Nam (source: *www.miss-saigon.com*). For an explanation of the mechanics of the helicopter on stage, see *www.sceneplay.com/reviews/MissSaigon*.
8. Such are the vagaries, over the decades, of critical authorship. This does not mean that criticism like Hugo Münsterberg's should be summarily discarded or blithely ignored but rather that such criticism itself must be viewed critically—or contextually. Hence, because Münsterberg's book *The Film: A Psychological Study* (1916) has dated, I have elected not to include an excerpt from it in this collection.
9. Although film has always embraced its inherent ability to shift place and time rapidly,

films such as *Run Lola Run* (1999) have extended this "fluidity" to include alternative streams or chronologies of action, dependent upon which character's perspective or choice of action is being adopted at any given moment.

10. As in all generalizations, there are exceptions to this rule. Jonathan Demme's *Swimming to Cambodia* (1987) is an excellent film of Spalding Gray's one-man theatrical performance. For those scholars interested in seeing the best video documentation of contemporary theater, the video collection at the Lincoln Center Library for the Performing Arts provides an invaluable service by preserving several thousand videotapes of significant New York productions since the 1970s, available for viewing at the Library with advance notice.

11. This depends, to a great extent, on the nature of the script and the approach to its production. A realistic script is more likely to convey a similar directorial sensibility in the majority of its productions than a nonrealistic one.

12. See *The Classical Hollywood Cinema* (New York: Columbia University Press, 1985).

13. Although *The Jazz Singer* (1927) was the first talking feature, short sound films were first exhibited in 1926 and silent films continued to be produced and exhibited until 1929. See Musser, *The Emergence of Cinema, 27*.

14. See page 39 in this volume.

15. See Jenkins, *What Made Pistachio Nuts?* (New York: Columbia University Press, 1992).

16. See Steve Seidman, *Comedian Comedy: A Tradition in Hollywood Film* (Ann Arbor, MI: UMI Research Press, 1981) on self-referentiality in comedy films.

17. Hugo Münsterberg, "The Means of the Photoplay," in *The Film: A Psychological Study.*

18. See Allardyce Nicoll, *Film and Theatre* (New York: Thomas Y. Crowell, 1936). Rather than anthologize an excerpt from this influential book, I have chosen to include Eric Bentley's lesser known but most convincing rebuttal to Nicoll's argument.

19. Sarah Bay-Cheng's essay in this volume supports Laura Mulvey's claim that different spectators relate to illusions depending upon their gender and sexual preference (and by extension, I would argue, class and a number of other personal characteristics) but notes that identification functions differently in film than in theater because of the selective nature of the camera's gaze as compared to the relative openness of the spectator's gaze in theater. Bay-Cheng's viewpoint represents an admirable advance over the influential work of feminist pioneers in theater studies, like Jill Dolan, who first applied Mulvey's theories to spectator-theory in theater.

20. See Richard Schechner, "Six Axioms for Environmental Theatre," *Drama Review* 12.3 (Spring 1968).

21. Although I personally have invested a great deal of my creative and scholarly energies in theater and film that are more physical and visual, I wonder if the critical bias that some film theorists have against words as communicators of psychological depth is a sign of anti-intellectualism. Or perhaps the bias against words is an indicator of theorists' preference for inarticulate characters, or audiences' own psychosocial inability to find words with which to confront the problems of life in today's world.

22. The concept of quality has gotten a bad reputation since postmodernism, as many now believe that quality is a purely subjective judgment. Yet I believe that quality is making a comeback, if you will, propelled by our need for some judgmental certainty in the post

9/11 world. Perhaps the destruction of the World Trade Center will pull us back from the brink of deconstruction, so that we may recover some truths, relative though they may be, on which to ground ourselves.

23. See page 135 in this volume.

24. See page 135 in this volume.

25. HBO has film projects of several other theater pieces in the works as of late 2003, including Patrick Marber's *Closer,* George C. Wolfe's *Jelly's Last Jam,* and Tony Kushner's *Homebody/Kabul.* See *American Theater* 20.1 (December 2003), 31.

26. See page 161 in this volume.

27. Henrik Ibsen, *Hedda Gabler,* trans. Jon Rabin Baitz (1890; reprinted Grove Press, 2000), act 2, 47.

Prelude The Director as Superstar

Vsevolod Meyerhold

Translated by Margorie L. Hoover

The reconstructed theatre, using every technical means at its disposal, will work with film, so that scenes played by the actor on stage can alternate with scenes he has played on screen. Going further, a dramatic production could become a kind of revue in which the actor uses dramatic, operatic, and film methods, as well as those of the ballet dancer, acrobat, gymnast, clown. And, of course, the play's division into acts, the inflexibility of conventional dramatic structure, must be superseded by episodes after the model of Shakespeare and the dramatists of the old Spanish theatre, making it possible to abandon the antiquated pseudo-classical unities of time and action. We are entering upon a new phase of playwriting. We are creating a new kind of play.

At this moment of transition the battle between movies and theatre is considerably greater than any they have fought before. In the West, particularly America and Germany, there are many more movie houses than dramatic theatres and opera houses, and many more peo-

Excerpted from Vsevolod Meyerhold, "Reconstruction of the Theater," *Drama Review* 11, no. 1 (Fall 1966): 186–188.

ple go to the movies than to any other kind of theatre. From this some conclude that the movies are proving a dangerous competitor of the theatre. I don't necessarily agree.

The movie-theatre owners, who had been drawing huge crowds, noticed one fine day that their audiences were beginning to be unenthusiastic. The public began to demand more than silent figures in motion, and technology gave in to its demands. In order to compete with the stage and with the live actor, the talkies were born; but this did not represent a victory over theatre for the movies. However attractive the screen's great freedom to move action from one scene to another, change night to day, perform miracles of transformation for the actor—it all wasn't enough. The audience insisted that the actor, whom it idolized, speak, and with the silent film's surrender to the sound film the international significance of the movies was lost. A Chaplin who was understood in America, the USSR, and Holland became incomprehensible as soon as he began to speak English. The Russian peasant now refuses to accept Chaplin, the Englishman, although Chaplin had been close and comprehensible to him as long as he only mimed. The film's progress is therefore a step backward. . . .

The theatres we know in our country are not those we shall have in the future. We shall abandon the structures inherited from the Tzarist period, when the peep-show illusionistic stage was built and productions staged so that the audience might relax, doze, flirt, and gossip. Today we who build theatres in competition with the movies say: let us "cinematify" the theatre, let us use in the theatre all the technical means of the screen—but not just in the sense that we install a screen in the theatre. We must move into theatre spectacle—and we shall stage productions attracting audiences as large as those in the movie theatres. The revolution to "reconstruct" the contemporary theatre in form and content has come to a halt only for lack of the means to re-equip stage and auditorium.

We must satisfy the contemporary spectator's need to see a play not in the company of three to five hundred persons—the proletariat will not go to "intimate" or "miniature" theatres—but surrounded by tens of thousands. Instead of today's football, we must devise tomorrow's theatricalized "sport." The electric charge which the contemporary spectator demands of the lecture must be increased to the high tension suitable for large masses of people. The technique of both contemporary playwriting and directing makes use of the audience as well as of the actors and stage machinery. I intentionally produce plays so that they seem on stage to be incomplete, for I know that the most significant revision of a play is done by the audience. The playwright and director regard the work of staging as preparation for the work done day by day during the run by two most effective forces in the theatre: actor and audience. The staging must not impose itself or compel, but allow free collaboration between these forces. Everything sketched in during rehearsal is only approximate, and therefore it is essential that the audience be large.

This is also how movies work. When an important film is made in Holly-wood, it is given a surprise pre-release showing in some large movie theatre. When people have been seated, the announced feature is cancelled and in its stead the film to be tested is shown. Agents from the studio are planted among the spectators to take notes, and thus they test the film with an unprejudiced audience, not one "selected" like that at a theatrical first night. After this the movie is revised, and only then released.

What will be the future development of the screen and stage? It is obvious that the theatre cannot surrender its position just as it is about to realize the technical stage equipment it so badly needs. The theatre must go further to-ward "cinematification," but the movies, I fear, must encounter the barrier al-ready described: the actor playing in the talkies will realize one fine day that he is losing his international public, and wish to return to the silent pictures.

When we reconstruct dramatic and operatic stages in the only way suitable for producing the new revolutionary plays, we face the enormous difficulty that our theatre is not yet industrialized. We do not have the means necessary to per-fect a technically still imperfect stage. Govozdev says: "Piscator is not afraid to bring theatre and movies together." Can we do what Piscator has done?

One **Historical Influences**

Realism, Romance, and the Development
of the Motion Picture

A. Nicholas Vardac

Art in any of its many forms cannot be considered in terms of static manifestation. It must forever be viewed in the light of its dynamics, its flow, and its changing social origins. The birth of the need for the motion picture, the expression of this need in the related arts of the times, its growth, and eventually its transition from the related arts to the screen must be considered as a study in aesthetic dynamics.

The spirit which dominated the nineteenth century arose from the intellectual upheavals of the eighteenth. Through the mid-years of the 1700's realistic rebellion and intellectual inquisition were breeding. The universe was questioned and dissected and its fabric examined. The modern objective and scientific point of view was in the process of birth. Its most immediate and sensational manifestations may indeed have been in the political arena, with revolutions flaring upon two continents within a matter of decades, but the power of this new

---

Excerpted from A. Nicholas Vardac, *Stage to Screen: Theatrical Origins of Early Film: David Garrick to D. W. Griffith* (Cambridge: Harvard University Press, 1949), xvii–xxvi.

spirit, pervading the eighteenth-century horizon, found a ready reflection in aesthetic areas as well.

In the arts of the theatre this spirit, beginning with the work of David Garrick, stimulated the growth of a new realism in staging and acting. As the objective or scientific point of view dominated society, finding its outlet in the flood of scientific invention of the nineteenth century, the cycle of realistic theatrical presentation inaugurated by Garrick marched in close step. Garrick's new aesthetic departure, stated simply, was that of achieving a greater pictorial realism in staging. This intention is indicated by the many stagings made for him by P. J. de Loutherbourg, by the withdrawal of his production into the proscenium picture frame, as well as by changes in lighting and in character interpretation. He was aiming at theatrical production pictorial, thus cinematic, in conception. Can the motion picture, then, be considered as the ultimate aesthetic expression of a cycle of realistic-pictorial theatrical production which had been a part of the rebirth of the objective spirit in the middle of the eighteenth century and which was to mature through the nineteenth-century age of invention?

The theory of the persistence of vision upon which the motion picture is based is said to have been understood and demonstrated by Ptolemy in 130 A.D.[1] But the cinema was born of a different era. Is there connection between the arrival of the motion picture in the late nineteenth century (1895) and theatrical production surrounding and preceding its arrival? Is it true that the cycle of nineteenth-century stage realism stemming from Garrick was the early expression of the same aesthetic need that gave rise to the cinema? Is there, first of all, any coincidence between the course of the development of realism in staging arising with Garrick and the course of progress in the invention of the motion picture? Any study of the transition of theatrical method from stage to screen must attempt to answer these questions.

Progress in the invention of the motion picture falls into three distinct periods. The first period produced animated pictures; the second, animated photographs; and the third, the culminating phase, the continuous projection of objects photographed in motion,[2] or motion pictures.

In 1824 Peter Mark Roget presented before the Royal Society a paper entitled "The Persistence of Vision with Regard to Moving Objects." In 1829 Joseph Nicéphore Niepce joined in a pact with Louis Jacques Mandé Daguerre for the furtherance of photography. The thaumatrope had already been demonstrated in 1825. A series of devices calculated to create the illusion of motion followed, with the eventual development of the phenakistoscope by Joseph Antoine

Plateau and the stroboscope by Simon Ritter von Stampfer. Thus the period 1824–1832 saw the achievement of animated pictures.

With the consummation of this preliminary goal, activity if not interest subsided and for over twenty years nothing of significance in the direction of the motion picture seems to have been precipitated. Progress came in well-defined surges. The second period started in 1853, when Baron Franz von Uchatius projected the phenakistoscopic pictures of Plateau with a magic-lantern apparatus. In 1857 a patent was issued in France to Leon Scott for a phonautograph. In 1860 Désvignes patented a zoëtrope. On numerous blades of a paddle wheel he mounted successively posed photographs. Then the wheel was spun. On February 5, 1861, a United States patent was granted to Coleman Sellers for a zoëtropic machine known as the kinematoscope. Thus with the animation of successively posed "stills," the second stage from 1853 to 1861 was completed.

In 1864 a patent is said to have been issued to Louis Arthur du Hauron anticipating the entire scheme of the motion picture. This and the combination of photography with magic-lantern projection in the phasmatrope of Henry Renno Heyl in 1870 opened the third and final period. Successively posed stills were projected. Once the relationship between photography and projection was established, progress quickened. Muybridge, working from 1872 to 1877, eventually utilized John D. Isaacs' battery of twenty-four cameras, shutters timed in succession, to photograph the movement of a galloping horse for Leland Stanford. And in 1881 Meissonier projected these stills at a private showing in Paris, using a zoöpraxiscope. In 1887 Edison joined W. E. L. Dickson in an attempt to photograph and project motion. Two years later William Friese-Greene patented photography on celluloid, and at the same time Eastman's celluloid film became available for still photography. Edison saw the possibilities and on October 6, 1889, demonstrated an Edison-Dickson kinetoscope at West Orange, New Jersey, utilizing a strip of Eastman's film with frames moving as fast as forty per second between a magnifying lens and a light source. In 1895 Thomas Armat projected an Edison kinetoscopic film upon a screen with his vitascope, and in the same year Edison, joined now with Armat, exhibited an improved form of the vitascope named, oddly enough, the kinetoscope. And so the final phase in the projection of the photography of motion was completed in the period from 1864 to 1895.

From this brief examination of the line of inventive progress, which gathered momentum through the nineteenth century and culminated, toward its end, in the motion picture, a rough over-all coincidence appears between the invention of cinema and the nineteenth-century cycle of theatrical realism stemming from Garrick. That the birth of cinema should have come at the end of a grad-ual process of invention running from 1824 to 1895 is, when we turn to examine conditions in the contemporaneous related arts, not surprising. The necessity for greater pictorial realism in the arts of theatre appears as the logical impetus to the invention of cinema. This necessity, an "aesthetic" tension of the nine-teenth century, found its preliminary satisfaction in the theatrical forms pre-ceding and surrounding the arrival of the film.

During the nineteenth century the related literary arts of the novel and the drama tended both toward the romantic and the realistic modes. While on one hand greater and more glamorous escape was offered, on the other we find re-action and an effort, despite the traditional rose-colored glasses of a romantic age, to view and appraise real values of the day. Paradoxical as it may appear, however, this dual character of certain nineteenth-century art forms presented but a single problem to the scenic artist. Romantic conceptions of the play-wrights might become more and more exaggerated in their never-ending quest for escape, but it would never do for the scene builder to follow a similar pat-tern. His job was to render believable upon the stage the increasingly glam-orous, unreal, and spectacular ideas of the romantic playwrights. The more ro-mantic the subject matter the more realistic must be its presentation upon the boards, else the entire effect would be lost. The conventional staging methods, forced upon audiences and producers alike by the stage building itself, were a serious limitation to realism, but were agreeably tolerated for their capacity in pictorializing the most romantic conceptions of the age. Within the limitations of the conventions and as the century progressed, the essential goal of the scenic artist became that of providing an ever larger and more elaborate pictorial real-ism. Thus, strange as it may seem, the nineteenth century witnessed a union of romanticism and realism in the arts of the drama and of staging.

In the face of this combined front, the waning pseudoclassic temper of eigh-teenth-century staging was rapidly spent, and even before the turn of the cen-tury the new realism found increasing support. The aural productions of the pseudoclassicists gave way before the visual productions of either realist or ro-manticist. Charles Macklin had already played *Macbeth* in kilts. David Garrick combined his realistic reforms in staging with the pictorial, spectacular scenic conceptions of M. de Loutherbourg, fresh from the baroque staging methods of Parisian theatres. Soon came the archaeological innovations of William Capon. In the drama, similar graphic inclinations were reflected in the work of the realist-sentimentalists, Thomas Holcroft and Mrs. Inchbald, and the ro-manticist, George Colman, the younger. Under the influence of Kotzebue, he managed such a piece as *The Iron Chest* in 1796. The novel, too, demonstrated the growing graphic bias of the new objective spirit. Again the pictorial approach, including realistic pictures of romantic subjects and romanticized pictures of subjects from immediate life, appeared in the work of Samuel Richardson, Henry Fielding, Tobias Smollett, Samuel Johnson, Oliver Goldsmith, "Monk" Lewis, and Horace Walpole, among others. Seeds of cinema, thus found in the realistic and romantic pictorial leanings of novel, drama, and theatre, were sown even before the arrival of the nineteenth century.

The pattern of this realistic-romantic movement, with its increasing stress upon pictorial values, harmonized throughout the nineteenth century with the three phases in the invention of the motion picture. Modern theatrical realism is said to have begun with the archaeologically authentic costume production of *King John* by J. R. Planché at Covent Garden, January 19, 1824.[3]

Planché's production and Roget's paper on the persistence of vision appeared in the same year, both apparently reflections of that social tension which was bringing about an aesthetic preference for the visual, the graphic, the pictorial illusion. Looking further into the Planché-Roget coincidence, we find that a new peak in realistic-romantic activity in theatrical production occurred simultaneously with the first phase in the development of cinema. Neither Planché nor Roget was an isolated phenomenon. Chronological parallels, of course, must be viewed with care, yet it may be of certain interest that the early nineteenth-century boom in pictorial theatre, marked by the work of Charles Macready, Edmund Kean, Edwin Forrest, Madame Vestris, and Charles J. Mathews, ran concurrently with the first phase in the invention of the motion picture. In novel and drama surrounding the 1824–1832 period, great activity appeared in the same pictorial direction. J. S. Knowles's *Virginius* appeared in 1820, and *The Hunchback* in 1832. Hugo's *Hernani* (1830) was translated into English for private production in 1831. Shelley's *Cenci* appeared in 1819. Miss Mitford moved into the scene of the twenties, Scribe filled the twenties and thirties, and Browning the thirties. Byron's *Sardanapalus* and *Marino Faliero* came in 1821, and his *Werner* in 1823. The *Waverley Novels* appeared from 1814 to 1831, and the work of James Fenimore Cooper, highly cinematic in conception and execution, was concentrated in the years from 1821 to 1826. Activity in these arts, to be sure, was of a continuous nature, yet the grouping within this period is sufficiently marked to justify consideration. It is not at all strange that the first phase in the development of the motion picture, the achievement of animated drawings, was begun and completed in the years from 1824 to 1832, for during the same period social tensions and the resultant aesthetic preferences sponsored a boom in pictorialism, both romantic and realistic, in these related arts. This concentration of activity directed toward a pictorial aesthetic expression offers the first indication in the century of that necessity which pointed to the invention of cinema.

With the completion of the initial stage in the invention of the motion picture, activity subsided while success was assimilated. Meanwhile, the graphic proclivities of this realistic-romantic trend in theatrical arts continued in an unbroken line until, with the work of Charles Kean, a second peak in activity and achievement was reached. Kean entered the Princess' Theatre in 1850. The success of his authentic pictorial productions continued into the next decade. Surrounding him in the theatre of London were such luminaries as Samuel Phelps at Sadler's Wells and Charles Fechter at the Lyceum. A younger Booth, Edwin, a more restrained and realistic performer than his forebear, made his debut in Boston in 1849 in *Richard III*. In the same decade Thackeray became firmly established. Darwin's *Origin of Species* was published in 1859. Dumas *père* built his own Théâtre Historique in Paris in 1847, and the design of this theatre, a sharp break from contemporary practice, reveals again the growing interest in staging realism. George Boker and the Philadelphia romanticists flourished through the fifties. Thus the decade of the fifties appears as a second period of achievement in the upward cycle of realism and romanticism.

Again coincidence is to be noted, for during the years from 1853 to 1861 the second phase in the invention of cinema, animated photographs, was completed. This coincidence carries a certain significance, for it would indicate that both the need for cinema and for greater pictorial realism in the theatre came in response to a single stimulus, a similar aesthetic, or, as Waldemar Kaempffert has applied the term, "social tension."[4] Two apparently independent developments, both sponsoring a greater pictorial realism for the arts of theatre, appeared simultaneously. The relationship so well demonstrated by Kaempffert to exist between the "social tension" of an age and its scientific progress also holds for its aesthetic growth. Progress in the invention of cinema came when the need for pictorial realism in the theatre was at a peak. Thus, while the second phase in its development did not provide the projection of motion pictures, such advance as did occur was so closely allied with the social tensions and aesthetic preferences of the times that there would seem to have been an impulse to supply, through scientific progress, a greater pictorial realism for the arts of the theatre.

The final phase in the invention of cinema and the final phase in the progress of the realistic-romantic theatrical cycle which had been going forward during the century were both inaugurated at about the same time, the former in 1864 and the latter in 1865. In 1864 M. du Hauron was issued a patent covering the scheme of cinema. In 1865 the Bancrofts' production of *Society* was given at the Prince of Wales's. With these two events began the final surge in the two related developments.

In staging method, the ultimate in nineteenth-century pictorial realism came with the productions of the Bancrofts and Henry Irving in England, of Augustin Daly, Steele MacKaye, and David Belasco in America, and with the Saxe-Meiningen group, the Théâtre-Libre of Antoine, and the Moscow Art Theatre as vanguard on the Continent. The Bancrofts may have used genuine falling leaves to complete a realistic picture, but Antoine included beeves fresh from the slaughterhouse for his stage butcher shop, and Steele MacKaye in America used real ships on real water. A parallel expression can be seen in the novel among such realists as George Eliot, George Meredith, Henry James, and Thomas Hardy, and such romanticists as Robert Louis Stevenson, A. Conan Doyle, H. Rider Haggard, Rudyard Kipling, and James M. Barrie. In the drama, Ibsen, Chekhov, and Strindberg are the outstanding figures of the cycle, surrounded by a multitude of lesser lights—Hauptmann, Masefield, Zola, Brieux, Augier, Robertson, Bernstein, Jones, Pinero, Granville-Barker, Houghton, and Galsworthy. Boucicault, Herne, Belasco, Stephen Phillips, and Maeterlinck supply a colorful romantic counterpoint, while the Irish playwrights are both realistic and romantic. Thus, at the moment of the arrival of the motion picture, pictorial realism and romanticism in these related arts had attained a pinnacle. The cinema came at the very crest of the realistic-romantic cycle which had been introduced a century before by Garrick. In marking time with this cycle, the invention of cinema seemed to have come in response to that same need for greater pictorial realism born with Garrick. When it finally did arrive, the cinema, as shall be seen, challenged the realistic-pictorial stage producers and took over the creations of the romantic authors.

The arrival of the motion picture cannot be looked upon as an isolated and haphazard expression of scientific progress. Two fundamental relationships now appear which indicate that the arrival of cinema, viewed in the light of growing social tensions and changing aesthetic preferences, came at a most logical phase in the evolutionary pattern of world theatre. The first relationship is simply the over-all coincidence between the realistic-romantic theatrical cycle in the nineteenth century and the invention of the motion picture. Both were devoted to the creation of visual or pictorial illusion, and both ran a similar course from 1824 to 1895, coinciding nearly to the year. Secondly, to cement this over-all similarity, the three separate stages in the development of cinema—animated pictures, animated photographs, and the projection of photographed motion—each coincided with three peaks in realistic-romantic activity in the related arts of the novel, drama, and theatre. Progress in the cinematic direction and progress in this pictorial cycle moved in response to a similar audience need. When, however, realism and romanticism had, toward the end of the century, attained real leaves, beeves, and ships, the stage could go no further. But the need for pictorial realism on an ever greater scale remained. Only the motion picture with its reproduction of reality could carry on the cycle.

In the face of such a theatrical presentation as Alexander Black's *Miss Jerry*[5] on October 10, 1894, the arrival of cinema would appear to have been preordained. The time was fully ripe and waited only upon the proper combination of technical knowledge and skill. *Miss Jerry* was a strange kind of play, a "picture-play." Current staging methods were apparently failing to satisfy the full pictorial preference of the late nineteenth-century audience. The play itself had now become less important than the realism of its pictorial aspects, for it was read by Black in a darkened hall. On a screen at one end were projected more than three hundred photographs taken from life. These pictures, shown in about two hours at a rate somewhat above two per minute, imparted life, vitality, and probably even imaginative motion to the play. The need for pictorial realism was apparently so great that, lacking motion pictures, a succession of "stills" was substituted.

That the motion picture finally made its appearance in response to the insistence of social pressure for a greater pictorial realism in the theatre is indicated still further by the manner of its arrival. This pressure was so great and so diversified that if Edison had not been available others would have pioneered. From a variety of quarters, almost simultaneously, the cinema sprang. In 1890 William Friese-Greene developed and printed successfully the first moving picture photographed on celluloid. In 1891 C. Francis Jenkins perfected a motion-picture machine complete with cogs, gears, and lenses, and in 1894 projected a film called *Annabelle the Dancer*. This machine, improved by Armat, was refused a patent in 1895. Jenkins bought out Armat for $2500. In 1895 and 1896 Jenkins, now sponsored by Edison, exhibited the machine as the Edison vitascope. In France the Lumière brothers patented a projection machine in 1895. In the same year in London, Robert Paul exhibited a machine along other lines. The times rather than the men controlled the ultimate arrival of the motion picture, for at just the point beyond which stage realism would have broken down and in many instances did, the cinema came to meet the need for a greater pictorial realism. By coming at the very peak of the nineteenth-century cycle of realism, it upset normal expectations in the theatre itself. For in accordance with the principle of organic change which is regularly found in theatrical art, one might have expected, in the early twentieth century, the rapid development of newer experimental forms with the consequent breakdown of both the realistic and the spectacular styles. Just at the time, however, that such a change might have been expected, the regular development of theatrical forms was checked and thwarted by the appearance of the motion picture. Naturally, in these early years, the film and the stage were hardly differentiated from one another; the cinema frequently borrowed from the theatre, while the theatre, in an attempt to counter the new attraction, in its turn borrowed from the film. From the beginning the cinema was recognized as a highly realistic and representational medium with, paradoxically, the means of proceeding in the romantic direction many degrees beyond the stage. The result was that the two styles which defined the nineteenth-century theatre, realism and romanticism, and which most probably would have seen alteration in the early years of the twentieth century, were given a new lease on life.

Did the cinema take over the audience of the nineteenth-century pictorial stage? Did this pictorial stage disappear? How did early twentieth-century theatrical producers combat the encroachment of the film? Was there a change in style? How do the sporadic reactionary experiments of the "producers' theatre" in the early 1900's fit into the picture? These and other questions evaluating stage and screen during the years of their aesthetic merger should be elaborated and clarified. If the roots of the cinema are examined, a better understanding of the relationship between stage and screen will eventually appear.

NOTES

1. B. J. Lubschez, *Story of the Motion Picture* (New York, 1920), p. 10.
2. For the history and description of various inventions in the development of motion pictures given in the paragraphs below, see Terry Ramsaye's article "History" under "Motion Pictures," *Encyclopaedia Britannica* (14th ed., 1946), XV, 855–856; Lubschez, *Story of the Motion Picture,* pp. 10ff.; F. A. Talbot, *Moving Pictures; How They Are Made and Worked* (Philadelphia, 1914), chaps. ii–iv; Robert Grau, *The Theatre of Science* (New York, 1914), pp. 30ff.; and Maurice Bardèche and Robert Brasillach, *The History of Motion Pictures,* translated by Iris Barry (New York: W. W. Norton and Co., and the Museum of Modern Art, 1938).

3. Described by J. R. Planché in *Recollections and Reflections* (2 vols.; London, 1901), I, 52–57.

4. Waldemar Kaempffert, "Invention as a Social Manifestation," chap. ii, p. 21, in C. A. Beard (ed.), *A Century of Progress* (New York, 1935).

5. Lubschez, *Story of the Motion Picture,* p. 51.

The Cinema of Attractions Early Film, Its Spectator, and the Avant-Garde

Tom Gunning

Writing in 1922, flushed with the excitement of seeing Abel Gance's *La Roue,* Fernand Léger tried to define something of the radical possibilities of the cinema. The potential of the new art did not lie in "imitating the movements of nature" or in "the mistaken path" of its resemblance to theatre. Its unique power was a "matter of *making images seen.*"[1] It is precisely this harnessing of visibility, this act of showing and exhibition, which I feel cinema before 1906 displays most intensely. Its inspiration for the avant-garde of the early decades of this century needs to be re-explored.

Writings by the early modernists (Futurists, Dadaists, and Surrealists) on the cinema follow a pattern similar to Léger: enthusiasm for this new medium and its possibilities; and disappointment at the way it has already developed, its enslavement to traditional art forms, particularly theatre and literature. This fascination with the *potential* of a

Excerpted from Tom Gunning, "The Cinema of Attractions," *Wide Angle* 8, no. 3/4 (1986), 63–70. Copyright © Ohio University: Athens Center for Film and Video. Reprinted by permission of the Johns Hopkins University Press.

medium (and the accompanying fantasy of rescuing the cinema from its en-slavement to alien and passé forms) can be understood from a number of view-points. I want to use it to illuminate a topic I have also approached before, the strangely heterogeneous relation that film before 1906 (or so) bears to the films that follow, and the way a taking account of this heterogeneity signals a new conception of film history and film form. My work in this area has been pur-sued in collaboration with André Gaudreault.[2]

The history of early cinema, like the history of cinema generally, has been written and theorized under the hegemony of narrative films. Early filmmakers like Smith, Méliès, and Porter have been studied primarily from the viewpoint of their contribution to film as a storytelling medium, particularly the evolu-tion of narrative editing. Although such approaches are not totally misguided, they are one-sided and potentially distort both the work of these filmmakers and the actual forces shaping cinema before 1906. A few observations will indi-cate the way that early cinema was not dominated by the narrative impulse that later asserted its sway over the medium. First there is the extremely important role that actuality film plays in early film production. Investigation of the films copyrighted in the U.S. shows that actuality films outnumbered fictional films until 1906.[3] The Lumière tradition of "placing the world within one's reach" through travel films and topicals did not disappear with the exit of the Ciné-matographe from film production. But even within non-actuality filming—what has sometimes been referred to as the "Méliès tradition"—the role narra-tive plays is quite different from in traditional narrative film. Méliès himself declared in discussing his working method:

> As for the scenario, the "fable," or "tale," I only consider it at the end. I can state that the scenario constructed in this manner has *no importance,* since I use it merely as a pretext for the "stage effects," the "tricks," or for a nicely arranged tableau.

Whatever differences one might find between Lumière and Méliès, they should not represent the opposition between narrative and non-narrative film-mak-ing, at least as it is understood today. Rather, one can unite them in a concep-tion that sees cinema less as a way of telling stories than as a way of presenting a series of views to an audience, fascinating because of their illusory power (whether the realistic illusion of motion offered to the first audiences by Lu-mière, or the magical illusion concocted by Méliès), and exoticism. In other words, I believe that the relation to the spectator set up by the films of both Lu-mière and Méliès (and many other film-makers before 1906) had a common basis, and one that differs from the primary spectator relations set up by narrative film after 1906. I will call this earlier conception of cinema, "the cinema of attractions." I believe that this conception dominates cinema until about 1906–7. Although different from the fascination in storytelling exploited by the cinema from the time of Griffith, it is not necessarily opposed to it. In fact the cinema of attractions does not disappear with the dominance of narrative, but rather goes underground, both into certain avant-garde practices and as a component of narrative films, more evident in some genres (e.g. the musical) than in others.

What precisely is the cinema of attractions? First, it is a cinema that bases itself on the quality that Léger celebrated: its ability to *show* something. Contrasted to the voyeuristic aspect of narrative cinema analysed by Christian Metz,[5] this is an exhibitionist cinema. An aspect of early cinema which I have written about in other articles is emblematic of this different relationship the cinema of attractions constructs with its spectator: the recurring look at the camera by actors. This action, which is later perceived as spoiling the realistic illusion of the cinema, is here undertaken with brio, establishing contact with the audience. From comedians smirking at the camera, to the constant bowing and gesturing of the conjurors in magic films, this is a cinema that displays its visibility, willing to rupture a self-enclosed fictional world for a chance to solicit the attention of the spectator.

Exhibitionism becomes literal in the series of erotic films which play an important role in early film production (the same Pathé catalogue would advertise the Passion Play along with "scènes grivoises d'un caractère piquant," erotic films often including full nudity), also driven underground in later years. As Noël Burch has shown in his film *Correction Please: How We Got into Pictures* (1979), a film like *The Bride Retires* (France, 1902) reveals a fundamental conflict between this exhibitionistic tendency of early film and the creation of a fictional diegesis. A woman undresses for bed while her new husband peers at her from behind a screen. However, it is to the camera and the audience that the bride addresses her erotic striptease, winking at us as she faces us, smiling in erotic display.

As the quote from Méliès points out, the trick film, perhaps the dominant non-actuality film genre before 1906, is itself a series of displays, of magical attractions, rather than a primitive sketch of narrative continuity. Many trick films are, in effect, plotless, a series of transformations strung together with little connection and certainly no characterization. But to approach even the plotted trick films, such as *Voyage dans la lune* (1902), simply as precursors of later narrative structures is to miss the point. The story simply provides a frame upon which to string a demonstration of the magical possibilities of the cinema.

Modes of exhibition in early cinema also reflect this lack of concern with creating a self-sufficient narrative world upon the screen. As Charles Musser has shown,[6] the early showmen exhibitors exerted a great deal of control over the shows they presented, actually re-editing the films they had purchased and supplying a series of offscreen supplements, such as sound effects and spoken commentary. Perhaps most extreme is the Hale's Tours, the largest chain of theatres exclusively showing films before 1906. Not only did the films consist of non-narrative sequences taken from moving vehicles (usually trains), but the theatre itself was arranged as a train car with a conductor who took tickets, and sound effects stimulating the click-clack of wheels and hiss of air brakes.[7] Such viewing experiences relate more to the attractions of the fairground than to the traditions of the legitimate theatre. The relation between films and the emergence of the great amusement parks, such as Coney Island, at the turn of the century provides rich ground for rethinking the roots of early cinema.

Nor should we ever forget that in the earliest years of exhibition the cinema itself was an attraction. Early audiences went to exhibitions to see machines demonstrated (the newest technological wonder, following in the wake of such widely exhibited machines and marvels as X-rays or, earlier, the phonograph), rather than to view films. It was the Cinématographe, the Biograph, or the Vitascope that were advertised on the variety bills in which they premièred, not *Le Déjeuner de bébé* or *The Black Diamond Express*. After the initial novelty period, this display of the possibilities of cinema continues, and not only in magic films. Many of the close-ups in early film differ from later uses of the technique precisely because they do not use enlargement for narrative punctuation, but as an attraction in its own right. The close-up cut into Porter's *The Gay Shoe Clerk* (1903) may anticipate later continuity techniques, but its principal motive is again pure exhibitionism, as the lady lifts her skirt hem, exposing her ankle for all to see. Biograph films such as *Photographing a Female Crook* (1904) and *Hooligan in Jail* (1903) consist of a single shot in which the camera is brought close to the main character, until they are in mid-shot. The enlargement is not a device expressive of narrative tension; it is in itself an attraction and the point of the film.[8]

To summarise, the cinema of attractions directly solicits spectator attention, inciting visual curiosity, and supplying pleasure through an exciting spectacle—a unique event, whether fictional or documentary, that is of interest in itself. The attraction to be displayed may also be of a cinematic nature, such as the early close-ups just described, or trick films in which a cinematic manipulation (slow motion, reverse motion, substitution, multiple exposure) provides the film's novelty. Fictional situations tend to be restricted to gags, vaudeville numbers, or re-creations of shocking or curious incidents (executions, current events). It is the direct address of the audience, in which an attraction is offered to the spectator by a cinema showman, that defines this approach to film making. Theatrical display dominates over narrative absorption, emphasizing the direct stimulation of shock or surprise at the expense of unfolding a story or creating a diegetic universe. The cinema of attractions expends little energy creating characters with psychological motivations or individual personality. Making use of both fictional and non-fictional attractions, its energy moves outward towards an acknowledged spectator rather than inward towards the character-based situations essential to classical narrative.

The term "attractions" comes, of course, from the young Sergei Mikhailovich Eisenstein and his attempt to find a new model and mode of analysis for the theatre. In his search for the "unit of impression" of theatrical art, the foundation of an analysis which would undermine realistic representational theatre, Eisenstein hit upon the term "attraction."[9] An attraction aggressively subjected the spectator to "sensual or psychological impact." According to Eisenstein, theatre should consist of a montage of such attractions, creating a relation to the spectator entirely different from his absorption in 'illusory depictions."[10] I pick up this term partly to underscore the relation to the spectator that this later avant-garde practice shares with early cinema: that of exhibitionist confrontation rather than diegetic absorption. Of course the "experimentally regulated and mathematically calculated" montage of attractions demanded by Eisenstein differs enormously from these early films (as any conscious and oppositional mode of practice will from a popular one).[11] However, it is important to realize the context from which Eisenstein selected the term. Then, as now, the "attraction" was a term of the fairground, and for Eisenstein and his friend Yutkevich it primarily represented their favourite fairground attraction, the roller coaster, or as it was known then in Russia, the American Mountains.[12]

The source is significant. The enthusiasm of the early avant-garde for film was at least partly an enthusiasm for a mass culture that was emerging at the beginning of the century, offering a new sort of stimulus for an audience not acculturated to the traditional arts. It is important to take this enthusiasm for popular art as something more than a simple gesture to *épater les bourgeois*. The enormous development of the entertainment industry since the 1910s and its growing acceptance by middle-class culture (and the accommodation that made this acceptance possible) have made it difficult to understand the liberation popular entertainment offered at the beginning of the century. I believe that it was precisely the exhibitionist quality of turn-of-the-century popular art that made it attractive to the avant-garde—its freedom from the creation of a diegesis, its accent on direct stimulation.

Writing of the variety theatre, Marinetti not only praised its aesthetics of astonishment and stimulation, but particularly its creation of a new spectator who contrasts with the "static," "stupid voyeur" of traditional theatre. The spectator at the variety theatre feels directly addressed by the spectacle and joins in, singing along, heckling the comedians.[13] Dealing with early cinema within the context of archive and academy, we risk missing its vital relation to vaudeville, its primary place of exhibition until around 1905. Film appeared as one attraction on the vaudeville programme, surrounded by a mass of unrelated acts in a non-narrative and even nearly illogical succession of performances. Even when presented in the nickelodeons that were emerging at the end of this period, these short films always appeared in a variety format, trick films sandwiched in with farces, actualities, "illustrated songs," and, quite frequently, cheap vaudeville acts. It was precisely this non-narrative variety that placed this form of entertainment under attack by reform groups in the early 1910s. The Russell Sage Survey of popular entertainments found vaudeville "depends upon an artificial rather than a natural human and developing interest, these acts having no necessary and as a rule, no actual connection."[14] In other words, no narrative. A night at the variety theatre was like a ride on a streetcar or an active day in a crowded city, according to this middle-class reform group, stimulating an unhealthy nervousness. It was precisely such artificial stimulus that Marinetti and Eisenstein wished to borrow from the popular arts and inject into the theatre, organizing popular energy for radical purpose.

What happened to the cinema of attractions? The period from 1907 to about 1913 represents the true *narrativization* of the cinema, culminating in the appearance of feature films which radically revised the variety format. Film clearly took the legitimate theatre as its model, producing famous players in famous plays. The transformation of filmic discourse that D. W. Griffith typifies bound cinematic signifiers to the narration of stories and the creation of a self-enclosed diegetic universe. The look at the camera becomes taboo and the devices of cinema are transformed from playful "tricks"—cinematic attractions (Méliès gesturing at us to watch the lady vanish)—to elements of dramatic expression, entries into the psychology of character and the world of fiction.

However, it would be too easy to see this as a Cain and Abel story, with narrative strangling the nascent possibilities of a young iconoclastic form of entertainment. Just as the variety format in some sense survived in the movie palaces of the 20s (with newsreel, cartoon, sing-along, orchestra performance, and sometimes vaudeville acts subordinated to, but still coexisting with, the narrative *feature* of the evening), the system of attraction remains an essential part of popular film-making.

The chase film shows how, towards the end of this period (basically from 1903 to 1906), a synthesis of attractions and narrative was already underway. The chase had been the original truly narrative genre of the cinema, providing a model for causality and linearity as well as a basic editing continuity. A film like Biograph's *Personal* (1904, the model for the chase film in many ways) shows the creation of a narrative linearity, as the French nobleman runs for his life from the fiancées his personal column ad has unleashed. However, at the same time, as the group of young women pursue their prey towards the camera in each shot, they encounter some slight obstacle (a fence, a steep slope, a stream) that shows them down for the spectator, providing a mini-spectacle pause in the unfolding of narrative. The Edison Company seemed particularly aware of this, since they offered their plagiarized version of this Biograph film (*How a French Nobleman Got a Wife Through the New York Herald "Personal" Columns*) in two forms, as a complete film or as separate shots, so that any one image of the ladies chasing the man could be bought without the inciting incident or narrative closure.[15]

As Laura Mulvey has shown in a very different context, the dialectic between spectacle and narrative has fuelled much of the classical cinema.[16] Donald Crafton in his study of slapstick comedy, "The pie and the chase," has shown the way slapstick did a balancing act between the pure spectacle of gag and the development of narrative.[17] Likewise, the traditional spectacle film proved true to its name by highlighting moments of pure visual stimulation along with narrative. The 1924 version of *Ben Hur* was in fact shown at a Boston theatre with a timetable announcing the moment of its prime attractions:

8.35 *The Star of Bethlehem*
8.40 *Jerusalem Restored*
8.59 *Fall of the House of Hur*
10.29 *The Last Supper*
10.50 *Reunion*[18]

The Hollywood advertising policy of enumerating the features of a film, each emblazoned with the command, "See!" shows this primal power of the attraction running beneath the armature of narrative regulation.

We seem far from the avant-garde premises with which this discussion of early cinema began. But it is important for the radical heterogeneity which I find in early cinema not to be conceived as a truly oppositional programme, one irreconcilable with the growth of narrative cinema. This view is too sentimental and too ahistorical. A film like *The Great Train Robbery* (1903) does point in both directions, towards a direct assault on the spectator (the spectacularly enlarged outlaw unloading his pistol in our faces), and towards a linear narrative continuity. This is early film's ambiguous heritage. Clearly in some sense recent spectacle cinema has reaffirmed its roots in stimulus and carnival rides, in what might be called the Spielberg-Lucas-Coppola cinema of effects.

But effects are tamed attractions. Marinetti and Eisenstein understood that they were tapping into a source of energy that would need focusing and intensification to fulfil its revolutionary possibilities. Both Eisenstein and Marinetti planned to exaggerate the impact on the spectators, Marinetti proposing to literally glue them to their seats (ruined garments paid for after the performance) and Eisenstein setting firecrackers off beneath them. Every change in film history implies a change in its address to the spectator, and each period constructs its spectator in a new way. Now in a period of American avant-garde cinema in which the tradition of contemplative subjectivity has perhaps run its (often glorious) course, it is possible that this earlier carnival of the cinema, and the methods of popular entertainment, still provide an unexhausted resource—a Coney Island of the avant-garde, whose never dominant but always sensed current can be traced from Méliès through Keaton, through *Un Chien andalou* (1928), and Jack Smith.

NOTES

1. Fernand Léger, "A critical essay on the plastic qualities of Abel Gance's film *The Wheel*," in Edward Fry (ed.), *Functions of Painting*, trans. Alexandra Anderson (New York: Viking Press, 1973), p. 21.
2. See my articles "The non-continuous style of early film," in Roger Holman (ed.), *Cinema 1900–1906* (Brussels: FIAF, 1982), and "An unseen energy swallows space: the space in early film and its relation to American avant garde film" in John L. Fell (ed.), *Film Before Griffith* (Berkeley: University of California Press, 1983), pp. 355–66, and our collaborative paper delivered by A. Gaudreault at the conference at Cerisy on Film History (August 1985) "Le cinéma des premiers temps: un défi à l'histoire du cinéma?." I would also like to note the importance of my discussions with Adam Simon and our hope to investigate further the history and archaeology of the film spectator.
3. Robert C. Allen, *Vaudeville and Film: 1895–1915, A Study in Media Interaction* (New York: Arno Press, 1980), pp. 159, 212–13.

4. Méliès, "Importance du scénario," in Georges Sadoul, *Georges Méliès* (Paris: Seghers, 1961), p. 118 (my translation).

5. Metz, *The Imaginary Signifier: Psychoanalysis and the Cinema,* trans. Celia Britton, Annwyl Williams, Ben Brewster, and Alfred Guzzetti (Bloomington: Indiana University Press, 1982), particularly pp. 58–80, 91–7.

6. Musser, "American Vitagraph 1897–1901." *Cinema Journal,* vol. 22 no. 3, Spring 1983, p. 10.

7. Raymond Fielding, "Hale's tours: Ultrarealism in the pre-1910 motion picture," in Fell, *Film Before Griffith,* pp. 116–30.

8. I wish to thank Ben Brewster for his comments after the original delivery of this paper which pointed out the importance of including this aspect of the cinema of attractions here.

9. Eisenstein, "How I became a film director," in *Notes of a Film Director* (Moscow: Foreign Language Publishing House, n.d.), p. 16.

10. "The montage of attractions," in S. M. Eisenstein, *Writings 1922–1934,* edited by Richard Taylor (London: BFI, 1988), p. 35.

11. Ibid.

12. Yon Barna, *Eisenstein* (Bloomington: Indiana University Press, 1973), p. 59.

13. "The variety theater 1913" in Umbro Apollonio (ed.), *Futurist Manifestos* (New York: Viking Press, 1973), p. 127.

14. Michael Davis, *The Exploitation of Pleasure* (New York: Russell Sage Foundation, Dept. of Child Hygiene, Pamphlet, 1911).

15. David Levy, "Edison sales policy and the continuous action film 1904–1906," in Fell, *Film Before Griffith,* pp. 207–22.

16. "Visual pleasure and narrative cinema," in Laura Mulvey, *Visual and Other Pleasures* (London: Macmillan, 1989).

17. Paper delivered at the FIAF Conference on Slapstick, May 1985, New York City.

18. Nicholas Vardac, *From Stage to Screen: Theatrical Method from Garrick to Griffith* (New York: Benjamin Blom, 1968), p. 232.

Berkeleyesque Traditions

Martin Rubin

Traditional chroniclers of the stage musical—Gerald Bordman, David Ewen, Stanley Green, Richard Kislan, Cecil Smith, etc.—commonly interpret its history in idealistic terms as a progressive development toward an ever greater and more seamless integration of plot and music, with shows such as *Show Boat* (1927), *Oklahoma!* (1943), and *My Fair Lady* (1956) frequently cited as milestones in this evolution.[1] Kislan's *The Musical: A Look at the American Musical Theater* contains a representative statement of the traditional pro-integration position:

> What emerged was a more fluid and compact union of song and story. Many called it the new musical comedy; in reality, it was a new form, the musical play. . . . Within the book, no elements were intended to function without the others. . . . Character, situation, mood, and theme were placed ahead of hit song, star, gags, and formula. To weave music deeper

Excerpted from Martin Rubin, *Showstoppers: Busby Berkeley and the Tradition of Spectacle* (New York: Columbia University Press, 1993), 12–19. Reprinted with permission of the publisher.

into the fabric of the musical drama, [*Show Boat* composer Jerome] Kern drew on the example of the "leitmotif" theory from opera composition. The songs that were once adjacent to or companions of the drama now became an essential part of the drama. Music began to personify character, foreshadow mood, echo emotion, underscore dialogue, and parallel the libretto's emerging patterns of action and rest.[2]

Analysts of the film musical have generally followed this lead, stating the matter in terms of the mastering of disruptive spectacle elements by other, integrative elements. These can be narrativization (Patricia Mellancamp), "internal narrative logic" (Thomas Schatz), thematic unity (Stanley J. Solomon), the body and voice of the singer/star (Jacque Schultz), "transformative energy" (J. P. Telotte), connections of musical performance to ordinary life (Michael Wood), a utopian dissolving of oppositions (Rick Altman), or an overall fusion of all the elements of the musical (Timothy E. Scheurer).[3] In each case, the primary value is placed upon a unifying principle that serves to transcend the inherently divided structure of the musical.

However, it could be argued that nonintegration—a built-in and formalized resistance to the ultimate homogeneity or hierarchy of discourse—is essential to the musical genre, which is based precisely on a shifting and volatile dialectic between integrative and nonintegrative elements.[4] Viewed in this way, the history of the musical becomes not so much a relentless, uni-directional drive toward effacing the last stubborn remnants of nonintegration, but a succession of different ways of articulating the tension and interplay between integrative (chiefly narrative) and nonintegrative (chiefly spectacle) elements.

This interpretation of the musical corresponds to a vision of genres as being based on the maintenance of certain central, unresolved tensions (which may be formal, structural, ideological, or thematic). Genres that resolve their central "problems" too definitively often eliminate their raison d'être at the same time, as the recent decline and near-extinction of the movie western has demonstrated. In a similar way, any such complete and universally applied "solution" of the problem of integration would probably spell the end of the musical genre. Musicals would then be supplanted by mere films-with-music, which are quite a different thing.

If integration were indeed the goal of the musical genre, then a question might be raised regarding the examples provided by eighteenth- and nineteenth-century prototypical forms such as ballad opera, comic opera, and operetta.[5] These early forms of the musical were all relatively cohesive and integration-oriented in form, and they pointed a clear path for the developing genre to follow.

However, the musical genre declined to rush toward the promised land of integration. As has happened so often in its history, for every step taken forward along the road to integration, another was taken backward. One possible reason for this recalcitrance might be that forms such as ballad opera, comic opera, and operetta are *too* well-integrated to be considered true musicals. They diminish that element of problematic, semiautonomous spectacle which, in tandem and constant struggle with the impulse toward integration, supplies the central dynamic that propels the musical genre.

The history of the evolution of the musical is not only the history of relatively integrated forms but also of those elements that pull in the opposite direction, that work to deintegrate and problematize the unity of the discourse of the narrative. These deintegrative elements should not necessarily be seen negatively, as crude and embarrassing drawbacks that need to be effaced. They can also be seen as essential elements in the musical genre's continuing and enriching struggle between integration and nonintegration, between the contradictory demands of narrative and spectacle.

The intention here is not to go to the opposite extreme and aggrandize certain types of musical simply for their hardy primitivism and their lack of bourgeoisified integrative elements. The idea, rather, is to point out that most histories of the musical, in their zeal to elevate its integration-oriented side, often overlook or underestimate the importance of nonintegration in the dynamic of the genre. These nonintegrative elements are a significant factor in the systems of virtually all individual musicals, including the predominantly integration-oriented ones, such as *Show Boat* and *Oklahoma!* In addition, those musicals in which nonintegrative elements are dominant need not be simply dismissed as stumbling blocks on the road to integration. Collectively, they form an important and lively tradition demonstrating that musicals can have much to offer outside the achievement of consistency.

It is to this spectacle-oriented, nonintegrative tradition that the Berkeleyesque is essentially linked. Indeed, in the cinema Busby Berkeley was that tradition's most prominent perpetrator. Accordingly, at this point it is appropriate to trace the development of that somewhat disreputable tradition, which Berkeley did so much to transfer to the screen.

AGGREGATE FORMS

> Do I contradict myself?
> Very well then. . . . I contradict myself;
> I am large. . . . I contain multitudes.
> —*Walt Whitman,*
> "Song of Myself"[6]

The spectacle-oriented mode of the musical (and, on a broader level, the entire musical genre) owes its genesis not only to the evolution of early musical forms such as ballad opera and comic opera but also to more general trends in nineteenth-century American popular culture. These trends spawned a whole series of related entertainment forms in a mode that might be termed (per *Webster's Ninth New Collegiate Dictionary*) a *conglomeration* ("a mixed coherent mass") or, perhaps better, the *aggregate* ("a mass or body of units or parts somewhat loosely associated with one another").

One of the pioneers in the evolution of nineteenth-century aggregate forms was the showman P. T. Barnum, a key figure in the history of American popular culture. Although today Barnum's name is mainly associated with the circus, his most important contribution to the world of entertainment concerned another type of institution: the so-called dime museum (Barnum actually charged a quarter). In 1841, Barnum acquired Scudder's American Museum in downtown Manhattan, a typical collection of natural history exhibits, scientific displays, and assorted curiosities. Renaming the place Barnum's American Museum, he converted it into a sensationally popular attraction by adding to the existing stock of educational exhibits diverse elements of the "freak" show, the circus, and the variety show.[7]

Barnum's American Museum was an early example of an aggregate entertainment form. It was a place where heterogeneity ruled, where as much diversity as possible was included under one roof. Rather than attempting to figure out what his customers wanted, then selecting and organizing the exhibits accordingly, Barnum operated on the principle of simply overwhelming his customers by including everything. In addition to the exhibits themselves, the museum also included a theater, which presented continuous performances of variety acts (singers, acrobats, animal acts, etc.), popular plays, and melodramas. All told, a patron of Barnum's American Museum could expect to receive an extraordinarily plentiful and diverse range of entertainment for the single admission price. In his autobiography, Barnum included this Whitmanesque catalogue of some of the bounty offered his customers:

> The transient attractions of the Museum were constantly diversified, and educated dogs, industrious fleas, automatons, jugglers, ventriloquists, living statuary, tableaux, gipsies, albinos, fat boys, giants, dwarfs, rope-dancers, live "Yankees," pantomime, instrumental music, singing and dancing in great variety, dioramas, panoramas, models of Niagara, Dublin, Paris, and Jerusalem; Hannington's dioramas of the Creation, the Deluge, Fairy Grotto, Storm at Sea; the first English Punch and Judy in this country, Italian fantoccini, mechanical figures, fancy glass-blowing, knitting machines and other triumphs of the mechanical arts; dissolving views, American Indians, who enacted their warlike and religious ceremonies on the stage—these, among others, were all exceedingly successful.[8]

After Barnum's American Museum was destroyed by fires in 1865 and 1868, he became primarily associated with the institution for which he is most famous today: the circus. Operating concurrently and sometimes in partnership with other leading showmen such as George A. Bailey, W. C. Coup, Dan Castello, and Adam Forepaugh, Barnum was involved in a major transformation of the circus form in the latter part of the nineteenth century. Previously, the circus had been based primarily on skilled performers displaying their acts one at a time, much like in a variety show. Beginning in the 1870s, the American circus turned in a direction where spectacle, extravagance, and opulence were stressed as much as were individual skills. Hundreds of performers were paraded, first in two rings, then in three, with the idea of presenting the audience with a *superabundance,* with more than could possibly be absorbed at a single sitting by any single spectator.[9]

It is this concept of superabundance that links the three-ring circus to Barnum's American Museum and to other aggregate entertainment forms. As Barnum wrote of his Museum:

> No one could go through the halls, as they were when they came under my proprietorship, and see one-half there was worth seeing in a single day; and then, as I always justly boasted afterwards, no one could visit my Museum and go away without feeling that he had received the full worth of his money. . . .
>
> From the first, it was my study to give my patrons a superfluity of novelties, and for this I make no special claim to generosity, for it was strictly a business transaction. To send away my visitors more than doubly satisfied, was to induce them to come again and to bring their friends. I meant to make people talk about my museum; to exclaim over its wonders; to have men and women all over the country say: "There is

not another place in the United States where so much can be seen for twenty-five cents as in Barnum's American Museum."[10]

Another important example of the aggregate tradition is the minstrel show, which reigned as the most popular American entertainment form in the period 1840–80. The minstrel show was a collection of comic and musical elements organized very loosely around a fixed format that consisted of three main parts. In the first part (which is the part corresponding to the subsequent popular image of the minstrel show), a group of performers in blackface seated themselves in a semicircular arrangement. Dominated by the central emcee (known as the Interlocutor) and the two disruptive end men (known as Tambo and Bones), this group presented a program of song, dance, and comedy tied to a heavily mythicized vision of the antebellum South. This first part was then followed by the olio (a series of variety acts) and the afterpiece (a one-act skit, usually a type of parody or burlesque common to the theatrical practice of the period).[11]

The minstrel show was very much in the aggregate vein: a conglomeration of diverse parts in which each act was presented as a self-contained unit designed to stop the show.[12] As Gerald Bordman writes of the minstrel show: "The show was held together by an external framework—what today's jargon would call a format—rather than by any internal cohesion or organically dictated form. Its devil-may-care indifference to even the vaguest dramatic unities helped establish a not altogether healthy slapdash tradition in the American Musical Theatre."[13] Centering on the two main elements of music and comedy, the minstrel show in some ways prefigured the nascent form of musical comedy, although two key elements were still lacking: narrative and spectacle.[14] These were supplied by the seminal 1866 show *The Black Crook,* which will be discussed below.

The next dominant form of American entertainment, vaudeville, was basically an extension of the minstrel show's olio: a series of separate acts in the music, comedy, and novelty modes.[15] American vaudeville differed from its French and British equivalents (known as music hall) in that music hall shows were less diversified, tailored more for specific class strata, and directed more toward establishing a sense of intimacy and rapport with the audience (often reinforced by having an emcee or host figure to tie the show together). American vaudeville did not feature an emcee; its variegated acts, pitched at a heterogeneous mass audience, succeeded each other without introductions or bridging elements; and it was generally a more objective and compartmentalized form than were its European equivalents.[16]

However, this does not mean that American vaudeville was merely an undifferentiated hodgepodge. The several acts (usually between seven and nine) of the standard vaudeville show were structured according to certain principles of logic and design, based on pacing, orchestration, and a consciousness of audience response, with the aim of creating an optimum overall impression of diversity and abundance.[17]

Other nineteenth-century-derived aggregate forms include the medicine show (something of a small-scale vaudeville show), the Wild West show (combining elements of the western, the circus, and vaudeville, and most famously represented by Buffalo Bill Cody's Wild West Show), the Tom Show (in which touring companies used the familiar story of *Uncle Tom's Cabin* as an elastic format allowing for the casual inclusion of novelty, specialty, and song-and-dance acts), and burlesque (which aggregated music, dance, comedy, and display of the female body).

Also of relevance to the aggregate tradition is the amusement park, particularly the type of self-enclosed, spectacular, all-inclusive bazaar pioneered by the opening of Coney Island's Steeplechase Park in 1897. It is worth noting some direct connections between the amusement park and the turn-of-the-century musical/spectacular stage. Frederic Thompson and Skip Dundy, founders of the legendary Hippodrome in New York, had previously made their mark by building Luna Park, the most beautiful and spectacular of Coney Island's great parks, in 1903. Florenz Ziegfeld, the most important figure in the creation of the American spectacular revue, got his show business start in the fairground/amusement-park field, first as a talent scout for the 1893 World's Columbian Exposition in Chicago and then as the promoter of strongman Eugene Sandow.[18]

Even the mainstream dramatic theater of the eighteenth and nineteenth centuries partook heavily of this aggregate impulse. Music, songs, and dances were freely interpolated into virtually every form of play. Between acts of plays, audiences were usually regaled with variety acts (singing, dancing, juggling, satire, pantomime, etc.), no matter whether the play was a Shakespeare tragedy or a potboiler melodrama.[19]

The texts of the plays themselves were often treated in a similar manner. Nineteenth-century performance style was based on treating each scene, each big speech, as a self-enclosed high point, almost in the manner of a vaudeville show.[20] Accordingly, a nineteenth-century production of a Shakespeare play might become something on the order of selected big moments from the play, with a few new songs and other interpolations thrown in for good measure.

One of the most striking examples of this casual approach to the unities of dramatic structure occurred during the 1888 Broadway revival of Johann Strauss's *Prince Methusalem,* a period Ruritanian operetta set in the requisite mythical European principality. During the show's run, the lead actor, De Wolf Hopper, bought performance rights to a new poem by Ernest L. Thayer entitled "Casey at the Bat," a recitation of which Hopper inserted forthwith into the middle of the second act.[21] It is perhaps difficult to imagine today how audiences of the time accommodated this sudden transition from Ruritania to Mudville, but they did accommodate it—indeed, it became the popular highlight of the show. Notions of unity and narrative consistency were not as paramount in the nineteenth-century theater as they have been in other times. Audiences of the day were more receptive to the concept of a theatrical show as a collection of powerful, autonomous moments and spectacular effects.

Although these aggregate forms are by no means completely random and disorganized in their structure, they generally lack the overriding sense of centrality and homogeneity that characterizes more strongly narrativized forms. A useful analogy (frequently called upon in recent art theory and criticism) concerns the idea of Renaissance perspective as the dominant system in Western representational painting (and photography), based on the use of a single dominant center (the vanishing point) to direct the viewer's gaze. This system can be contrasted with other systems of representation, such as Cubism or Oriental art, which are based more on the balance and arrangement of elements, and on a series of multiple "centers" dispersed throughout the frame. Narrative can be seen as a centering device analogous to Renaissance perspective, with a similar function of directing attention and containing the potential disruptiveness of heterogeneous elements.[22]

The types of arrangements used in alternative representational systems (such as pre-Renaissance, "primitive," Oriental, and Cubist art) bear a certain analogy to the nineteenth-century aggregate forms discussed above, which are based on a concept of multiple centers and which strive to make each unit, each act, each number, a self-contained highlight—a "showstopper." The very phrase "stopping the show" (frequently used to describe the effect of musical numbers) is itself of great interest in relation to these issues, especially when compared to the concept of narrativity, which is based on principles of sustained continuity and temporal flow.

To a certain extent, all musicals bear the mark of their ancestry in nineteenth-century aggregate forms, with the musical numbers functioning as a series of self-contained highlights that work to weaken the dominance of a homogeneous, hierarchical narrative continuity. In a similar sense, all musical numbers are spectacles, by virtue of the way in which they function as semi-autonomous exhibitions somewhat distinct from the discourse of the narrative.

It is important to emphasize that here the concept of "spectacle" need not be limited to the large-scale but may include anything that sets itself apart from the dominant narrative flow and calls attention to itself as an object of display. In these broad terms, something as simple as a provocatively garbed (or ungarbed) female body or a musical performer turning to address a song directly to the audience can function as an element of spectacle.

While all musicals bear the mark of their aggregate heritage, and all musical numbers are to a certain extent spectacles, certain musicals work to efface as much as possible the marks of spectacle and aggregation. These musicals belong to the tradition of the "integrated" musical, generally esteemed by critics and historians as the more modern, sophisticated, and artful tradition: ballad opera, opéra bouffe, comic opera, operetta, the Princess Theatre shows, *Show Boat, Oklahoma!*, etc.[23] The other major tradition in the evolution of the musical (and one generally viewed as the more primitive, unsophisticated, and artless) works to maximize heterogeneity, excess, and spectacle in the manner of nineteenth- and early twentieth-century aggregate entertainment forms.

The pleasure offered by these aggregate forms is largely directed toward creating feelings of copiousness, superabundance, variety, heterogeneity, inclusiveness, and blatant spectacle, based around a loosely organized series of self-enclosed units or climactic moments. In aggregate forms these qualities are stressed more than in integrated forms where the spectator's pleasure is more directly based on a unified, hierarchical, centered, closure-oriented experience, leading the spectator along a continuous path that organizes, arranges, and absorbs the various elements of the show/film/narrative.

Although recent film and narrative theory has placed major emphasis on the primacy of these latter, integrative elements in mainstream modes of art and entertainment, the example of divergent aggregate forms suggests that the narrative/integrative impulse ("integrated" being essentially just another term for narrative-dominated) has not always or necessarily been such a dominant force in a work of entertainment. The musical genre itself—something of a holdover from these more archaic entertainment forms—remains more or less in a state of unresolved suspension between aggregative and conventional narrative impulses. A major stylistic and structural choice in a musical therefore concerns

Fig. 2. Chorus girls revolve on a rotating multilevel wheel in *Footlight Parade* (1933),
directed by Busby Berkeley. Based on his stage production. Berkeley's choreography lent
itself beautifully to film, where high camera placements captured the symmetry of his
geometric use of bodies. Courtesy of Billy Rose Theatre Collection, The New York Public
Library for the Performing Arts, Astor, Lenox and Tilden Foundations.

the type of interrelationship it establishes between these two aspects of the genre.

NOTES

1. Gerald Bordman, *American Musical Theatre: A Chronicle* (New York: Oxford University Press, 1978); David Ewen, *The Story of America's Musical Theater,* rev. ed. (New York: Chilton, 1968); Stanley Green, *The World of Musical Comedy,* 4th ed. (New York: A. S. Barnes, 1980); Richard Kislan, *The Musical: A Look at the American Musical Theater* (Englewood Cliffs, N.J.: Prentice-Hall, 1980); Cecil Smith, *Musical Comedy in America,* 1950 (New York: Theatre Arts Books, 1981).

2. Kislan, *The Musical: A Look at the American Musical Theater,* 113.

3. Patricia Mellancamp, "Spectacle and Spectator: Looking through the American Musical Comedy," *Cine-Tracts* 1 (Summer 1977): 28–35; Thomas H. Schatz, *Hollywood Genres: Formula, Film Making, and the Studio System* (New York: Random House, 1981), 194–212; Stanley J. Solomon, *Beyond Formula: American Film Genres* (New York: Harcourt, Brace, and Jovanovich, 1976), 71–75; Jacque Schultz, "Categories of Song," *Journal of Popular Film and Television* 8 (Spring 1980): 24–25; J. P. Telotte, "A Sober Celebration: Song and Dance in the 'New' Musical," *Journal of Popular Film and Television* 8 (Spring 1980): 2–5; Michael Wood, *America in the Movies* (New York: Basic Books, 1975), 156; Rick Altman, *The American Film Musical* (Bloomington: Indiana University Press, 1987), 74–89; Timothy J. Scheurer, "The Aesthetics of Form and Convention in the Movie Musical," *Journal of Popular Film* 3 (Fall 1974): 308–17.

   A notable exception to the integrationist consensus is Gerald Mast's *Can't Help Singin': The American Musical on Stage and Screen* (Woodstock, N.Y.: Overlook Press, 1987). Although it is not a central element in his overall argument, Mast seems to accept quite cheerfully the inherent contradictions of the musical genre. For example, of George M. Cohan he writes: "He never quite left vaudeville behind—but neither have the very best American musical shows in some way or other. . . . But the problem of unity in this inherently disunified form is more paradoxical than later historians of the musical have been willing to admit" (p. 34). Most refreshingly, Mast sees such integrationist sacred-cows as Rodgers and Hammerstein's *Oklahoma!, Carousel,* and *South Pacific* as representing more loss than gain for the genre in the final balance (pp. 201–18).

   Jerome Delamater, in his essay "Performing Arts: The Musical" in *American Film Genres,* ed. Stuart Kaminsky (Dayton, Ohio: Pflaum, 1974), 120, calls integration the "Platonic ideal" of the genre but acknowledges that this ideal can be too restrictive.

4. "Discourse," a frequently used term in recent critical studies, refers to a distinct system of addressing the reader/spectator. Classical or conventionally realistic forms of art are commonly seen as those in which one mode of discourse is dominant. In musicals, the narrative/dialogue passages constitute one mode of discourse, while the singing/dancing passages constitute another, quite distinct way of addressing the spectator. The dominance of one discourse over the other in the musical is questionable or, at best, weakly resolved, and this is the beginning of the problem.

5. In ballad opera, spoken dialogue is combined with preexisting popular tunes to which

new lyrics are added (e.g., *The Beggar's Opera*). Comic opera is similar to ballad opera but uses original music that is more central to the narrative (e.g., Gilbert and Sullivan's works). Operetta is related to the comic opera, but with greater emphasis on romance and melodrama.

6. Walt Whitman, *Leaves of Grass: The First* (1855) *Edition*, ed. Malcolm Cowley (New York: Viking Press, 1959), 85.

7. P. T. Barnum, *Struggles and Triumphs: Or, The Life of P. T. Barnum*, ed. George S. Bryan (New York: Alfred A. Knopf, 1927), 1;183–97; Robert C. Toll, *On with the Show: The First Century of Show Business in America* (New York: Oxford University Press, 1976), 25–34.

8. Barnum, *Struggles and Triumphs*, 1:195.

9. George L. Chindahl, *A History of the Circus in America* (Caldwell, Idaho: Caxton Printers, 1959), 92–95; John Culhane, *The American Circus: An Illustrated History* (New York: Henry Holt, 1990), 95–107; Neil Harris, *Humbug: The Art of P. T. Barnum* (Chicago: University of Chicago Press, 1973), 235–76; Toll, *On with the show*, 46–47, 61–62.

Historians offer differing interpretations of Barnum's contribution to the spectacularization of the American circus. Neil Harris and Robert C. Toll see Barnum as chiefly a publicist and figurehead for the various circuses he fronted, with Barnum's early partner W. C. Coup credited as the main innovative force. However, John Culhane's exhaustively researched history accords Barnum a more central creative role in his circuses.

10. Barnum, *Struggles and Triumphs*, 1:193, 197–98.

11. Dailey Paskman, *"Gentlemen, Be Seated!": A Parade of American Minstrels* (New York: Clarkson N. Potter, 1976), 21–31, 83–88; Robert C. Toll, *Blacking Up: The Minstrel Show in Nineteenth-Century America* (London: Oxford University Press, 1974), 52–57; Carl Wittke, *Tambo and Bones: A History of the American Minstrel Stage* (Durham, N.C.: Duke University Press, 1930), 135–58.

12. Toll, *On with the Show*, 86.

13. Bordman, *American Musical Theatre*, 12. The final remark about the "not altogether healthy slapdash tradition" can be considered an example of pro-integration rhetoric.

14. Another key element (especially crucial to Berkeleyesque spectacle) that was minimized in minstrel shows was sex. The linking of sexuality with representations of African-Americans was a touchy area for white audiences of the time. The claims by some authors (e.g., Erenberg and McLean) that a sexual dimension was absent in minstrel shows seem overstated; there was apparently a limited opportunity for such material in the form of female impersonations and double entendre jokes. See Lewis A. Erenberg, *Steppin' Out: New York Nightlife and the Transformation of American Culture, 1890–1930* (Chicago: University of Chicago Press, 1984), 19; Albert F. McLean, Jr., *American Vaudeville as Ritual* (Lexington: University of Kentucky Press, 1965), 29; Paskman, *"Gentlemen, Be Seated!,"* 85–88.

15. Some writers use the terms "vaudeville and "variety" interchangeably. However, it is generally considered more accurate to use "variety" to denote an earlier, rowdier, less respectable phase of the form, before it was "cleaned up" (c. 1880) in order to broaden its appeal. See, for instance, Charles W. Stein, ed., *American Vaudeville as Seen by Its Contemporaries* (New York: Alfred A. Knopf, 1984), 3–5, 6–9, 98–99.

16. Stuart Hall and Paddy Whannel, *The Popular Arts* (New York: Pantheon, 1965), 56–57; Peter Leslie, *A Hard Act to Follow: A Music Hall Review* (New York: Paddington Press, 1978), 36–42, 49–50; McLean, *American Vaudeville as Ritual,* 34: Toll, *On with the Show,* 189–92.

    Several writers have linked the compartmentalized diversity of American vaudeville with the evolution of a heterogeneous mass urban audience in the late nineteenth-century United States. This connection would seem to be applicable to other aggregate entertainment forms as well. See John E. DiMeglio, *Vaudeville U.S.A.* (Bowling Green, Ohio: Bowling Green University Popular Press, 1973), 44, 197–99; McLean, *American Vaudeville as Ritual,* 3–15, 33–37; Robert W. Snyder, *Voice of the City: Vaudeville and Popular Culture in New York* (New York: Oxford University Press, 1989), xiii–xvi.

17. DiMeglio, *Vaudeville U.S.A.,* 35–37; George Gottlieb, "Psychology of the American Vaudeville Show from the Manager's Point of View," *Current Opinion* 60 (April 1926), reprinted in Stein, ed., *American Vaudeville,* 179–81; McLean, *American Vaudeville as Ritual,* 93–105; Snyder, *Voice of the City,* 66–68; Marian Spitzer, "The Business of Vaudeville," *Saturday Evening Post,* May 24, 1924 (reprinted as "The Mechanics of Vaudeville" in Stein, ed., *American Vaudeville,* 173–76); Toll, *On with the Show,* 276–77.

18. Charles Higham, *Ziegfeld* (Chicago: Henry Regnery, 1972), 10–18; John F. Kasson, *Amusing the Million: Coney Island at the Turn of the Century* (New York: Hill and Wang, 1978), 57–72; Gary Kyriazi, *The Great American Amusement Parks: A Pictorial History* (Secaucus, N.J.: Citadel Press, 1976), 42–65.

19. Foster Rhea Dulles, *A History of Recreation: America Learns to Play,* 2nd ed. (New York: Appleton-Century-Crofts, 1965), 112; Harlowe R. Hoyt, *Town Hall Tonight* (Englewood Cliffs, N.J.: Prentice-Hall, 1955), 19; Julian Mates, *The American Musical Stage Before 1800* (New Brunswick, N.J.; Rutgers University Press, 1962), 136–37, 154–55, 180; Toll, *On with the Show,* 9.

20. Toll, *On with the show,* 9.

21. Bordman, *American Musical Theatre,* 95.

22. Jean-Louis Baudry, "Ideological Effects of the Basic Cinematographic Apparatus," *Film Quarterly* 28 (Winter 1974–75): 41–42; Stephen Heath, "Lessons from Brecht," *Screen* 15 (Summer 1974): 21–22; Stephen Heath, "Narrative Space," *Screen* 17 (Autumn 1976): 83, 90–100; Bill Nichols, *Ideology and the Image* (Bloomington: Indiana University Press, 1981), 18–19, 49–57.

23. Opéra bouffe was a blend of satire, farce, song, and spoken dialogue that was especially popular in France during the Second Empire; its most famous practitioner was Jacques Offenbach. The Princess Theatre shows were an influential series of American musical comedies created by composer Jerome Kern, lyricist P. G. Wodehouse, and librettist Guy Bolton in 1915–18. Tailored to the confines of the diminutive Princess Theatre on West 39th Street, they downplayed spectacle in favor of intimacy and unity.

Buster Keaton in the Context of Stage Vaudeville and Silent Film Comedy

Robert Knopf

In his study of early sound comedy, Henry Jenkins suggests, "Perhaps, the habits of watching classical Hollywood texts had become so ingrained that spectators looked for causally integrated narratives even within films not primarily interested in telling stories."[1] If spectators watching early sound comedies, which frequently valued performers' virtuosity over narrative, found it difficult to break the habit of concentrating on narrative values, then spectators of Keaton's films, which hold narrative and gag values in a more precarious balance, may find it even more difficult to overcome the tendency to focus on narrative. Yet in order to see the vaudeville in Keaton's films, we must do precisely that: resist, albeit temporarily, the lure of the narrative. By doing so, I seek to answer the following questions about the influence of vaudeville on Keaton's films: 1) what elements of vaudeville influenced Keaton's filmmaking and remained in his films in some form?; 2) how did Keaton adapt his vaudevillian skills to film?; and 3) what

---

Excerpted from Robert Knopf, *The Theater and Cinema of Buster Keaton* (Princeton, N.J.: Princeton University Press, 1999), 36–40, 76–83.

attributes of film attracted Keaton and how did he use these attributes to expand and otherwise change his artistic vision?

One of the primary vaudevillian influences on Keaton's filmmaking may not
be immediately apparent: his use of improvisation. For Keaton, as with many
of the vaudeville performers who left the stage to make silent films, the practice
of improvising was central to his working process. "Vaudeville acts were rarely
scripted in advance or written down," notes David Robinson. "Generally they
were developed in performance, and perfected against the reactions of an audience."[2] By polishing their acts during performances, vaudevillians exerted
artistic control with unmatched immediacy. Although many of The Three
Keatons' routines had a basic shape, Joe [Buster's father] liked to change their
act almost every night and encouraged Buster to improvise. Keaton observed,
"We never bothered to do the same routines twice in a row. We found it much
more fun to surprise one another by pulling any crazy, wild stunt that came into
our heads."[3]

From the beginning of his filmmaking apprenticeship with Roscoe Arbuckle, Keaton learned to approach filmmaking with the same improvisatory
skills upon which he depended in vaudeville. Like Keaton, Arbuckle started
out as a vaudeville performer and, together with the less structured studio apparatus Joe Schenck had developed, this led Arbuckle to incorporate into his
filmmaking the methods of improvisational comedy-making he learned during
his stage work.[4] Arbuckle allowed Keaton to improvise extensively, so that
when Schenck put Keaton in charge of his own studio in 1920 Keaton's use of
improvisation was a firmly established part of his filmmaking approach.

To permit himself the freedom to improvise in his filmmaking, Keaton developed particular stylistic preferences that had practical as well as visual aims. By
using full or long shots, for example, Keaton allowed himself the opportunity
to improvise at will during the production of his silent films, since these shots
provided him with the physical space within the frame to improvise. The director and cameramen did not have to know what he would do next, so Keaton
maintained the immediacy of his vaudeville act. Medium and close-up shots
demanded that the cameramen know where Keaton would move next; long
shots, by contrast, allowed him to move within a larger area and gave him the
latitude to change his mind and follow his impulses. In addition, the full or
long shot in film most closely replicates the vaudeville stage in terms of the performer's physical relationship to the frame.[7] Keaton's preference for long shots
stems not only from the oft-quoted observation that tragedy is a close-up and

comedy a long shot, but also from the complementary notion that long shots emphasize the body in space. By choosing the long shot for his most extraordinary physical gags and stunts, Keaton focuses the audience's attention insistently on his physical virtuosity as a performer.

To allow himself as much artistic freedom as possible in front of the camera, Keaton insisted that his cameramen continue to shoot film until he said to stop. As Bruckman told Blesh, "The cameramen . . . knew one thing: never stop cranking until Bus said, 'Cut!' Anything might happen. Once into action, it would unfold in his mind, developing as he went along, germinating from a gag to a scene, from a minor scene to a master scene."[8] By insisting upon this rule and retaining control over the editing process and final cut, Keaton retained artistic control even when he had a co-director: as long as the camera caught the action, it remained Keaton's choice whether to include the improvised footage later.

The nature of this artistic control arose from the unique aesthetics of vaudeville. Vaudeville bills were structured in a completely different fashion from theatrical bills; vaudeville producers valued different qualities in performers from those encouraged and emphasized on the "legitimate" stage. By the end of the nineteenth century, the emerging trend in legitimate theater favored ensemble acting as part of a desire for greater verisimilitude.[9] As Jenkins notes, "The focus shifted from the individual performer's ability to 'stop the show,' to 'command the stage,' toward a theater perceived as 'group art,' where each element had to assume its particular place within the overall work."[10] The rise of the director as the locus of artistic control subdued the virtuosic performances by lead actors that had dominated theater for much of the nineteenth century. As legitimate theater strove for greater realism, the interaction among actors took precedence over the power and artistic expression of any one actor. Theatrical conventions were modified to accommodate the change in aesthetic values: actors no longer addressed the audience directly, for example, imagining the presence of an invisible "fourth wall" separating the stage from the audience.

Vaudeville, however, maintained a set of conventions directly opposed to the trends of the legitimate stage. Vaudeville performers addressed the audience directly, soliciting immediate responses to their every joke, stunt, and move. The vaudeville aesthetic was based on "affective immediacy"[11]—performers looked for immediate response from the audience and altered their act from night to night, theater to theater, and town to town depending upon the audience's reactions.[12] This led to a necessarily flexible structure for each act. As one teacher of vaudeville writing suggested, routines could be written down, a joke at a time, on index cards and reshuffled on demand to fit the needs of particular audiences, bills, and venues:

> Have as many cards or slips of paper as you have points or gags. Write only one point or gag on one card or slip of paper. On the first card, write "Introduction" and always keep that card first in your hand. Then take up a card and read the point or gag on it as following the introduction, the second card as the second point or gag, and so on until you have arranged your monologue in an effective manner. . . . By shuffling the cards you may make as many arrangements as you wish and eventually arrive at the ideal routine.[13]

The order of the cards was manipulated for purely emotional effect. Vaudeville producers judged each act's worth by the audible and visible reactions of the audience.[14] Producers shared this information among themselves and with the booking agencies that dominated vaudeville from the turn of the century. This information played a major part in the establishment of the reputation of each act, so that the audience's reactions shaped not only the act's nightly performance, but also its future marketability, salary, and placement on the bill. Vaudeville acts, therefore, had to be structurally fluid to adapt to the differing tastes of individual audiences. The livelihood of the performers depended upon their ability to constantly shift the focus of their material for greater impact: more laughs, more gasps, more applause.

Although vaudeville performers retained artistic control over the content of their acts, the producer of each vaudeville theater selected and arranged the acts on the bill for any given week. An evening of vaudeville was never organized with a narrative throughline or any sort of thematic coherence; instead, the producer arranged the acts with an eye toward constant variety.[15] As Brooks McNamara notes, "The organization of acts on a bill was governed by practical considerations about balancing the elements of a show, by traditions about the location of certain kinds of material within the show's framework, and by the attempt to create a 'rising action' as the evening progressed, building toward a climactic act at or near the end of the show."[16] The shape not only of the vaudeville bill, but also of each of the acts contained within it, was developed along this rising curve. Each act tried to finish its routine with a topper: a final gag, joke, or stunt that capped their performance by evoking the largest audience response yet. Thus, an evening of vaudeville was designed to elicit a series of rising curves, each one the length of a vaudeville routine—fifteen to twenty minutes in duration. The overall pattern of the vaudeville bill replicated the shape of an act, building audience response toward the "headliner," the best-known and hopefully best-received act of the evening, which operated as a topper for the evening's entertainment. Usually the topper was followed by a closing act or two that settled down the audience. Needless to say, the spots following the headliner were not considered desirable by performers because they functioned as a sort of anticlimax.

Keaton's films reveal a variety of approaches to transferring this structure to film. Sometimes, as in *Our Hospitality* and *The General,* the vaudeville structure is blended with a strong narrative line, the positioning of the gags and stunts supporting rather than challenging the dominance of the more linear, causally linked narrative. Other films display a more complex and equivocal relationship between the two structures. Yet another group of films, which includes many of Keaton's silent shorts and a few of his feature-length silent films, appears to depend upon vaudeville structure—the rise in pure emotional and comic effect—for cohesiveness, using narrative as a pretext for extended gag sequences.

Buster Keaton began making films with Roscoe Arbuckle in 1917, as the American film industry was in the midst of a massive stylistic and economic transformation—from a "cinema of attractions"[17] to classical Hollywood cinema; from a loose association of independent producers into what was becoming the Hollywood industry. Bordwell, Staiger, and Thompson's seminal work, *The Classical Hollywood Cinema,* marks 1917 as the beginning of the classical Hollywood era, when the classical Hollywood style and industry came of age. As Thompson suggests, "The formulation of the classical mode began quite early, in the period around 1909–11, and . . . by 1917, the system was complete in its basic narrative and stylistic premises. During the early and mid-teens, older devices lingered, but classical norms began to coalesce."[18] Keaton's introduction to filmmaking comes at this crucial juncture in the history of American filmmaking, just as his loss of independence as a filmmaker when he signed with MGM in 1928 coincides with the next major phase in the development of classical Hollywood cinema—the introduction of sound films. Although Keaton's sound films at MGM were financially successful, he was never again given the opportunity to direct his own work. His reputation as a film director is therefore based on the silent films he made during the 1920s, the so-called "classic era" of slapstick film comedy.

Neale and Krutnik observe, however, that the classic era of slapstick comedy is not nearly as stylistically monolithic as scholars have traditionally portrayed it. Instead they argue that "these films are a specific and unstable combination of slapstick and narrative elements rather than the final flowering of an authentic slapstick tradition, which is how they have generally tended to be seen."[19] Perhaps because the first sound comedies in the late 1920s and early 1930s exhibit a more disruptive relationship between gag and narrative, the silent comedies of the 1920s appear in contrast to be more firmly classical than they actually are. It may be more accurate, therefore, to view the silent comedies of the 1920s as part of an ongoing negotiation between gags and narrative, one that shifts its favor toward gags with the onslaught of stand-up comedians from vaudeville into film at the beginning of the sound era.

Although Keaton developed stronger narratives after he made the transition to feature-length films, his vaudeville training—his knowledge and love of gags, gag structure, acrobatics, and improvisation—remained a dominant part of his film practice. And to understand the shifting relationship between gags and narrative in Keaton's films, we must first locate his work within the historical evolution of Hollywood cinema as an industry and a form.

The films produced from the advent of cinema in 1894 through approximately 1908 have been labeled "primitive" by many film historians. In recent years, scholars have challenged the suitability of this term.[20] Tom Gunning cogently argues that film historians view these films as primitive only in retrospect.[21] Once film historians have assumed that the tight linear causality of later cinema is the inevitable form of filmmaking, they then find early cinema lacking in this regard. Gunning emphasizes the roots of early cinema in vaudeville and popular entertainment and advances the theory that early cinema, rather than being a nascent form of narrative-based film, comes from an entirely different tradition, one that valued variety over unity. During this transition, "The US cinema moved from a narrative model derived largely from vaudeville into a filmmaking formula drawing upon aspects of the novel, the popular legitimate theater, and the visual arts, and combined with specifically cinematic devices."[22]

Because of early cinema's dependence on the vaudeville theater as an exhibition site, vaudeville exerted a strong influence on the forms of early cinema: "Exhibition circumstances, short length, and small-scale production facilities dictated the creation of films which modeled themselves largely on types of stage acts: the variety act, the fictional narrative, the scenic (views of interesting locales), the topical (presentations of current events), and the trick film."[23] From 1903 to 1908, films began to exhibit one of the fundamental features of narrative—linear causality—with the chase film emerging as one of the first genres to temporally extend a single action across an entire short film. As Thompson observes, "Rather than confining itself to a simple, brief slapstick fight, the film might prolong its action by having one combatant flee, with the other chasing and passersby joining in."[24] Two vaudeville forms—the vaudeville skit and the playlet—exerted a powerful influence on the forms of early cinema. A vaudeville skit "usually involved a couple of comics performing verbal and sight gags in a relatively static situation."[25] Vaudeville playlets told a story in extremely compressed form—a "highly episodic series of highlights from existing works."[26] Neither skits nor playlets encouraged the tight and prolonged line of cause-and-effect seen in classical Hollywood cinema, however; skits were too brief, while playlets were too episodic and depended too much on coincidence to prolong the action.[27]

As the film industry expanded, several factors encouraged producers to switch from vaudeville structure to a more classical structure inspired by fiction and drama. First, producers increased the length of their films in order to meet audience demand for more of their product. As Thompson observes, the film industry rapidly discovered that narrative films were the most cost-effective and reliable form to expand to greater length: "Because of film's success, more footage was needed, and it proved more predictable to manufacture staged films than documentaries. In addition, all other things being equal, a longer narrative film was proportionately cheaper than a short one, since the same sets and personnel could be used to create a greater amount of footage."[28] Second, classical narrative films were much easier to mass produce than documentaries because of the classical narrative's reliance on formulaic plot constructions.

Full-length dramatic films became the norm after 1915, while comedy was mostly confined to shorter films of one- and two-reel length: "Relatively few feature-length comedies were produced before 1920, and even in 1925, the year of *The Gold Rush, The Freshman,* and *Seven Chances,* almost one thousand reels of short comedies were released."[29] As early as 1914, Mack Sennett produced the feature-length comedy *Tillie's Punctured Romance,* starring Mabel Normand and Charlie Chaplin, but this one-time experiment was not repeated for several years. The few feature-length comedies produced in the late 1910s, such as those of Douglas Fairbanks, tended to be more realistic and character-based comedies, as compared to the gag-based shorts popularized by Chaplin, Lloyd, and Arbuckle in the mid- to late 1910s. Richard Koszarski notes that high and low comedy were polarized in the film industry during this time: "Audiences now began to see two distinct types of comedy. The more 'high-class' comedy descended from Broadway adaptations and portrayed recognizable characters in believable situations. It was generally to be seen only in features. Short films were the province of 'low comedy,' a continuation of the slapstick tradition of nickelodeon days."[30]

With the popular success of *The Kid* (1921), Chaplin proved that a slapstick comedian could produce a commercially viable full-length comedy. Although Chaplin did not release another feature-length comedy until 1925, Lloyd began releasing one or two features per year in 1921 and Keaton proceeded at the same pace beginning in 1923 with *The Three Ages*.[31] In order to overcome the industry-wide reluctance to produce feature-length films by slapstick comedians, the comedians (and their producers) incorporated stronger narrative elements into their feature films. Yet even as he introduced more developed narratives into his feature films, Keaton retained much of the spirit of his vaudeville routines in his gag sequences, which were sometimes quite extensive. For this reason, his films exhibit a wide range of relationships between gag and narrative, as he experimented with different ways of balancing the demands of vaudeville and Hollywood.

KEATON IN CONTEXT: KEATON, CHAPLIN, AND LLOYD

Keaton was only one of the many vaudeville comedians who tried their hands at blending slapstick comedy with traditional narrative in the 1920s. By the time Keaton began making features, classical Hollywood cinema had become entrenched as an industry and a style, both in dramatic features and in the genteel comedies of actors such as Sidney Drew. It was left for comedians such as Keaton, Chaplin, and Lloyd to find the means to blend slapstick into traditional narratives, though each of them did so in a somewhat different way.[32]

Because Lloyd's films were heavily influenced by the classical style of director and producer Hal Roach, his films consistently subordinate gags to narrative. As Frank Krutnik cogently argues, in Lloyd's films "gags tend to *arise from* the narrative rather than competing with it. Both the status of Lloyd-as-comedian and the gags themselves are 'naturalized' within a narrative process."[33] His gags therefore lose much of their power to disrupt. Conversely, Chaplin—primarily because of the great freedom he enjoyed as an independent director—was less concerned with the unity and driving force of the narratives in his feature-length films than he was with the dynamism of individual scenes and his own performance. Chaplin constructed his films by a method of accretion rather than depending upon the strict causality of classical narrative structure.[34]

Keaton was more concerned with narrative structure than Chaplin, yet he was less classical than Lloyd in his subordination of gags to narrative. As he displayed in *The General* (1927), Keaton was capable of constructing classical narratives, yet he enjoyed enough freedom under producer Joe Schenck to diverge into extended gag and stunt sequences. He was therefore able to combine the most fantastic gags and stunts with traditional narratives.

For the most part, Keaton's vaudeville—the gags, acrobatics, and optical illusions Keaton learned in vaudeville with The Three Keatons—provided the inspiration for his disruptive flights of fantasy, while his realism came from film, or more accurately from the attributes of film to which Keaton was attracted: long shots, long takes, and the composition of shots within the mise-en-scène. By its nature, vaudeville (particularly The Three Keatons' style of knockabout comedy) was disruptive and chaotic. In contrast, while film is not inherently orderly, Keaton created his short and feature films in Hollywood, where the commercial film industry was rapidly turning its filmmaking process into inarguably the most systematic or standardized style of storytelling in movie history—classical Hollywood cinema. As a result, Keaton's films evince a fundamental conflict between vaudeville and Hollywood, gags and narrative, fantasy and realism. In using the word "conflict," I do not mean to depict this relationship in Keaton's films as counterproductive. On the contrary, I believe that Keaton's unique combination of theatrical slapstick and visual realism goes to the heart of his achievement as a film artist.

Like Keaton, Chaplin groomed his skills on the stage—specifically, in the British music-hall—before he started making films. Chaplin, however, remained much more closely wed to his popular entertainment roots than Keaton. In Chaplin's films we see music-hall gags transferred to the screen fairly intact; his routines retain much of their original scale and style. He rarely uses film to enlarge the physical scale of his gags. On the contrary, he brings in the camera in order to focus more closely on smaller-scale gags. While Keaton's camera captures his body in relationship to a very real and potent world, Chaplin's camera tends to isolate him from the world so that we can revel in the charm and physical grace of his performance. We need only think of each comedian's most famous gag to understand this basic distinction: the "Oceana Roll" from Chaplin's *The Gold Rush* (1925) and the falling-wall sequence from Keaton's *Steamboat Bill, Jr.* (1928). In the former, Chaplin executes a classic transformation gag, spearing two dinner rolls with the ends of two forks and moving the forks and rolls as if they were a pair of dancing legs. The scene is captured in a medium shot (almost a close-up) of Charlie at a dinner table. The closeness of the camera to him allows Chaplin to emphasize the delicate motions of the dancing rolls. This scene is emblematic of Chaplin's approach to transferring his vaudeville to film: he uses film to bring the audience closer to the action. He also achieves greater intimacy through his use of medium and close-up shots, a preference that supports his somewhat sentimental narratives as well as his fine, detailed gag work.

Conversely, Keaton's trademark gag, the falling wall, evinces a different aesthetic. Rather than moving the camera closer for greater detail and intimacy, Keaton pulls it back in order to capture Buster's relationship to his environment. While Chaplin uses medium and close-up shots to create audience empathy for the plight of his character, Keaton prefers to use the long shot to create a larger image, one that visually exceeds the boundaries of his body. Particularly in his climactic sequences, Keaton's use of extreme long shots provides the audience with greater emotional distance from his character, a quality that is amplified by his understated acting style. Buñuel commends this aspect of Keaton's work when he designates him "the great specialist against all sentimental infection."[35] While Chaplin usually concludes his feature films with an emotional catharsis naturally deriving from the story (as in the close-up shot at the end of *City Lights*), Keaton frequently fails to provide the emotional release of the sentimental ending. Instead, he resolves his films in physical chases executed on the largest possible scale, depending on his acrobatic grace for closure rather than the audience's emotional identification with his character.

The larger physical scale of Keaton's gags and stunts contributes to their status as attractions. On the basis of sheer size alone, Keaton's gags tend to break free of the confines of his narratives. From the rotating house in *One Week* (1920) to the multiple Busters of *The Playhouse* (1921) to the cyclone in *Steamboat Bill, Jr.,* Keaton's films demonstrate his decided preference for sequences that are more concerned with showing than telling. In comparison, although Chaplin's gags may also be disruptive of the narrative, he is still bound to the aesthetic of the music-hall. Chaplin makes little attempt to transform his vaudeville aesthetic visually; he is more concerned with developing the emotional and social aspects of the story than with exploring film's ability to enlarge the visual realism or physical scale of his comedy. In *The Gold Rush,* for example, Chaplin juxtaposes the realistic opening sequence of the westward migration for gold with artificial-looking studio shots of the interior of the cabin as well as exterior shots in which he makes no attempt whatsoever to disguise his use of a rather flimsy-looking model of the cabin. When Chaplin does move to the larger scale, therefore, his films rarely inspire in us a sense of wonder as to how he created the world as a performer, creating in the words of Dan Kamin a "one-man show."[36] In Keaton's films, the world itself is an integral part of the show, and consequently the world embraces the illogic of his vaudeville comedy rather than serving merely as a background for it.

Although Keaton and Chaplin shared a background on the popular stage, their differences were already evident in their vaudeville and music-hall stage acts. We must resist the temptation to lump all comic performers from the variety stage into the single category of "comedian." The variety stage (I include both vaudeville and music-hall in the larger category of "variety") encompassed diverse types of performers within every category of performance. Not only was variety comprised of musicians, comedians, magicians, dancers, and specialty acts, but each category contained subcategories. Just as the larger category of dancing acts include everything from tap dancing to chorus lines, so did "comedians" include double-talk teams, stand-up comedians, and mimes.

Despite the range of work that The Three Keatons performed, Keaton was primarily a knockabout comedian—a comic acrobat. Because of the spatial requirements of his family's acrobatics, Keaton learned to work in a deep stage space early in his career. Whereas Keaton rarely performed without his family, Chaplin frequently worked as a solo act on stage and was always the center of the theatrical attention. He was first and foremost a mime.[37] From his early days as the star of Fred Karno's comedy troupe "Karno's Komics," he grew accustomed to being the driving force of the comic action, while Keaton learned to collaborate, building comic action in reaction to a larger power (his father). In silent film comedy, Keaton displaced the driving force of his father into the world around him, while Chaplin remained the disruptive center of attention in a smaller world that revolved around him.

Like Keaton, Harold Lloyd sought to expand the physical scale of his comedy, particularly in his feature films. Yet Lloyd's approach differed from Keaton's in several key respects. First, Lloyd did not use long shots and long takes for stunts as frequently as Keaton did. Lloyd simply was not as skilled an acrobat as Keaton, and therefore he was forced to construct many of his most daring sequences in the editing room. When the three-story wall falls on Buster in *Steamboat Bill, Jr.,* there is no doubt that Keaton actually performed the stunt. When Lloyd clings to the hands of the tower clock in *Safety Last* (1923), the action is shown predominantly in deceptive full shots. The director used progressively higher camera angles to suggest a height that is illusory—Lloyd later admitted that he was only two stories off the ground with a padded platform beneath him—and chose a building that was located at the top of a hill, so that the buildings below the hill contributed to the visual deception.[38] Whereas Lloyd's use of the full shot draws attention away from the larger world and toward his own character, Keaton's use of the long shot emphasizes the patterns his stunts create. His stunts become inseparable from his environment, drawing our focus to the mechanisms of the world he inhabits. By projecting his comic vision onto the world rather than keeping it contained within his character, as do Chaplin and Lloyd, Keaton suggests that the world itself may function according to the irrational and ephemeral dictates of vaudeville.

NOTES

1. Henry Jenkins, *What Made Pistachio Nuts?: Early Sound Comedy and the Vaudeville Aesthetic* (New York: Columbia University Press, 1992), 107.
2. David Robinson, *Buster Keaton* (Bloomington: Indiana University Press, 1969), 18. See Jenkins, *What Made Pistachio Nuts?*, 75.
3. Buster Keaton with Charles Samuels, *My Wonderful World of Slapstick* (New York: Doubleday, 1960), 33.
4. Tom Dardis, *Keaton: The Man Who Wouldn't Lie Down* (London: André Deutsch, 1979; W. H. Allen, 1989), 38.
5. Kevin Brownlow, *The Parade's Gone By* (New York: Alfred Knopf, 1968), 270.
6. "Keaton Interview," eds. Joan and Bob Franklin (New York: Oral History Project of Columbia University, 1958), 19–20.
7. Early silent film was shot almost entirely in long shots, reflecting the influence of theater on film. David Bordwell, Janet Staiger, and Kristin Thompson, *The Classical Hollywood Cinema* (New York: Columbia University Press, 1985), 214.
8. Rudi Blesh, *Keaton* (New York: Macmillan, 1966), 214.
9. Helen Krich Chinoy, "The Emergence of the Director," in *Directors on Directing: A Sourcebook of the Modern Theater* (rev. ed.), eds. Toby Cole and Helen Krich Chinoy (New York: Macmillan, 1963), 22–31.
10. Jenkins, *What Made Pistachio Nuts?*, 67.
11. Ibid., 61.
12. Ibid., 73–77.
13. Brett Page, *Writing for Vaudeville* (Springfield, Mass.: Home Correspondence School, 1913), 86.
14. Jenkins, *What Made Pistachio Nuts?*, 79.
15. As vaudeville grew as an economic institution, the demand for variety within each act increased too. Performers were required to incorporate more and more specialties within their acts in order to distinguish themselves from competing acts. See Jenkins, *What Made Pistachio Nuts?*, 69–70. The Keatons followed this trend, blending knockabout comedy with eccentric dancing, imitations, songs, and music.
16. Brooks McNamara, ed. *American Popular Entertainments.* (New York: Performing Arts Journal, 1983), 17.

17. Tom Gunning, "The Cinema of Attractions: Early Film, Its Spectator, and the Avant-Garde," *Wide Angle* 8.3/4 (1986): 63–70.

18. Bordwell, Staiger, and Thompson, *The Classical Hollywood Cinema,* 157.

19. Steve Neale and Frank Krutnik, *Popular Film and Television Comedy* (New York: Routledge, 1990), 5.

20. See Bordwell, Staiger, and Thompson, *Classical Hollywood Cinema,* 158. "The term 'primitive' is in many ways an unfortunate one, for it may imply that these films were crude attempts at what would later become classical filmmaking. While I use the word because of its widespread acceptance, I would prefer to think of primitive films more in the sense that one speaks of primitive art, either produced by native cultures (e.g., Eskimo ivory carving) or untrained individuals (e.g., Henri Rousseau). That is, such primitive art is a system apart, whose simplicity can be of a value equal to more formal aesthetic traditions."

21. Gunning, "Cinema of Attractions," 64.

22. Bordwell, Staiger, and Thompson, *Classical Hollywood Cinema,* 157.

23. Ibid., 159. See also Robert C. Allen, *Vaudeville and Film 1895–1912: A Study in Media Interaction* (New York: Arno, 1980), on the economic interaction between the two media from the advent of film until 1912.

24. Ibid., 160.

25. Ibid., 159.

26. Ibid., 160.

27. Ibid., 160.

28. Ibid., 162.

29. Richard Koszarski, *An Evening's Entertainment: The Age of the Silent Feature Picture, 1915–1928.* Vol. 3, *History of the American Cinema* (New York: Charles Scribner's Sons, 1990), 174.

30. Ibid., 175.

31. Arbuckle starred in features produced by Adolf Zukor starting with *The Round Up* (1920), but the films were hastily made and unsuited for him, particularly in their emphasis on dialogue titles over slapstick. See Koszarski, *Evening's Entertainment,* 178.

32. Although I have kept references to other film comedians to a minimum throughout this book, I feel that it is necessary to compare Keaton to his contemporaries at this point in order to isolate the particular qualities of Keaton's blend of vaudeville and film. Most scholars of silent film comedy limit themselves to discussing Keaton in the context of the films of his two or three more famous rivals: Charlie Chaplin, Harold Lloyd, and occasionally Harry Langdon. I will follow this tradition for the following reasons. First, few if any slapstick comedians other than the "big four" had demonstrable artistic control over their films. Roscoe Arbuckle, for example, lost almost all artistic control over his films when he began making features for Paramount in 1920. Many of the next tier of comedians (in terms of box-office success) never made feature films, and although I do not mean to equate running time with quality, short films necessarily curtail the extent of our inquiry into the gag-narrative relationship. Langdon will also be excluded from my comparisons, for, despite the influence he exerted on his films as a comic performer, they

were directed by the strong-willed Frank Capra, and it is therefore difficult to attribute any cinematic innovations solely to Langdon. For a detailed analysis of Langdon's influence on the mise-en-scène of his films, see Joyce Rheuban, *Harry Langdon: The Comedian as Metteur-en-Scène* (Rutherford, N.J.: Fairleigh Dickinson University Press, 1983).

33. Frank Krutnik, "A Spanner in the Works?: Genre, Narrative and the Hollywood Comedian," in *Classical Hollywood Comedy,* ed. Kristine Brunovska Karnick and Henry Jenkins (New York: Routledge, 1995), 19. Italics in original. In his tribute to Larry Semon, Petr Král contrasts the nonconformism of Semon's films with Lloyd's films, which he characterizes as "healthy, classically balanced *white* humour," crediting Lloyd's style to Roach. Petr Král, "Larry Semon's Message," trans. Paul Hammond, in *The Shadow and Its Shadow: Surrealist Writing on the Cinema,* 2nd ed., ed. Paul Hammond (Edinburgh: Polygon, 1991), 177. Král attributes Roach's commercial success in the 1930s to his essential conformism, asserting that Roach's films provided a sense of stability for audiences living in the economic uncertainty of the Depression.

34. Donald W. McCaffrey, *Four Great Comedians: Chaplin, Lloyd, Keaton, Langdon* (New York: A. S. Barnes, 1968), 165.

35. Luis Buñuel, "Buster Keaton's College," trans. David Robinson, in *The Shadow and Its Shadow: Surrealist Writing on the Cinema,* 2nd ed., ed. Paul Hammond (Edinburgh: Polygon, 1991), 64.

36. Dan Kamin, *Charlie Chaplin's One-Man Show* (Carbondale: Southern Illinois University Press, 1984).

37. See ibid., for a detailed analysis of the mechanics of Chaplin's work as a mime.

38. Walter Kerr, *The Silent Clowns* (New York: Knopf, 1975), 198.

An Embarrassment of Riches The Impact of the Classical Stage on Early Japanese Cinema

Keiko I. McDonald

Does there exist an unbridgeable gap, even opposition, between the two arts? Is there something genuinely "theatrical," different in kind from what is genuinely "cinematic"?[1]

In her seminal essay of 1964, "Theater and Film," Susan Sontag posed these engaging questions, which have occupied many Western film critics for forty years and more. I cannot pretend to theorize away the sometimes troubled relationship between film and theater, although, obviously, I have set myself the task of dealing with their kinships. I do not even mean to tender a theory to explain the separate paths these two arts have taken, closely related as they are. Rather, I would like to break new ground by charting the influence of Japanese classical theater on its national cinema and assess the consequences for filmic art. I do hope that one pleasure this book has to offer is a heightened awareness in the West of the contributions made by Japanese classical

Excerpted from Keiko I. McDonald, *Japanese Classical Theater in Films* (Rutherford, N.J.: Fairleigh Dickinson University Press, 1994), 18–37.

theater to a cinematic tradition already known worldwide for its outstanding achievements and unique character.

Japanese classical theater embraces three distinct genres that have made Japan's art very much her own: Noh, with its emphasis on the aesthetic ideal of simplicity; Bunraku, with its near life-size puppet and chanter; and the colorful Kabuki, with its female impersonators. The viewer steeped in these traditional dramatic forms will undoubtedly notice many aspects of their stage conventions in Japanese cinema, and it is precisely this intimacy that makes the aesthetic/intellectual experience of such films more enriching and enlightening.

As Donald Richie has noted, "from the first the cinema [in Japan] was regarded as an extension of the stage, a new kind of drama, and not as in the West a new kind of photography."[2] Indeed, early Japanese cinema was greatly indebted to formal properties of the classical stage, especially Kabuki, and also to the Kabuki/Bunraku repertoire.

Of course this relationship could scarcely be as close or extensive as that between Japanese cinema and literature, since Japanese film is famously receptive to many adaptations of literary masterpieces, especially fiction. Film versions from the well-known Noh, Bunraku, and Kabuki repertoires, however, show the valuable effects that these dramatic forms have had on filmmaking.

Readers will naturally want to know at the outset what Noh, Bunraku, and Kabuki represent in Japanese culture. A number of works in English explain all three very well.[3] Those who need essential background information should pause to search it out before plunging into the work at hand. The first four chapters of Part 1 include information on each kind of theater, as demanded by the discussion. Even so, it seems a good idea to offer a brief overview here.

Noh drama developed out of a synthesis of various religious rituals and mimetic forms with roots in aristocratic and plebeian life alike. Thus *dengaku* (literally "field music") represented a kind of agricultural ritual related to hopes of good harvest. *Sangaku* ("variety music") combined feats of juggling, acrobatics, and magic. *En'nen* were prayers wishing long life to persons of high rank.

The present form of Noh is considered to be the creation of a father and son: Kan'ami (1333–84) and Zeami (1363–1443). As a dramatic form representative of the Muromachi period (1333–1573), Noh shares that era's aesthetic ideal of simplicity with arts such as monochromatic painting, landscape gardening, and flower arrangement. As shall be seen, its origins in the Japanese *locus classicus* of simplicity endowed Noh theater with notions of economy in props and backdrops, cast of characters, and expressive devices like masks.

Whereas Noh represents an art developed under auspices of power and privilege—various shoguns from the Ashikaga Clan—Bunraku and Kabuki came up from under, as it were. Both are associated with the cultural milieu of commoners in the Tokugawa period (1600–1868). Bunraku and Kabuki reflect a desire on the part of successful townsmen—merchants and artisans—to see their culture come to life on stage. Thus those who rose to economic power in the mid-seventeenth century helped bring about the blossoming of creative arts identified with the Genroku Era (1688–1703).

The Bunraku seen today is the traditional puppet form that uses half-life-size dolls manipulated by as many as three black-robed puppeteers. By convention, the black color is considered invisible. This art takes its name from the Bunraku-za in Osaka. Founded in the Edo period, this theater survives today as the only commercial theater devoted exclusively to the performance of Bunraku plays.

Bunraku itself grew out of various folk art performances involving puppet shows and musical and narrative features. The earliest puppeteers were groups of strolling players known as Kugutsu. They were essentially vagabonds, the men known for skill at hunting, the women being available as prostitutes. It is thought that they started giving puppet shows at shrine and temple festivals. The puppets they used were crude clay dolls worked by hand in a repertory limited to wrestling, swordplay, and some episodic drama.[4] By the eleventh century, Kugutsu were found throughout Japan, even on remote Awaji, which is known to this day for the primitive puppet art.

In the Bunraku theater, action onstage is explained by a chanter, the *gidayu.* He sits on the left side of the stage, accompanied by a *samisen* player. The narration, generally known as *joruri,* continues a venerable oral tradition. During the medieval period, blind monks gave strolling performances of recited tales. They were accompanied by tunes on a *biwa,* an instrument introduced from China. The material included Buddhist sermons and tales of war. Especially famous were recitations derived from the epic *Heike Monogatari (The Tale of the Heike),* whose subject concerned the rise and fall of the Taira Clan.

By the beginning of the sixteenth century, this oral tradition gave way to a new form called *joruri.* The most famous piece in this form was the twelve-part *Jorurihime Monogatari (The Tale of the Princess Joruri),* the story of romance between a divine princess and a young warrior. The success of this work bestowed its name on the new genre.

Sometime between 1558 and 1569, the *samisen* was introduced from Okinawa. Its percussive tone proved more suitable as a guide for the emotions of an audience, so the *biwa* gave way to it. It is not evident when puppeteering was incorporated in *joruri,* but some scholars think that puppet *joruri* performances were offered in Kyoto in 1596. Around 1580, both stringed marionettes and mechanical dolls were invented, and, twenty years later, an early form of the puppet drama Bunraku emerged, through a synthesis of the *joruri* narration, *samisen* music, and puppetry. In early Bunraku, each doll was manipulated by a single puppeteer concealed by a partition at the front of the stage. By 1734, it had achieved its present-day convention of the three-man system. As dolls became more expressive this way, they grew larger, to about half human-size.

The development of Bunraku theater is greatly indebted to two men, Gidayu Takemoto (1651–1714) and Monzaemon Chikamatsu (1653–1724). Takemoto opened the Takemoto-za, a Bunraku theater, in Osaka. He attempted to modernize the medieval *joruri* narration, which, by his time, had degenerated into a mere mannerism. Takemoto enriched the given *joruri* style with chanting techniques derived from popular folk songs and New Year festivity performances. His creation was given the very personal label: *gidayu* singing.

Chikamatsu wrote for both Bunraku and Kabuki stage. He broke with the tradition of plots based on supernatural and spectacular action. In the course of his career he produced more than a hundred Bunraku plays. Seventy-nine were classified as *jidaimono* (historical drama), which dealt with events in the lives of samurai and aristocrats. Twenty-four were classified as *sewamono* (domestic drama) since they depicted sensational events and scandals among commoners.

Critics commonly point to two salient features of Chikamatsu's plays: an exquisite literary style, and a vivid portrayal of individuals torn between the opposing values of *giri* (social obligation) and *ninjo* (personal inclination.)[5] His sympathies lie inevitably with those who choose *ninjo* and are crushed accordingly, since the society in Chikamatsu's world defined *giri* as the paramount value.

Although nurtured by commoners, the modes of representation in Bunraku and Kabuki were controlled in important ways by those in power. The development of *onnagata,* or female impersonators, is a case in point. Kabuki began with the song and dance performances of a priestess named Okuni, who was attached to a Shinto shrine in Izumo.[6] The main repertoire of Okuni and her troupe offered group dances, often intermitted by short, episodic plays. Okuni specialized in male impersonation. Wearing a long, Buddhist rosary ornamented with a cross, she acted the part of a man who flirted with courtesans. Performance was given in a hut and the staging was exceedingly simple without props. This phenomenon appeared in Kyoto at the end of the sixteenth century. Okuni and her troupe became so popular that they gave a command performance at the imperial court in residence there.[7]

This mode of performance came to be known as Okuni Kabuki or Onna Kabuki (female Kabuki). The emphasis was on sensual charm, readily shading into rawer forms of sex appeal as performers took up a far older profession of prostitution. Emboldened by Okuni's popularity, similar theatrical performances appeared. Among them was one called quite frankly Yujo Kabuki (Courtesan Kabuki). This sort of thing led the Tokugawa Shogunate to ban female Kabuki on moral grounds in 1629. In its place, Wakashu Kabuki (Young Men's Kabuki) came to the fore. Then it, too, became a source of scandal as the boy performers expanded their repertoire to all the arts of pleasing. The authorities forbade their appearance on stage in 1652.

The following year, however, officials yielded to collective pressure from theater owners. They restored Kabuki on two conditions: that young men not appear on stage with bangs, and that acting be limited to nonsensual mime. Since cutting off bangs was a sign of change from boyhood to manhood, the newly restricted art was christened Yaro Kabuki (Men's Kabuki). The lure of purely physical charms no longer being the main attraction, players were forced to exhibit real theatrical talent. Playwrights, too, had to enrich their offerings. Fortunately, Kabuki responded to these challenges, making rapid progress to become the sophisticated dramatic form known today. Another interesting result of Kabuki's original social context was the subsequent development of sophisticated specialty roles such as the *tachiyaku* or *tateyaku* (strong male hero) and the *onnagata* (female impersonator).

Important stage conventions of Kabuki include the *hanamichi* (passage from the stage to the rear of an auditorium) and the *mawaributai* (rotating stage). The *hanamichi* is used for entrances and exits of star performers and for certain dramatic actions. It began in the 1660s as a platform from the center stage to a point midway into the theater. In 1664, a system of curtains was introduced. This *tsuzuki kyogen* (literally, play with many curtains) helped develop more complex plots as each act concluded with a curtain. The rotating stage was introduced in 1713. It added speed and efficiency to scene changes, replacing the system of curtains.

Kabuki reached its high point as an art form in the Genroku period, thanks to the talents of a number of performers. Danjuro Ichikawa I (1660–1704), for example, initiated the *aragoto* (or "rough stuff") style of acting. It featured a bold and bombastic, he-man style popular with the townspeople of Edo. In contrast, Tojuro Sakata I (1647–1709) developed the *wagoto* (or "soft touch") style. Its keynote was a genteel, elegant manner more suited to the sophisticated cultural milieu of his native Kansai region. One notable *onnagata* was Ayame Yoshizawa I (1673–1729), who did much to sophisticate the art of impersonation.

Kabuki was considerably fortified by elements borrowed from the other two classical theaters. The plays themselves owed much to distinctions dating from the Genroku period. Thus both Kabuki *jidaimono* and *sewamono* were influenced by Bunraku. Many, in fact, were written first for Bunraku and later adapted for Kabuki. The dance drama called *shosagoto* developed from the Noh repertoire. This happened because the manners of everyday life had not yet been given artistic choreography in the Genroku period.[8] Kabuki, however, created its own variety of *sewamono*. This was *kizewamono* ("living" domestic plays). These dealt with the seamy side of life among the lowest orders of society. This genre fed on slice-of-life thrills like theft, murder, and incest. It reached for these depths in the mid-nineteenth century, long after Bunraku had reached its prime. It was now Kabuki's turn to hold sway, and it did.

Even so, Kabuki borrowed from Noh and Bunraku in creative ways and modified the received stylistic conventions. When a play from Bunraku is being performed in Kabuki, for example, the *gidayu* chanter, accompanied by *samisen* players, is seated on a dais on the stage left apron. This form of narration is called *degatari* ("visible narration"). In some instances, the narrator and players are placed in an alcove set on stage left and screened from view by a bamboo blind. The Kabuki play derived from Noh calls for *debayashi* (musicians and singers on stage); the narrator and players are placed on a rostrum at the back. These performers serve the function of the chorus used in Noh. The singers explain events for the benefit of the audience. They also speak for characters and give voice to their inner thoughts and feelings. Noh theater also contributed its instrumental combination of flute, hand drums, and stick drums.

As far as anyone can tell, the first attempt to make a Japanese film with the *cinématographe* dates back to the summer of 1897. The idea was to film two Kabuki *shosagoto* (dance) plays.[9] That attempt failed, but a successful first film was made towards the end of the same year. It offered glimpses of various sites in Tokyo, notably the famous Nihonbashi bridge. In 1898, seventy feet of film became the first commercial Japanese moving picture. It showed center-front shots of three geisha dancing. Japan's first "dramatic film" soon followed: a 150-foot-long depiction of a detective arresting a thief.

Japanese cinema spent its first decade stealing from the stage, since theatrical traditions were so strong that the new art form could not conceive dramatic conventions all its own. As a result, the burden of tradition retarded the formation of a specifically cinematic grammar, even as the continuity between old art forms and new made for something like an easier transition. Donald Richie has this to say about the situation:

> The West was given time to develop at least the rudiments of film grammar and vocabulary before the stage took over; in Japan the influence of stage upon screen was from the first complete. Since no two arts forms are further apart, the effect upon the infant Japanese cinema could have been disastrous.[10]

Critics commonly identify the three major characteristics of early Japanese cinema as *onnagagta* (female impersonators), *benshi* (commentators), and center-front, long shots following strict continuity. They also note the importance of cues taken from the Kabuki and related sources. Directors in the early days—especially until 1912—quite naturally turned to Kabuki with its rich theatrical resources and audiences well-prepared to respond to them for subject matter. Similarly, it seems only natural that Kabuki acting styles continued to give Japanese actors their cues for many years even after 1912.

These important characteristics are well documented in Richie's recent book *Japanese Cinema: An Introduction.*[11] Noël Burch also offers thought-provoking, if often dogmatic observations on these early practices.[12] The aim here is to complement the work of both these critics, with additions and modifications.

The unique Kabuki tradition of *onnagata* dates all the way back to the mid-Edo period, 1629, when the Tokugawa Shogunate banned women not only from Kabuki but from all other theatrical performances.[13] Early filmmakers, however, were not restricted to Kabuki female impersonators. Some *onnagata* came to the screen via actor training schools and the Shimpa stage. These performers were cast in *jidaigeki* (period films) and contemporary screenplays derived from the Shimpa tradition. Itself born out of reaction against Kabuki stage conventions, Shimpa made use of modern settings for a wide range of plays, with comedy and suspense among them. The Shimpa mainstay, however, was melodrama, most often derived from domestic novels of unrequited love.

The aspect of impersonation in female roles was "upstaged" onscreen, where the illusion of realism was strengthened by some of the conventions borrowed from the theater. Thus the female impersonator was often present to the viewer as "herself," not "himself," thanks to a distant camera recording the action in a series of long shots subject to rigid continuity. The Nikkatsu Company (established in 1912), for example, became an early major studio thanks to a repertory

Fig. 3. On the right, Tatsuya Nakadai, in Akira Kurosawa's *Ran* (1985), a retelling of Shakespeare's *King Lear*. In this film, Kurosawa blends the spectacle of Kabuki with the story of Shakespeare's tragedy, while shifting the gender of Lear's children from female to male. Courtesy of Billy Rose Theatre Collection, The New York Public Library for the Performing Arts, Astor, Lenox and Tilden Foundations.

of stereotypical tearjerkers. Popular themes involved the cruel stepmother and the woman divorced for reasons of incompatibility. The camera ground slowly through repetitious long shots focused on a weepy female impersonator whose body language of despair was given voice by the lugubrious commentary of the *benshi.* An example of this phenomenon would be *Konjiki Yasha* (*The Golden Demon,* 1917) whose theme was revenge for a lover's betrayal. Similarly, *Shinho-togogisu* (*The Cuckoo,* 1917) got its power from a tale of a wife separated by war from a loving husband whose mother is classically domineering.

The audience in those early days thought nothing odd in seeing the role of the fragile heroine in *The Cuckoo* played by a man, Teijiro Tachibana. Having begun his career in childhood on the Shimpa stage, this actor joined the Nikkatsu Company after graduating from actors' training school. He came to specialize in depicting delicate beauties—helped, it is said, by having the fragile constitution of a consumptive. His best surviving performance is in *Fukkatsu* (*Resurrection,* 1914), based on Tolstoy's novel. This film shows the in-fluence of the New Theater Movement, especially in the acting technique inspired by Stanislavsky; but Shimpa still dominates in a highly melodramatic treatment of social questions.

Resurrection is also notable as being among the earliest films in which female impersonators appeared in Western dress. The setting, too, was Westernized. Even the *benshi* followed suit, learning to imitate the woman on the screen singing the popular song "Kachusha Kawai ya" (Katyusha, my love). This was novelty to spare in a film 360 feet long.

The ample entertainment values of *Resurrection* were apparently typical of offerings (and audience responses) in the early *gendaigeki* films, whose contemporary settings feature heroines played by impersonators. There were, however, voices to be heard in opposition to this practice. The harshest criticism came from those involved in the Shingeki (New Theater) movement.[14] Hogetsu Shimamura, an advocate of Ibsen's realism, spoke out this way:

> Why don't Japanese filmakers use close-ups? . . . Why do Japanese films focus on a setting in which the actor looks like a tiny doll in motion against a vast background? . . . I have seen Teijiro Tachibana playing the heroine in *Resurrection* and thought it interesting in the love duels between Katyusha and Nevdulov. In the New Theater, however, we must have actresses; a female impersonator spoils any sense of realism. The same is true in films. Only when these horrible *benshi* give way to music used to enhance artistic effect, will we have films which appeal to the intelligence of the spectator, and realize the potential of this medium.[15]

The drama critic Kitaro Oka had very severe opinions about the films then in circulation. He was especially irked by their "presentational aspect."

> I dislike Japanese films, especially those featuring female impersonators in wigs. The female character herself is realistic while her impersonator is a fake. A wig like those worn in the West might possibly pass, but the ones our impersonators use are made of artificial hair which only serves to emphasize the masquerade. A film captures "reality." . . . Props, costumes, and setting are all real, but the female impersonator we have moving against this realistic background is unreal, and out of balance with the rest.[16]

The Japanese word *"jisshashugi"* conveys what these critics meant by realism here, namely a photographic fidelity to images. Such a spirit of fidelity did establish itself gradually, through in measure that varied from studio to studio. Nikkatsu was slow to replace its female impersonators with actresses who became studio "policy" only in 1928, when the *onnagata* joined the *benshi* in a strike that gave the company its chance to be rid of them both. Interestingly, the rival Shochiku Company (established in 1920), noted for its innovative approach to cinema, used "real" actresses from the outset. Even so, Shochiku made incidental use of *onnagata.*

The early years of the film were presided over by the *benshi,* whose complex functions scholars have been at pains to define. Don Kirihara, for example, claims that the *benshi* served not as a "neutral 'explainer'" nor as a dominant narrator, but rather "to reinforce, interrupt, counterpoint, and in any case to intercede."[17] Joseph Anderson cites the three major roles given the *benshi* by Japanese critics: "a narrator and voice actor," "commentator-reader," and "audience representative." For these critics, the *benshi* in his first capacity helps the viewer to achieve a "fuller sensual experience" by "appealing to senses other than sight." The third role relates to the *benshi*'s rendition of his own responses to the film as a viewer, not as a commentator.[18] From a semiotic point of view, Noël Burch argues that *benshi* was a fragmentation of the signifier.[19]

These views constitute an interesting testing ground for contemporary film theory on audience positioning. The Imaginary, a unifying function of the spectator, operates on an external unity, an intelligible discourse (movie), and positions him as "a unified, autonomous subject."[20] Thus his psyche is sensitized by features of film (images and narrative structure, for example) to create a sense or illusion of wholeness. Burch's deduction is based on the idea of the audience as a unified subject. On the contrary, Anderson's view presupposes the *benshi* rather than his audience as such.

Conversely, Don Kirihara brings some important cultural specifics to this discussion by explaining that *benshi* and spectators in those early days did not go to the movies equipped with the intellectual "positioning" one might assume today. Most *benshi,* in fact, were poorly educated, many having stopped their education in primary school. The *benshi*'s role was to make it possible for audiences seeking theatrical experience to enjoy the presentational aspects of film. In this capacity, the *benshi* was easily reduced to his own actual limitations, offering "legibility" to an audience itself far from ideal and therefore attentive to his performance, no matter how redundant or even erroneous his interpretation might have been.

Anderson and Richie also discuss the autonomy of the *benshi.* They point out that early audiences were eager spectators of foreign films that did more than quicken their desire to be entertained by novel scenes from the West: they needed someone to explain the West to them, even as its "evidence" appeared on the screen. The *benshi* did that too.[21] They also explain how the *benshi* constituted an important link between Japanese theater audiences and the emerging new technology of the movies, especially those made before 1902.

When the movies came, the West dropped its equivalent of the *benshi,* but Japan still felt the need for someone to explain. For one thing, the audience was not sure how the projector worked, and this they had to be told, since the ordinary Japanese, unfailingly curious, is usually interested in machinery. Furthermore, Japan has a theatrical convention of treating the necessary mechanism as a part of the performance itself, as in the Kabuki, where sets are charged with the curtain up. This interest in the machine rather than in the content of the film shown was most apparent when one of early showmen placed the projector on the right side of the stage and the screen on the left. Most of the spectators, if they could see the screen at all, viewed it quite obliquely, but at least they had an excellent view of the projection crew in action.[22]

Another cultural specific that explains the easy acceptance of the all-knowing *benshi* is the age-old Japanese tradition of storytelling. This essentially plebeian activity had already enriched many other forms of performance entertainment: Bunraku theater; the *narimono* musical accompaniment and chorus in Kabuki; and specific narrative traditions such as the historical *kodan,* the tuneful *naniwabushi,* and the comic *rakugo* tales.[23]

In the Bunraku theater, the narrator-chanter sits on the right-hand side of stage, exposed to the audience. Accompanied by the percussive *samisen,* he speaks not just for the puppet, but also for the entire dramatic action, rendering it more intelligible. Since Kabuki actors very rarely engage in singing or playing an instrument, the singers and musicians perform a similar function. In a Kabuki dance play (*shosagoto*) based on a Noh drama, for example, singers and *samisen* players sit on a rostrum at the rear of the stage. Players of the other instruments are placed at floor level in front of the rostrum.[24] In Kabuki plays derived from Bunraku, however, a narrator-chanter takes over from the musicians. He is seated on the *yuka,* a small elevation on the right-hand side of the stage. The musicians are sometimes placed in an alcove set on stage left behind a bamboo blind. The accompaniment (*narimono*) of Kabuki is itself important for clarifying dramatic highlights, using sounds of bells, drums, and wooden clappers.

Rakugo originated as comical tales accentuated with equally funny gestures and vocalizations in the late sixteenth century. This genre made great progress towards the end of the seventeenth century, gradually shifting audiences from feudal lords to the man in the street.

Naniwabushi is another Edo period entertainment, being essentially an oral narrative with occasional song accompanied by *samisen.* After the Meiji restoration, this genre became a more sophisticated kind of folk art, thanks to gifted narrators like the celebrated Kumoemon Tochuken.

Yet another Edo period form of popular storytelling is *kodan,* with its repertory of adventures of heroic samurai, most having to do with family feuds and vendettas. Its thematic concentration on military tales gave it a different name—*gundan*—at the beginning.

Prior to the Meiji period, all three of these popular narrative forms, each with its own storytelling mode, found a common venue called *yose.* One might think of it as a kind of storytellers' vaudeville.

The rise and fall of the *benshi* may best be illustrated by the changing phases of early Japanese cinema itself. The earliest film of any length at all was called *"engeki jissha eiga"* (film of ongoing stage action). This was an immediate success in 1908. The connection to established stage conventions made for obvious transfers and some creative evolution, too. Thus segments of Kabuki performance onstage were billed as "Kyugeki" or "old drama." In 1917 the Shinkokugeki Troupe was founded in response to modern drama movements of Shingeki and Shimpa. Its repertoire ranged from plays with modern settings to those set in pre-Meiji times. In staging the latter, the Shinkokugeki Troupe introduced a new, realistic style of swordfighting to replace the more abstract, formal, Kabuki-style choreography seen in Kyugeki films. And since swashbuckling needs a vehicle, the *jidaigeki,* or "period film," soon followed.

These films of ongoing stage action borrowed three important devices from the theater. The functions of Bunraku/Kabuki chanter, *naniwabushi* reciter, and *kodan* narrator were taken over by two kinds of specialists dividing their work between them, as it were. *Kowairo* were those who took charge of dialogue directly by imitating or in effect dubbing the real voices of actors appearing on the silent screen. Though these specialists were themselves low-paid actors or even vaudeville entertainers, they satisfied a public familiar with the voices of famous actors known from popular (and similar) scenes from the Kabuki and Shimpa repertories. The other half of the spoken work was done by the *benshi,* who followed the Bunraku/Kabuki custom of describing ongoing action and even, in full ceremonial Kabuki style, introducing the piece to be offered. In this latter function, the *benshi* might be thought of as providing a run of the "credits" with full pomp and circumstance, along with an impressive synopsis of the coming attraction. The third borrowed element combined a *narimono* adaptation of Kabuki-like sound effects of bells and drums along with *gidayu*-style samisen played in unison.[25] Solo *benshi* and groups of *kowairo* worked behind the stage at the cinema. Both jobs in fact fell to actors from local small theaters. This transfer might be thought of as resembling the crossover employment of symphony and movie palace orchestra players of the silent era in the West.

The popularity of this transfer of presentation from theater to cinema was vastly increased by *Soga Kyodai: Kariba no Akatsuki (Soga Brothers)*, a Kabuki stage performance filmed in 1908 on improvised location. The troupe involved was an all-female one called Musume Bidan (Group of young beauties).[26] The "set" consisted of a large tentlike curtain hung in a temple yard, with rough straw mats for staging. A total of 1,700 feet of film was shot against this backdrop. Since the aim of the film was to give the masses a sampling of Kabuki performance (most could not afford to see otherwise), the onstage illusion was given by a camera fixed at one point.

Purely by chance, one of the producers, Hideo Honda, thought of having actresses (actual female "Young Beauties," not impersonated ones) stand by the screen and provide a synchronized dialogue.[27] Needless to say, this was a piquant innovation in a *kowairo* field of narration still dominated by males.

The combined art of *kowairo* narration and *benshi* commentary was later used to highlight dramatic effects for *Soga Brothers,* paving the way for the basic *kowairo* film presentation form, the form in which dialogue among characters is spoken by several live *kowairo* specialists while the narration is accompanied by a single *benshi.* For better or for worse, the immense popularity of this early piece linked cinema to stage drama in a dependent friendship that was to hold the art of film captive for a long time.

An interesting manifestation of this pairing was the *rensa-geki,* or "chain drama," in which a stage performance was presented in segments live and in footage onscreen in the theater. Moviehouse programs from 1910 to 1917 featured this genre, along with a newsreel, some footage of street scenes, a foreign film, and a domestic "dramatic" picture.

The effect of this eclectic offering was described by one critic this way:

> From behind the curtain we hear various voices dubbed by *kowairo,* who use even "vulgar" language. We also hear *gidayu* from Kabuki. Flutes, drums big and small, and bells are all there. When a scene depicts a violin being played, we hear the instrument itself from behind the curtain. The viewers who love "sensational" effects respond to these devices, with applause and hilarity.
>
> At a moment of climax, or at the end of a tragedy, the screen is removed so that real actors can appear onstage to re-enact the scene. . . . This is real-live drama. The unsophisticated spectator sobs, clutching her hanky.[28]

This chain drama format—an admixture of the filmic and the theatrical—could impart more of a sense of motion and variety to a basically static series of long takes in which actors appeared so distantly, acting in accord with strict continuity.

The chain drama also featured another innovation, this time borrowing from the popular *naniwabushi* genre of tales of derring-do. A Kyugeki, or "old drama" version of the classical samurai saga *Chuchingura (Loyal Forty-Seven Ronin,* Matsunosuke's version, 1912), was filmed with inclusions taken from footage of a stage performance by the famous reciter Naramaru Yoshida. This hybrid performance was given a recorded sound track (played on a phonograph behind the screen) featuring Naramaru's delivery as recreated by his apprentice.

Despite its lack of artistic values, the chain drama continued to satisfy the masses. In 1917 some films appeared with promise of better fare in the genre, among them a version of Pushkin's novel, *The Captain's Daughter.* In that same year, however, the end of chain drama was announced by several factors working together. Budget restrictions limited the live drama portions, which resulted in stereotypical plots, correspondingly tedious. Then the police stepped in to enforce new safety regulations. In July 1917, all chain drama theaters under their jurisdiction were in fact cited as fire hazards, not being properly equipped to handle both their drama and cinema functions.[29]

Other types of cinema prospered, however, as productions and movie theaters increased in number, as did the power of the *benshi* with them. There were two thousand of these performers in 1918, and seven thousand by 1920, the year of their greatest prosperity.[30] The *benshi* soon proved to be very self-important. In movie theatres owned by the studios, a *benshi* could restructure a film to suit his own display. If a shot turned out to be too short to allow his storytelling gift full play, he could demand a longer retake. With some minor exceptions, however, the influence of *benshi* extended to exhibition not to production. The commonest practice involved *benshi* lording it over projectionists. Film speed might then be adjusted, as when a somewhat slower pace at a climax gave a *benshi* more scope for working his vocal magic. Similarly, unwanted scenes might even be spliced away.

Interestingly enough, an early experiment with subtitles originated with a *benshi*-turned-director. This was Shinzaburo Iwafuji, who combined work as a *benshi* for foreign films with directing his own *Nihon Zakura (Japanese Cherry Blossoms).* In this work, he dispensed both with dubbing and with commentary, splicing in the brief subtitles used in silent era pictures from the West. The year was 1910, too early for Japanese audiences to respond. A few years later, more films with intertitles appeared, but the *benshi* saw to it that this threat to their profession was short-lived.

Certainly the *benshi* had their work cut out for them. A typical theater billing of around 1915 consisted of a feature in the style of the film of ongoing stage action, together with two or three works each in the other staple categories of comedy, action films, old drama, and Shimpa domestic melodrama. A *benshi* apprentice would take charge of the first two, leaving the rest to a "star" performer. If a Shimpa drama had seven characters, the *benshi* would narrate and dub in the protagonist's voice, leaving the *kowairo* actors to speak for the other six.

Before each film began, all these live performers would line up in front of the screen to be introduced according to role by the principal *benshi,* with full benefit of pomp. These introductions amounted to a roll of credits, complete with soundtrack accompaniment—here, by *narimono* players in the Kabuki manner. The analogue was with the opening of a special Kabuki program, with the principal actor offering a ceremonious greeting to the audience, introducing new players or perhaps announcing someone's inheritance of a distinguished actor's name.

The superstar Matsunosuke Onoe was turning out as many as seven films a month at the height of his popularity around 1915, yet even he had to accommodate the wishes of a *benshi* like the legendary Shoju Tsuchiya, noted for his mastery of the seven distinct voices. Tsuchiya also sang. His song about a boatman was an unfailing hit. A contemporary newspaper writer described the storm of applause that greeted his appearance onstage, adding that moviegoers were "moved to tears" by his storytelling.[31]

A favorite Tsuchiya vehicle was *The Golden Demon,* a tale of revenge for unrequited love. Based on a work by the popular Meiji novelist Koyo Ozaki, the story concerns a man whose fiancée jilts him in order to marry for wealth and social position. He avenges himself on her and a money-hungry society by succeeding in the despised profession of moneylender.

The following passages show how Tsuchiya interpreted or acted out in his role of *benshi,* standing on the dark stage, summoning up his voices as narrator and *kowairo* in the climactic long take:

NARRATOR. This is Japan's famous sentimental drama, *The Golden Demon.* The scene is set on Atami Beach.

KOWAIRO *(for the hero).* Miya, tonight I speak to you for the very last time. Remember the date: January 17th. I will remember this night for the rest of my life. How could I ever forget? A year from now, two years I'll cloud the moon with my tears. When you see that cloudy moon, think of me weeping, hating you.

KOWAIRO *(for the heroine).* Don't say sad things like that . . . I won't forget you.

KOWAIRO *(for the hero).* I don't want to listen to you . . . This is a dream, a bad dream I have dreamed.

NARRATOR. Kanichi walked silently along the beach, hanging his head. Omiya could not help herself. She followed him.

KOWAIRO *(for the hero)*. Why shouldn't I weep?

KOWAIRO *(for the heroine)*. If I marry Tomiya, what will you say?

KOWAIRO *(for the hero)*. Then, you're all set to marry him! What a fickle flirt you are!

NARRATOR. Kanichi, overcome with rage, kicks the fragile Omiya. . . .[32]

Benshi commonly supplied dialogue and narration, composing them before-hand or improvising to suit. However, this creative license could be abridged when the given material came from a source familiar to the audience. This would have been the cause with Tsuchiya's performance as given above.

Tradition also dictates that this climactic moment will merge with the sound of waves and a distant temple gong, as again the popular song is heard: "It's the sound of farewell. (*Gong rings.*) Just give her up. These lovers don't know when they will meet again. Now they hear only the wind sighing in the pines and waves lapping on the beach."[33]

The treatment of such scenes as essentially stage effects captured in long take and long shot showed a significant aspect of the symbiotic relationship between Japan's traditional theater and film. Theatrical tradition was that much in con-trol of early Japanese cinema, which considered itself in the light of a stage play whose effect would be damaged by the moving camera and close-up.[34]

Three decades later directors like Mizoguchi enjoyed the luxury of drawing the best performances from actors and actresses capable of sustaining a single take. Their predecessors were not so fortunate. Early actors and female imper-sonators in Japanese cinema had training only in presentational acting forms, rather than in transparent realism. They came on screen as they came onstage, prepared to exhibit those exaggerated facial expressions and the grandiose ges-ticulations seen in Kabuki. Moreover, those were elements of unsophisticated pantomime reminiscent of *sarugaku,* the age-old art of mimicry often high-lighted by acrobatics (one of the origins of Noh drama). Similar infelicitites were in effect a parody of sacred *kagura* dancing performed at Shinto shrines. In a scene depicting two persons getting ready to leave, for example, one would point an index finger at the other, then to himself, and then show two fingers before the pair moved away.

Despite the traditional theater's hold on the cinema, some critics and direc-tors were urging change fairly early on. In 1916 a movement was launched for the purpose of demanding technical innovations in service of more artistic cin-ema. Subtitles were to replace the *benshi* and *kowairo.* Western music would displace the traditional *narimono*. Acting would become more realistic, and female impersonators yield to actresses. More shots per film would also be used, with emphasis on cross-cutting and close-ups.

This trend undoubtedly owed much to literary and dramatic circles then advocating movement towards "the modern." The success of such early efforts may be measured by pioneering naturalistic novels such as Katai Tayama's *Futon* (*The Quilt*, 1907) and Toson Shimazaki's *Hakai* (Broken Commandment, 1906). As mentioned earlier, the Modern Theater Movement led by Kaoru Osanai established the Jiyugekijo (Liberty Theater) in 1908. Among Osanai's contemporaries who joined his movement were the film director Eizo Tanaka, the writer Junichiro Tanizaki, and the young film connoisseur Norimasa Kaeriyama.

Criticizing a Shimpa tragedy issued by Nikkatsu, Eizo Tanaka had this to say:

> The minute you enter a movie theater, you hear *kowairo* voices from both sides of the screen . . . mingling with the sounds of the *narimono*. A wooden clapper bangs out every subtitle change. The spectator could experience the same atmosphere in a traditional theater. . . . Cross-cuts are rarely used, and the need of *benshi* and *kowairo* to display their vocal talents determines the standard one-scene, one-shot method. Even a film of five or six reels contains only twenty-two to thirty-three scenes. . . . One film exists, in fact, which was shot as a single long take lasting an entire 800 foot reel. The camera just kept rolling for over twenty minutes while the two actors delivered a dialogue script twelve pages long. . . . I refer to the film *Yuwaku* (*Seduction*) based on Shusei Tokuda's novel serialized in the newspaper.[35]

In 1917, a major studio like Nikkatsu could attract another seminal influence in the person of Norimasa Kaeriyama. He published a book entitled *Katsudo Shashingeki no Seisaku to Satsueiho* (The creation of photography of the moving picture drama). This work made a significant contribution to the argument that Japanese cinema should break free of traditional theater. Kaeriyama shared the views of other modernists urging innovation. According to them, a director must maximize the essence of "the moving picture" itself, freeing himself from reliance on *benshi* and *narimono*. Kaeriyama also provided illustrations to explain cross-cutting, close-ups, and long shots as used so effectively by D. W. Griffith and discussed scriptwriting and matters of continuity.

Kaeriyama also persuaded Nikkatsu to let him direct *Sei no Kagayaki* (*The Glory of Life*, 1919), his first chance to put his ideas into effect. He used no studio set, but moved to a room in the Christian Youth Hall (YMCA), to employ tungsten lamps for the first time, and elsewhere to film on location. He also played a bit part himself.[36]

The Glory of Life was a melodrama that delivered an oblique social message. An aristocratic youth falls in love with a country girl who becomes pregnant by him. He abandons her in order to marry a banker's daughter. The jilted girl attempts suicide, but is rescued from drowning by a commoner who happens to be a friend of the aristocratic youth. The girl is married by her rescuer, although her baby dies soon after its birth. Five years pass. The hardworking young couple now run a successful factory. They are visited by the aristocratic youth whose plebeian friend lectures him on a sense of fulfillment that comes from a productive life—in contrast to the spoiled existence of the idle upper class like his. As the film ends, the couple open a window and gaze out on the smoke rising up from the factory chimneys, as if in affirmation of their own life.

Although some critics accused Kaeriyama of merely imitating Western models, his debut film enjoyed a moderate success with the general public. He made two more films the same year (1919): *Miyama no Otome* (*Maid of the Deep Mountain*) and *Shiragiku Monogatari* (*The Tale of the White Chrysanthemum*). Both films met with severe criticism, especially the latter, which was opposed with great vigor by the powerful *benshi* lobby.

Nevertheless other experimental films influenced by the new trend soon followed. Among them were *Taii no Musume* (*The Captain's Daughter*) and *Dokuso* (*Poisonous Grass*), both directed by Masao Inoue in 1920. Originally an actor in chain drama productions and also a long-established Shimpa stage actor, this director became a modernist bent on freeing films from the domination of the *benshi*. He himself was inspired to make these two works by reading *Eiga no Sekai* (The world of cinema), the most widely circulated film journal of its day.

In *The Captain's Daughter*, Inoue played the male role while *onnagata* were cast for other female roles. He also repeated the role in the 1936 sound version. *The Captain's Daughter* was adapted from a popular German film *Gendarme Moebius* (released in Japan as early as 1912), which was based on Viktor Grutgen's drama. The heroine returns to her native village after a year away in service as a maid. She looks forward to a reunion with her fiancé and the baby she has borne him. She arrives to discover that he is in fact preparing to marry someone else. Moreover, their child has died. Driven to despair, she sneaks into the wedding and sets fire to the hall. Her father, an army captain, persuades her that she must turn herself in to the police or commit suicide. The daughter, however, rejects that line of reasoning. Overcome with despair, he drowns himself.

Although *The Captain's Daughter* had been produced before as a chain drama, Inoue treated it as pure film. The *kowairo*'s roles were supplied by the new techniques of flashback and close-ups. These occurred, for example, in the scenes when the daughter remembers her fiancé and dead baby, and when her father imagines the life she has led. Inoue also used a dolly shot in the scene showing the father escorting his daughter to the police station. The effect was innovative enough, but premature in technique. *Poisonous Grass,* based on a popular newspaper serial with the same title, took on the familiar theme of a mother-in-law bent on tormenting her son's wife. Three major companies vied with one another with screen adaptations, but Inoue's was the one that broke free of traditional stage conventions. He used frequent close-ups, even focusing on important props like the calendar and straw doll used by the old woman to call up evil spirits with which to haunt her daughter-in-law. Inoue also combined subtitles with illustrations used for the original novel. A critic in the film journal *Katsudo no Sekai* (The world of cinema) provides these notes on the film's use of modern innovations.

> Close-ups are effectively used in some scenes. . . . When Oshina (the heroine) first meets Kichizo (the hero), the director shows them from the waist up. This helps the plot along by giving the audience a clear indication of the importance of this meeting. In several scenes, the setting of room partitions and an alcove is shown obliquely . . . which gives evidence of the director's efforts to create pictorial and realistic effects in full perspective, eliminating flat composition. The close-ups of female impersonators, however, were in most instances a failure.[37]

Determined as Inoue was to be innovative, he was forced to compromise. He did use *benshi,* who, as was the custom with foreign films, explained only the major events onscreen. Moreover, pressure from *benshi* and the distributing theaters forced him to include *kowairo* as well.

The arrival of Japanese cinema's age of realism was hastened by young directors who were fascinated with the mode of representation they saw in foreign films. They were anxious to adopt it. In 1921, for example, the Shochiku Kinema School of Art, which had been established a year earlier with Kaoru Osanai as its head, was reorganized as the Shochiku Kinema Study Center. Film directors under Osanai's supervision were youths about twenty, including Minoru Murata and Tsunehiko Ushiwara. Some of them were strongly attracted to those editing techniques like cross-cutting and parallel montage that D. W. Griffith employed in *Intolerance.*[38] But this urge for change from inside was also assisted by those who were trained overseas. Among returning directors and cameramen were Henry Kotani and Thomas Kurihara. In their book *The Japanese Cinema: Art and Industry* Anderson and Richie offer a most informative discussion of this aspect, so only a few films made by these Japanese from the West will be considered here.[39]

Henry Kotani had been trained by Sycoff, considered by many the "father" of cameramen. The Shochiku Company put Kotani to work on a pioneer work in their own movement towards "pure drama." This was *Shima no Onna (Island Woman,* 1920), the story of a fisherman's daughter whose lover is pursued by another woman. In order to prevent this, she swims from her island to be reunited with him. The heroine was played by an actress, Yoshiko Kawada, a "first" innovation matched by Kotani's use of American-style flashbacks and close-ups, together with subtitles.

Island Woman was in fact a failure. Its innovations and editing did not really fit the Japanese style of acting and made the plot seem rather ambiguous. At its premier in the prestigious Kabuki Theater in Tokyo, the audience laughed at the close-ups. One critic sees several factors at work in this response. For a start, the sketchy filmscript led to blunders in editing, making the story seem somewhat unnatural. Then too, Kotani was trained as a cameraman; the director's role was unfamiliar, especially in matters of general overview. As a result, close-ups were not well planned and tended to appear untimely.[40]

Kotani's second work was *Gubijinso (Poppy,* 1921), a forerunner of the Sochiku commercial melodrama. This eclectic work retained many familiar elements of the Shimpa tragedy in its story line: the heroine suffers the tyranny of a mother-in-law, degradation to the position of concubine, and a final self-sacrifice to promote her husband's social advancement. She commits a convenient suicide.

A number of new expressive devices do give *Poppy* a fresh touch, however. Kotani connects the small-scale, interior setting of the domestic drama with a background as large as the great outdoors. For a battle scene involving two generals, he uses a large Chinese-style castle foundation built on a beach, with masses of extras.[41] A close-up of scattered cigarette butts is used to signal the fact that the hero has been stood up by the heroine. And of course, the long take of Shimpa stage action has yielded to film footage characterized by rapid cutting.

Even so, *Poppy* was a popular success chiefly because of an innovation of another kind: the impression made by the amateur actress Sumiko Kurishima. Cast as the heroine, she gave a natural performance that made her an instant popular favorite. Kotani had drawn from this actual actress something different from the stage-mannered performances used here and there by directors drawing on the talents of women from the Shingeki (New Theater) or all-girl stage revue troupes.

Nikkatsu was the last of the major studios to turn from the long tradition of *benshi* and female impersonators to actresses. They did issue a few new style works, among them *Tsuma to Tsuma* (*Two Wives*) of 1922. The inevitable showdown between modernists and traditionalists at the studio took place that same year, resulting in a mass walkout of female impersonators.

Even so, in 1922, the modernist Eizo Tanaka issued a memorable work, *Kyoya Erimise* (*Kyoya Collar Shop*). This film might stand as a celebration of the androgynous beauty of female impersonators.[42] With the exception of Sadao Yamanaka's sound picture *Machi no Irezumimono* (*The Outlaw in the Village*, 1935) in which Kunitaro Kawarazaki was cast as a geisha, this film by Tanaka was the last prewar Japanese film featuring an oonnagata. A three-part tragedy in the Shimpa mold, *Kyoya Collar Shop* focused on the typical love triangle: the proprietor of an old, well-respected business marries his favorite geisha after his wife's death. His son and daughter rebel, leaving home with their respective lovers. The new wife continues to see her younger lover; and worse, the old man's shop is destroyed by fire.

Tanaka was at pains to make his picture a showcase of the "stylistic beauty" of the Shimpa stage in setting, costumes, and *onnagata* acting. The overall effect of the film is that of a picture scroll imparting a rhythmical flow to the story.

This film was also influenced for its vivid transposition onto screen of a theme for which Japanese classical theater is noted. One might call it love-turned-to-hatred and say that here it is given the benefit of a traditional aesthetics of killing. In the final scene of revenge, for example, one sees the husband near the *shoji* door. It catches fire as he struggles with his wife. He has grabbed her by the hair, pinning her against the door in the hallway. The door gives way, falling out into the yard. A cut to the outside shows the husband emerging from the smoke-filled room, clutching a swatch of bloody hair. The wife staggers toward the gate and struggles to open it. Her husband catches up and stabs her in the stomach with a butcher knife. He stands over her fallen body, holding the knife, a sinister smile fixed on her face.[43]

However successful this Shimpa-style film with *onnagata* was, the Japanese film industry was ready for change. By 1923 even the powerful *benshi* and female impersonators found themselves cast adrift in the transitional climate that would completely force them out of business in 1928. The latter was the first to go. In 1923, stirred by Shochiku's success in films with actresses, Nikkatsu abolished the employment of *onnagata* in favor of natural performers.

NOTES

1. Susan Sontag, "Theatre and Film," in her *Styles of Radical Will* (New York: Dell, 1978), p. 99.
2. Donald Richie, *Japanese Cinema: An Introduction* (Hong Kong and New York: Oxford University Press, 1989), p. 8.
3. Standard references in English on these three dramatic genres include Yoshinobu Inoura and Toshio Kawatake, *The Traditional Theater of Japan* (New York and Tokyo: Weatherhill, 1981), and Faubion Bowers, *Japanese Theatre* (Rutland, Vt., and Tokyo: Tuttle, 1974).
4. As a standard reference on Bunraku, see Donald Keene's *Bunraku: The Art of the Japanese Puppet Theatre* (Tokyo: Kodansha, 1973).
5. For background information on Chikamatsu and his plays, see Donald Keene, trans., *Major Plays of Chikamatsu* (New York and London: Columbia University Press, 1961), pp. 1–38.
6. Yasuji Toida, *Onnagata no Subete* (Everything you want to know about female impersonators) (Tokyo: Shunshundo, 1990), p. 22. Other sources suggest that Okuni was more like a prostitute than a priestess. The two professions were not in fact clearly separate in feudal Japan.
7. Shigetoshi Kawatake, *Gaesetsu Nihon Engekishi* (A survey of the history of Japanese drama) (Tokyo: Iwanami, 1966), p. 232.
8. Ibid., p. 288.
9. Junichiro Tanaka, *Nihon Eiga Hattatsushi* (History of the development of Japanese cinema) (Tokyo: Chuo Koron, 1976), 1: 67–68.
10. Donald Richie, *Japanese Cinema: Film Style and Natural Character* (Garden City, N.Y.: Anchor Books, 1971), p. 5. For further information on the early stages of Japanese cinema, see Joseph L. Anderson and Donald Richie, *The Japanese Film: Art and Industry*, expanded edition (Princeton: Princeton University Press, 1982), pp. 22–34.
11. Donald Richie, *Japanese Cinema: An Introduction* (Hong Kong: Oxford University Press, 1989), pp. 1–20.
12. Noël Burch, *To the Distant Observer: Form and Meaning in the Japanese Cinema* (Berkeley and Los Angeles: University of California Press, 1979), pp. 57–86.
13. For a further study of the development of *onnagata*, see Shigetoshi Kawatake, *Gaisetsu Nihon Engekishi*, pp. 258–62.
14. Shingeki, which literally means a new theater, occurred as a part of the Meiji enlightenment. A leader of this New Theater Movement was Shoyo Tsubouchi (1859–1935), an advocate of realism in fiction and drama, who formed Bungei Kyokai (Association for Literature and Art) in 1906. Tsubouchi's follower Hogetsu Shimamura (1873–1918) upheld a theory of European naturalism as a basis for the modern theater. Together, they were instrumental in introducing many European plays, especially those of Ibsen. Hogetsu's production of Ibsen's *A Doll's House* with the actress Sumako Matsui made an important contribution to the development of Shingeki. The Geijutsuza, the Fine Art Theater, was also cofounded by the two. Kenji Mizoguchi's *Joyu Sumako no Koi* (*The Love of Sumako the Actress*, 1947) and Teinosuke Kinugasa's *Joyu* (*Actress*, 1947) portrayed the couple's in-

volvement in the Shingeki movement. The culmination of the Shingeki drive came in 1908 with the organization of Jiyugekijo, the Liberty Theater, by Kaoro Osanai (1881–1928) and Sadanji Ichikawa II (1880–1940). Together, they introduced modern plays by Ibsen, Chekov, and Hauptmann, and Osanai was also instrumental in fostering the Stanislavskian acting style. For further information on Shingeki, see Thomas Rimer, *Toward a Modern Theatre: Kishida Kunio* (Princeton: Princeton University Press, 1974) and Edward Pultzar, *Japanese Literature: A Historical Outline* (Tuscon: The University of Arizona Press, 1973), p. 190, 198.

15. Quoted in Tanaka, *Nihon Eiga Hattatsushi,* pp. 233–34. The translation is mine.
16. Quoted in Tanaka, *Nihon Eiga Hattatsushi,* pp. 236–37.
17. Don Kirihara, "A Reconsideration of the Institution of the Benshi," *Film Reader,* no. 6 (1985): 48.
18. Joseph Anderson, "Spoken Silents in the Japanese Cinema," *Journal of Film and Video* 40, no. 1 (winter 1988): 23–26.
19. Burch, *To the Distant Observer,* p. 84.
20. For a summary and criticism of this Althusserian-Lacanian approach to the unified subject, see Carroll, *Mystifying Movies,* pp. 53–88.
21. Anderson and Richie, *The Japanese Film,* pp. 23–24. It has been pointed out that their comments on *benshi*'s machine-cum-machine role quoted here are relevant to early films introduced before 1902.
22. Ibid., pp. 24–25.
23. For more information on these genres, see Joseph Anderson, "Spoken Silents in the Japanese Cinema," pp. 21–22.
24. The term *gidayu* is attributed to Gidayu Takemono (1651–1714) who established his Bunraku theater, the Takemotoza, in Osaka in 1685. *Gidayu* is a style of narration that reflects ordinary conversation of townspeople in the Edo period. *Gidayu* narration is often used in contrast to the *joruri* narration, which prevailed in the earlier days of Bunraku. The samisen used for *gidayu* is larger and thicker in its neck than the one for other types of narration such as *tokiwazu, kiyomoto,* and *nagauta.* See Inoura and Kawatake, *The Traditional Theater of Japan,* pp. 148–49.
25. Sometimes, the dais has two tiers, and singers occupy the upper and musicians the lower. See Shoichi Yamada, *Kabuki Ongaku Nyumon* (Introduction to Kabuki music) (Tokyo: Ongaku no Tomo-sha, 1986), pp. 155–56.
26. The name of the troupe is rather misleading. Those in the troupe were not fullgrown actresses, but little girls playing adult roles. See Chieo Yoshida, *Mo Hitotsu no Eigashi: Katsuben no Jidai* (Another history of cinema: the period of *benshi*) (Tokyo: Jiji Tsushin, 1978), p. 46.
27. Tanaka, *Nihon Eiga Hattatsushi,* p. 160.
28. Shiran Wakazuki, "Tokyo Nenju Gyoji 2" (Annual events in Tokyo: 2); quoted in Nobuo Chiba et al., *Sekai no Eiga Sakka: Nihon Eigashi* (Film directors of the world: history of Japanese cinema) (Tokyo: Kinema Jumpo, 1976), 31: 11.
29. Tanaka, *Nihon Eiga Hattatsushi,* pp. 245–46.
30. Chiba et al., *Sekai no Eiga Sakka,* p. 15.
31. Tanaka, *Nihon Eiga Hattatsushi,* p. 182.

32. Ibid., pp. 182–83.

33. Ibid., p. 183.

34. Yoshida, *Mo Hitotsu no Eigashi,* p. 77.

35. Quoted in Tanaka, *Nihon Eiga Hattatsushi,* 1: 235–36.

36. Ibid., p. 286.

37. Ibid., pp. 273–74.

38. Chiba et al., *Sekai no Eiga Sakka,* pp. 27–29.

39. Anderson and Richie, *The Japanese Film,* pp. 39–43. Also see Donald Richie, *The Japanese Movie,* revised edition (Tokyo, New York, and San Francisco: Kodansha International, 1982), pp. 18–20.

40. Tanaka, *Nihon Eiga Hattatsushi,* pp. 317–18.

41. Ibid., p. 342.

42. Ibid., p. 365.

43. Kaneto Shindo, "Shinario Tanjo Zengo" (Around the time of the birth of the scenario) in *Shohei Imamura et al., eds., in Nihon Eiga no Tanjo* (The birth of Japanese cinema) (Tokyo: Iwanami, 1985), 1: 213.

Interlude: The Filmmaker as Creator "Moving Pictures Can Get Nothing from the Stage"; "Griffith's Reply to Two Questions"; "Some Prophecies: Film and Theatre, Screenwriting, Education"

D. W. Griffith

MOVING PICTURES CAN GET NOTHING FROM THE STAGE

Moving pictures can get nothing from the so-called legitimate stage because American directors and playwrights have nothing to offer. The former are, for the most part, conventional and care nothing for natural acting. They don't know how to make use of even the material they have, limited as that is. Of course, there are a few, a very few, exceptions. As for American playwrights, we can get our ideas from the same sources they do. We need to depend on the stage for our actors and actresses least of all. How many of them make you believe they are real human beings? No, they "act," that is, they use a lot of gestures and make a lot of sounds such as are never seen or heard anywhere else. For range and delicacy, the development of character, the quick transition

---

Excerpted from "A Poet Who Writes on Motion Picture Film," *The Theatre* XIX (June 1914): 311–312, 314, 316. Robert Grau, *The Theatre of Science* (New York, 1914), 85–87. D. W. Griffith, "Five Dollar 'Movies' Prophesized," *The Editor* (April 24, 1915): 407–410.

Fig. 4. Lillian Gish in D. W. Griffith's *Way Down East* (1920). Griffith frequently denied the influence of stage on film, but his early training was as a stage actor, and *Way Down East* itself is adapted from a play. Courtesy of the National Film Archive, London.

from one mood to another, I don't know an actress now on the American stage, I don't care how great her reputation, who can begin to touch the work of some of the motion picture actresses. And I'll give you the names if you want them.

As far as the public is concerned, there is no real competition between the stage and the motion picture. It doesn't exist. The latter makes an appeal which the former never has and never can hope to meet, not only because of its physical limitations, but because most of its managers, directors, and actors are bound by tradition. They don't know human nature and they don't care to find out about it. James A. Herne,[1] who wrote plays with real people in them, is only just beginning to be rightly appreciated years after his death. Wonderful Mrs. Fiske is, of course, one of the exceptions, too.

GRIFFITH'S REPLIES TO TWO QUESTIONS

You ask me: "Do you think the stage and its craft are the best means of productivity for the cameraman?" No, I do not. The stage is a development of centuries, based on certain fixed conditions and within prescribed limits. It is needless to point out what these are. The motion picture, although a growth of only a few years, is boundless in its scope and endless in its possibilities. The whole world is its stage, and time without end its limitations. In the use of speech alone it is at a disadvantage, but the other advantages of the motion picture over the stage are so numerous and powerful that we can well afford to grant the stage this one point of superiority. The conditions of the two arts being so different, it follows that the requirements are equally dissimilar. Stage craft and stage people are out of place in the intense realism of motion-picture expression, but it may well be that a little motion-picture realism would be of immense advantage to the stage.

To your second question, "After the plays of other days are exhausted, who will supply the needs of thirty thousand theatres?" I would refer you to the opinion expressed in the foregoing paragraph. The plays of other days are not essential to the motion picture, and I am not sure that they are not proving a positive harm. If motion picture producers had no access to stage plays, they would be obliged to depend upon their own authors for their material, and, since the picture dramas that would thus result would be composed entirely for picture production, they could not fail to much more nearly reach a perfection of art than could ever be hoped for while writers and directors are trying in vain to twist stage dramas into condition for picture use. When the plays of other days, and of these days are exhausted, as they will be, motion pictures will come into their own. They are valued now only for advertising purposes, and, when a stage play is reproduced in pictures with any success, it is inevitably found that often the plot and always the manner of treatment have been entirely departed from.

SOME PROPHECIES: FILM AND THEATRE,
SCREENWRITING, EDUCATION

The regular theatre . . . will, of course, always exist, but not, I believe, as now. The [moving] pictures will utterly eliminate from the regular theatre all the spectacular features of production. Plays will never again appeal to the public for their scenery, or their numbers of actors and supernumeraries. Pictures have replaced all that.

The only plays that the public will care to see in the regular theatre will be the intimate, quiet plays that can be staged in one or two settings within four walls, and in which the setting is unimportant, while the drama will be largely subjective. Objective drama, the so-called melodrama, will be entirely absorbed in the pictures. . . .

Imagine a public library of the near future, for instance. There will be long rows of boxes or pillars, properly classified and indexed, of course. At each box a push button and before each box a seat. Suppose you wish to "read up" on a certain episode in Napoleon's life. Instead of consulting all the authorities, wading laboriously through a host of books, and ending bewildered, without a clear idea of exactly what did happen and confused at every point by conflicting opinions about what did happen, you will merely seat yourself at a properly adjusted window, in a scientifically prepared room, press the button, and actually see what happened.

There will be no opinions expressed. You will merely be present at the making of history. All the work of writing, revising, collating, and reproducing will have been carefully attended to by a corps of recognized experts, and you will have received a vivid and complete expression.

Everything except the three R's, the arts, and possibly the mental sciences can be taught in this way—physiology, chemistry, biology, botany, physics, and history in all its branches. . . .

NOTE

1. James A. Herne (1839–1901); perhaps his most notable realist dramas are *Margaret Fleming* (1890) and *Shore Acres* (1892).

Two Comparisons and Contrasts

Realism and the Cinema

Eric Bentley

Although realism has long been the dominant mode of modern drama, there are two inventions which could—and, according to many authorities, should—put an end to realism in the theater. One is the cinema. The other is the electric lamp.

Just as the abstract painter argues that photography removed the need for representational painting by doing the job much better, so, it is argued, cinematography removes the need for realist theater. Now about the same time as the cinematograph came into use—around 1900—the electric lamp began to replace the gas lamp on the stage. It revolutionized the theatrical medium. It created magical new worlds. At the same time as the stage was outdone by the movies in the representation of objects, it received, by way of compensation, a new power over the non-realistic realm through electricity. Playwrights, accordingly, should—so the argument is clinched—unlearn realism, revive poetic drama, or create new styles for the new settings.

Excerpted from Eric Bentley, *The Playwright as Thinker* (New York: Reynal & Hitchcock, 1946).

Since it is clear that physical changes in the theater and in society have many times in the past modified and even revolutionized the art of drama, it is fair to give these two recent inventions our best attention. First, the cinema. What effect does it have on the art of drama in general? And does it, in particular, render stage obsolete?

When the nineteenth-century invention of the cinematograph led to the twentieth-century invention of the cinema there arose a new art, not to mention a new business, which in many respects could carry out the aims of certain types of dramatic performance much more fully than the theater. Some felt from the beginning that the motion picture would be the dramatic art of the twentieth century, and this opinion was not hard to support even in the days of the silent screen. Before the talkies were a decade old, even the kind of people who had earlier despised the screen began to see in it the successor to the living actor. In this belief, it is said, Clifford Odets left Broadway for Hollywood: the drama was a thing of the past, the future belonged to the motion picture. A more subtle analysis of the relation of stage and screen was given by Allardyce Nicoll in his interesting and informative book *Film and Theatre*. He tries to find a place for both stage and screen by assigning to each its proper style. The style of the screen is realism, he says, the theater should accordingly be non-realistic. The argument is worth quoting at length:

> If we seek for and desire a theater which shall possess qualities likely to live over generations, unquestionably we must decide that the naturalistic play, made popular towards the close of the nineteenth century and still remaining in our midst, is not calculated to fulfill our highest wishes.
>
> Of much greater importance, even, is the question of the position this naturalistic play occupies in its relations to the cinema. At the moment it still retains its popularity, but, we may ask, because of cinematic competition, is it not likely to fail gradually in its immediate appeal? The film has such a hold over the world of reality, can achieve expression so vitally in terms of ordinary life, that the realistic play must surely come to seem trivial, false, and inconsequential. The truth is, of course, that naturalism on the stage must always be limited and insincere. Thousands have gone to *The Children's Hour* and come away fondly believing that what they have seen is life; they have not realized that here too the familiar stock figures, the type characterizations, of the theater have been presented before them in modified forms. From this the drama cannot escape; little possibility is there of its delving deeply into the recesses of the individual spirit. That is the realm reserved for cinematic exploitation, and, as the film more and more explores this territory, does it not seem likely that theater audiences will become weary of watching shows which, although professing to be "lifelike," actually are inexorably bound by the restrictions of the stage? Pursu-

ing this path, the theater truly seems doomed to inevitable destruction. Whether in its attempt to reproduce reality and give the illusion of actual events or whether in its pretense toward depth and subtlety in character-drawing, the stage is aiming at things alien to its spirit, things which so much more easily may be accomplished in the film that their exploitation on the stage gives only an impression of vain effort.

Is, then, the theater, as some have opined, truly dying? Must it succumb to the rivalry of the cinema? The answer to that question depends on what the theater does within the next ten or twenty years. If it pursues naturalism further, unquestionably little hope will remain. . . .

These are weighty sentences, but are they really unquestionable? One might question whether the drama has always been incapable of delving into those "recesses of the individual spirit," whether the movie, even in the best hands, has in fact shown itself any more capable? But my prime interest is in Mr. Nicoll's remarks about "naturalism." A generation of movies has given to "naturalism" a popular success such as no dramatic style has ever had before. *A Tree Grows in Brooklyn,* movie version, is, one might say, pure Zola. Mr. Nicoll's strongest point, perhaps, is that the screen gives the illusion of actuality itself. The screen actor is not thought to act. He does not act. He is himself and, the argument runs, rightly so, since the screen must seem to be life itself. Such is the power of the camera. In support of his argument Mr. Nicoll adduces the fact that plays fail on the screen, and that movie actors haven't a style that can be parodied as Henry Irving had. The screen play, more than any other form of art, is just such a "slice of life" as the naturalists had always wished to cut.

This is Mr. Nicoll's argument, but does it all ring true? After all, we *do* praise acting on the screen; many of the screen's best actors are also stage stars and they are not always so very different in the two mediums; they *can* be parodied, and a parody of Charles Laughton the filmstar is not very different from one of Charles Laughton the actor; and good plays—witness Shaw's *Pygmalion*—have been successfully transferred to the screen with little alteration. Nor do audiences believe that what happens on the screen is really happening or that it has happened—at least no more than theater audiences do. After all, it was in the theater that the proverbial man in the gallery told Othello to leave the lady alone, and it was on the radio that the announcement of the end of the world was taken literally. These are abnormal responses. Normally an audience does not give full credence to fiction on the air, the stage, or the screen. I have known a movie audience to catch its breath at the sight of wounded soldiers in a newsreel and to be quite unperturbed by the same sight in a fictional movie.

In short, and Mr. Nicoll to the contrary notwithstanding, I think there is no radical distinction between stage and screen illusion. At best the difference is one of degree. The usual Hollywood product does seek to be a convincing illusion of actuality, but so does the usual Broadway product. This is a matter not of stage or screen, but of the style chosen by the director or author or producer. On either stage or screen he may choose, with great effectiveness, to be "naturalistic" or the reverse. It is also a matter of audience. An untrained audience, an audience of children, might want to save Desdemona's life in the theater, as at the movies it might believe that it is actually present in Greta Garbo's bedroom. That is the trouble with being untrained and childish.

What Mr. Nicoll says is true of current movies and of many audiences, but not of all possible movies and all possible audiences. At present, it is true, we go to the movies to witness certain illusions and to share them. We do not go for imaginative experience. Years ago the Lynds found out how the movie magnates appealed to Middletown, via the *Saturday Evening Post,* in such advertisements as this:

> Go to a motion picture . . . and let yourself go. Before you know it you are *living* the story—laughing, loving, hating, struggling, winning! All the adventure, all the romance, all the excitement you lack in your daily life are in Pictures. They take you completely out of yourself into a wonderful new world . . . Out of the cage of everyday existence! If only for an afternoon or an evening—escape!

This is not Zola's naturalism in subject matter and aim, for it is frankly "romantic" and remote from everyday life. It is the naturalism of the movies. It is Mr. Nicoll's naturalism. And it stems not, as Mr. Nicoll thinks, from the medium, but purely from social factors. The movie is an extension of gossip and daydream. It influences life as no art ever has because it influences not as art at all but as suggestion, almost as hypnotism. Clark Gable is found to have no undershirt on, and the underwear trade of America suffers a fifty-percent loss for a year. Ingrid Bergman has her hair cut short, and the women's hairdressers of the nation have to send for more scissors. Not that the theater, on its part, has held aloof from such nonartistic matters. Actors and actresses have often been foci of mass emotion and sometimes leaders of fashion. All that Hollywood has done in this, as in so many other matters, is to systematize what had been haphazard and to make a mania out of a tendency.

The escapist realism of the movies is only that of most popular art. William Dieterle's movie *The Hunchback of Notre Dame* is not different in kind from Sardou's play *Patrie.* What is new is that we have in movies an art form so exclusively given over to Sardoodledom that a man can think Sardoodledom in-

grained in the celluloid. Sardoodledom—or escapist realism—always consisted of concealing flattering, sentimental hokum in a setting of the most solid
and beefy reality, thus conferring upon hokum the status of the actual and the
real. This, it is very true, the film can do even better than David Belasco, because its realism can be at once more varied and more intimate. The camera can
find the needle in the haystack and the fly in the ointment, and, above all, the
camera—like Mr. Lee Shubert's box office—cannot lie. Aided by the camera,
and abetted by popular prejudice in favor of the tangible, a director is able to
wrap the maximum of nonsense in the maximum of verisimilitude, a combination as dangerous as the atomic bomb.

We must distinguish between the predilections of Hollywood and the nature
of the medium. If the screen is able to be more realistic than the stage, it is also
able to be more fantastic. If the Hollywood director is a super-Belasco, the Disney cartoon is a super-Punch-and-Judy, and Eisenstein is a super–Gordon
Craig.

Mr. Nicoll makes the movie so completely natural that it is no longer art. He
takes the "slice of life" theory too seriously. If we want life, we have it without
making works of art at all. We need not pay our fifty cents for it; we necessarily
pay in our hearts' blood. The *theory* of Zolaist naturalism has nearly always
been astray here, though Zola himself was prepared to define art as "a part of life
seen through a temperament" and the last three words are an important pro-
viso. There is art only if the material of life is selected and intelligently arranged.
Such arrangement is of course artificial. It imposes form on the formless. And
the understanding of art depends upon a prior understanding of this fact.
Nothing, therefore, that we take for reality can we also take for art. In a good
movie, as in any good work of art, we *are* aware of the "artificial" elements—
structure, selection, characterization, cutting—or rather, we can be. In actual
fact very few moviegoers are aware of any of these things; but the same is true of
novel readers and theatergoers.

A more astute way of arguing that film and theater are utterly different is by
pointing to the conditions of production. A movie is manufactured in little
bits, the bits forming a jigsaw puzzle which is put together later; on the stage
the unity of a single complete performance is the director's chief end in view.
This distinction between the two media, like the others we have examined, is
not a necessary distinction. It is to equate the present doings of studios with the
exigencies of the medium. The degree of decentralization that exists in Hollywood is not a technical necessity. Many Russian directors, for example, have
done their own cutting. And, for that matter, joint authorship, in the form of

impudent revisions perpetrated by hacks and businessmen, and lack of integration in the directing and producing of plays—these are the bane of Broadway as well as Hollywood.

What then *is* the difference between film and theater? Or should one not rather ask: what are the differences? Let us be content with the reply that the screen has two dimensions and the stage three, that the screen presents photographs and the stage living actors. All subtler differences stem from these. The camera can show us all sorts of things—from close-ups of insects to panoramas of prairies—which the stage cannot even suggest, and it can move from one to another with much more dexterity than any conceivable stage. The stage, on the other hand, can be revealed in the unsurpassable beauty of three-dimensional shapes, and the stage actor establishes between himself and his audience a contact real as electricity. From these basic differences one might elaborate many others. Here I wish only to reiterate that there is no such difference as is suggested by the antithesis of realistic and non-realistic theater. One cannot say, with Mr. Nicoll, that undecorated reality suits the screen, and fine words the stage. Such a belief is a hangover from the days of silent films. On the talking screen the aural is not necessarily subordinate to the visual. One could just as easily argue that the *stage* should stick to the natural, since on the stage the possibilities of fantasy are physically limited, while the screen should go in for poetic fantasy, since it can show anything in this world or the next with its cameras and can reproduce the merest murmurs and the subtlest intonations with its sound apparatus. All such distinctions are arbitrary. The truth is that dramatic art is possible on both stage and screen. On both it could fulfill its function of presenting an account of human experience deeply and truly. On both it would require the services of an artist—I think we may say a dramatist—to plan the whole work as a unity beforehand and of an interpreter or director to see that the unity is faithfully reproduced.

Is the film the dramatic art of the twentieth century then, or is it not? If as yet it is not, could it still grow to be so? My answers to these questions, which we started from, must now be evident. The movies as a whole, like plays as a whole, are a matter of business, not of art at all. The occasional artistic movie, like the occasional artistic play, is one legitimate and welcome form of twentieth-century art. It is not the only one. Moreover, while playwrights have demonstrated for centuries the potentialities of the stage, the screen is as yet an only partly explored territory. We have still to learn what its possibilities are. I have acknowledged that they are different from those of the stage, especially in certain kinds of emphasis. But they may not be as different as many have supposed. And there is no reason to assume that the art of the screen is a threat to the art of the stage, naturalistic or otherwise. Let us question Mr. Nicoll's unquestionable proposition. Although the movie industry can threaten the theater industry, the one *art* cannot be threatened by the other. So long as an art is alive it will be cherished and kept going by the minority that is interested in the arts. "The answer," Mr. Nicoll said, "depends on what the theater does within the next ten or twenty years. If it pursues naturalism further, unquestionably little hope will remain. . . ." About ten years have passed since these words were written. Today one of the few live spots in the drama is the Epic Theater of Bertolt Brecht, which is a new form of realism. That the Epic dramatist believes also in combining the use of stage and screen in the theater is an additional sign that the two media need not part company according to the prescriptions of the doctors.

Theater and Cinema

André Bazin

The leitmotiv of those who despise filmed theater, their final and apparently insuperable argument, continues to be the unparalleled pleasure that accompanies the presence of the actor. "What is specific to theater," writes Henri Gouhier, in *The Essence of Theater*, "is the impossibility of separating off action and actor." Elsewhere he says "the stage welcomes every illusion except that of presence; the actor is there in disguise, with the soul and voice of another, but he is nevertheless there and by the same token space calls out for him and for the solidity of his presence. On the other hand and inversely, the cinema accommodates every form of reality save one—the physical presence of the actor." If it is here that the essence of theater lies then undoubtedly the cinema can in no way pretend to any parallel with it. If the writing, the style, and the dramatic structure are, as they should be, rigorously conceived as the receptacle for the soul and being of the flesh-and-blood actor, any attempt to substitute the shadow and reflection

---

Excerpted from André Bazin, *What Is Cinema?* vol. 1, trans. Hugh Gray (Berkeley: University of California Press, 1967), 95–124.

of a man on the screen for the man himself is a completely vain enterprise. There is no answer to this argument. The successes of Laurence Olivier, of Welles, or of Cocteau can only be challenged—here you need to be in bad faith—or considered inexplicable. They are a challenge both to critics and philosophers. Alternatively one can only explain them by casting doubts on that commonplace of theatrical criticism "the irreplacable presence of the actor."

THE CONCEPT OF PRESENCE

At this point comments seem called for concerning the concept of "presence," since it would appear that it is this concept, as understood prior to the appearance of photography, that the cinema challenges.

Can the photographic image, especially the cinematographic image, be likened to other images and in common with them be regarded as having an existence distinct from the object? Presence, naturally, is defined in terms of time and space. "To be in the presence of someone" is to recognize him as existing contemporaneously with us and to note that he comes within the actual range of our senses—in the case of cinema of our sight and in radio of our hearing. Before the arrival of photography and later of cinema, the plastic arts (especially portraiture) were the only intermediaries between actual physical presence and absence. Their justification was their resemblance which stirs the imagination and helps the memory. But photography is something else again. In no sense is it the image of an object or person, more correctly it is its tracing. Its automatic genesis distinguishes it radically from the other techniques of reproduction. The photograph proceeds by means of the lens to the taking of a veritable luminous impression in light—to a mold. As such it carries with it more than mere resemblance, namely a kind of identity—the card we call by that name being only conceivable in an age of photography. But photography is a feeble technique in the sense that its instantaneity compels it to capture time only piecemeal. The cinema does something strangely paradoxical. It makes a molding of the object as it exists in time and, furthermore, makes an imprint of the duration of the object.

The nineteenth century with its objective techniques of visual and sound reproduction gave birth to a new category of images, the relation of which to the reality from which they proceed requires very strict definition. Even apart from the fact that the resulting aesthetic problems cannot be satisfactorily raised without this introductory philosophical inquiry, it would not be sound to treat the old aesthetic questions as if the categories with which they deal had in no way been modified by the appearance of completely new phenomena. Common sense—perhaps the best philosophical guide in this case—has clearly understood this and has invented an expression for the presence of an actor, by adding to the placards announcing his appearance the phrase "in flesh and blood." This means that for the man in the street the word "presence," today, can be ambiguous, and thus an apparent redundancy is not out of place in this age of cinema. Hence it is no longer as certain as it was that there is no middle stage between presence and absence. It is likewise at the ontological level that the effectiveness of the cinema has its source. It is false to say that the screen is incapable of putting us "in the presence of" the actor. It does so in the same way as a mirror— one must agree that the mirror relays the presence of the person reflected in it— but it is a mirror with a delayed reflection, the tin foil of which retains the image.[1] It is true that in the theater Molière can die on the stage and that we have the privilege of living in the biographical time of the actor. In the film about Manolete however we are present at the actual death of the famous matador and while our emotion may not be as deep as if we were actually present in the arena at that historic moment, its nature is the same. What we lose by way of direct witness do we not recapture thanks to the artificial proximity provided by photographic enlargement? Everything takes place as if in the time-space perimeter which is the definition of presence. The cinema offers us effectively only a measure of duration, reduced but not to zero, while the increase in the space factor reestablishes the equilibrium of the psychological equation.

OPPOSITION AND IDENTIFICATION

An honest appraisal of the respective pleasures derived from theater and cinema, at least as to what is less intellectual and more direct about them, forces us to admit that the delight we experience at the end of a play has a more uplifting, a nobler, one might perhaps say a more moral, effect than the satisfaction which follows a good film. We seem to come away with a better conscience. In a certain sense it is as if for the man in the audience all theater is "Corneillian." From this point of view one could say that in the best films something is missing. It is as if a certain inevitable lowering of the voltage, some mysterious aesthetic short circuit, deprived us in the cinema of a certain tension which is a definite part of theater. No matter how slight this difference it undoubtedly exists, even between the worst charity production in the theater and the most brilliant of Olivier's film adaptations. There is nothing banal about this observation and the survival of the theater after fifty years of cinema, and the prophecies of Marcel Pagnol, is practical proof enough. At the source of the disenchantment which follows the film one could doubtless detect a process of depersonalization of the spectator. As Rosenkrantz wrote in 1937, in *Esprit*, in an article profoundly original for its period, "The characters on the screen are quite naturally objects of identification, while those on the stage are, rather, objects of mental opposition because their real presence gives them an objective reality and to transpose them into beings in an imaginary world the will of the spectator has to intervene actively, that is to say, to will to transform their physical reality into an abstraction. This abstraction being the result of a process of the intelligence that we can only ask of a person who is fully conscious." A member of a film audience tends to identify himself with the film's hero by a psychological process, the result of which is to turn the audience into a "mass" and to render emotion uniform. Just as in algebra if two numbers equal a third, they they are equal to one another, so here we can say, if two individuals identify themselves with a third, they identify themselves with one another. Let us compare chorus girls on the stage and on the screen. On the screen they satisfy an unconscious sexual desire and when the hero joins them he satisfies the desire of the spectator in the proportion to which the latter has identified himself with the hero. On the stage the girls excite the onlooker as they would in real life. The result is that there is no identification with the hero. He becomes instead an object of jealousy and envy. In other words, Tarzan is only possible on the screen. The cinema calms the spectator, the theater excites him. Even when it appeals to the lowest instincts, the theater up to a certain point stands in the way of the creation of a mass mentality.[2] It stands in the way of any collective representation in the psychological sense, since theater calls for an active individual consciousness while the film requires only a passive adhesion.

These views shed a new light on the problem of the actor. They transfer him from the ontological to the psychological level. It is to the extent to which the cinema encourages identification with the hero that it conflicts with the theater. Put this way the problem is no longer basically insoluble, for it is a fact that the cinema has at its disposal means which favor a passive position or on the other hand, means which to a greater or lesser degree stimulate the consciousness of the spectator. Inversely the theater can find ways of lessening the psychological tension between spectator and actor. Thus theater and cinema will no longer be separated off by an unbridgeable aesthetic moat, they would simply tend to give rise to two attitudes of mind over which the director maintains a wide control.

Examined at close quarters, the pleasure derived from the theater not only differs from that of the cinema but also from that of the novel. The reader of a novel, physically alone like the man in the dark movie house, identifies himself with the character. That is why after reading for a long while he also feels the same intoxication of an illusory intimacy with the hero. Incontestably, there is in the pleasure derived from the cinema and novel a self-satisfaction, a concession to solitude, a sort of betrayal of action by a refusal of social responsibility.

The analysis of this phenomenon might indeed be undertaken from a psychoanalytic point of view. It is not significant that the psychiatrists took the term catharsis from Aristotle? Modern pedagogic research on psychodrama seems to have provided fruitful insights into the cathartic process of theater. The ambiguity existing in the child's mind between play and reality is used to get him to free himself by way of improvised theater from the repressions from which he suffers. This technique amounts to creating a kind of vague theater in which the play is of a serious nature and the actor is his own audience. The action that develops on these occasions is not one that is divided off by footlights, which are undoubtedly the architectural symbol of the censor that separates us from the stage. We delegate Oedipus to act in our guise and place him on the other side of a wall of fire—that fiery frontier between fantasy and reality which gives rein to Dionysiac monsters while protecting us from them. These sacred beasts will not cross this barrier of light beyond which they seem out of place and even sacrilegious—witness the disturbing atmosphere of awe which surrounds an actor still made up, like a phosphorescent light, when we visit him in his dressing room. There is no point to the argument that the theater did not always have footlights. These are only a symbol and there were others before them from the cothurnus and mask onwards. In the seventeenth century the fact that young nobles sat up on the stage is no denial of the role of the footlights, on the contrary, it confirms it, by way of a privileged violation so to speak, just as when today Orson Welles scatters actors around the auditorium to fire on the audience with revolvers. He does not do away with the footlights, he just crosses them. The rules of the game are also made to be broken. One expects some players to cheat.[3] With regard to the objection based on presence and on that alone, the theater and the cinema are not basically in conflict. What is really in dispute are two psychological modalities of a performance. The theater is indeed based on the reciprocal awareness of the presence of audience and actor, but only as related to a performance. The theater acts on us by virtue of our participation in a theatrical action across the footlights and as it were under the protection of their censorship. The opposite is true in the cinema. Alone, hidden in a dark room, we watch through half-open blinds a spectacle that is unaware of our existence and which is part of the universe. There is nothing to prevent us from identifying ourselves in imagination with the moving world before us, which becomes *the* world. It is no longer on the phenomenon of the actor as a person physically present that we should concentrate our analysis, but rather on the ensemble of conditions that constitute the theatrical play and deprive the spectator of active participation. We shall see that it is much less a question of actor and presence than of man and his relation to the decor.

BEHIND THE DECOR

The human being is all-important in the theater. The drama on the screen can exist without actors. A banging door, a leaf in the wind, waves beating on the shore can heighten the dramatic effect. Some film masterpieces use man only as an accessory, like an extra, or in counterpoint to nature which is the true leading character. Even when, as in *Nanook* and *Man of Aran,* the subject is man's struggle with nature, it cannot be compared to a theatrical action. The mainspring of the action is not in man but nature. As Jean-Paul Sartre, I think it was, said, in the theater the drama proceeds from the actor, in the cinema it goes from the decor to man. This reversal of the dramatic flow is of decisive importance. It is bound up with the very essence of the *mise-en-scène.* One must see here one of the consequences of photographic realism. Obviously, if the cinema makes use of nature it is because it is able to. The camera puts at the disposal of the director all the resources of the telescope and the microscope. The last strand of a rope about to snap or an entire army making an assault on a hill are within our reach. Dramatic causes and effects have no longer any material limits to the eye of the camera. Drama is freed by the camera from all contingencies of time and space. But this freeing of tangible dramatic powers is still only a secondary aesthetic cause, and does not basically explain the reversal of value between the actor and the decor. For sometimes it actually happens that the cinema deliberately deprives itself of the use of setting and of exterior nature— we have already seen a perfect instance of this in *Les Parents terribles*—while the theater in contrast uses a complex machinery to give a feeling of ubiquity to the audience. Is *La Passion de Jeanne d'Arc* by Carl Dreyer, shot entirely in close-up, in the virtually invisible and in fact theatrical settings by Jean Hugo, less cinematic than *Stagecoach?* It seems to me that quantity has nothing to do with it, nor the resemblance to certain theater techniques. The ideas of an art director for a room in *Les Dames aux camélias* would not noticeably differ whether for a film or a play. It's true that on the screen you would doubtless have some close-ups of the blood-stained handkerchief, but a skillful stage production would also know how to make some play with the cough and the handkerchief. All the close-ups in *Les Parents terribles* are taken directly from the theater where our attention would spontaneously isolate them. If film direction only differed from theater direction because it allows us a closer view of the scenery and makes a more reasonable use of it, there would really be no reason to continue with the theater and Pagnol would be a true prophet. For it is obvious that the few square yards of the decor of Vilar's *La Danse de la mort* contributed as much to the drama as the island on which Marcel Cravene shot his excellent film. The fact is that the problem lies not in the decor itself but in its nature and function. We must therefore throw some light on an essentially theatrical notion, that of the dramatic place.

There can be no theater without architecture, whether it be the cathedral square, the arena of Nîmes, the palace of the Popes, the trestle stage on a fairground, the semicircle of the theater of Vicenza that looks as if it were decorated by Bérard[4] in a delirium, or the rococo amphitheaters of the boulevard houses. Whether as a performance or a celebration, theater of its very essence must not be confused with nature under penalty of being absorbed by her and ceasing to be. Founded on the reciprocal awareness of those taking part and present to one another, it must be in contrast to the rest of the world in the same way that play and reality are opposed, or concern and indifference, or liturgy and the common use of things. Costume, mask, or make-up, the style of the language, the footlights, all contribute to this distinction, but the clearest sign of all is the stage, the architecture of which has varied from time to time without ever ceasing to mark out a privileged spot actually or virtually distinct from nature. It is precisely in virtue of this *locus dramaticus* that decor exists. It serves in greater or less degree to set the place apart, to specify. Whatever it is, the decor constitutes the walls of this three-sided box opening onto the auditorium, which we call the stage. These false perspectives, these façades, these arbors, have another side which is cloth and nails and wood. Everyone knows that when the actor "retires to his apartment" from the yard or from the garden, he is actually going to his dressing room to take off his make-up. These few square feet of light and illusion are surrounded by machinery and flanked by wings, the hidden labyrinths of which do not interfere one bit with the pleasure of the spectator who is playing the game of theater. Because it is only part of the architecture of the stage, the decor of the theater is thus an area materially enclosed, limited, circumscribed, the only discoveries of which are those of our collusive imagination.

Its appearances are turned inward facing the public and the footlights. It exists by virtue of its reverse side and of anything beyond, as the painting exists by virtue of its frame.[5] Just as the picture is not to be confounded with the scene it represents and is not a window in a wall. The stage and the decor where the action unfolds constitute an aesthetic microcosm inserted perforce into the universe but essentially distinct from the Nature which surrounds it.

It is not the same with cinema, the basic principle of which is a denial of any frontiers to action.

The idea of a *locus dramaticus* is not only alien to, it is essentially a contradiction of the concept of the screen. The screen is not a frame like that of a picture but a mask which allows only a part of the action to be seen. When a character moves off screen, we accept the fact that he is out of sight, but he continues to exist in his own capacity at some other place in the decor which is hidden from us. There are no wings to the screen. There could not be without destroying its specific illusion, which is to make of a revolver or of a face the very center of the universe. In contrast to the stage the space of the screen is centrifugal. It is because that infinity which the theater demands cannot be spatial that its area can be none other than the human soul. Enclosed in this space the actor is at the focus of a two-fold concave mirror. From the auditorium and from the decor there converge on him the dim lights of conscious human beings and of the footlights themselves. But the fire with which he burns is at once that of his inner passion and of that focal point at which he stands. He lights up in each member of his audience an accomplice flame. Like the ocean in a sea shell the dramatic infinities of the human heart moan and beat between the enclosing walls of the theatrical sphere. This is why this dramaturgy is in its essence human. Man is at once its cause and its subject.

On the screen man is no longer the focus of the drama, but will become eventually the center of the universe. The impact of his action may there set in motion an infinitude of waves. The decor that surrounds him is part of the solidity of the world. For this reason the actor as such can be absent from it, because man in the world enjoys no a priori privilege over animals and things. However there is no reason why he should not be the mainspring of the drama, as in Dreyer's *Jeanne d'Arc,* and in this respect the cinema may very well impose itself upon the theater. As actions *Phèdre* or *King Lear* are no less cinemato-gaphic than theatrical, and the visible death of a rabbit in *La Règle du jeu* affects us just as deeply as that of Agnès' little cat about which we are merely told.

But if Racine, Shakespeare, or Molière cannot be brought to the cinema by just placing them before the camera and the microphone, it is because the han-dling of the action and the style of the dialogue were conceived as echoing through the architecture of the auditorium. What is specifically theatrical about these tragedies is not their action so much as the human, that is to say the verbal, priority given to their dramatic structure. The problem of filmed theater at least where the classics are concerned does not consist so much in transpos-ing an action from the stage to the screen as in transposing a text written for one dramaturgical system into another while at the same time retaining its effec-tiveness. It is not therefore essentially the action of a play which resists film adaptation, but above and beyond the phases of the intrigue (which it would be easy enough to adapt to the realism of the screen) it is the verbal form which aesthetic contingencies or cultural prejudices oblige us to respect. It is this which refuses to let itself be captured in the window of the screen. "The the-ater," says Baudelaire, "is a crystal chandelier." If one were called upon to offer in comparison a symbol other than this artificial crystal-like object, brilliant, intricate, and circular, which refracts the light which plays around its center and holds us prisoners of its aureole, we might say of the cinema that it is the lit-tle flashlight of the usher, moving like an uncertain comet across the night of our waking dream, the diffuse space without shape or frontiers that surrounds the screen.

The story of the failures and recent successes of theater on film will be found to be that of the ability of directors to retain the dramatic force of the play in a medium that reflects it or, at least, the ability to give this dramatic force enough resonance to permit a film audience to perceive it. In other words, it is a matter of an aesthetic that is not concerned with the actor but with decor and editing. Henceforth it is clear that filmed theater is basically destined to fail whenever it tends in any manner to become simply the photographing of scenic representa-tion even and perhaps most of all when the camera is used to try and make us forget the footlights and the backstage area. The dramatic force of the text, in-stead of being gathered up in the actor, dissolves without echo into the cine-matic ether. This is why a filmed play can show due respect to the text, be well acted in likely settings, and yet be completely worthless. This is what hap-pened, to take a convenient example, to *Le Voyageur sans baggages*. The play lies there before us apparently true to itself yet drained of every ounce of energy, like a battery dead from an unknown short. But over and beyond the aesthetic of the decor we see clearly both on the screen and on the stage that in the last analysis the problem before us is that of realism. This is the problem we always end up with when we are dealing with cinema.

THE SCREEN AND THE REALISM OF SPACE

The realism of the cinema follows directly from its photographic nature. Not only does some marvel or some fantastic thing on the screen not undermine the reality of the image, on the contrary it is its most valid justification. Illusion in the cinema is not based as it is in the theater on convention tacitly accepted by the general public; rather, contrariwise, it is based on the inalienable realism of that which is shown. All trick work must be perfect in all material respects on the screen. The "invisible man" must wear pyjamas and smoke a cigarette.

Must we conclude from this that the cinema is dedicated entirely to the representation if not of natural reality at least of a plausible reality of which the spectator admits the identity with nature as he knows it? The comparative failure of German expressionism would seem to confirm this hypothesis, since it is evident that *Caligari* attempted to depart from realistic decor under the influence of the theater and painting. But this would be to offer an oversimplified explanation for a problem that calls for more subtle answers. We are prepared to admit that the screen opens upon an artificial world provided there exists a common denominator between the cinematographic image and the world we live in. Our experience of space is the structural basis for our concept of the universe. We may say in fact, adapting Henri Gouhier's formula, "the stage welcomes every illusion except the illusion of presence," that "the cinematographic image can be emptied of all reality save one—the reality of space."

It is perhaps an overstatement to say "all reality" because it is difficult to imagine a reconstruction of space devoid of all reference to nature. The world of the screen and our world cannot be juxtaposed. The screen of necessity substitutes for it since the very concept of universe is spatially exclusive. For a time, a film is the Universe, the world, or if you like, Nature. We will see how the films that have attempted to substitute a fabricated nature and an artificial world for the world of experience have not all equally succeeded. Admitting the failure of *Caligari* and *Die Nibelungen* we then ask ourselves how we explain the undoubted success of *Nosferatu* and *La Passion de Jeanne d'Arc,* the criterion of success being that these films have never aged. Yet it would seem at first sight that the methods of direction belong to the same aesthetic family, and that viewing the varieties of temperament and period, one could group these four films together as expressionist as distinct from realist. However, if we examine them more closely we see that there are certain basic differences between them. It is clear in the case of R. Weine and Murnau. *Nosferatu* plays, for the greater part of the time, against natural settings whereas the fantastic qualities of *Caligari* are derived from deformities of lighting and decor. The case of Dreyer's *Jeanne d'Arc* is a little more subtle since at first sight nature plays a nonexistent role. To put it more directly, the decor by Jean Hugo is no whit less artificial and theatrical than the settings of *Caligari;* the systematic use of close-ups and unusual angles is well calculated to destroy any sense of space. Regular cinéclub goers know that the film is unfailingly introduced with the famous story of how the hair of Falconetti was actually cut in the interests of the film and likewise, the actors, we are told, wore no make-up. These references to history ordinarily have no more than gossip value. In this case, they seem to me to hold the aesthetic secret of the film; the very thing to which it owes its continued survival. It is precisely because of them that the work of Dreyer ceases to have anything in common with the theater, and indeed one might say, with man. The greater recourse Dreyer has exclusively to the human "expression," the more he has to reconvert it again into Nature. Let there be no mistake, that prodigious fresco of heads is the very opposite of an actor's film. It is a documentary of faces. It is not important how well the actors play, whereas the pockmarks on Bishop Cauchon's face and the red patches of Jean d'Yd are an integral part of the action. In this drama-through-the-microscope the whole of nature palpitates beneath every pore. The movement of a wrinkle, the pursing of a lip are seismic shocks and the flow of tides, the flux and reflux of this human epidermis. But for me Dreyer's brilliant sense of cinema is evidenced in the exterior scene which every other director would assuredly have shot in the studio. The decor as built evoked a Middle Ages of the theater and of miniatures. In one sense, nothing is less realistic than this tribunal in the cemetery or this drawbridge, but the whole is lit by the light of the sun and the gravedigger throws a spadeful of real earth into the hole.[6]

It is these "secondary" details, apparently aesthetically at odds with the rest of the work, which give it its truly cinematic quality.

If the paradox of the cinema is rooted in the dialectic of concrete and abstract, if cinema is committed to communicate only by way of what is real, it becomes all the more important to discern those elements in filming which confirm our sense of natural reality and those which destroy that feeling. On the other hand, it certainly argues a lack of perception to derive one's sense of reality from these accumulations of factual detail. It is possible to argue that *Les Dames du Bois de Boulogne* is an eminently realistic film, though everything about it is stylized. Everything, except for the rarely noticeable sound of a windshield-wiper, the murmur of a waterfall, or the rushing sound of soil escaping from a broken vase. These are the noises, chosen precisely for their "indifference" to the action, that guarantee its reality.

The cinema being of its essence a dramaturgy of Nature, there can be no cinema without the setting up of an open space in place of the universe rather than as part of it. The screen cannot give us the illusion of this feeling of space without calling on certain natural guarantees. But it is less a question of set construction or of architecture or of immensity than of isolating the aesthetic catalyst, which it is sufficient to introduce in an infinitesimal dose, to have it immediately take on the reality of nature.

The concrete forest of *Die Nibelungen* may well pretend to be an infinite expanse. We do not believe it to be so, whereas the trembling of just one branch in the wind, and the sunlight, would be enough to conjure up all the forests of the world.

If this analysis be well founded, then we see that the basic aesthetic problem of filmed theater is indeed that of the decor. The trump card that the director must hold is the reconversion into a window onto the world of a space oriented toward an interior dimension only, namely the closed and conventional area of the theatrical play.

It is not in Laurence Olivier's *Hamlet* that the text seems to be rendered superfluous or its strength diminished by directorial interpretations, still less in Welles' *Macbeth,* but paradoxically in the stage productions of Gaston Baty, to the precise extent that they go out of their way to create a cinematographic space on the stage; to deny that the settings have a reverse side, thus reducing the sonority of the text simply to the vibration of the voice of the actor who is left without his "resonance box" like a violin that is nothing else but strings. One would never deny that the essential thing in the theater is the text. The latter conceived for the anthropocentric expression proper to the stage and having as its function to bring nature to it cannot, without losing its raison d'être, be used in a space transparent as glass. The problem then that faces the filmmaker is to give his decor a dramatic opaqueness while at the same time reflecting its natural realism. Once this paradox of space has been dealt with, the director, so far from hesitating to bring theatrical conventions and faithfulness to the text to the screen will find himself now, on the contrary, completely free to rely on them. From that point on it is no longer a matter of running away from those

Fig. 5. Adolph Caesar and Denzel Washington in *A Soldier's Story* (1984), adapted by
Charles Fuller from his drama *A Soldier's Play* (1982). Jewison combined the authenticity of
on-location shooting with a flashback-structure in this film adaptation. Directed by
Norman Jewison. Courtesy of Billy Rose Theatre Collection, The New York Public Library
for the Performing Arts, Astor, Lenox and Tilden Foundations.

things which "make theater" but in the long run to acknowledge their existence
by rejecting the resources of the cinema, as Cocteau did in *Les Parents terribles*
and Welles in *Macbeth,* or by putting them in quotation marks as Laurence
Olivier did in *Henry V.* The evidence of a return to filmed theater that we have
had during the last ten years belongs essentially to the history of decor and editing. It is a conquest of realism—not, certainly, the realism of subject matter or
realism of expression but that realism of space without which moving pictures
do not constitute cinema.

AN ANALOGY FROM PLAY-ACTING

This progress in filmed theater has only been possible insofar as the opposition
between them did not rest on the ontological category of presence but on a psychology of "play." In passing from one to the other, one goes from the absolute
to the relative, from antinomy to simple contradiction. While the cinema cannot offer the spectator the community feeling of theater, a certain knowledge of

direction will allow him finally, and this is a decisive factor, to preserve the meaning and force of the text. The grafting of the theatrical text onto the decor of cinema is an operation which today we know can be successful. There remains that awareness of the active opposition existing between the spectator and the actor which constitutes the "play" of theater and is symbolized by scenic architecture. But there is a way of reducing even this to the psychology of the cinematic.

The reasoning of Rosenkrantz concerning opposition and identification requires in effect an important correction. It carries with it, still, a measure of equivocation. Rosenkrantz seems to equate identification with passivity and escape—an accepted fact in his time because of the condition of the cinema but less and less so in its present stage of evolution. Actually the cinema of myth and dream is now only one variety of production and one that is less and less frequent. One must not confuse an accidental and historical social condition with an unalterable psychological one—two activities, that is to say, of the spectator's consciousness that converge but are not part of one another. I do not identify equally with Tarzan and Bresson's curé. The only denominator common to my attitude to these two heroes is that I believe that they really exist, that I cannot refuse, except by staying away from the film, to share their adventures and to live them through with them, inside their universe, a universe that is not metaphorical and figurative but spatially real. This interior sharing does not exclude, in the second example, a consciousness of myself as distinct from the person from whom I chose to be alienated in the first example. These factors originating in the affective order are not the only ones that argue against passive identification; films like *L'Espoir* or *Citizen Kane* require in the spectator an intellectual alertness incompatible with passivity. The most that one can suggest is that the psychology of the cinematographic image offers a natural incline leading towards a sociology of the hero characterized by a passive identification. But in the arts as in morals, inclines are also made to be climbed. While the contemporary man of the theater often tries to lessen the sense of theatricality in a performance by a kind of realism in the production—just as those who love to go to the Grand Guignol play at being frightened but hold on at the very height of the horror to a delicious awareness of being fooled—the film director discovers on his side means of exciting the awareness of the spectator and of provoking him to reflection. This is something which would set up a conflict at the very heart of the identification. This private zone of consciousness, this self-awareness at the height of illusion, creates a kind of private footlights. In filmed theater it is no longer the microcosm of the play which is set over against nature but the spectator who is conscious of himself. On the screen *Hamlet* and *Les Parents terribles* cannot nor should they escape from the laws of cinematic perception; Elsinore and "La Roulotte" really exist but I pass through them unseen, rejoicing in that equivocal freedom which certain dreams allow us. I am walking but moving backwards.

Certainly the possibility of a state of intellectual self-awareness at the moment of psychological identification should never be confused with that act of the will which constitutes theater, and that is why it is foolish to identify stage and screen as Pagnol does. No matter how conscious of myself, how intelligent a film can make me, it is not to my will that it appeals—only at most to my good will. A film calls for a certain effort on my part so that I may understand and enjoy it, but it does not depend on me for its existence. Nevertheless it would certainly seem, from experience, that the margin of awareness allowed by the cinema is enough to establish an acceptable equivalent to the pleasure given by theater, at least enough to preserve what is essential to the artistic values of the play. The film, while it cannot pretend to be a complete substitute for the stage performance, is at least capable of assuring the theater a valid artistic existence and can offer us a comparable pleasure. There can never be question of anything more than a complex mechanical aesthetic where the original theatrical effectiveness is almost never directly applied, rather it is preserved, reconstituted, and transmitted thanks to a system of circuits, as in *Henry V,* of amplification as for example in *Macbeth,* of induction or interference. The true filmed theater is not the phonograph, it is its Martenot wave.[7]

MORALITY

Thus the practice (certain) like the theory (possible) of successful filmed theater reveals the reasons for former failures. Straightforward animated photography of theater is a childish error recognized as such these thirty years and on which there is no point in insisting further. The heresy of film adaptation has taken longer to smoke out. It will continue to have its dupes but we now know where it leads—to aesthetic limbos that belong neither to film nor to theater, to that "filmed theater" justly condemned as the sin against the spirit of cinema. The true solution, revealed at last, consists in realizing that it is not a matter of transferring to the screen the dramatic element—an element interchangeable between one art and another—of a theatrical work, but inversely the theatrical quality of the drama. The subject of the adaptation is not that of the play, it is the play precisely in its scenic essence. This truth, apparent at last, will allow us to reach a conclusion concerning three propositions seemingly paradoxical at first, but which on reflection are seen to be quite evident.

(1) THEATER AN AID TO CINEMA

The first proposition is that so far from being a corruption of cinema, filmed theater serves on the contrary to enrich and elevate it. Let us first look at the matter of theater. It is alas only too certain that the level of film production is intellectually much below, if not that of current dramatic production—think of Jean de Létraz and Henry Bernstein—at least of the living heritage of the-ater, even if only because of its great age. True, our century is no less that of Charlie Chaplin than was the seventeenth century that of Racine and Molière, but after all the cinema has only half a century of literature behind it while the theater has twenty-five. What would the French theater be like today if, as is the case with the cinema, it had nothing to offer but the production of the past decade? Since the cinema is undeniably passing through a crisis of subject mat-ter it is not risking anything by employing screen writers like Shakespeare or even Feydeau. Let us not labor the subject. The case is only too clear. However, the inferiority is less evident in the realm of form. If the cinema is a major art with its own laws and language, what can it gain by submitting to the laws and language of another art? A great deal! And precisely to the extent to which, lay-ing aside all its vain and puerile tricks, it is seriously concerned to subordinate itself and render a service. To justify this point of view completely, one should really discuss it within the framework of the aesthetic history of influence in art in general. This would almost certainly reveal, we feel, that at some stage in their evolution there has been a definite commerce between the technique of the various arts. Our prejudice about "pure art" is a critical development of rel-atively recent origin. But the authority of these precedents is not indispensable to our argument. The art of direction, the mechanics of which in relation to certain major films, as we have had to explain earlier, more even than our theo-retical hypotheses, supposes on the part of the director a grasp of the language of cinematography equalled only by his knowledge of what theater is. If the *film d'art* failed where Olivier and Cocteau have succeeded, it is first of all be-cause they have at their disposal a much more developed means of expression, but they also know how to use it more effectively than their contemporaries. To say of *Les Parents terribles* that it is perhaps an excellent film but that it is not cinema because it follows the play step by step is critical nonsense. On the con-trary, it is precisely for this reason that it is cinema. It is *Topaze* by Marcel Pagnol—in its most recent style—which is not cinema, precisely because it is no longer theater. There is more cinema, and great cinema at that, in *Henry V* alone than in 90% of original scripts. Pure poetry is certainly not that which has nothing to say, as Cocteau has so well demonstrated: all the examples of pure poetry given by the Abbé Brémond illustrate the exact opposite. *La Fille de Minos et Pasiphae* is as informative as a birth certificate. There is likewise a way, unfortunately not yet practiced, of reciting this poem on the screen which would be pure cinema because it would respect, in the most intelligent way, its true theatrical value.

The more the cinema intends to be faithful to the text and to its theatrical requirements, the more of necessity must it delve deeper into its own language. The best translation is that which demonstrates a close intimacy with the genius of both languages and, likewise, a mastery of both.

(2) THE CINEMA WILL SAVE THE THEATER

That is why the cinema will give back to the theater unstintingly what it took from her, if it has not already done so. For if the success of filmed theater supposes that dialectical progress had been made with the cinematic form, it implies both reciprocally and a fortiori a reevaluation of the essentially theatrical. The idea exploited by Marcel Pagnol according to which the cinema will replace the theater by "canning it" is completely false. The screen cannot replace the stage as the piano has supplanted the clavichord. And to begin with, replace the theater for whom? Not for the filmgoing public that long ago deserted the theater. The divorce between public and theater does not date, so far as I know, from that historic evening at the Grand Café in 1895. Are we talking then about the privileged minority of culture and wealth which actually makes up the theater audiences? But we see that Jean de Létraz is not bankrupt and that the visitor to Paris from the provinces does not confuse the breasts of Françoise Arnoul that he has seen on the screen with those of Nathalie Nattier at the Palais-Royal, although the latter may be covered by a brassière; but they are there, if I may say so, "in the flesh." Ah! The irreplaceable presence of the actor! As for the "serious" theaters, say the Marigny or the Français, it is clearly a question of a public that, for the most part, does not go to the cinema and, for the others, of people who go to both without confusing the pleasure to be derived from each. The fact is, if any ground has been taken over it is not the territory of the theatrical spectacle as it exists, it is much more the taking over of the place abandoned long ago by the now-defunct forms of popular theater. So far from being a serious rival to the stage, the cinema is in process of giving back, to a public that had lost it, a taste and feeling for theater.[8]

It is possible that canned theater had something to do at the time with the disappearance of touring companies from the road. When Marcel Pagnol makes a film of *Topaze,* there is no doubt about his intentions, namely to make his play available to the provinces with a "Paris cast" at the price of a cinema seat. It is often the same with the boulevard plays. Their successful run finished, the film is distributed to those who were unable to see the play. In those areas where the Baret touring companies performed with a second-rate cast, the film offers at a very reasonable price not only the original cast, but even more magnificent sets. But this illusion was really successful for only a few years and we now see provincial tours on the road again, the better for their experience. The public they have recaptured, made blasé by the cinema and its glamorous casting and its luxurious sets, has, "come to," as they say, and is looking for something that is, more or less, theater.

But the popularizing of Paris successes is still not the ultimate end of the theatrical revival nor is it the chief merit of the "competition" between screen and stage. One might even say that this improvement in the situation of the touring companies is due to badly filmed theater. It is the defects of these films that have finally turned the stomachs of a section of the public and sent them back into the theaters.

It was the same situation with regard to photography and painting. Cinema dispensed photography from what was aesthetically least essential to it: likeness and anecdote. The high standard and the lower cost of photography and the ease with which pictures are taken, has at last contributed to the due evaluation of painting and to establishing it unalterably in its proper place. But this is not the end of the benefits derived from their coexistence. The photographers have not just served as the helots of the painters. At the same time, as it became more conscious of itself, painting absorbed something of photography. It is Degas and Toulouse-Lautrec, Renoir and Manet, who have understood from the inside, and in essence, the nature of the photographic phenomenon and, prophetically, even the cinematographic phenomenon. Faced with photography, they opposed it in the only valid way, by a dialectical enriching of pictorial technique. They understood the laws of the new image better than the photographers and well before the movie-makers, and it is they who first applied them.

Nevertheless this is not all and photography is in process of rendering services to the plastic arts that are even more decisive still. Their fields henceforth
clearly known and delimited, the automatic image multiplies and renews our
knowledge of the pictorial image. Malraux has said what needed to be said on
this. If painting has been able to become the most individual of arts, the most
onerous, the most independent of all compromise while at the same time the
most accessible, it is thanks to color photography.

The same process applies to the theater; bad "canned theater" has helped
true theater to become aware of its own laws. The cinema has likewise contributed to a new concept of theatrical production. These are results henceforth
firmly established. But there is a third result which good filmed theater permits
us to look for, namely the remarkable increase in breadth of understanding of
theater among the general public. What then is a film like *Henry V?* First of all,
it is Shakespeare for everybody. Furthermore, and supremely, it is a blazing
light thrown onto the dramatic poetry of Shakespeare—the most effective and
brilliant of theater lessons. Shakespeare emerges from the process twice himself.
Not only does the adaptation of the play multiply his potential audience in the
same way that the adaptation of novels makes the fortune of publishers, but
also, the public is far better prepared than before to enjoy the stage play. Laurence Olivier's *Hamlet* must obviously increase the audience for Jean-Louis
Barrault's *Hamlet* and sharpen the critical sense. Just as there is a difference that
can never be bridged between the finest modern reproduction of a painting and
the pleasure of owning the original, seeing Hamlet on the screen cannot take
the place of a performance of the play by, say, a group of English students. But
you need a genuine education in theater to appreciate the real-life performance
by amateurs, that is to be able truly to share in what they are doing. So the more
successful the filmed theater, the deeper it probes into the essence of theater, the
better to serve it, the more clearly it will reveal the unbridgeable gulf between
stage and screen. It is, on the contrary, the canned theater on the one hand and
mediocre popular theater on the other that give rise to the confusion. *Les Parents terribles* never misleads its audience. There is not a sequence in it that is not
more effective than its stage counterpart, while there is not one which does not
allude by implication to that indefinable pleasure that I would have had from
the real thing. There is no better propaganda for the real theater than well-
filmed theater. These truths are henceforth indisputable and it would have been
ridiculous of me to have spent so much time on them if the myth about filmed
theater did not still survive too frequently in the form of prejudice, of misun-
derstanding, and of minds already made up.

(3) FROM FILMED THEATER TO
CINEMATOGRAPHIC THEATER

My last argument, I realize, will be the boldest. So far we have considered the theater as an aesthetic absolute to which the cinema can come close in a more or less satisfactory fashion, but only in all circumstances and under the best possible conditions, as its humble servant. However, we can see in slapstick the rebirth of dramatic forms that had practically disappeared, such as farce and the *Commedia dell'Arte*. Certain dramatic situations, certain techniques that had degenerated in the course of time, found again, in the cinema, first the sociological nourishment they needed to survive and, still better, the conditions favorable to an expansive use of their aesthetic, which the theater had kept congenitally atrophied. In making a protagonist out of space, the screen does not betray the spirit of farce, it simply gives to the metaphysical meaning of Scarpin's stick its true dimensions, namely those of the whole universe. Slapstick is first and foremost, or at least is also, the dramatic expression of the tyranny of things, out of which Keaton even more than Chaplin knew how to create a tragedy of the Object. But it is true that the forms of comedy create something of a special problem in the history of filmed theater, probably because laughter allows the audience to become aware of itself and to use this to experience a measure of the opposition that theater creates between actor and audience. In any case, and that is why we have not gone farther into the study of it, the grafting together of cinema and comedy-theater happened spontaneously and has been so perfect that its fruit has always been accepted as the product of pure cinema.

Now that the screen can welcome other kinds of theater besides comedy without betraying them, there is no reason to suppose that it cannot likewise give the theater new life, employing certain of the stage's own techniques. Film cannot be, indeed must not be, as we have seen, simply a paradoxical modality of theater production, but stage structures have their importance and it is not a matter of indifference whether *Julius Caesar* is played in the arena at Nîmes or in a studio; but certain dramatic works, and by no means the least of them, have suffered in a very material way these thirty to fifty years from a discord between contemporary taste and the style of the staging that they call for. I am thinking particularly of tragedy. There, the handicap we suffer from is due especially to the disappearance of the race of traditional tragedians of the old school—the Mounet-Sullys and the Sarah Bernhardts, that is, who disappeared at the beginning of the century like prehistoric creatures of the secondary period. By a stroke of irony, it is the cinema that has preserved their bones, fossilized in the *films d'art*. It has become a commonplace to attribute their disappearance to the cinema and for two converging reasons: one aesthetic, the other sociological. The screen has certainly modified our feeling about verisimilitude in interpretation. It is enough to see one of the little films of Bernhardt or Bargy to understand that this type of actor was still trussed up to all intents and purposes in cothurnus and mask. But the mask is simply an object of laughter while a close-up can drown us in a tear, and the megaphone is ridiculous when the microphone can produce at will a roar from the feeblest vocal chords. Thus we are accustomed to the inner naturalness which only allows the stage actor a slender margin of stylization beyond verisimilitude. The sociological factor is probably even more decisive. The success and effectiveness of a Mounet-Sully was undoubtedly due to his talent but helped on by the consenting complicity of the public. It was the phenomenon of the *monstre sacré* which is today diverted almost exclusively to the cinema. To say that the classes at the Conservatory do not produce any more tragedians doesn't by any means imply that no more Sarah Bernhardts are being born, only that their gifts and the times do not consort well. Thus, Voltaire wore out his lungs plagiarizing the tragedy of the seventeenth century because he thought that it was only Racine who had died when actually it was tragedy itself. Today we see not the slightest difference between Mounet-Sully and a ham from the provinces because we could not recognize a tragedian of the old school when we saw one. Only the "monster" survives in the *film d'art* for a young man today. The sacred quality has departed.

In the circumstances it is not surprising that Racine's tragedy is in a period of eclipse. Thanks to its conservative attitude, the Comédie Française is in the fortunate position of being able to guarantee him a reasonable life, but no longer a triumphal one.[9] Furthermore, this is only because of an interesting filtering-through of traditional values, their delicate adaptation to modern tastes, and not by a radical renewal straight out of the period. As for ancient tragedy, it is paradoxically to the Sorbonne and to the archeological enthusiasm of students that it owes the fact that it moves us once more. But it is important to see in these experiments by amateurs an extremely radical reaction against the actor's theater.

Thus, is it not natural to think that if the cinema has completely turned to its own advantage the aesthetic and the sociology of the sacred monster, that it might return them if the theater came looking for them? It is reasonable enough to dream what an Athalie could have been with Yvonne de Bray and Jean Cocteau directing!

But doubtless it would not be just the style of the interpretation of tragedy that would find its raison d'être once more on the screen. One could well imagine a corresponding revolution on the stage which, without ceasing to be faithful to the spirit of the theater, would offer it new forms in keeping with modern taste and especially at the level of a great mass audience. Film theater is waiting for a Jean Cocteau to make it a cinematographic theater.

Thus not only is theater on film from now on aesthetically founded in truth and fact, not only do we know that henceforth there are no plays that cannot be brought to the screen, whatever their style, provided one can visualize a reconversion of stage space in accordance with the data. But it may also be that the only possible modern theatrical production of certain classics would be on the screen. It is no chance matter that some of the best filmmakers are also the best stage directors. Welles and Olivier did not come to the cinema out of cynicism, snobbery, or ambition, not even, like Pagnol, to popularize theatrical works. Cinema is for them only a complementary form of theater, the chance to produce theater precisely as they feel and see it.

NOTES

1. Television naturally adds a new variant to the "pseudopresences" resulting from the scientific techniques for reproduction created by photography. On the little screen during live television the actor is actually present in space and time. But the reciprocal actor-spectator relationship is incomplete in one direction. The spectator sees without being seen. There is no return flow. Televised theater, therefore, seems to share something both of theater and of cinema: of theater because the actor is present to the viewer, of cinema because the spectator is not present to the actor. Nevertheless, this state of not being present is not truly an absence. The television actor has a sense of the millions of ears and eyes virtually present and represented by the electronic camera. This abstract presence is most noticeable when the actor fluffs his lines. Painful enough in the theater, it is intolerable on television since the spectator who can do nothing to help him is aware of the unnatural solitude of the actor. In the theater in similar circumstances a sort of understanding exists with the audience, which is a help to an actor in trouble. This kind of reciprocal relationship is impossible on television.
2. Crowd and solitude are not antinomies: the audience in a movie house is made up of solitary individuals. Crowd should be taken here to mean the opposite of an organic community freely assembled.
3. Here is a final example proving that presence does not constitute theater except in so far as it is a matter of a performance. Everyone either at his own or someone else's expense has known the embarrassment of being watched without knowing it or in spite of knowing it. Lovers who kiss on public benches offer a spectacle to the passerby, but they do not care. My concierge who has a feeling for the *mot juste* says, when she sees them, that it is like be-

ing at the movies. Each of us has sometimes found himself forced to his annoyance to do something absurd before other people. On those occasions we experience a sense of angry shame which is the very opposite of theatrical exhibitionism. Someone who looks through a keyhole is not at the theater; Cocteau has rightly demonstrated in *Le sang d'un poète* that he was already at the cinema. And nevertheless there are such things as "shows," when protagonists are present to us in flesh and blood but one of the two parties is ignorant of the fact or goes through with it reluctantly. This is not "play" in the theatrical sense.

4. Christian Bérard: A French painter (1902–1949) whom Louis Jouvet and Jean Cocteau persuaded, with some difficulty, to undertake designing theater sets. He designed sets for *La Voix humaine* (1930) and *La Machine infernal* (1934). He also created the sets for Cocteau's film *La Belle et la bête*. His illustrations of the works of Rimbaud are well known.

5. The ideal historical example of this theory of theater architecture and its relations to the stage and the decor is provided by the Palladium with the extraordinary Olympic Theater of Vicenza, making of the ancient amphitheater open to the sky a purely architectural *trompe-l'oeil*. There is not a single element, including the entrance to the auditorium, which is not an affirmation of its essentially architectural nature. Built in 1590, inside an old barracks donated by the town, outwardly the Olympic Theater appears to be just red-brick walls, that is, a purely utilitarian piece of architecture which one might describe as amorphous in the sense in which chemists distinguish between the amorphous state and the crystal state of the same body. The visitor going in by what appears to be a hole in the wall cannot believe his eyes when he finds himself all of a sudden in the extraordinary hollowed-out grotto which constitutes the semicircle of the theater. Like those blocks of quartz or amethyst which outwardly look like common stones whereas inside they are a composite of pure crystal, secretly oriented inward, the theater of Vicenza is conceived according to the laws of an aesthetic and artificial space polarized exclusively towards the center.

6. This is why I consider the graveyard scene in *Hamlet* and the death of Ophelia bad mistakes on Olivier's part. He had here a chance to introduce sun and soil by way of counterpoint to the setting of Elsinore. Does the actual shot of the sea during the soliloquy of Hamlet show that he had sensed the need for this? The idea, excellent in itself, is not well handled technically.

7. Martenot waves: Name of a radio-electrical instrument which was an advance on the theremin. It is one of many electro-phonic instruments on which, at will, the player may make notes whose origin is to be traced to electro-magnetic vibrations ultimately converted into sound waves by some form of loudspeaker.

8. The case of the Théâtre Nationale Populaire offers another unexpected and paradoxical example of support for the theater by the cinema. I presume that Jean Vilar (well-known French actor, formerly director of the Théâtre Nationale Populaire) would not dispute the undoubted help his enterprise gets from the film fame of Gérard Philipe. Actually in doing this the cinema is only paying back to the theater a part of the capital it borrowed some forty years ago in the heroic period when the infant film industry, an object of contempt, had recourse to stage celebrities who could provide the artistic discipline and pres-

tige it needed before it could be taken seriously. Certainly the situation was soon enough reversed. The Sarah Bernhardt of the years between the wars went by the name of Greta Garbo and it is now the theater that is willing to advertise the name of a film star on its marquees.

9. Triumph is precisely what *Henry V* is, thanks to color film. If one were searching through *Phédre* for an example of cinematic potentiality, the recital of Theramine, a verbal reminiscence of the *tragicomédie à machines,* considered as a dramatically literary piece, dramatically out of place, would find, visually, a new raison d'être on the screen.

•

Film and Theatre

Susan Sontag

The big question is whether there is an unbridgeable division, even opposition, between the two arts. Is there something genuinely "cinematic"?

Almost all opinion holds that there is. A commonplace of discussion has it that film and theatre are distinct and even antithetical arts, each giving rise to its own standards of judgment and canons of form. Thus Erwin Panofsky argues, in his celebrated essay "Style and Medium in the Motion Pictures" (1934, rewritten in 1946), that one of the criteria for evaluating a movie is its freedom from the impurities of theatricality. To talk about film, one must first define "the basic nature of the medium." Those who think prescriptively about the nature of live drama, less confident in the future of their art than the *cinéphiles* in theirs, rarely take a comparably exclusivist line.

The history of cinema is often treated as the history of its emancipation from theatrical models. First of all from theatrical "frontality"

Excerpted from *Drama Review* 11, no. 1 (Fall 1966): 24–37.

(the unmoving camera reproducing the situation of the spectator of a play fixed in his seat), then from theatrical acting (gestures needlessly stylized, exaggerated—needlessly, because now the actor could be seen "close up"), then from theatrical furnishings (unnecessary "distancing" of the audience's emotions, disregarding the opportunity to immerse the audience in reality). Movies are regarded as advancing from theatrical stasis to cinematic fluidity, from theatrical artificiality to cinematic naturalness and immediacy. But this view is far too simple.

Such over-simplification testifies to the ambiguous scope of the camera eye. Because the camera *can* be used to project a relatively passive, unselective kind of vision—as well as the highly selective ("edited") vision generally associated with movies—cinema is a "medium" as well as an art, in the sense that it can encapsulate any of the performing arts and render it in a film transcription. (This "medium" or non-art aspect of film attained its routine incarnation with the advent of television. There, movies themselves became another performing art to be transcribed, miniaturized on film.) One *can* film a play or ballet or opera or sporting event in such a way that film becomes, relatively speaking, a transparency, and it seems correct to say that one is seeing the event filmed. But theatre is never a "medium." Thus, because one can make a movie "of" a play but not a play "of" a movie, cinema had an early but, I should argue, fortuitous connection with the stage. Some of the earliest films were filmed plays. Duse and Bernhardt and Barrymore are on film—marooned in time, absurd, touching; there is a 1913 British film of Forbes-Robertson playing Hamlet, a 1923 German film of *Othello* starring Emil Jannings. More recently, the camera has "preserved" Helene Weigel's performance of *Mother Courage* with the Berliner Ensemble, the Living Theatre production of *The Brig* (filmed by the Mekas brothers), and Peter Brook's staging of Weiss's *Marat/Sade*.

But from the beginning, even within the confines of the notion of film as a "medium" and the camera as a "recording" instrument, a great deal other than what occurred in theatres was taken down. As with still photography, some of the events captured on moving photographs were staged but others were valued precisely because they were *not* staged—the camera being the witness, the invisible spectator, the invulnerable voyeuristic eye. (Perhaps public happenings, "news," constitute an intermediate case between staged and unstaged events; but film as "newsreel" generally amounts to using film as a "medium.") To create on film a *document* of a transient reality is a conception quite unrelated to the purposes of theatre. It only appears related when the "real event" being recorded is a theatrical performance. And the first use of the motion picture camera was to make a documentary record of unstaged, casual reality: Louis Lumière's films of crowd-scenes in Paris and New York made in the 1890's antedate any use of film in the service of plays.

The other paradigmatic non-theatrical use of film, which dates from the earliest activity of the motion-picture camera, is for the creation of *illusion,* the construction of fantasy. The pioneer figure here is, of course, Georges Méliès. To be sure, Méliès (like many directors after him) conceived of the rectangle of the screen on analogy with the proscenium stage. And not only were the events staged; they were the very stuff of invention: imaginary journeys, imaginary objects, physical metamorphoses. But this, even adding the fact that Méliès situated his camera "in front of" the action and hardly moved it, does not make his films theatrical in an invidious sense. In their treatment of persons as things (physical objects) and in their disjunctive presentation of time and space, Méliès' films are quintessentially "cinematic"—so far as there is such a thing.

The contrast between theatre and films is usually taken to lie in the materials represented or depicted. But exactly where does the difference lie? It's tempting to draw a crude boundary. Theatre deploys artifice while cinema is committed to reality, indeed to an ultimately physical reality which is "redeemed," to use Siegfried Kracauer's striking word, by the camera. The aesthetic judgment that follows this bit of intellectual map-making is that films shot in real-life settings are better (*i.e.,* more cinematic) than those shot in a studio (where one can detect the difference). Obviously, if Flaherty and Italian neo-realism and the *cinema verité* of Vertov, Rouch, Marker, and Ruspoli are the preferred models, one would judge rather harshly the period of 100% studio-made films inaugurated around 1920 by *The Cabinet of Dr. Caligari,* films with ostentatiously artificial landscapes and decor, and deem the right direction to be that taken at the same period in Sweden, where many films with strenuous natural settings were being shot "on location." Thus, Panofsky attacks *Dr. Caligari* for "prestylizing reality," and urges upon cinema "the problem of manipulating and shooting unstylized reality in such a way that the result has style."

But there is no reason to insist on a single model for film. And it is helpful to notice that, for the most part, the apotheosis of realism, the prestige of "unstylized reality," in cinema is actually a covert political-moral position. Films have been rather too often acclaimed as the democratic art, the art of mass society. Once one takes this description very seriously, one tends (like Panofsky and Kracauer) to want movies to continue to reflect their origins in a vulgar level of the arts, to remain loyal to their vast uneducated audience. Thus, a vaguely

Marxist orientation jibes with a fundamental tenet of romanticism. Cinema, at once high art and popular art, is cast as the art of the authentic. Theatre, by contrast, means dressing up, pretense, lies. It smacks of aristocratic taste and the class society. Behind the objection of critics to the stagy sets of *Dr. Caligari,* the improbable costumes and florid acting of Renoir's *Nana,* the talkiness of Dreyer's *Gertrud,* as "theatrical," lay the feeling that such films were false, that they exhibited a sensibility both pretentious and reactionary which was out-of-step with the democratic and more mundane sensibility of modern life.

Anyway, whether aesthetic defect or not in the particular case, the synthetic look in films is not necessarily a misplaced theatricalism. From the beginning of film history, there were painters and sculptors who claimed that cinema's true future resided in artifice, construction. It lay not in figurative narration or story-telling of any kind (either in a relatively realistic or in a "surrealistic" vein), but in abstraction. Thus, Theo van Doesburg in his essay of 1929, "Film as Pure Form," envisages film as the vehicle of "optical poetry," "dynamic light architecture," "the creation of a moving ornament." Films will realize "Bach's dream of finding an optical equivalent for the temporal structure of a musical composition." Today, a few film-makers—for example, Robert Breer—continue to pursue this conception of film, and who is to say it is not cinematic?

Could anything be farther from the scope of theatre than such a degree of abstraction? It's important not to answer that question too quickly.

Some locate the division between theatre and film as the difference between the play and the filmscript. Panofsky derives this difference from what he takes to be the most profound one: the difference between the *formal* conditions of seeing a play and those of seeing a movie. In the theatre, says Panofsky, "space is static, that is, the space represented on the stage, as well as the spatial relation of the beholder to the spectacle, is unalterably fixed," while in the cinema "the spectator occupies a fixed seat, but only physically, not as the subject of an aesthetic experience." In the cinema, the spectator is "aesthetically . . . in permanent motion as his eye identifies with the lens of the camera, which permanently shifts in distance and direction."

True enough. But the observation does not warrant a radical dissociation of theatre from film. Like many critics, Panofsky is assuming a "literary" conception of theatre. To a theatre which is conceived of basically as dramatized literature, texts, words, he contrasts cinema which is, according to the received phrase, primarily "a visual experience." In effect, we are being asked to acknowledge tacitly the period of silent films as definitive of cinematic art and to identify theatre with "plays," from Shakespeare to Tennessee Williams. But many of the most interesting movies today are not adequately described as images with sound added. And what if theatre is conceived of as more than, or something different from, plays?

Panofsky may be over-simplifying when he decries the theatrical taint in movies, but he is sound when he argues that, historically, theatre is only one of the arts that feeds into cinema. As he remarks, it is apt that films came to be known popularly as moving *pictures* rather than as "photoplays" or "screen plays." Movies derive less from the theatre, from a performance art, an art that already moves, than they do from works of art which were stationary. Bad nineteenth-century paintings and postcards, wax-works à la Madame Tussaud, and comic strips are the sources Panofsky cites. What is surprising is that he doesn't connect movies with earlier narrative uses of still photography—like the family photo-album. The narrative techniques developed by certain nineteenth-century novelists, as Eisenstein pointed out in his brilliant essay on Dickens, supplied still another prototype for cinema.

Movies are images (usually photographs) that move, to be sure. But the distinctive unit of films is not the image but the principle of connection between the images, the relation of a "shot" to the one that preceded it and the one that comes after. There is no peculiarly "cinematic" as opposed to "theatrical" mode of linking images.

Panofsky tries to hold the line against the infiltration of theatre by cinema, as well as vice versa. In the theatre, not only can the spectator not change his angle of vision but, unlike movies, "the settings of the stage cannot change during one act (except for such incidentals as rising moons or gathering clouds and such illegitimate reborrowings from film as turning wings or gliding backdrops)." Were we to assent to this, the ideal play would be *No Exit,* the ideal set a realistic living room or a blank stage.

No less dogmatic is the complementary dictum about what is illegitimate in films—according to which, since films are "a visual experience," all components must be demonstrably subordinate to the image. Thus, Panofsky asserts: "Wherever a poetic emotion, a musical outburst, or a literary conceit (even, I am grieved to say, some of the wisecracks of Groucho Marx) entirely lose contact with visible movement, they strike the sensitive spectator as, literally, out of place." What, then, of the films of Bresson and Godard, with their allusive, densely thoughtful texts and their characteristic refusal to be visually beautiful?

How could one explain the extraordinary rightness of Ozu's relatively immobilized camera?

The decline in average quality of films in the early sound period (compared with the level reached by films in the 1920's) is undeniable. Although it would be facile to call the sheer uninterestingness of most films of this period simply a regression to theatre, it is a fact that film-makers did turn more frequently to plays in the 1930's than they had in the preceding decade. Countless stage successes like *Outward Bound, Dinner at Eight, Blithe Spirit, Faisons un Rêve, Twentieth Century, Boudu Sauvé des Eaux, She Done Him Wrong, Anna Christie, Marius, Animal Crackers, The Petrified Forest,* were filmed. The success of movie versions of plays is measured by the extent to which the script rearranges and displaces the action and deals less than respectfully with the spoken text—as do certain films of plays by Wilde and Shaw, the Olivier Shakespeare films (at least *Henry V*), and Sjöberg's *Miss Julie.* But the basic disapproval of films which betray their origins in plays remains. A recent example: the outright hostility which greeted Dreyer's latest film, *Gertrud.* Not only does *Gertrud,* which I believe to be a minor masterpiece, follow a turn-of-the-century play that has characters conversing at length and quite formally, but it is filmed almost entirely in middle-shot.

Some of the films I have just mentioned are negligible as art; several are first-rate. (The same for the plays, though no correlation between the merits of the movies and those of the "original" plays can be established.) However, their virtues and faults cannot be sorted out as a cinematic versus a theatrical element. Whether derived from plays or not, films with complex or formal dialogue, films in which the camera is static or in which the action stays indoors, are not necessarily theatrical. *Per contra,* it is no more part of the putative "essence" of movies that the camera must rove over a large physical area, than it is that movies ought to be silent. Though most of the action of Kurosawa's *The Lower Depths,* a fairly faithful transcription of Gorki's play, is confined to one large room, it is as cinematic as the same director's *Throne of Blood,* a very free and laconic adaptation of *Macbeth.* The quality of Melville's claustrophobic *Les Enfants Terribles* is as peculiar to the movies as Ford's *The Searchers* or a train journey in Cinerama.

What does make a film theatrical in an invidious sense is when the narration becomes coy or self-conscious: compare Autant-Lara's *Occupe-Toi d'Amélie,* a brilliant cinematic use of the conventions and materials of theatricality, with Ophuls' clumsy use of similar conventions and materials in *La Ronde.*

Fig. 6. Anita Bjork and Ulf Palme in *Miss Julie* (1950), adapted and directed by Alf Sjöberg, from the play by August Strindberg (1888). Sjöberg mentored Ingmar Bergman and remained a major influence on Bergman's theater and film style throughout the latter's career. Courtesy of Billy Rose Theatre Collection, The New York Public Library for the Performing Arts, Astor, Lenox and Tilden Foundations.

Allardyce Nicoll, in his book *Film and Theatre* (1936), argues that the difference may be understood as a difference in kinds of characters. "Practically all effectively drawn stage characters are types [while] in the cinema we demand individualization and impute greater power of independent life to the figures on the screen." (Panofsky, it might be mentioned, makes exactly the opposite point: that the nature of films, in contrast to plays, requires flat or stock characters.)

Nicoll's thesis is not as arbitrary as it may at first appear. I would relate it to the fact that often the indelible moments of a film, and the most potent elements of characterization, are precisely the "irrelevant" or unfunctional details. (A random example: the ping-pong ball the schoolmaster toys with in Ivory's *Shakespeare Wallah*.) Movies thrive on the narrative equivalent of a technique familiar from painting and photography, off-centering. It is this that creates the pleasing disunity of fragmentariness (what Nicoll means by "individualization"?) of the characters of many of the greatest films. In contrast, linear "coherence" of detail (the gun on the wall in the first act that must go off by the end of the third) is the rule in Occidental narrative theatre, and gives rise to the sense of the unity of the characters (a unity that may appear like the statement of a "type").

But even with these adjustments, Nicoll's thesis seems less than appealing when one perceives that it rests on the idea that "When we go to the theatre, we expect theatre and nothing else." What is this theatre-and-nothing-else? It is the old notion of artifice. (As if art were ever anything else. As if some arts were artificial but others not.) According to Nicoll, when we are in a theatre "in every way the 'falsity' of a theatrical production is borne in upon us, so that we are prepared to demand nothing save a theatrical truth." In the cinema, however, every member of the audience, no matter how sophisticated, is on essentially the same level; we all believe that the camera cannot lie. As the film actor and his role are identical, so the image cannot be dissociated from what is imaged. Cinema, therefore, gives us what is experienced as the truth of life.

Couldn't theatre dissolve the distinction between the truth of artifice and the truth of life? Isn't that just what the theatre as ritual seeks to do? Isn't that what is being sought when theatre is conceived as an *exchange* with an audience?—something that films can never be.

If an irreducible distinction between theatre and cinema does exist, it may be this. Theatre is confined to a logical or *continuous* use of space. Cinema (through editing, that is, through the change of shot—which is the basic unit of film construction) has access to an alogical or *discontinuous* use of space. In the theatre, people are either in the stage space or "off." When "on," they are always visible or visualizable in contiguity with each other. In the cinema, no such relation is necessarily visible or even visualizable. (Example: the last shot of Paradjanov's *In the Shadows of Our Ancestors.*) Some films considered objectionably theatrical are those which seem to emphasize spatial continuities, like Hitchcock's virtuoso *Rope* or the daringly anachronistic *Gertrud.* But closer analysis of both these films would show how complex their treatment of space is. The longer and longer "takes" toward which sound films have been moving are, in themselves, neither more nor less cinematic than the short "takes" characteristic of silents.

Thus, cinematic virtue does not reside in the fluidity of the positioning of the camera nor in the mere frequency of the change of shot. It consists in the arrangement of screen images and (now) of sounds. Méliès, for example, though he didn't get beyond the static positioning of his camera, had a very striking conception of how to link screen images. He grasped that editing offered an equivalent to the magician's sleight of hand—thereby suggesting that one of the features of film (as distinct from theatre) is that *anything* can happen, that there is nothing that can't be represented convincingly. Through editing, Méliès presents discontinuities of physical substance and behavior. In his films, the discontinuities are, so to speak, practical, functional; they accomplish a transformation of ordinary reality. But the continuous *re*invention of space (as well as the option of temporal indeterminacy) peculiar to film narration does not pertain only to the cinema's ability to fabricate "visions," to show us a radically altered world. The most "realistic" use of the motion-picture camera also involves a discontinuous account of space.

Film narration has a "syntax," composed of the rhythm of associations and disjunctions. As Cocteau has written, "My primary concern in a film is to prevent the images from flowing, to oppose them to each other, to anchor them and join them without destroying their relief." (But does such a conception of film syntax entail, as Cocteau thinks, our disavowal of movies as "mere entertainment instead of a vehicle for thought"?)

In drawing a line of demarcation between theatre and films, the issue of the continuity of space seems to me more fundamental than the difference that might be pointed out between theatre as an organization of movement in three-dimensional space (like dance) versus cinema as an organization of plane space (like painting). The theatre's capacities for manipulating space and time are, simply, much cruder and more labored than film's. Theatre cannot equal the cinema's facilities for the strictly-controlled repetition of images, for the duplication or matching of word and image, and for the juxtaposition and overlapping of images. (Through advanced lighting techniques, one can now "dissolve" on the stage. But as yet there is no equivalent, not even through the most adept use of scrim, of the "lap dissolve.")

Theatre has been described as a mediated art, presumably because it usually consists of a pre-existent play mediated by a particular performance which offers one of many possible interpretations of the play. Film, in contrast, is regarded as unmediated—because of its larger-than-life scale and more unrefusable impact on the eye, and because (in Panofsky's words) "the medium of the movies is physical reality as such" and the characters in a movie "have no aesthetic existence outside the actors." But there is an equally valid sense which shows movies to be the mediated art and theatre the unmediated one. We see what happens on the stage with our own eyes. We see on the screen what the camera sees. In the cinema, narration proceeds by ellipsis (the "cut" or change of shot); the camera eye is a unified point of view that continually displaces itself. But the change of shot can provoke questions, the simplest of which is: from *whose* point of view is the shot seen? And the ambiguity of point of view latent in all cinematic narration has no equivalent in the theatre.

Indeed, one should not neglect to emphasize the aesthetically positive role of disorientation in the cinema. Examples: Busby Berkeley dollying back from an ordinary-looking stage already established as some thirty feet deep to disclose a stage area three hundred feet square. Resnais panning from character X's point of view a full 360°, to come to rest upon X's face.

Much may be made of the fact that, in its concrete existence, cinema is an *object* (a *product,* even) while theatre is a *performance.* Is this so important? In a way, no. Whether objects (like films or paintings) or performances (like music or theatre), all art is first a mental act, a fact of consciousness. The object aspect of film, the performance aspect of theatre are merely means—means to the experience, which is not only "of" but "through" the film and the theatre-event. Each subject of an aesthetic experience shapes it to his own measure. With respect to any *single* experience, it hardly matters that a film is usually identical from one projection of it to another while theatre performances are highly mutable.

The difference between object-art and performance-art lies behind Panofsky's observation that "the screenplay, in contrast to the theatre play, has no aesthetic existence independent of its performance," and characters in movies *are* the stars who enact them. It is because the film is an object, a totality that is set, that movie roles are identical with the actors' performances; while in the theatre (in the West, an additive rather than an organic art?) only the written play is "fixed," an object and therefore existing apart from any staging of it. Yet this dichotomy is not beyond dispute. Just as movies needn't necessarily be designed to be shown in theatres at all (they can be intended for more continuous and casual looking), a movie *may* be altered from one projection to the next. Harry Smith, when he runs off his own films, makes each projection an unrepeatable performance. And, again, it is not true that all theatre is only about written plays which may be given a good or a bad production. In Happenings and other recent theatre-events, we are precisely being offered "plays" identical with their productions in the same sense as the screenplay is identical with the film.

Yet, a difference remains. Because the film is an object, it is totally manipulable, totally calculable. A film is like a book, another portable art-object; making a film, like writing a book, means constructing an inanimate thing, every element of which is determinate. Indeed, in films, this determinacy has or can have a quasi-mathematical form, like music. (A shot lasts a certain number of seconds, a change of angle of so many degrees is required to "match" two shots.) Given the total determinacy of the result on celluloid (whatever the extent of the director's conscious intervention), it was inevitable that some film directors would want to devise schemas to make their intentions more exact. Thus, it was neither perverse nor primitive of Busby Berkeley to have used only one camera to shoot the whole of each of his mammoth dance numbers. Every "set-up" was designed to be shot from only one exactly calculated angle. Bresson, working on a far more self-conscious level of artistry, has declared that, for him, the director's task is to find the single correct way of doing each shot. An image cannot be justified in itself, according to Bresson; it has an exactly specifiable relation to the temporally adjacent images, which relation constitutes its "meaning."

But the theatre allows only the loosest approximation to this sort of formal concern. (And responsibility. Justly, French critics speak of the director of a film as its "author.") Because they are performances, something always "live," theatre-events are not subject to a comparable degree of control, do not admit a comparably exact integration of effects.

It would be foolish to conclude that the best films are those which arise from the greatest amount of conscious planning; the plan may be faulty; and with some directors, instinct works better than any plan. Besides, there is an impressive body of "improvised" cinema. (To be distinguished from the work of some film-makers, notably Godard, who have become fascinated with the "look" of improvised cinema.) Nevertheless, it seems indisputable that cinema, not only potentially but by its nature, is a more rigorous art than theatre.

Thus, not merely a failure of nerve accounts for the fact that theatre, this seasoned art, occupied since antiquity with all sorts of local offices—enacting sacred rites, reinforcing communal loyalty, guiding morals, provoking the therapeutic discharge of violent emotions, conferring social status, giving practical instruction, affording entertainment, dignifying celebrations, subverting established authority—is now on the defensive before movies, this brash art with its huge, amorphous, passive audience. Meanwhile, movies continue to maintain their astonishing pace of formal articulation. (Take the commercial cinema of Europe, Japan, and the United States simply since 1960, and consider what audiences have become habituated to in the way of increasingly elliptical story-telling and visualization.)

But note: this youngest of the arts is also the one most heavily burdened with memory. Cinema is a time machine. Movies preserve the past, while theatres—no matter how devoted to the classics, to old plays—can only "modernize." Movies resurrect the beautiful dead; present intact vanished or ruined environments; employ, without irony, styles and fashions that seem funny today; solemnly ponder irrelevant or naïve problems. The historical flavor of anything registered on celluloid is so vivid that practically all films older than two years or so are saturated with a kind of pathos. (The pathos I am describing, which overtakes animated cartoons and drawn, abstract films as well as ordinary movies, is not simply that of old photographs.) Films age (being objects) as no theatre-event does (being always new). There is no pathos of mortality in theatre's "reality" as such, nothing in our response to a good performance of a Mayakovsky play comparable to the aesthetic role the emotion of nostalgia has when we see a film by Pudovkin.

Also worth noting: compared with the theatre, innovations in cinema seem to be assimilated more efficiently, seem altogether to be more shareable—and not only because new films are quickly and widely circulated. Also, partly because virtually the entire body of accomplishment in film can be consulted in the present, most film-makers are more knowledgeable about the history of their art than most theatre directors are about the recent past of theirs.

The key word in many discussions of cinema is "possibility." A merely classifying use of the word occurs, as in Panofsky's engaging judgment that, "within their self-imposed limitations the earlier Disney films . . . represent, as it were, a chemically pure distillation of cinematic possibilities." But behind this relatively neutral sense lurks a more polemical sense of cinema's "possibility." What is regularly intimated is the obsolescence of theatre, its supercession by films.

Thus, Panofsky describes the mediation of the camera eye as opening "up a world of possibility of which the stage can never dream." Artaud, earlier, thought that motion pictures may have made the theatre obsolete. Movies "possess a sort of virtual power which probes into the mind and uncovers undreamt of possibilities. . . . When this art's exhilaration has been blended in the right proportions with the psychic ingredient it commands, it will leave the theatre far behind and we will relegate the latter to the attic of our memories."

Meyerhold, facing the challenge head on, thought the only hope for theatre lay in a wholesale emulation of the cinema. "Let us 'cinematify' the theatre," he urged. The staging of plays must be "industrialized," theatres must accommodate audiences in the tens of thousands rather than in the hundreds, etc. Meyerhold also seemed to find some relief in the idea that the coming of sound signalled the downfall of movies. Believing that their international appeal depended entirely on the fact that screen actors didn't speak any particular language, he couldn't imagine in 1930 that, even if that were so, technology (dubbing, sub-titling) could solve the problem.

Is cinema the successor, the rival, or the revivifier of the theatre?

Art forms *have* been abandoned. (Whether because they became obsolete is another question.) One can't be sure that theatre is not in a state of irremediable decline, spurts of local vitality notwithstanding. But why should it be rendered obsolete by movies? It's worth remembering that predictions of obsolescence amount to declaring that a something has one peculiar task (which another something may do as well or better). Has theatre one peculiar task or aptitude?

Those who predict the demise of the theatre, assuming that cinema has engulfed its function, tend to impute a relation between films and theatre reminiscent of what was once said about photography and painting. If the painter's job had been no more than fabricating likenesses, the invention of the camera might indeed have made painting obsolete. But painting is hardly just "pictures," any more than cinema is just theatre for the masses, available in portable standard units.

In the naïve tale of photography and painting, painting was reprieved when it claimed a new task, abstraction. As the superior realism of photography was supposed to have liberated painting, allowing it to go abstract, cinema's superior power to represent (not merely to stimulate) the imagination may appear to have emboldened the theatre in a similar fashion, inviting the gradual obliteration of the conventional "plot."

Actually, painting and photography evidence parallel developments rather than a rivalry or a supercession. And, at least in principle, so have theatre and film. The possibilities for theatre that lie in going beyond psychological realism, in seeking greater abstractness, are not less germane to the future of narrative films. Conversely, the notion of movies as witness to real life, testimony rather than invention, the treatment of collective situations rather than the depiction of personal "dramas," is equally relevant to the stage. Not surprisingly, what follows some years after the rise of *cinema verité*, the sophisticated heir of documentary films, is a documentary theatre, the "theatre of fact." (Cf. Hochhuth, Weiss's *The Investigation*, recent projects of the Royal Shakespeare Company in London.)

The influence of the theatre upon films in the early years is well known. According to Kracauer, the distinctive lighting of *Dr. Caligari* (and of many subsequent German silents) can be traced to an experiment with lighting Max Reinhardt made shortly before, in his production of Sorge's play, *The Beggar.* Even in this period, however, the impact was reciprocal. The accomplishments of the "Expressionist film" were immediately absorbed by the Expressionist theatre. Stimulated by the cinematic technique of the "iris-in," stage lighting took to singling out a lone player, or some segment of the scene, masking out the rest of the stage. Rotating sets tried to approximate the instantaneous displacement of the camera eye. (More recently, reports have come of ingenious lighting techniques used by the Gorki Theatre in Leningrad, directed since 1956 by Georgi Tovstonogov, which allow for incredibly rapid scene changes taking place behind a horizontal curtain of light.)

Today traffic seems, with few exceptions, entirely one way: film to theatre. Particularly in France and in Central and Eastern Europe, the staging of many plays is inspired by the movies. The aim of adapting neo-cinematic devices for the stage (I exclude the out-right use of films within the theatre production) seems mainly to tighten up the theatrical experience, to approximate the cinema's absolute control of the flow and location of the audience's attention. But the conception can be even more directly cinematic. Example: Josef Svoboda's production of *The Insect Play* by the Capek brothers at the Czech National Theatre in Prague (recently seen in London) which frankly attempted to install a mediated vision upon the stage, equivalent to the discontinuous intensifications of the camera eye. According to a London critic's account, "the set consisted of two huge, faceted mirrors slung at an angle to the stage, so that they reflect whatever happens there defracted as if through a decanter stopper or the colossally magnified eye of a fly. Any figure placed at the base of their angle becomes multiplied from floor to proscenium; farther out, and you find yourself viewing it not only face to face but from overhead, the vantage point of a camera slung to a bird or a helicopter."

Perhaps the first to propose the use of film itself as *one* element in a theatre experience was Marinetti. Writing between 1910 and 1914, he envisaged the theatre as a final synthesis of all the arts; and as such it had to use the newest art form movies. No doubt the cinema also recommended itself for inclusion because of the priority Marinetti gave to the use of existing forms of popular entertainment, such as the variety theatre and the *café-chantant*. (He called his projected art form "the Futurist Variety Theatre.") And cinema, at that time, was not considered as anything other than a vulgar art.

Soon after, the idea begins to occur frequently. In the total-theatre projects of the Bauhaus group in the 1920's (Gropius, Piscator, etc.), film had a regular place. Meyerhold insisted on its use in the theatre. (He described his program as fulfilling Wagner's once "wholly utopian" proposals to "use all means available from the other arts.") Film's actual employment has by now a fairly long history, which includes "the living newspaper," "epic theatre," and "happenings." This year marked the introduction of a film sequence into Broadway-type theatre. In two highly successful musicals, London's *Come Spy with Me* and New York's *Superman,* both parodic in tone, the action is interrupted to lower a screen and run off a movie showing the pop-art hero's exploits.

Thus far, the use of film within live theatre-events has tended to be stereotyped. Film is employed as *document,* supportive of or redundant to the live stage events (as in Brecht's productions in East Berlin). Or else it is employed as *hallucinant;* recent examples are Bob Whitman's Happenings, and a new kind of nightclub situation, the mixed-media discothèque (Andy Warhol's The Plastic Inevitable, Murray the K's World). The interpolation of film into the theatre-experience may be enlarging from the point of view of theatre. But in terms of what film is capable of, it seems a reductive, monotonous use of film.

Every interesting aesthetic tendency now is a species of radicalism. The question each artist must ask is: What is *my* radicalism, the one dictated by *my* gifts and temperament? This doesn't mean all contemporary artists believe that art progresses. A radical position isn't necessarily a forward-looking position.

Consider the two principal radical positions in the arts today. One recommends the breaking down of distinctions between genres: the arts would eventuate in one art, consisting of many different kinds of behavior going on at the same time, a vast behavioral magma or synaesthesis. The other position recommends the maintaining and clarifying of barriers between the arts, by the intensification of what each art distinctively is; painting must use only those means which pertain to painting, music only those which are musical, novels those which pertain to the novel and to no other literary form, etc.

The two positions are, in a sense, irreconcilable. Except that both are in-voked to support a perennial modern quest—the quest for the definitive art form. An art may be proposed as definitive because it is considered the most rigorous, or most fundamental. For these reasons, Schopenhauer suggested and Pater asserted that all art aspires to the condition of music. More recently, the thesis that all the arts are leading toward one art has been advanced by enthusi-asts of the cinema. The candidacy of film is founded on its being so exact and, potentially, so complex—a rigorous combination of music, literature, and the image.

Or, an art may be proposed as definitive because it is the most inclusive. This is the basis of the destiny for theatre held out by Wagner, Marinetti, Artaud, John Cage—all of whom envisage theatre as nothing less than a total art, po-tentially conscripting all the arts into its service. And as the ideas of synaesthe-sia continue to proliferate among painters, sculptors, architects, and com-posers, theatre remains the favored candidate for the role of summative art. So conceived, of course, theatre's claims do contradict those of cinema. Partisans of theatre would argue that while music, painting, dance, cinema, the speaking of words, etc. can all converge on a "stage," the film-object can only become bigger (multiple screens, 360° projection, etc.) or longer in duration or more internally articulated and complex. Theatre can be anything, everything; in the end, films can only be more of what they specifically (that is to say, cinemati-cally) are.

Underlying the competing apocalyptic expectations for both arts, one de-tects a common animus. In 1923 Béla Balázs, anticipating in great detail the the-sis of Marshall McLuhan, described movies as the herald of a new "visual cul-ture" that will give us back our bodies, and particularly our faces, which have been rendered illegible, soulless, unexpressive by the centuries-old ascendancy of "print." An animus against literature, against "the printing press" and its "culture of concepts," also informs most of the interesting thinking about the theatre in our time.

What's important is that no definition or characterization of theatre and cin-ema, even the most self-evident, be taken for granted.

For instance: both cinema and theatre are temporal arts. Like music (and un-like painting), everything is *not* present all at once.

Could this be modified? The allure of mixed-media forms in theatre suggests not only a more elongated and more complex "drama" (like Wagnerian opera) but also a more compact theatre-experience which approaches the condition of painting. This prospect of increased compactness is broached by Marinetti; he calls it simultaneity, a leading idea of Futurist aesthetics. In becoming a final synthesis of all the arts, says Marinetti, theatre "would use the new twentieth-century devices of electricity and the cinema; this would enable plays to be extremely short, since all these technical means would enable the theatrical synthesis to be achieved in the shortest possible space of time, as all the elements could be presented simultaneously."

A pervasive notion in both advanced cinema and theatre is the idea of art as an act of violence. Its source is to be found in the aesthetics of Futurism and of Surrealism; its principal "texts" are, for theatre, the writings of Artaud and, for cinema, the two classic films of Luis Buñuel, *L'Age d'Or* and *Un Chien Andalou.* (More recent examples: the early plays of Ionesco, at least as conceived; the "cinema of cruelty" of Hitchcock, Clouzot, Franju, Robert Aldrich, Polanski; work by the Living Theatre; some of the neo-cinematic lighting techniques used in experimental theatres; the sound of late Cage and LaMonte Young.) The relation of art to an audience understood to be passive, inert, surfeited, can only be assault. Art becomes identical with aggression.

This theory of art as assault on the audience—like the complementary notion of art as ritual—is understandable, and precious. Still, one must not neglect to question it, particularly in the theatre. For it can become as much a convention as anything else; and end, like all theatrical conventions, by reinforcing the deadness of the audience. (As Wagner's ideology of a total theatre played its role in confirming the stupidity and bestiality of German culture.)

Moreover, the depth of the assault must be assessed honestly. In the theatre, this entails not "diluting" Artaud. Artaud's writings represent the demand for a totally open (therefore, flayed, self-cruel) consciousness of which theatre would be *one* adjunct or instrument. No work in the theatre has yet amounted to this. Thus, Peter Brook has astutely and forthrightly disclaimed that his company's work in London in the "Theatre of Cruelty," which culminated in his celebrated production of Weiss's *Marat/Sade,* is genuinely Artaudian. It is Artaudian, he says, in a trivial sense only. (Trivial from Artaud's point of view, not from ours.)

For some time, all useful ideas in art have been extremely sophisticated. Like the idea that everything is what it is, and not another thing. A painting is a painting. Sculpture is sculpture. A poem is a poem, not prose. Etcetera. And the complementary idea: a painting can be "literary" or sculptural, a poem can be prose, theatre can emulate and incorporate cinema, cinema can be theatrical.

We need a new idea. It will probably be a very simple one. Will we be able to recognize it?

Notes on Theater-and-Film

Stanley Kauffmann

For a number of years I have spent a lot of time going to plays and films, sometimes one of each on the same day, so the two forms are constantly juxtaposed for me. There are some received ideas on the subject of theater-and-film—or theater versus film—that can use a quizzical look. My intent is not hierarchical ranking, which seems to me bone-headed, simply investigation. Here are some notes.

ATTENTION

The art of film lives by controlling attention, we are told, and are told truly except when there is an implication that the theater lives otherwise. The film director controls attention irrevocably; you cannot look at anything in the scene except what he permits you to look at. But the theater director wants to have exactly the same power over you. His job is harder because he has to *earn* your attention. If you

Reprinted from *Performance* 1, no. 4 (September–October 1972): 104–109. Reprinted by permission of the author.

look elsewhere than where he wants you to be looking at any given moment, the production is wobbling as badly as when the film in a projector jitters.

The difference between the two arts here is certainly not in intent but in means. Temperament sometimes enables a director to use both sets of means—Bergman and Visconti, for just two instances—sometimes not. Antonioni once told me that he had directed a few plays, and I asked him whether he wanted to do more theater work. "No," he said. "Always the same shot."

The film's ability to vary the shots, to command our shifts of attention with no chance of our demurral, is a happy slavery when the right person is given the orders. But the notion advanced by some film writers that the very idea of holding attention on specific points for specific lengths of time *began* with film is aesthetic and pragmatic nonsense.

TIME

The synoptic powers of film in regard to time are much greater than in the theater. The actor crossing the room on stage has to cross it, step by step; the film actor can come in the door and immediately be on the other side of the room. Film can juggle the present, past, and future effortlessly, and can repeat the moment, *à la* Resnais. The theater can try all these things to some degree (I have even seen the Resnais effect on stage), but it has to breathe hard in the attempt.

Much has been made, quite rightly, of these temporal powers in film. Much has been scanted, almost as if by contrasting obligation, of the temporal powers in the theater. The strength, not the limitation, of the stage is that, in any given scene, time does elapse there, moment by moment. Obviously, figurative time has been used in the theater—mostly between scenes—ever since the first break with Aristotle; still, a strength of the theater is that you feel and see time passing. This is a component of theatrical structure, enrichment, companionship.

It's interesting that in the film form, which can play with time, few works run over two hours. In the theater, which mostly must accept time as it comes, chunk by chunk, many works run over two hours. To see a picture like the recent Russian film of *Uncle Vanya* which, among other barbarisms, chopped the play to bits, is to miss the theater's power of letting lives flow before us in simulated passage, the theater's function as the place where such things can happen effectively.

Also, theatrical time works to the actor's advantage in many cases. A scintillating example was Rosalind Russell's performance in *Auntie Mame*. On stage it

Fig. 7. Russ Tamblyn and the Jets in *West Side Story* (1961), adapted by Ernest Lehman from the musical play by Arthur Laurents (1957). On film, Jerome Robbins opened up his choreography so that it could explode across the streets of New York. Directed by Robert Wise and Jerome Robbins. Courtesy of Billy Rose Theatre Collection, The New York Public Library for the Performing Arts, Astor, Lenox and Tilden Foundations.

was not only a dazzling entertainment but a marathon event. Almost the same performance on screen was less effective because we knew it had been done in bits and pieces over a period of months, and the soft silent hum of wonder as the evening progressed was missing. Almost the only thing wrong for me with Peter Brook's film of *Marat/Sade* was the fact that I knew it had been made in seventeen days—a whirlwind in filmmaking time but a far distance from the span of one theater performance.

"OPENING UP"

To continue with a comparison of plays and filmed plays, a relation that is not only commonplace but revealing: The surest sign of the cliché mind in film-making is a feeling of obligation to "open up" plays when they become films and a conviction that this process proves superiority, that a play really comes into its own when it is filmed. We can really go to Italy in Zeffirelli's film of *Romeo and Juliet,* so it supersedes placebound theater productions. We can dissolve and cross-fade more easily in the film of *Death of a Salesman,* so the theater is once again just a tryout place for later perfect consummation. We can go outside the house in the film of *Who's Afraid of Virginia Woolf?,* and once again the theater is shown up as cribbed and confined.

The trouble here is a confusion in aesthetic logic, an assumption that we are comparing apples and apples when we are really comparing apples and pears. Fundamentally, the film takes the audience to the event, shifting the audience continually; the theater takes the event to the audience, shifting it never. Just as the beauty of poetry often lies in tensions between free flight and form-as-preserver, so the beauty of drama often lies in tensions between imagination and theatrical exigency, theater form as a means of preservation, of *availability.* To assume that the film's extension of a play's action is automatically an improvement is to change the subject: from the way the theater builds upward, folding one event on another in almost perceptible vertical form, to the film's horizontal progression. The theater works predominantly by building higher and higher in one place. The film, despite the literally vertical progress of the frames, works predominantly in lateral series of places.

The very necessity for the dramatist to arrange to get the right people together at the right time in his one place becomes, for the appropriate talent, a means to beauty rather than a burden. (See any Chekhov or Shaw play.) It is muddled to think that, by "unfolding" these careful arrangements, the film inevitably enlarges the original work. This "unfolding" can be successful when the filmmaker knows clearly what he is doing and treats his film as a new work from a common source, as in the admirable Lester-Wood film of *The Knack*. But most adapters seem to think that any banal set of film gimmicks constitutes a liberation for which the poor cramped play ought to be grateful.

DEEP FOCUS

To oversimplify only somewhat: there are two basically different views of film-making—montage and deep focus. Directors nowadays often use both, but we are well aware of the mixture when we see it. In the earliest days of film, when it was discovering itself, montage was prized because it is exclusively cinematic. Griffith, who did not invent it, developed it tremendously; and the great Soviet directors of the twenties used it wonderfully and theorized about it extensively.

This exaltation of montage wavered in the mid-thirties, for two reasons. Technically, the use of sound seemed to inhibit montage; the soundtrack couldn't be snipped to keep up with fast-changing shots. (This difficulty was soon overcome with different approaches to sound.) Culturally, the film became more self-confident, less anxious to prove itself. By the time we get to Renoir, we find a different mode: the held shot, in which the camera may itself move but which is for a relatively long time uncut, into and out of which actors enter and exit, and which has within it different planes. Many critics, including André Bazin, expatiated on this as a new realization in film aesthetics. In fact, however, it was at bottom a realization that the film could use, when appropriate, the 2500-year-old "deep focus" of the theater. The film had come to utilize, along with its dominant horizontal movement, a cinematized adaptation of the vertical.

FRAMING

We often read some version of the following: A difference between stage and screen is that the stage contains all of the place where the event occurs, but the screen frames only part of the film's reality, which continues away from its borders on all sides.

One can see why this idea would grow out of film scenes shot on location. The cowhand who steps before the camera steps out of all Colorado into a tiny portion of it. It is harder to credit this idea when a film actor steps onto a set, even though the camera may eventually go into the next room or outside the house.

The theater audience knows that, literally, what is out of sight is the back-stage area. The film audience knows that, literally, what is out of sight—even in Colorado—is a different set of mechanical means: grips, gaffers, reflectors, sound men, and a mechanical omnipresence that the theater never has, the camera.

Seemingly desperate for distinctive aesthetics, desperate, too, to formulate a mystique, the film lays claim here to an imaginative exclusivity that is invalid except to the dull-minded. When Barbara Loden in her film *Wanda* roamed through coal-fields and coal towns, she did not suggest any more real places out of sight than Ruby Dee in Fugard's *Boesman and Lena* telling us of the towns she had tramped through in her lifetime. In both cases there was a literal frame of mechanics and techniques; in both cases there was an imaginative world that stretched endlessly outside the frame.

THINGS AS ACTORS

The difference here is one of degree, not—as is frequently implied—of kind. Vachel Lindsay, with an enthusiasm that was admirable and probably necessary at the time, said of *The Cabinet of Dr. Caligari* in 1922: "It proves in a hundred new ways the resources of the film in making all the inanimate things which, on the spoken stage, cannot act at all, the leading actors in the films." The discovery was important, though overstated. One can forgive "cannot act at all" and "leading actors" in a prophet of 1922; the claim is less forgivable when repeated without modulation fifty years later.

How beautifully Kurosawa, Welles, Ford use *things* in their films—a breeze, a sled, a gun. This is quite outside the competence, or business, of the theater. Although objects acquire metaphoric significance on the stage simply by virtue of having been selected to be there, no one could maintain that they become "actors"—as the splinter in the rain barrel seems to become an actor in *Eclipse*.

But Lindsay's pronunciamento, parroted without qualification, tries to sweep away the affective power of such "things" in the theater as costume and setting. Rex Harrison's cardigan in *My Fair Lady* was a "thing" that functioned for me as well on stage as on screen. Places, which of course are things, can be more easily enlisted in the aid of the whole work on stage. (Excepting the exceptions, like *Caligari* itself.) Inarguably, set design is important in film, and all sets are not equally good. But John Bury's setting for *The Homecoming,* which was a collection of "things," contributed to the drama in a way that was theatrically valid but would have been cinematically obtrusive.

WORDS

Many have noted, myself among them, that words often fight films, which is why classic plays are hard to film. Let's define "classic" in old theatrical terms: The classic style is one in which you must play on the line, not between the lines. In films the action usually stops for the words, the words for the action. In addition, the camera brings classic language too close, as the camera brings the music too close in films of opera. But the facile implication behind this, in much film criticism, is that prolixity doesn't matter in the theater. In fact, as all theater people know, a superfluous line in the theater is, in its own scale, as impedimental as it would be on film.

Further, when language is designed for film and is understood as contributory dynamics, it is as cinematic as any other film element. Bibi Andersson's account of the sex orgy in *Persona,* many of the dialogues in *My Night at Maud's* and *Claire's Knee,* Gielgud's speeches in *The Charge of the Light Brigade,* Ray Collins' farewell at the railroad station in *The Magnificent Ambersons,* these are only a few of the instances where words, understood and controlled, become film components.

Of course there are still some who think that the film art died the moment Jolson sang. A quite valid case can be made to show that the silent and the sound film are aesthetically separate; but it is a different case from the one that words are intrinsically and inevitably the enemy of the sound film.

THE NEED FOR AN AUDIENCE

We may be coming to the end of the age in which film acting is judged by theater standards. X is not an actor, we are told, even though successful in films, because on stage he could not project beyond the third row; or because cameraman and editor patched together a performance out of his efforts; or because he has to work out of sequence; or because he has the chance to try things a dozen times and to preserve only the best effort. (This last reason would prove that Rubinstein is not a good pianist on records.) Now we are beginning to judge acting by standards appropriate to the particular medium.

Still all performing media have certain standards in common. This can be shown empirically, and it destroys a sentimentality to which the theater clings: that an actor cannot really act unless he has an audience. Think of Mastroianni in *The Organizer,* Huston in *Treasure of the Sierra Madre,* Oscarsson in *Hunger,* Baranovskaia in *Mother,* Garbo in *Camille* . . . and on and on and on. No matter the sequence in which each of those films were shot, can one say that those are not sustained performances? And can one imagine how they could possibly have been improved by being done in front of an audience?

Conversely, there are theater performances that seem to proceed wonderfully without any real cognizance of or relation to an audience. The three plays of the Grotowski company that I saw were among the few really momentous theater experiences of my life, but it is hard to believe that those actors play to and with an audience. They reveal certain matters; the audience takes them up or not. I cannot think that *Akropolis* would be played differently if there were no audience present, or that different audiences affect the performances.

The one element that "live" acting inevitably contains is the possibility of mistake. We are never really aware of the confidence that an actor earns until he fluffs a line; and it usually takes considerable time before he gets us back in his grip. The fissure is in a way pleasurable because it underscores the fact of the making of the art right before us and gives us a kind of added pride in the actors who have not fluffed.

Theater comedy must, of course, take account of laughs, and directors of film comedy have to develop some sense of how to anticipate what the laughs will be so that they don't smother or rush them. But laughter is an overt response. Other tensions, sensations, "feels" are more often than not theater sentimentalities, as far as the actor's need for them is concerned.

To settle the matter subjectively, which is at last the only way, my response to film actors is never less than to theater actors just because the former are on film. The medium is never the reason for response or lack of it. And the fact that film actors *can* move me, and often do, is sufficient proof to me that they don't need my presence at the time they are acting in order to create.

Most talk by actors about the nourishment they get from the audience affects me much like Don Marquis' Mehitabel reminiscing about the old theater days, putting her hand on her heart, and saying, "They haven't got it here." The theater has unalterable powers: it doesn't need to cling to claptrap.

ACTOR AND ROLE

Any play that we see, we can see again with a different cast; most films never. This is wonderful and terrible, for both the theater and the film.

The London production of *Old Times* did little for me; the New York production did a good deal. Individual actors improve in the same role: Christopher Walken's Caligula, which was good to begin with, was even better when I sampled it again some weeks later. On the other hand, there are numberless plays that have seemed lesser later on because of cast or whole company changes; and the same actor can deteriorate in a part. (Not a rarity.)

In films the performance is fixed, for good or ill. When I urge people, as I do, to see Peter O'Toole in *Brotherly Love* if ever it is revived, I know they will see precisely the same performance I saw. When I urge people to see a play, I hope they will go on a good night.

When I saw *Sugar,* I thanked providence that the performances of Jack Lemmon and Tony Curtis and Marilyn Monroe in *Some Like It Hot* were fixed immutably. When I sat through Welles's *Macbeth* and *Othello* films, I thanked providence that the scripts weren't fixed immutably to those performances.

As has often been noted, most film roles, if they are memorable at all, are inseparable from their performances. The role has no separate conceptual existence, even if the performance is more than a personality display. Who can conceive of an actor other than George C. Scott playing in *The Hospital,* if a re-make were ever conceivable? A film role has no separate existence; most theater roles are apprehensible as entities, even during original productions, because the theater is a place where actor and role meet and, eventually, part. Concepts of actor and role in film may be in as much need of change, *vis-à-vis* the theater, as standards of acting.

GLAMOUR

No contest. Film actors now have it, some of them, theater actors do not. This is a serious loss to the theater, not frivolous baggage. The mythopoeic quality of actors was an instrument in the mythopoeic functioning of the theater. The theater now gets no such assistance from its casts, no matter whose name is above the title—unless of course it's a film or TV star!

Possibly one of the reasons, among many, for the latter-day theater interest in ensemble work and matrix performance, is the realization that the actor's persona, as armatured by the playwright, is no longer a prime power.

DEATH

No contest. The effects of death belong entirely to the film. Anyone who saw *Wild Strawberries* before Victor Sjöstrom died and saw it again afterward knows that his performance, the whole film, took on added poignancy and truth. Last January I read of Dita Parlo's death shortly before I saw *La Grande Illusion* again; when I saw the film and she came into the barn, I felt suddenly as if more were being given me than I knew how to cope with. It was more than moving, it seemed to confirm the death of the actress herself in a very cruel appropriative way and to confirm, by the very fact that what was on the screen was invulnerable, the certainty of my and my fellow-viewers' deaths.

In the theater, play scripts and photographs are souvenirs of productions, no more, if one happens to have seen the now-dead performers. In film, as TV movies demonstrate every night, inevitabilities laugh at us all.

CRITICISM

The crucial historical difference between theater and film is this: the theater began as a sacred event and eventually included the profane. The film began as a profane event and eventually included the sacred.

No serious person objects to the theater's being judged by sacred standards (as the term is relevant here) because of its origins. But many serious people object to the film's being judged by sacred standards because of its origins.

It is tyrannical and priggish and self-cheating to militate against the profane. But it is a curious critical gift that militates against the sacred, or, more curious, equivocates by insisting that the sacred is *in* the profane.

The theater's struggle is not to forget its past. The film's struggle is not to be afraid of its future. This difference in origins is, at worst, hard luck for the film, not aesthetic or spiritual hierarchy. No Dionysus happened to be available when the film was beginning, but, fundamentally, it was born out of the same needs and to comparable ends. Its extra burden is that it has had to fashion its Dionysus as it goes, fitfully, patchily. But what a proof of its power and its potentiality that it has been able to do it. Why should film be reproved or patronized for this? Why should the one art born in this century be scolded for treating *everything* that anguishes and exalts human beings in this century? Or, more strangely, why should some of its devotees apply critical standards that implicitly urge it to aim low? What a price to pay for being apt!

Following the Gaze: The Influence (and Problems) of Feminist Film Theory in Theater Criticism

Sarah Bay-Cheng

Men look at women. Women watch themselves being looked at. This determines not only most relations between men and women but also the relation of women to themselves. The surveyor of woman in herself is male: the surveyed female. Thus she turns herself into an object—and most particularly an object of vision: a sight.
—John Berger, *Ways of Seeing*

Men's eyes were made to look, and let them gaze.
—William Shakespeare, *Romeo and Juliet*

Among the many essays, articles, and books devoted to feminist theories of dramatic writing and performance, there is one problematic aspect that has been largely ignored: the use of feminist film theory to analyze and critique live performance. Although drama and cinema are clearly two very different forms of representation, theater was considered a virtually parallel phenomenon to film by early feminist the-

---

Published here for the first time, with permission of Sarah Bey-Cheng, Colgate University.

ater critics. Initial feminist theater theory drew on a number of interdiscipli-
nary sources for its initial inspiration, including psychoanalysis, literary theory,
and semiotics, as well as previous theater theorists such as Brecht.[1] However,
one of the most influential sources was undoubtedly film theory. Feminist theater critics widely excerpted the writing of Laura Mulvey, Mary Ann Doane,
and Teresa de Lauretis in the mid-to-late 1980s, using theory devoted exclusively to film to explain and explore live performance and drama. In particular,
these writings followed film theory's concept of the male "gaze," which was
based on the belief that the technological apparatus of the film camera had a
distinct ideological position. This position of the film camera was unilaterally
male, phallic, and harmful to the women, both as onscreen objects (or fetishes)
and as unwitting spectators. Although the concept of the gaze opened up new
avenues of criticism in feminist studies of theater and performance, the application of film theory to live performance is fundamentally flawed. As such, the
use of "the gaze" in theater criticism deserves a closer examination than it has
previously received.

During the 1990s feminist theater theory gradually shifted away from its
early reliance on film, embracing an increasingly multifaceted critical approach
to both dramatic literature and performance. However, the influence of film
theory, most often explored through the concept of the male gaze, is still evident in most feminist theorizing about drama and performance. For example,
in her study of feminist performance art titled *The Explicit Body in Performance*
(1997), Rebecca Schneider writes in language that deliberately echoes filmic
discourse. She uses filmic metaphor to explain the role of the (male) spectator,
describing him as a "seeing eye [that] is unseen" and a "gaze [that] is rendered
active, phallic" (62). Her discussion of live performance through the seen and
the unseen, and, of course, through the gaze itself, has its origins in film theory.[2] Thus, despite feminist theater theory's movement away from film, cinema
clearly has left a distinct imprint on the evolution of feminist theater theory
and criticism. To fully understand feminist theater theory and its evolution, it
is therefore essential to examine its theoretical predecessors in film.

Perhaps the most influential of these filmic forerunners was Laura Mulvey.
Many of the concepts critical to feminist theory in both film and theater first
appeared in her groundbreaking essay "Visual Pleasure and Narrative Cinema"
(1975). In it, she introduced psychoanalysis to film theory and created a model
for critiquing not only representations of women in film, but also the mechanism that created those representations. Whereas Mulvey readily admitted the
limitations of psychoanalysis, particularly in theorizing female development,

she noted that "at this point, psychoanalytic theory as it now stands can at least advance our understanding of the status quo, of the patriarchal order in which we are caught" (23).

Mulvey considered the pleasure film creates through three interrelated psychoanalytic experiences: scopophilia (the pleasure of looking), voyeurism (the pleasure from looking at sexual acts), and ego libido (the formation of identification). She argued that in film three distinct "looks" make up the male gaze and creates the male's "visual pleasure." The camera looks at the profilmic event, the spectator looks at the film image, and the characters on screen look at each other. To create maximum pleasure for the (male) spectator, these first two looks are rendered invisible, allowing the male viewer to identify with the active male protagonist—who solves problems, gains possession of the woman (or women) on screen, and frequently emerges triumphant at the conclusion of the film—without interruption. By denying the existence of the camera (as well as the controlling agent behind it) and the existence of the audience, the spectator can imagine that the protagonist on screen is simply a more perfect vision of himself.[3] Similarly, because the woman (with her lack of a penis) threatens to provoke castration anxiety in the male spectator, she is frequently fetishized on screen, existing as only a face (Greta Garbo) or a pair of legs (Marlene Dietrich), to relieve the spectator's anxiety. The woman is presented directly to the spectator as a sexual object, allowing him to possess the image visually, just as his screen counterpart will possess the woman through a romantic or sexual relationship, thereby reinforcing the spectator's identification with the film's protagonist.

At first glance, Mulvey's argument and the subsequent discourse that it inspired among feminist film theorists appears to be an ideal method for critiquing traditional theater. Like the narrative Hollywood cinema that she critiques, commercial theater presents women for viewing by an audience of anonymous spectators. The plots of both mainstream plays and films overwhelmingly present active male protagonists and passive female objects of desire. In the cinema and its burgeoning feminist theory, feminists in theater studies found a seemingly parallel form and a body of critical literature that addressed issues of both performance and spectatorship. Unlike literary theory, which lacks the visual aspect so critical to theater, film theory considers both the content of a story and the unique form in which it is visualized, as well as the role of the audience. Perhaps even more importantly, feminist theater critics discovered a body of theory that had already processed the "looks" of film through the lens of psychoanalysis. As Jeanie Forte writes in her essay "Women's Performance Art," "Much of the feminist theory regarding notions of fetishism has come from the world of film theory, wherein the cinematic image provides a clear paradigm for the workings of fetishism in a patriarchal—and psychoanalytically encoded—culture" (262).

From psychoanalytic theory and its repeated emphasis on looking during psycho-sexual development, early film feminists constructed a theory of "the gaze" to describe both how an individual watches films and how the films themselves construct images to appeal to the (male) spectator.[4] This gaze was explicitly male, aimed at women, and based on the childhood development theories of Freud and Lacan. Freud's theory of the Oedipal complex and fetishism provided an explanation for the woman as icon on screen, and Lacan's theory of the "mirror stage" explored the process of identification between the viewer and the male characters on screen. Since most theater also has male viewers and displays women on stage, it must have seemed quite logical for feminist theater theorists also to consider the role of the male gaze in performance.

But the application of film theory to theater is not as simple as theater theorists have implied. First, there is the problem of the camera and the role that its technical apparatus plays in constructing the gaze. This point is frequently addressed in theater theory, but quickly dismissed. For example, in her analysis of Richard Foreman's work, Jill Dolan writes, "In some ways, Foreman's construction of images cannot be parallel to that of the cinematic apparatus because he cannot control the spectator's gaze as carefully. . . . Foreman's scenography, however, is intended to force the spectator's eye to scan the stage picture and in some respects to control the gaze by playing with focus" (49–50). Similarly, even though Mulvey herself describes her three "looks" as unique to cinema, Gayle Austin writes, "Scopophilia and narcissism are just as actively at work in live performance as in film, perhaps more today than in earlier decades because of the use of filmic devices on the stage" (85).

In fact, Mulvey's proposed "first blow" against the oppressive conventions of narrative cinema is "to free the look of the camera into its materiality in time and space and the look of the audience into dialectics, passionate detachment" (33). In her consideration of the cinematic apparatus, Mulvey advocates for a camera that does not invisibly and omnipotently direct the gaze, but instead acts as a visible and temporal mechanism for looking. Similarly, she wants spectators to view a cinematic scene without over-identifying with the characters on screen, to watch without losing themselves in the illusion of the screen image. In other words, Mulvey wants film to behave more like theater.

In theater the spectator has much greater freedom to look at whatever appears interesting. The eye has the freedom to scan the entire stage area with much greater freedom than in film. Furthermore, because more light is required in the theater to see people and objects clearly on stage, the audience itself is more visible to the spectator. A variety of seating arrangements, such as theater in the round, allow, and even encourage, audience members to look at each other. In fact, this type of audience arrangement creates the audience dialectic that Mulvey sought for film. Audience members watch other members watch the performance and, in a sense, are thus aware of their own gaze. Unlike their counterparts at the cinema, theater audiences are allowed an unbridled gaze. Audience members may choose to look at each other, their programs, or elements of the set.

A clear example of this occurs in Dolan's description of seeing Richard Foreman's productions. She notes that during his "performances, he would sit at a console in front of the playing space, running the lights and sound" (53). It is true that sitting in the audience at Foreman's shows, one can quite easily see Foreman at his console table, controlling the various elements at work on stage. He makes no secret of his presence; indeed, he often introduces productions. Dolan further writes that Foreman "was the active male who controlled the production and was able to secure his desire" (53). This is also true. But, unlike his cinematic counterparts, Foreman is *visible* to the audience and he does not attempt to be otherwise. He openly takes credit for writing, directing, and designing nearly all of his productions himself. Foreman may control the audience's gaze or manipulate the elements of production to control both actor and audience, but the fact remains that he is visible while doing it. He is not the unseen and unrecognized camera, or even the unseen playwright or director, but instead operates as the very visible and recognizable manipulator of the performance.

Perhaps a more accurate cinematic context in which to consider Foreman's work can be found in the apparatus theory of Jean-Louis Baudry. In his essay "Ideological Effects of the Basic Cinematographic Apparatus," Baudry argues that the viewer watching the film unfold will not identify with the characters on screen (as Mulvey argues), but instead with the omnipotent force directing the view. It is with this powerful unseen force that the viewer aligns him- or herself. Baudry cites Jean Mitry, who writes in *Esthétique et psychologie du cinéma* (1965), "In the cinema I am simultaneously in this action and *outside* it, in this space and out of this space. Having the power of ubiquity, I am everywhere and nowhere" (emphasis in Baudry, 297). Thus the viewer of film identifies with what Baudry calls the "eye-subject," the unseen force that propels the viewer through space with the mobility of the camera, creating a world that opens up for the viewer more so than for any character locked within the screen's frame. In this context, the work of Richard Foreman works against the ideological effects of the cinema that Mulvey and Dolan cite. Foreman makes himself visible in the same space as his production and thereby invites the spectator to see the production as the product of his efforts. He is less a director, perhaps, than an orchestral conductor and, as such, he invites the viewer to see his productions as projections of his own imagination.

If, however, one accepts the argument that theater, with such quasi-filmic framing devices as spotlights and proscenium arches, does in fact direct the eye much like film, there are still problems with the application of cinematic apparatuses to theater theory. The most glaring of these is the fragmentation of the female form on screen. One of the key distinctions Mulvey makes between men and women on screen is the difference between the spaces they occupy. Whereas "the active male figure . . . demands a three-dimensional space" (28), the image of a woman on screen is frequently fragmented, creating "the quality of a cutout or icon rather than verisimilitude [on] screen" (27). In the context of psychoanalysis, this fragmentation is thought to be the fetishization of the woman necessary to alleviate the (unacknowledged) castration anxiety of the male viewer. As Mulvey writes, "The male unconscious has two avenues of escape from this castration anxiety: preoccupation with the re-enactment of the original trauma (investigating the woman, demystifying her mystery) . . . or else complete disavowal of castration by the substitution of a fetish object, or turning the represented figure itself into a fetish object so that it becomes reassuring rather than dangerous—hence overevaluation, the cult of the female star" (29). When the film director employs the close-up, both "avenues of escape" are available to the viewer. The disconnected body parts are presented as fetish objects and, similarly, the deconstruction of the female body implies a power of discovery in the viewer. Thus, the close-up functions in much the same way as a microscope.[5] By viewing the female body in close-up, the viewer is able to investigate the female form and demystify it.

In the theater, however, this fragmentation of the woman and the space she occupies is very different. In virtually every live performance, the women on stage occupy the same space as the men. The viewer sees both men and women as whole and intact beings that move through space with mostly equal access. Certainly, there are plays that restrict women to isolated parts of the stage or restrict their movement through clothing like corsets, high heels, etc., and there are, of course, plays in which women are never visible at all. However, there is no parallel to the shifting borders of the film screen in theater. Whereas men and women in film may occupy vastly difference spaces depending on the framing of the shot, space on the stage is fundamentally equal. In live performance, women cannot be broken apart and contained by the theater apparatus, as can their counterparts on film.[6]

In addition to its control of space, cinema also has the ability to adjust the scale of images of men and women on screen. Not only can a woman on film be visually cut into disconnected body parts; those parts can also equal or even exceed the amount of space her entire body occupies. For example, a close-up of Marlene Dietrich's legs in *The Blue Angel* (1930) takes up more space on the screen than her body as an integrated whole ever does. Hence not only can the image of a woman on film be fragmented, but it can also be grossly distorted. Her body parts can be prioritized both by time (as in the duration of a close-up of Dietrich's legs) and by size (her legs being equal to, or exceeding, the value of her entire body). Dietrich's legs do not simply exceed her integrated body size on screen, they are taller than a single story building! Her whole becomes literally less than the sum of her parts. Conversely, the power of the male protagonist—who has the freedom to move through space—is amplified because of the screen's enormous scale. His size, his power, and his mobility are all exaggerated by the film screen's size. It is this manipulation of the female body in time and space to which Mulvey refers when she writes that, "Playing on the tension between film as controlling the dimension of time (editing, narrative) and film as controlling the dimension of space (changes in distance, editing), cinematic codes create a gaze, a world and an object, thereby producing an illusion cut to the measure of desire" (32–33). Thus, the gaze to which Mulvey devotes so much critical energy is a distinctly filmic phenomenon.

These manipulations of time and space are clearly the exclusive domain of film. In the theater, time, space, and the human beings who inhabit the stage are fundamentally more integrated than their film counterparts. Although one can cite the occasional theatrical fracturing of the human form—the Italian Futurist play "Feet" (1915, by Filippo Tommaso Marinetti), for example—the fractured body parts never exceed their natural size. There are, of course, avant-garde plays that do challenge these limitations of space and size. For example, Eugene Ionesco's *Amédée or How to Get Rid of It* (1954) presents a dead man who grows so large that his feet crash through the wall of his neighbor's living room. But even here size is progressive. The dead man's feet get progressively larger, but he is never reintegrated and his body clearly operates outside the realm of "reality." In short, Ionesco's feet will never become Dietrich's legs. theater is fundamentally incapable of achieving the verisimilitude of film and mimicking its ability to promote and maintain male pleasure through the manipulations of the female form.

Because of these fundamental *visual* differences between theater and film, it is clear that the gaze aimed at film is necessarily very different from the gaze aimed at live bodies on stage. In fact, although film theory has clearly left its mark on feminist theater scholarship, the limited applicability of film theory to live performance studies was never entirely lost on feminist theater scholars. Elin Diamond, for example, in her essay "Brechtian Theory/Feminist Theory: Toward a Gestic Feminist Criticism," recognizes that the means with which to dismantle the male gaze in theater are themselves present in theater. She writes, "Feminist film theorists, fellow-traveling with psychoanalysis and semiotics, have given [theater feminist theorists] a lot to think about, but we, through Brechtian theory, have something to give them: a female body in representation that resists fetishization and a viable position for the female spectator" (83). Diamond finds greater possibilities for feminist performance in the dramatic theories of Bertolt Brecht than in theories of the cinematic gaze. According to Diamond, Brecht's concept of *Verfremdungseffekt,* or defamiliarization, challenges normative gender ideology on stage and creates the opportunity for a more critical viewing of gender by the theater audience. Based on her examination of Brechtian gesture, Diamond argues for "a theater-specific feminist criticism" (83).

What is most interesting about Diamond's move from Mulvey to Brecht is that Mulvey herself seems to draw from Brecht.[7] When Mulvey advocates for the audience's "passionate detachment" (33) in film, she appears directly to refer to Brecht's belief that theater audiences should not be carried away by a performance, but should instead view that performance as "unemotional experts." Indeed, the theories of Brecht and Mulvey are strikingly similar. Both Brecht and Mulvey consider their ideal audience to be self-aware and critical, and both desire to make visible the mechanisms of their respective apparatuses: Brecht through the use of titles, songs, and non-realistic acting; Mulvey through the visibility of the camera and the filmmaker. Paradoxically, theater theory rediscovers its own resistance to the "male gaze" through feminist film theory, which itself appears to borrow from theater.

From a reading of early feminist theater theory of the mid-to-late 1980s, it is clear that film theory prompted an important beginning for feminist theater criticism. Film theory's appropriation of psychoanalysis and its emphasis on the spectator exerted a strong influence on feminist theater studies and its first generation of scholar-critics. So much so, that the concept of a monolithic "gaze" has persisted throughout feminist theater theory even though, as I have attempted to demonstrate here, there are actually two distinct gazes—one for theater and one for film. When feminist theater theory claimed its own gaze in the 1990s, it established its own direction, one that more closely attended to the unique qualities of live performance in the theater. And, yet, many aspects of theater and film theory overlap, as in the case of Laura Mulvey and Bertolt Brecht. As theater performances increasingly reflect the influence of cinema and its technology, the new direction for feminist theory therefore seems to be toward a new intersection of film and theater theory.

NOTES

1. For more on Brecht and feminist theories of drama and performance, see Elin Diamond's "Brechtian Theory/Feminist Theory: Toward a Gestic Feminist Criticism" *The Drama Review* 32.1 (Spring 1988): 82–94, Janelle Reinalt's "Beyond Brecht: Britain's New Feminist Drama" *Theatre Journal* 38.1 (May 1986): 154–164, and her "Rethinking Brecht: Deconstruction, Feminism, and the Politics of Form" *Brecht Yearbook* 15 (1990): 99–110.

2. It is important to note that Schneider considers both live performance and film in her study, using much of her theory to knit the two forms of representation together without necessarily blurring the distinctions between them.

3. Mulvey draws a parallel here between the male spectator viewing the male protagonist on screen and the male child viewing himself in the mirror in what Lacan, quite aptly, called, the "mirror stage." Mulvey writes, "The mirror phase occurs at a time when the child's physical ambitions outstrip his motor capacity, with the result that his recognition of himself is joyous in that he imagines his mirror image to be more complete, more perfect than he experiences his own body" (25).

4. It is important to note that in Mulvey's theory the gaze of the spectator is always male, even when the spectator herself is not. Indeed, Mulvey's lack of consideration of the female spectator in the audience, as well as the unique viewing position of gay men and lesbians and their filmic desires, has been a major criticism of her essay. She responded to these criticisms in her later essay, "Afterthoughts on 'Visual Pleasure and Narrative Cinema' Inspired by King Vidor's *Duel in the Sun* (1946)" in her *Visual and Other Pleasures* (Bloomington: Indiana University Press, 1989), pp. 29–37.

5. In fact, Baudry makes just such a connection between the cinematic apparatus and "optical instruments, directly attached to scientific practice" (286).

6. For more on the relationship between space and feminist film theory, see Peggy Phelan's chapter "Spatial Envy: Yvonne Rainer's *The Man Who Envied Women*" in her *Unmarked: The Politics of Performance* (London: Routledge, 1993), pp. 71–92.

7. This move by Mulvey was not lost on Diamond, who writes, "Mulvey powerfully invokes Brechtian concepts" (83).

WORKS CITED

Austin, Gayle. *Feminist Theories for Dramatic Criticism.* Ann Arbor, Mich.: University of Michigan Press, 1990.

Baudry, Jean-Louis. "Ideological Effects of the Basic Cinematographic Apparatus." 1970. Trans. Alan Williams. *Film Quarterly* 28.2 (Winter 1974–75): 39–47. Rpt. in *Narrative, Apparatus, Ideology: A Film Theory Reader.* Ed. Philip Rosen. New York: Columbia University Press, 1986. 286–298.

Berger, John. *Ways of Seeing.* London: British Broadcasting Corporation, 1972.

Diamond, Elin. "Brechtian Theory/Feminist Theory: Toward a Gestic Feminist Criticism." *The Drama Review* 32.1 (Spring 1988): 82–94.

Dolan, Jill. *The Feminist Spectator as Critic.* Ann Arbor, Mich.: UMI Research Press, 1988.

Forte, Jeanie. "Women's Performance Art: Feminism and Postmodernism." In *Performing Feminisms: Feminist Critical Theory and Theatre.* Ed. Sue-Ellen Case. Baltimore, Md.: Johns Hopkins University Press, 1990. 251–269.

Hart, Lynda, ed. *Making a Spectacle: Feminist Essays on Contemporary Women's Theatre.* Ann Arbor, Mich.: University of Michigan Press, 1989.

Mitry, Jean. *Esthétique et psychologie du cinema.* Paris: Presses Universitaires de France, 1965.

Mulvey, Laura. "Visual Pleasure and Narrative Cinema." *Screen* 16.3 (Autumn 1975): 6–18. Rpt. in *The Sexual Subject: A Screen Reader in Sexuality.* Ed. *Screen.* London: Routledge, 1992. 22–43.

Schneider, Rebecca. *The Explicit Body in Performance.* London: Routledge, 1997.

Entr'acte: The Playwright as Film Critic
The Film, the Novel, and Epic Theatre

Bertolt Brecht

SOME PRECONCEPTIONS EXAMINED

I. "Art can do without the cinema"

We have often been told (and the court expressed the same opinion) that when we sold our work to the film industry we gave up all our rights; the buyers even purchased the right to destroy what they had bought; all further claim was covered by the money. These people felt that in agreeing to deal with the film industry we put ourselves in the position of a man who lets his laundry be washed in a dirty gutter and then complains that it has been ruined. Anybody who advises us not to make use of such new apparatus just confirms the apparatus's right to do bad work; he forgets himself out of sheer open-mindedness, for he is thus proclaiming his willingness to have nothing but dirt pro-

Excerpted from "The Film, the Novel, and Epic Theatre" from *Brecht on Theatre,* edited and translated by John Willett. Translation copyright © 1964, renewed 1992 by John Willett. Reprinted by permission of Hill and Wang, a division of Farrar, Straus and Giroux, LLC.

duced for him. At the same time he deprives us in advance of the apparatus which we need in order to produce, since this way of producing is likely more and more to supersede the present one, forcing us to speak through increasingly complex media and to express what we have to say by increasingly inadequate means. For the old forms of communication are not unaffected by the development of new ones, nor do they survive alongside them. The filmgoer develops a different way of reading stories. But the man who writes the stories is a filmgoer too. The mechanization of literary production cannot be thrown into reverse. Once instruments are used even the novelist who makes no use of them is led to wish that he could do what the instruments can: to include what they show (or could show) as part of that reality which constitutes his subject-matter; and above all, when he writes, to assume the attitude of somebody using an instrument.

For instance it makes a great difference whether the writer approaches things as if using instruments, or produces them "from within himself." What the film itself does, that is to say how far it makes its individuality prevail against "art," is not unimportant in this connection. It is conceivable that other kinds of writers, such as playwrights or novelists, may for the moment be able to work in a more cinematic way than the film people. Up to a point they depend less on means of production. But they still depend on the film, its progress or regress; and the film's means of production are wholly capitalist. Today the bourgeois novel still depicts "a world." It does so in a purely idealistic way from within a given *Weltanschauung:* the more or less private, but in any case personal outlook of its "creator." Inside this world every detail of course fits exactly, though if it were taken out of its context it would not seem authentic for a minute by comparison with the "details" of reality. What we find out about the real world is just as much as we find out about the author responsible for the unreal one; in other words we find out something about the author and nothing about the world.

The film cannot depict any world (the "setting" in which it deals is something quite different) and lets nobody express himself (and nothing else) in a work, and no work express any person. What it provides (or could provide) is applicable conclusions about human actions in detail. Its splendid inductive method, which at any rate it facilitates, could be of infinite significance to the novel, in so far as novels still signify anything. To the playwright what is interesting is its attitude to the person performing the action. It gives life to its people, whom it classes purely according to function, simply using available types that occur in given situations and are able to adopt given attitudes in them.

Character is never used as a source of motivation; these people's inner life is never the principal cause of the action and seldom its principal result; the individual is seen from outside. Literature needs the film not only indirectly but also directly. That decisive extension of its social duties which follows from the transformation of art into a paedagogical discipline entails the multiplying or the repeated changing of the means of representation. (Not to mention the Lehrstück proper, which entails supplying film apparatus to all those taking part.) This apparatus can be used better than almost anything else to supersede the old kind of untechnical, anti-technical "glowing" art, with its religious links. The socialization of these means of production is vital for art. . . .

To understand the position we must get away from the common idea that these battles for the new institutions and apparatus only have to do with one part of art. In this view there is a part of art, its central part, which remains wholly untouched by the new possibilities of communication (radio, film,

Fig. 8. *The Threepenny Opera* (1931), adapted by Leo Lania, Bela Balasz, and Ladislas Vajda from the play by Bertolt Brecht (1928), which itself is based on John Gay's *Beggar's Opera* (1728). Directed by G. W. Pabst. Courtesy of Billy Rose Theatre Collection, The New York Public Library for the Performing Arts, Astor, Lenox and Tilden Foundations.

book clubs, etc.) and goes on using the old ones (printed books, freely mar-
keted; the stage, etc.). Quite different from the other, technically-influenced
part where it is a matter of creation by the apparatus itself: a wholly new business, owing its existence in the first place to certain financial calculations and
thereby bound to them for ever. If works of the former sort are handed over to
the apparatus they are turned into goods without further ado. This idea, leading as it does to utter fatalism, is wrong because it shuts off so-called "sacrosanct
works of art" from every process and influence of our time, treating them as
sacrosanct purely because they are impervious to any development in communication. In fact, of course, the whole of art without any exception is placed in
this new situation; it is as a whole, not split into parts, that it has to cope with
it; it is as a whole that it turns into goods or not. The changes wrought by time
leave nothing untouched, but always embrace the whole. In short, the common preconception discussed here is pernicious.

2. A Film Must Have Some 'Human Interest'

This preconception is equivalent to the notion that films have got to be vulgar.
Such an eminently rational view (rational because nobody is going to make any
other kind of film, or look at it once made) owes its relevance to the inexorable
way in which the metaphysicians of the press, with their insistence on "art," call
for profundity. It is they who want to see the "element of fate" emphasized in all
dealings between people. Fate, which used (once) to be among the great concepts, has long since become a vulgar one, where the desired "transfiguration"
and "illumination" are achieved by reconciling oneself to circumstances—and
a purely class-warfare one, where one class fixes the fate of another. As usual,
our metaphysicians' demands are not hard to fulfil. It is simple to imagine
everything that they reject presented in such a way that they would accept it
with enthusiasm. Obviously if one were to trace certain love stories back to
Romeo and Juliet, or crime stories to Macbeth, in other words to famous plays
that need contain nothing else (need show no other kind of human behaviour,
use no other kind of energy to govern the world's movements), then they would
at once exclaim that vulgarity is determined by How and not What. But this "it
all depends how" is itself vulgar.

  This beloved "human interest of theirs, this How (usually qualified by the
word "eternal," like some indelible dye) as applied to Othello (my wife is my
property), Hamlet (better sleep on it), Macbeth (I'm destined for higher
things) and co., now seems like vulgarity and nothing more when measured on
a massive scale. If one insists on having it, this is the only form in which it can

be had; simply to insist is vulgar. What once determined the grandeur of such passions, their non-vulgarity, was the part they had to play in society, which was a revolutionary one. Even the impact which *Potemkin* made on such people springs from the sense of outrage which they would feel if their wives were to try to serve bad meat to them (I won't stand it, I tell you!), while Chaplin is perfectly aware that he must be "human," i.e. vulgar, if he is to achieve anything more, and to this end will alter his style in a pretty unscrupulous way (viz. the famous close-up of the doggy look which concludes *City Lights*).

What the film really demands is external action and not introspective psychology. Capitalism operates in this way by taking given needs on a massive scale, exorcizing them, organizing them and mechanizing them so as to revolutionize everything. Great areas of ideology are destroyed when capitalism concentrates on external action, dissolves everything into processes, abandons the hero as the vehicle for everything and mankind as the measure, and thereby smashes the introspective psychology of the bourgeois novel. The extrenal viewpoint suits the film and gives it importance. For the film the principles of non-aristotelian drama (a type of drama not depending on empathy, mimesis) are immediately acceptable. Non-aristotelian effects can be seen in the Russian film *The Road to Life,* above all because the theme (re-education of neglected children by specific socialist methods) leads the spectator to establish causal relationships between the teacher's attitude and that of his pupils. Thanks to the key scenes this analysis of origins comes so to grip the spectator's interest that he "instinctively" dismisses any motives for the children's neglect borrowed from the old empathy type of drama (unhappiness at home plus psychic trauma, rather than war or civil war). Even the use of work as a method of education arouses the spectator's scepticism, for the simple reason that it is never made clear that in the Soviet Union, in total contrast to all other countries, morality is in fact determined by work. As soon as the human being appears as an object the causal connections become decisive. Similarly in the great American comedies the human being is presented as an object, so that their audience could as well be entirely made up of Pavlovians. Behaviourism is a school of psychology that is based on the industrial producer's need to acquire means of influencing the customer; an active psychology therefore, progressive and revolutionary. Its limits are those proper to its function under capitalism (the reflexes are biological; only in certain of Chaplin's films are they social). Here again the road leads over capitalism's dead body; but here again this road is a good one.

NOTE

The above are two sections from Brecht's long account of his lawsuit over the making of Pabst's film version of *The Threepenny Opera*, which was heard in Berlin on 17 and 20 October 1930. The suit failed and Brecht lost his claim to dictate the treatment of the story, which would have been along the lines of his draft "Die Beule" (printed in the same volume). This draft became instead the basis of *The Threepenny Novel*, the only true novel that Brecht wrote.

The emphasis on contradictions in the opening quotation is new, and will become increasingly important in Brecht's writings. In Marxist language this term means the conflicting elements in any person or situation.

Nikolai Ekk's *The Road to Life,* one of the first Soviet sound films, was released on 1 June 1930. Brecht had met Eisenstein on his Berlin visit of 1929; later he came to know Chaplin in Hollywood. An earlier unpublished note on *The Gold Rush* entitled "Less Security" ("Weniger Sicherheit," *Schriften zum Theater 2,* p. 220) calls Chaplin a "document" and praises story and theme on the ground that the average theatre would at once reject anything so simple, crude and linear. "The cinema has no responsibilities, it doesn't have to overstrain itself. Its dramaturgy has remained so simple because a film is a matter of a few miles of celluloid in a tin box. When a man bends a saw between his knees you don't expect a fugue." Yet another early fragment (*Schriften zum Theater I,* pp. 163–164) on "The theatre of the big cities" concludes: "The only kind of art produced by these cities so far has been *fun:* Charlie Chaplin's films and jazz. Jazz is all the theatre it contains, as far as I can see."

In 1931 Brecht helped to make the (Communist) semi-documentary film *Kuhle Wampe,* which was directed by Slatan Dudow and banned in March of the following year. Probably this came closer to his ideas than any other film with which he was associated.

Three **Writing**

Growing Apart
From an Interview with Roger Blin

Erika Munk

Translated by J. Later Strahs

Q: *You worked with Artaud and were a friend of his. Is it possible that his concepts, ideals, and philosophy could be achieved better through film than in theatre?*

A: Perhaps, yes. There are certain films which Artaud might have liked. *Maitre Fou,* for example, a documentary by Jean Rouch. It is concerned with a group of people from Accra, who from time to time go into a clearing in the forest. There they indulge in exercises, in feasts: they drink and they are put into a trance, they eat dogs, they enter completely into another world. The next day they return to their work. It is a kind of rapid self-psychoanalysis. As for fiction films, I can't say. There are certain cruel films like Polanski's *Repulsion* and those of Buñuel. Buñuel, of course, comes from Spanish Cruelty, while the others are related to the German Expressionists, and thus to Romanticism with its phantoms and horrors. Movie production is so

Reprinted from *Drama Review* II, no. 1 (Fall 1966), 115–116. Translated by J. Later Strahs.

much compliance and compromise (perhaps there are a few happy exceptions), and financial imperatives exercise so much control, that you can't hope for anything great.

Q: *Why have Genet and Beckett written little for the film, when the French cinema's* auteur *theory would seem naturally attractive to such writers?*

A: Genet made an "underground" film once (*Un Chant d'Amour*). But he wants to be a complete *auteur*—to do this, he would have to know the entire craft of film-making. He found that he was too old to learn it, and that is why he doesn't write for the cinema. The same was true of Beckett, who is now beginning to get interested. He made that thing with Schneider and Buster Keaton in New York [T27]. Perhaps he has something, but the producers will never ask Beckett to write a film.

In cinema the producer comes to the writer with an idea and the writer has to know how to execute it. That's all. A producer couldn't do this with Beckett. If a producer accepted a Beckett scenario he'd know that it was a film for cinema clubs. The films that are selling, those which are *à la mode,* we get from young *cinéastes* who have talent and who are (or wish to become) *auteurs.* They experiment in their youth: boy and girl stories, love stories, action stories, war stories—things like that. But this is never the world of Beckett or of Genet—never . . . in the last analysis, that other world is very *nice.* Those *auteurs* have nothing important to say—nice little stories, and then that's all.

Q: *In many French cities the film has replaced the theatre in popularity. Do you feel that this represents a threat or a challenge to the theatre?*

A: It is a good thing for the theatres. Theatre audiences are small, but would have been smaller had it not been for the cinema. Many theatres are closed and many barely hang on to life, but at the same time there is a renewed interest in the theatre. The cinema has forced the theatre to be theatre. For me the true theatre is that which is *total* theatre, with no imitation of any other form, although special lighting effects can be permitted and sound recording, and dance, certainly: all the plastic things. Besides, cinema is now being influenced by theatre, as is television. What the theatre will have to do, in order to survive, is to improve its essential particulars. That will be good.

Q: *Even the young French writers, the ones with ideas and imagination, aren't writing for the cinema. Is this a trend peculiar to France, and have film and theatre grown very far apart?*

A: None of the talented young writers I know wish to be the intermediary for another *metteur-en-scène*. In the theatre they are able to work on the stage. The *metteur-en-scène* is usually a friend, so there is no great difference between his view and theirs. But in the cinema, the *metteurs-en-scène* appear to them to be magicians who possess some kind of secret, a secret which they haven't the right to approach. They don't want to be in this position, and the money doesn't interest them. Do you know that in France the production directors are in collusion with the exhibitors—those who own the studios and sell the film? In France a film is sold before it is begun. The writer hands over a script which will be examined by people who say: "Oh well, we must cut this, that won't do, the censor won't permit this, the public won't understand that. It's too tame, we'll have to put in a little ass so it'll sell in South America," and it comes out completely changed. If the guy says "Good, give me my money, I accept," then the film is done. If he doesn't, then it's not made. And no self-respecting author will accept this situation. This theatre and the cinema are two different worlds, two different pleasures. There are some theatre directors who work in the cinema: Peter Brook, Raymond Rouleau. There are many of them in America: Kazan and that whole New York crowd. And me? I would like to do some films. But I would do true films. I would not use the theatre at all. True films, without a theatrical origin. I think that the people who are now doing theatre, the *auteurs* of the theatre, will do cinema when they earn less money in the cinema than in the theatre. Then there would be a kind of nobility in cinema. One thinks immediately that theatre equals art and cinema equals money. Obviously this is a little idiotic.

Theatre and Film: The Misery of Comparison

Peter Handke

Pascal said, approximately: all misery comes from man's constantly believing that he must compare himself with the infinite. And another misery—Pascal did not say this—comes from man's believing that he must, in general, compare.

As I write this, I see, outside in the street, two streetsweepers cleaning the sidewalk with huge brooms. Both have orange and white striped uniforms *like bicycle racers,* both have white, crumpled stockings *like tramps* or *like characters in a Beckett play,* both have faces *like Southerners,* both wear caps *like those in photographs of prisoners of war from the First World War,* both walk stiffed-kneed *like bums,* all three— now a third joins them, and a fourth—wear black mittens *like the snow removal crew in the winter,* all five are alike with their gigantic brooms and shovels, which make them appear quite small, *like figures in a painting by Breughel.*

But—one of the streetsweepers swept *faster than* the other, and the

From Peter Handke, *Prosa, Gedichte, Theaterstücke, Hörspiel, Aufsatz,* trans. Donald Nordberg (Frankfurt, Germany: Suhrkamp Verlag, 1969).

other streetsweeper wore his cap *lower* on his face *than* the one, and the other other streetsweeper had a much *more German* face *than* the other streetsweeper, and the other other other streetsweeper seemed to perform his work *more unwillingly than* the other other streetsweeper, and finally—meanwhile the men have moved from my view—the last streetsweeper came to mind because he had, it seemed, shoved the broom forward *more powerfully than* the others.

How do we arrive at this need to compare, at this search? (And I call it a search.) Does it not originate in the inability to distinguish individual things immediately? And how does it come about that we, while we compare, also want to evaluate every time at the same time? Is it not true that we evaluate because we are unable at first to perceive an object *dis*valued by the comparison? Because we, in short, look at it blindly; and from an utter helplessness, if we cannot perceive it thus, we slip immediately into comparison? The objects seem to be there only to be played off against each other. They become abstracted to possibilities for comparison: one avoids becoming clear about them by thoughtlessly measuring them against other objects. In this way a hierarchy of objects arises mechanically in the consciousness of the perceiver, which, like a customer, collects the objects. The first thought following perception is not a first thought, but on the contrary a reflex of comparison, as if we were buyers in a department store, presented not so much with a world of individual wares as with a world of possibilities for comparison. And I too have been able to help myself by nothing other than comparing: yes, comparisons help.

And the models for comparison to which all comparisons and devaluations may be reduced are the following: "I would rather have this than that," and "I would rather be this than that." And finally (of use for all objects, situations, and incidents): "I like Negroes more than Chinamen," "I like the flatlands more than the mountains," "I like music more than painting," "I like democracy more than revolutions," "I like security more than insecurity," "I like my wife more than all movie stars put together," "I like the patriarch in Constantinople more than the Pope in Rome," "I like a strict order, in which everyone has his job and can eat until he is content more than a freedom in which . . ."—you can complete the sentences for yourself. It appears, then, that comparisons serve above all to talk away the compared object with a sentence. Any further preoccupation with it is unnecessary: it exists only as an object of comparison, as an object of value, as an object of feeling. The object transforms itself—it becomes an object of aversion. And the misery and the greatness of the art of comparison is that, with its help, every object becomes formalized in consciousness into an object of feeling and value. Every object in the world can come to be compared with every other object in the world. Everything is super- and sub-ordinated in the hierarchy of feeling—anything can be compared to anything else—nothing remains outside consciousness only because it is incomprehensible, strange, and complicated. Precisely because it is incomprehensible, strange, and complicated, no alternative remains but comparing. Comparison protects against preoccupation with the object. The incomprehensible object becomes an object of feeling; because it is incomprehensible other objects are preferable to it. For example, one's own skin, which one knows: everything is easily compared to one's own skin, and by the comparison is also in fact undeservingly trusted. The healthy perception celebrates its triumph—we can prove this later—in the great misery of comparison.

This seemingly long preface should only make us skeptical, and clarify the reaction mechanisms in a single, modest sentence. And it is the sentence whose model I wanted, tediously, to approach more and more closely. It is simply: "I like going to the movies more than to the theatre." (I would have liked to have been able to turn the sentence around, but it will be employed quite well in the following series.) What an expense about such a harmless sentence! "I like going to the movies more than to the theatre." I remember having already used the sentence myself repeatedly. I say "remember" because I have not used the sentence for some time. Does that mean that I now prefer going to the theater? No, it means only that I no longer use the sentence, that I am embarrassed by using such a sentence. I still like going to the movies more. So, now I have used this sentence, but the more frequently I use it the more it bores me. It seems to me that as you can go through the same stream only once, so can you use the same sentence only once. The second time it is already a mistake; by the next time it is a disgrace; and finally it is only an idiocy. And as there is a wise saying of Kierkegaard's that one is not able to go through the same stream even once, so there is perhaps the wise saying that there are specific sentences that one cannot use even once without their being immediately mistakes, disgraces, and idiocies. And they are all those sentences whose models are conveyor-belt products of consciousness. Another is the sentence about theatre and the movies, which is understandable, perhaps, as a cry, like "Ow!" or "Aha!" or "Oh!" or "O God!" As *sentence*, however, it can no longer say anything to me—I can say it well enough, but I cannot hear it anymore.

Moreover, the sentence has also become something like a first and last cry. With it, everything is said about theatre and film, beginning and end. It is a model sentence, a modal sentence for young writers, young filmmakers—and even young dramatists—or whoever else we care to name. At present, the theater is in the position of having to defend itself. But what does *the* theatre mean? The theatre which the detractors of theatre mean is nothing but a ceremonial running at idle and gradually running out. The fights, which are decided in it in the form of dialogues, conflicts, stage laughter, trembling voices, burdensome silences, and actual fights, are—this is the paradox—in *reality apparent* fights, and the softest and most restrained chamber plays are as material nothing but flashy principal and state actions, principal and state reactions in the East and West. Enough of metaphors, enough of scolding, that is as boring as this theatre itself. A short time ago the students in Paris, with a circular and self-referring system of metaphor, cleared out and occupied the Théâtre Odéon. To be sure, the photos of it show that the quality of its playing space is still overwhelming, that the debaters in it are themselves romantic ornaments: so easily the talk about the old metaphors can become distorted. But, as I said, I have little desire to grind sentences long known to be true against this hurdy-gurdy theatre. Much more noteworthy, it seems to me, is the overdevelopment of films to the point in time where it is precisely the progressive films which are attentive to the great dilemma of film. That dilemma is that film, over a long period of time, simply by showing images and not by *describing* in the literary manner—simply by the abundant showing of images—has arrived gradually, with every new film, at an order of images that one can call a film syntax. A film image is no longer a pure *image;* it has become, through the history of all the film images before it, a "shot" or point of view. That means it shows the conscious or unconscious point of view of the filmmaker toward the filmed object, which in this way becomes the object of the filmmaker. Filmed, the object is abstracted by the shot, dematerialized—the shot of the object serves as the *expression* of the filmmaker. Because of the series of shots that have been produced which carry the same meaning, the shot turns into, one can say, a film sentence, which is built after the model of film sentences which already exist. The shot, the film sentence, now stands in already firmly canonized relationships to the preceding and succeeding shots and film sentences. The history of moving pictures, it is true, is more than the history of the formation of a standardized (and also standardizing) film syntax. In the beginning one could perhaps have asserted that a film did not need a description. Since then, however, film has had its own history, and the images of objects, the shots of objects, present themselves to the skillful film viewer as *descriptions* of the objects! That applies especially well to films which belong to particular genres and hold completely to the rules of those genres, as in crime movies, spy movies, westerns, horror movies, and so forth. Each image in these films is an image sentence which sticks to the syntax already established. I think of the shot in horror movies in which a person is seen walking up to the camera, and as the face grows larger you become more frightened, and suddenly an inch in front of the camera, something horrible happens to the person, and in the action is the rule (I say: the rule!) that the huge contorted face must now open its eyes wide and scream chillingly, or in any case try to scream—at which point a hand, perhaps a gloved hand, instantly spreads over the face. The shot, of course, has another meaning if, some meters in front of the camera, the person turns to the left or right and disappears from view: this image sentence quiets us—nothing will happen to the person. The fright that we have in genre films when a person is shown from the rear, I do not need to recall in detail, nor the anxiety that we feel for the hero of westerns when he is shown riding along a rock ledge and the edge of the cliff above is still empty. I would mention, however, a flowery phrase of the film grammar introduced into the film language by Alfred Hitchcock. He not only shows close-ups of beautiful women such as Grace Kelly or Kim Novak "out of focus," he also makes especially threatening shots seem to be "behind a veil," "milky," inexact. I mention this for this reason: I heard some time ago that in the face of great anxiety, in a particularly dangerous situation, the frightened person is so upset that he becomes nearsighted. Hitchcock has therefore turned psychic events into an image sentence.

We can say that in the genre films mentioned the image language may have been cultivated early and also numbed into a fixed canon which is unchangeable and yet most flexible. It appears, however, that more and more—and for this reason it concerns me here—the so-called impartial films (we rightly call them problems films or artistic films), which pretend to show quite impartial images, unpleasant, sterile shots, mechanically repeated, which pretend not to describe and to have no normative language, are really biased. These artistic films, while pretending to give back the outer world of filmed objects in images, actually give back only the inner world, the rigidified grammar of film forms. Famous filmmakers like Ingmar Bergman work in this way; also Alain Resnais, who with his last film, *La Guerre est Finie*, and now with *Je t'aime, Je t'aime*, could not even repeat his own efforts, which after *Hiroshima, mon amour* had already been unpleasant enough. The completed grammar of these films turns out to be usable for only the most unpleasant, that is, the *simplest* meaning: that is, for unmitigated trash. Godard's film grammar, too, had become, one could say, "fixed." The sequence of shots which he has developed is so completely adaptable that with its help one can establish a new genre film—not a crime movie, nor a western or a horror movie—a Godard film. The dilemma of film is that its syntax grows harder and harder. The way out of this dilemma seems to be that this syntax should be given some thought, that it should be made conscious with the film, that it should be presented; yes, that the syntax of films should appear so abstract that it itself will be shown as the film. Here we can mention some experiments.

Francois Truffaut's *The Bride Wore Black* seems to me an inoffensive film. The plot is clear ahead of time. The story is not invented, it is found—that is, it is known to the viewer from other films. Here it is only brought forward to him as a *film* story; the formal conclusions are so clear that not a single variation seems possible. When a variation does become possible (in the shot in which the actual murderer of the bridegroom is arrested by the police just before the bride can shoot him), one is disappointed because one takes this occurrence as a reversal in the fiction. Later, of course, everything runs its natural course. What baffles me about Truffaut's film? It seems to me that the director, although he sees more sharply than others, is still too short-sighted; the film dramaturgy is in no way abstract, but is very simply exploited. In this way, surely against the will of the author, the film becomes a near parody, and often the contra*diction* between the idyllic quality of the actual shot and the threatening quality of the entire film reminded me only of the old *Ladykillers:* the idyllic was only comic, a little enervating, perhaps with the giddy atmosphere of an English crime comedy. While the comedy makes the dramaturgy clear, the dramaturgy does not make the film into a comedy. Truffaut's film is not much less inoffensive as a comedy; he lacks Hitchcock's exact sincerity. Even the scene in which Jeanne Moreau seals, airtight, with adhesive tape, the door behind which she has confined one of her victims is, in an irritating way, comic, without really working comically. Of course, the shots *earlier* in the film allow this shot to work like a fairy tale, too.

Other attempts to abstract film to its syntax and then, after the reduction, to show images as examples of the syntax, so that the shot actually makes clear the artfulness of the images, are radical. Jean-Marie Straub's *Chronik der Anna Magdalena Bach* has shown the astounding possibilities of film, coupling the strongest and most precise calculation of shots with the strongest and most precise gracefulness—or better put, this film has proved that the most precise artistry leads to the strongest gracefulness. Similar results have been reached by Klaus Lemke with his first film, *48 Hours to Acapulco;* his second film, *Negresco,* went awry because the images also went awry; that is, they were overdeveloped, and the dialogue was babbled.

Examples of showing the syntax of films as the films themselves seem to be manifest above all in American underground films. *The Illiac Passion,* by George Makropoulos, is constructed so that a series of shots is given in a manner similar to a slide lecture. These shots are not, however, thrown one after another on the screen, but gradually, individually, rhythmically repeated and by the repetition formalized into a sequence of shots. As soon as the sequence is made clear, made *visible* in its rhythm, a strange image is injected into the sequence, foreign to the sequence; this strange image now serves as the image which will be rhythmically repeated in the next shot, in which another new image will also appear, which will be repeated in the next rhythmic film unit, whereupon the viewer, who now grasps the syntax, waits in tension for the strange image of this sequence, and so forth. The enormous *affect*ation of these films *effects* an experience which the viewer also *affects* and in which he, in *effect,* participates. A similar tension in viewing operates in the excellent film *Wavelength,* by Michael Snow, in which for forty-five minutes the camera shows nothing but a scantily furnished room. This film presents itself as *affected;* people and objects are not allowed to act, but instead the materials of the film, the film itself, acts—the lighting changes rhythmically, the colors change, so that we see the buses passing on the street once *outside,* or the house address across the street *outside;* then, however, the window to the outside world goes blank again, and only the *inside* of the room can be seen. In addition, a ghastly note of a pipe rises in the course of the film until it reaches the limits of sound. Shortly before the end of the film, after the camera has turned slowly around to a picture on the wall, the note breaks off. The picture on the wall is exactly the film image: a photograph of the sea, which the viewer observes for some minutes: the screen crackles, it is now so still.

The advances of film continue, to be sure. We consider them political, though at the same time asocial—more asocial than the advances of theatre, of which we have yet to speak. And as in the theatre, the great "problem films"— those which concern themselves with (unfortunately) truly eternal questions— appear as art films. It no longer holds true, as Walter Benjamin claimed, that as a consequence of its technical reproducibility, film has nothing of the ritual artistic aura. This might still have been true in 1930; today, however, it seems that that very technical reproducibility of film has given it the ability to create illusions of the second grade, naive illusions which the theatre no longer achieves today. How often do you hear, for example, people say, who claim to have seen through the theatre's pretensions to Art, that they "prefer to go to the movies, only, of course, when a truly artistic film, a film worth seeing, is playing"? *Blow-Up,* the Bergman films, Fellini films, the films of Godard replace, for such people, the Hamlet-aura which, we understand, they can no longer endure. These films, precisely because they are reproducible and two-dimensional, raise for the public the great questions of being (three-dimensional). It seems that the formal three-dimensionality of the ordinary theatre conflicts with the promoted three-dimensionality of theme. The artistic quality of the flat screen, however, distances and allows the remaining *space* all the big questions. Problem films are the most dishonest genre films because they—in contrast to crime films and so forth—pretend to be so frightfully real and natural because they use the rules of play, but do not make them recognizable: a film about love, a film about suffering, a film about death—each is a genre film. Death, whenever filmed, has rules of play; most of these films do not show that. They have also become edifying experiences; even the cost of admission approximates that of the theatre.

What effect the restrictions of production have, I do not know, nor whether they are more serious in the theatre or in film. Already the costs of production are leading in the direction that the producer, if he wants to continue to produce, must eliminate every radical thought because of economic considerations. The asocially existing social film—the underground film—exists less easily than the asocially existing social theatre. The theatre can afford, in the economic sense, to exist a little asocially; even the small theatre has a position of some importance in the business structure. Underground films, however, have not yet created any such position of importance in business. Not only are they denied publicity; they are also denied publication. The self-proclaimed, as well as the actually, radical theatre, on the other hand, can count at least on worldwide publication if not, in fact, on publicity. The radical film, unfortunately, has been able to produce no public interest. Straub's film can be shown only in Sunday matinees before startled Bach lovers.

Theatre, on the other hand, has publicity. The business system is such that what happens on stage will be discussed in any case. Events of the theatre are, at least, made public. The theatre has a claim to publication from tradition. By a right of custom the theatre has become and remained an indirect means of mass communication. Had it, of course, by its reactionary method of communication forfeited that claim, it would need the administration of the State, and could not rely on so-called diversity of opinion. In this way the theatre has an unearned right to publicity which, however, its promoters earned. We will follow up on that. The administrator should earn this right to publicity! The theatre has a good possibility of squeezing through, because it also likes to be scornful as an institution. The theatre can be craftily employed—with it one can dispossess oneself from merely *private* expressions: one makes himself public. Of course, a blind self-exposure is insignificant in received dramaturgy and more painful than the same blindness in film. But there are examples of the possibility of theatre to display direct—not reproduced—movements, words, and actions, which have an effect only because they are presented live, not reproduced. If they were filmed, they would be artificial in a quite *natural, usual* manner, while in the theatre they operate immediately, directly, spatially. They are *artificially* artificial; they are *in the making* and not *made*. In Paris I recently saw the Bread and Puppet Theatre from New York, which convinced me of the possibilities, not of theatre, but of direct presentation of actions. The traditional dramaturgy, which recognizes only action and words which *serve* the story, is reduced to actions and words, noises and clangs themselves; they become incidents which show nothing else, but present themselves as theatrical events. Actions act themselves and words talk themselves. The viewer, who awaits in the theatre the resolution of every word and every action, the thematic sense, the story, will be left with the action alone. The raising of a hand is a story. Buzzing is a story. Sitting, lying, and standing are stories. A very exciting story is the striking of a hammer against iron. Every word, every sound, every movement is a story: they lead to nothing, they remain visible for themselves alone. Every utterance is *made;* no action results naturally from the preceding action; no utterance means anything other than itself—it signifies itself. An unheard-of simultaneity of sight, breath, and discrimination is created. The space forms a theatrical unity, in which one becomes increasingly self-conscious and tense, almost to the point that the socially protective adhesive tape with which everyone wraps himself is ripped, is no longer visible, not only without, but also within, in the consciousness of the viewer.

This intense artificiality is replaced in the movies by a technical artificiality: here the theatre, as direct presentation, has one possibility *more* than film. The theatre has the possibility of becoming more artificial, and in that way it is endlessly *unusual*, unfamiliar. It can fully utilize the mechanism of the viewer, in order to bring him to confusion. As long as it is that way, I prefer of course to go to the movies. But I less like to write a filmscript than a play. The misery of comparison.

A Conversation
with Harold Pinter

Mel Gussow

. . .

MG: *What are you working on now, in 1971?*

HP: Unfortunately, I'm not in a position to tell you. It is very, very likely that I'm going to enter into a film which is going to be the most difficult task I've ever had in my life—and one which is almost impossible. I'm pretty frightened, but I'm also excited. The thing is, it isn't absolutely concrete.

MG: *Would you be interested in directing a film?*

HP: Yes, I would. I've written one film script which I want to direct. But I can't get the money for it, not with the kind of artistic freedom I want. It's an adaptation of a novel by Aidan Higgins, called *Langrishe, Go Down*. It's a curious title. It's on a subject which doesn't seem to be very appealing. It's about three middle-aged spinsters living in a house in Ireland in the 1930s. At the lodge gate there's a cottage and a Ger-

Excerpted from Mel Gussow, *Conversations with Harold Pinter* (London: Nick Hern, 1994), 36–39, 45, 52–53, 72–73, 88–91, 100, 116–118, 134–139, 145–146.

man philosophy student in his thirties working on a thesis. Now they don't seem to feel this is the brightest subject. [Laugh.]

MG: Of course if you let them name three leading actresses—Vanessa Redgrave, Jane Fonda . . .

HP: Exactly. You hit the nail right on the head. That's the kind of freedom I'm talking about.

MG: How have you chosen your films? Or have they chosen you?

HP: They've been proposed to me.

MG: Not a case of you sitting down and reading The Servant *or* Accident *or* The Go-Between, *and saying I simply must do this?*

HP: It's always been Joe Losey who's given me the books to read. But of course I have been asked to do many other things and declined. These are quite rare items. I've chosen them because I thought something sparked.

MG: Do films act as a chance to get away from a certain part of yourself? The atmospheres are different than in your plays?

HP: I think you may be right. It never occurred to me, actually.

MG: Accident *and* The Go-Between *deal with time, as do your last three plays. Is there a correlation? Is the past much more of an artistic concern?*

HP: Oh, yes, it is. I think I'm more conscious of a kind of ever-present quality in life.

MG: Is it your age?

HP: It may be. It may be. I certainly feel more and more that the past is not past, that it never was past. It's present.

MG: What's future?

HP: I know the future is simply going to be the same thing. It'll never end. You carry all the states with you until the end.

MG: You're always the sum of your previous parts?

HP: But those previous parts are alive and present. The only time I can ever be said to live in the present is when I'm engaged in some physical activity. Really do forget.

MG: Like cricket?

HP: Yes, or squash, for instance. The concentration on the present seems to be absolutely total.

MG: You don't think about past cricket matches?

HP: Not when I'm absolutely engaged.

MG: You don't feel that when you're writing a play?

HP: No. When I'm writing a play I don't know what's coming in. It's coming from somewhere. It isn't the present moment alone, by any means. What it all comes down to is time—your original question. The whole question of time and all its reverberations and possible meanings really does seem to absorb me more and more.

MG: What's in your future?

HP: I don't know what I'll do. I have no idea what's to come, really. I've always been left with this empty space in front of me after finishing a play. And it gets longer and longer.

MG: After The Homecoming *did you feel you wouldn't write a play again?*

HP: Yes. I certainly did. Very, very depressing.

MG: What did you do?

HP: I kept busy I suppose, one way or the other. Films, I suppose. It's not quite the same thing as something really coming out from the bottom of your spine. Words anyway become more difficult all the time, the older you get. What else can one possibly write? Something seems to happen. I feel quite cheerful about the prospect in front of me.

. . .

MG: There's a phrase that Martin Esslin used about Betrayal—*the "fallibility of memory." In* Old Times, No Man's Land, *and* Betrayal, *you never know if certain things did or did not take place. The subject of memory seems to interest you more and more. Do you find yourself, in 1979, thinking about your past? Does your work on the screenplay for Proust's* Remembrance of Things Past *bear a responsibility here?*

HP: I wrote *Landscape* and *Silence and Old Times* before I wrote the Proust screenplay, and it is certainly true that those plays concern themselves with memory and the past. But Proust did open up a hell of a world for me. It was really a great year working on Proust, although the screenplay can never in any way rival the work which it served, and which is an evident masterpiece. I've just done another screenplay, by the way. *The French Lieutenant's Woman.* That's been bloody, bloody hard. It's a remarkable book. The problems involved in transposing it to film are quite considerable. It pretends to be a Victorian novel, but it isn't. It's a modern novel, and it's made clear by the author that he's writing it now. That whole idea had to be retained.

MG: *How did you do it? Does the novelist tell the story?*

HP: Ah, well, I'm not going to tell you the secret. Karel Reisz [the director] and I just stumbled upon a way of looking at it, which I hope mirrors what the author [John Fowles] does in his original.

MG: *Once again, you're dealing with the past, with memory. How is your memory?*

HP: I have a strange kind of memory. I think I really look back into a kind of fog most of the time, and things loom out of the fog. Some things I have to force myself to remember. I bring them back by an act of will. It appalls me that I've actually forgotten things, which at the time meant a great deal to me.

. . .

HP: I wrote *One for the Road* in 1984. It's taken me four years to write a twenty-minute play. [Laugh.] I must have been doing something else during all this time.

MG: *You've also been writing movies.*

HP: I've written three scripts in the last two years, 1986–1988, movies which all have to do, one way or another, with political states of affairs. *The Handmaid's Tale*—that's Margaret Atwood's projection into a possible United States twenty-five to thirty years from now. The one that's just been shot is *Reunion* by Fred Uhlman. He was a German painter who wrote this one novella, which is about Stuttgart in 1932, about a Jewish boy and a German boy who were great friends. The Jewish boy is sent away by his parents to New York and goes back to Germany fifty-five years later, and meanwhile his parents committed suicide and his best friend became a Nazi. The other one is an adaptation of *The Heat of the Day* by Elizabeth Bowen. It deals with a British officer who is working for the Germans; he believes the Germans are right.

MG: *These are in contrast to your earlier screenplays,* The Servant, Accident, The Go-Between, *which may have had some political message but* . . .

HP: *The Servant* is about the English caste system.

MG: Turtle Diary *has no political message.*

HP: No, *Turtle Diary* is about lonely people. But there's a link between all these concerns in the end. Don't you think?

MG: *A distinction could be made between your early plays and movies and your current ones.*

HP: I cannot say that every work I've written is political. There's nothing political about *Landscape*. What the hell is political about *Old Times?* I would say, nothing. But I feel the question of how power is used and how violence is used, how you terrorize somebody, how you subjugate somebody, has always been alive in my work.

. . .

MG: *Your next project is writing a screenplay of Kafka's* The Trial. *Why* The Trial *now, in 1989?*

HP: I read *The Trial* when I was a lad of eighteen, in 1948. It's been with me ever since. I don't think anyone who reads *The Trial*—it ever leaves them, although it can be curiously distorted by time. Speaking to a number of people, who remember having read it when they were young, they look back and think it's a political book. They rather tend to think it's like Arthur Koestler. In my view, it isn't at all. I admire Koestler, but I wouldn't be interested in writing a screenplay of *Darkness at Noon,* because it's so specifically of its time and place. But *The Trial* is not that case at all. I find it very difficult to talk about, except that it has been with me for forty years, and I've had a whale of a time over the last few months entering into Kafka's world. The nightmare of that world is precisely in its ordinariness. That is what is so frightening and strong.

So I don't regard *The Trial* as a particularly political work, though I think bureaucracy figures very strongly in it, obviously. There's a very deep religious conundrum in it. A lot of people think that Kafka was writing about Communism. He actually wrote the book before the Russian revolution. His reference of course was the Austro-Hungarian empire. Prague, which we see in the film, has those great pillars, the bank, a very strong solid world indeed, with a worm of anxiety in the very middle of it. Looking back, or rather, looking forward, you can see elements where a society in a very surreptitious and appalling way is grinding you into the dust.

MG: And you certainly are aware of Orson Welles's film.

HP: Yes. Orson Welles was a genius but I think his film was quite wrong because he made it into an incoherent nightmare of spasmodic half-adjusted lines, images, effects in fact. As I said, I don't think Kafka is at all about affect, effect, but about something that happens on Monday, and then on Tuesday, and then on Wednesday and then right through the week. This man in *The Trial* is arrested one morning in his bed by two people and he is then let out, he goes to his job, a case is taking place. There seems to be a kind of implacable but invisible force and he is finally executed. The important thing about it is that he fights like hell all the way along the line. It reminded me of the shot in John Ford's film, *The Grapes of Wrath,* when the man is protecting his shack as the tractor comes up: "If you go any further, I'll shoot your head off." The fellow takes off his goggles and says, "There's no point doing that because I'm going to knock your house down. I'm getting paid for that and if I don't do it there'll be another guy who will." He says, "I'll still knock your head off." "Then you'll have to shoot the other guy's head off. You've got to go to the bank in Oklahoma City, and you'll have to shoot all of them. Then you'll have to go to the bank in New York. How many people can you shoot?" He says, "Get out of my damn way," and he knocks the house down. One of the most terrible sequences in cinema, in a wonderful film. That's what Kafka's looking at: whom do you shoot?

MG: Would you ever have considered turning The Trial *into a play rather than a screenplay?*

HP: No. I can't do that. I never adapted anything to the stage. It's not my thing. I enjoy cinema very much. I always have. I've enjoyed all my work in the cinema, without exception really. I think I'm very fortunate in that of course, because I know what normally happens to writers working in the film industry. I've been fortunate—in the people with whom I've worked. Clive Donner, for instance, who directed the film of *The Caretaker.* You see, there's a sort of compulsion in film makers to "open out" (whatever that means) subjects that they set out to film. But we decided from the beginning that this approach was a blind alley. It seemed to us that within the situation, and within the relationships that developed between the characters, there was enough action, enough excitement seen through the eye of a film camera, without imposing conventional film action treatment. It seemed to us that when you have two people standing on the stairs and one asks the other if he would like to be caretaker in this house, and the other bloke, you know, who is work-shy, doesn't want in fact to say no, he doesn't want the job, but at the same time he wants to edge it around. . . . Now it seems to me there's an enormous amount of internal conflict within one of the characters and external conflict between them—and it's exciting cinema. The fact that it doesn't cover enormous landscapes and there aren't hordes of horses galloping in one direction and hordes of bison in the other has nothing to do with it. It's a different sort of action, but it's still action. And it's still capable of being encompassed in the cinema. You can say the play has been "opened out" in the sense that things I'd yearned to do, without knowing it, in writing for the stage, crystallized when I came to think about it as a film. Until then I didn't know that I wanted to do them because I'd accepted the limitations of the stage. For instance, there's a scene in the garden of the house, which is very silent; two silent figures with a third looking on. I think in the film one has been able to hit the relationship of the brothers more clearly than in the play.

MG: *Do you mean when you say that the film developed on what had happened for you in the theater, with particular reference to the relationship between the brothers, that the psychological richness of the original play was to a certain extent hampered by the need to project out into a theater?*

HP: Yes, I think the actors on the stage are under the delusion that they have to project in a particular way. There's a scene in the film, also in the play, when the elder brother asks the other if he'd like to be caretaker in the place. On film it's played in terms of great intimacy and I think it's extraordinarily successful. They speak quite normally, it's a quiet scene, and it works. But on stage it didn't ever work like that. The actors get a certain kind of comfort, I think, in the fact that they're so close to the camera.

MG: *Can't the cinema deal with that very much more subtly and specifically? Isn't the writing such that* The Caretaker *isn't a piece of theater, but can go further and further and discover more and more facts to the characters, so that rather than repeating what happened in the theater one can enrich and develop it much more surely?*

HP: I'm not sure I agree that the cinema will be able to gain in subtlety. I think that when one talks in these terms one thinks of a stage miles away with a vast audience and the characters very small. But I think you can be as subtle on a stage as you can in the film. You just do it in a different way. In this case the director understood what was necessary and what I, the fellow who had written it, meant. Which is a very rare thing. I'd always understood that everything is always bastardized in films, and that film people were a real lot of fakes, phonies, charlatans. The whole relationship between the people concerned was something I hadn't quite met in any medium.

MG: *Did you ever think you might do it in a studio?*

HP: No, never! I wish the actors were here to ask, but I'm sure that for them it was tremendous—I'm sorry to say this, it sounds rather strange, almost as if I'm asking for realism, which I'm not—but I think it did an awful lot for the actors to go up real stairs, open real doors in a house which existed, with a dirty garden and a back wall.

MG: *You were there every minute of the shooting?*

HP: Not entirely. I arrived late quite often. I don't know whether other script writers are there to the extent I was.

MG: *How did you react to it?*

HP: As a complete layman to the film medium, I found that looking around that room where one had to crouch to see what was going on (the whole film was shot in a kneeling or crouching posture)—I found there was a smell to it. Since then I've been down to a studio, Shepperton, and things are very different. You don't have to crouch, you don't have to kneel, you can absolutely stand up straight, there are lots of lights, the walls open, they float, that's the word, float, and you've got no worries at all. Well, I found the limitations on location, in this house, gave a freshness to the work. I think the actors found that, too. They found new answers, answers they hadn't been able to find or at least hadn't within the circumstances been able to find when they were playing it on the stage. What I'm very pleased about myself is that in the film, as opposed to the play, we see a real house and real snow outside, dirty snow, and the streets. We don't see them very often but they're there, the backs of houses and windows, attics in the distance. There is actually sky as well, a dirty one, and these characters move in the context of a real world—as I believe they do. In the play, when people were confronted with just a set, a room and a door, they often assumed it was all taking place in limbo, in a vacuum, and the world outside hardly existed, or had existed at some point but was only half-remembered. Now one thing which I think is triumphantly expressed in the film is Clive's concentration on the characters when they are outside the room, outside the house. Not that there aren't others. There are others. There are streets, there is traffic, shadows, shapes about, but he is for me concentrating on the characters as they walk, and while we go into the world outside it is almost as if only these characters exist.

MG: What struck me just now was your thoroughness in following the film through the editing stages.

HP: Well, this editing stage was for me, of course, completely new. It was the first time, and an absolute eye opener.

MG: I can see you were enjoying it.

HP: It's great. It's great that one can move from one thing to another, or duplicate it, or cut it out.

MG: But you must have been involved in television productions, and to that extent you must have had some feeling for what happened and what you could do. You know what pictures roughly you're going to use, in about the same way as you know in a film.

HP: But it's very primitive. All that's open to you is just a position of sequences, or possibly cuts, but you haven't got the flexibility that you have in films. For instance in this particular play, there was a moment on stage when the two brothers smiled at each other. That was it. One stood on one side of the stage and the other stood on the other, and they smiled briefly.

MG: That was written into the text?

HP: Oh yes. And then one of them exited and that was that. Now, on film, either you're going to hold both things, in other words, the two brothers smiling, then one goes out. But it isn't the same as the stage, you don't get the complex thing which makes it so much of a moment on the stage. The distance, the separation cannot be the same. The balance, the timing, and the rhythm to this, the silent music, as it were, are determined in so many different ways, and I know we both felt, Clive and I, that there was something to come there. I said something, I don't know what, and Clive said, "We want to go from one to the other, one to the other." Now the balance of the whole thing is that if you don't go to the other then there's no point made, but if you go from the other back to the first then the point is over-made. The balance, the editing balance, is crucial, as everyone knows, but it needs an eye and a relaxation which the film affords you, and no other medium can. You can sift it, you see, and the sifting is of value. Of course, on the stage, you can say to the girl, "Go out, this won't do, try another one . . ." And if you make a decision and you're proved wrong, you correct it. But in films you're dealing with something that's going to be finished once you make a decision. You cannot go on changing ad infinitum, and you may make a decision and six months later you say, "That was entirely wrong."

To a certain extent, in the theater, one entrusts the satisfactory presentation of this moment of the smile entirely to the actors. You expect that they have either consciously or intuitively sensed the way an audience is going with them and the play at a particular moment, and they can adjust their performance each night, to each audience. Now one of the things that actors feel terribly strongly about in the cinema is that their performances are taken out of their hands. They resent this, and I understand it completely. It seems to me a miserable thing to have to accept, particularly with the sort of actors we have in this film, who are extremely intelligent men, extremely successful, extremely creative. They do it, then they go away to other films, other projects, and leave us with the film to edit in a way that ultimately we have to take a decision alone. Well, as I say, you may decide at this moment that one thing is right, and six months later you see it, and you say, "I was wrong"—and actors, alas, have to accept this. Surely with this film, though, all the actors would subscribe to what is being done. Because we weren't asking them merely to go on there and give their performances as such; we were asking to examine how you should give your performance in relation to producing a finished film. To take creative responsibility, which is the aim of all these ventures, I think. In any event, *The Caretaker* has been preserved on film, I believe it's perfectly true to what I wrote, and I think it's funny.

. . .

MG: *1993's* Moonlight *is your first full-length play in fifteen years. Can you say what enabled you to overcome your writer's block?*

HP: I really would like to say something about this question of a writer's block. You're quite entitled to call it a writer's block, and a lot of people have been talking about a writer's block. But the fact is, I have written—whether people like them or not, or think they're "too short"—I have actually written six plays since 1978. I have also written seven screenplays, including *The French Lieutenant's Woman* and *The Trial.* Actually eight, including *The Remains of the Day,* which we'll come to later, so it's eight screenplays. Now in these screenplays, I don't just transcribe the novel; otherwise you might as well do the novel. In other words, these are acts of the imagination on my part!

As for the plays, I believe that, in their own ways, they are works of substance. If you write a poem, it really doesn't matter whether the poem is two pages long or four lines. I think this whole question of length has become an obsession.

MG: Every one of your screenplays has been an adaptation. Haven't you been tempted to write an original?

HP: No. I've never had the impulse.

MG: It's been a different author each time. How do you choose your films?

HP: They're almost invariably offered to me. Ironically, the only one that wasn't offered to me was *The Remains of the Day*. I read the book in proof and bought an option. Then it became a best seller. There were a number of inquiries which I didn't want to pursue. Then Mike Nichols suddenly called and said I just read this book and tried to find out who had the film rights and it turned out to be you. I said that's right. He and I worked together. I did a screenplay. Mike simply couldn't get a budget that would suit him. It started to wobble. Suddenly, Ivory-Merchant came into it, wanted to do it, and that all went immediately like that [snaps fingers] because *Howard's End* had been a big success. Tony Hopkins was already in it. I met Ivory and Merchant once and they didn't really discuss the screenplay, which they'd read, obviously. We talked about locations and actors, and we parted, and I never heard another word. I got one letter about three or four months later. They just went to Ruth Prawer Jhabvala, who wrote them a totally new screenplay, which they're doing. There's one thing for the record. Merchant has been saying one thing: that I approve and I'm a part of it. It's not so. I've withdrawn my name from the film.

MG: Did they want to credit the screenplay to the two of you?

HP: Yes. But I wouldn't. I've never done that in my life. It's her screenplay, though they have used a number of my scenes.

MG: Your Losey films stand up.

HP: Oh, I think so too. *The Servant, Accident,* and *The Go-Between*—and *Proust.* I worked with him a great deal and still miss him. That was a really rich working relationship, and I was very fond of him . . .

MG: Do you go to the movies often?

HP: Not often . . . You know American movies meant an awful lot to me. I was brought up on them. I had a very rich cinematic education, much more than the theatre. I never went to the theatre.

MG: What movies did you see?

HP: I'm talking about the 1940s. I saw all the American black-and-white gangster films, which were great.

MG: Bogart, Cagney, Robinson?

HP: Oh, yeah. I didn't miss one. And later William Bendix, Alan Ladd, Brian Donlevy. *The Glass Key.* All those B films. Franchot Tone, Elisha Cook, Jr. I saw *The Ox-Bow Incident* and John Ford's *The Grapes of Wrath.* Then *The Long Voyage Home,* which left a great impression on me. At the same time, at the age of fourteen, I joined the local film club, and I ran right into Eisenstein and Pudovkin and Dovzhenko, *The Cabinet of Dr. Caligari*—and Buñuel and Cocteau. I saw *L'Âge d'Or* and *Chien Andalou* when I was fourteen. That was my language, apart from reading. The theatre didn't really come into it until much later.

MG: Have films been an influence on your work? Buñuel on Party Time?

HP: I suppose I never ask myself that. The American thrillers, there was something to do with the language then, very sharp, very terse [snaps fingers] and Hemingwayish. I was reading Hemingway at the time.

MG: It was the American not the British movies.

HP: I omitted one other element, the British war films. I don't know if you ever saw *The Way Ahead.* It was a great British war film, with David Niven, Carol Reed directed it, and Peter Ustinov wrote the script. Vivien [Merchant] was in it. She was nine. She played Stanley Holloway's daughter. He came back from the war. There's a scene where she's nine years old and playing the radio. She was a funny looking little girl. It was a nice little scene. She would always tell the story that she was taken by her mother, and she was called back and called back and she finally got the part. She said to herself, I must be the prettiest girl here. Actually quite the opposite was the case. But it was a damned good film. And the French cinema. Carné. Duvivier. *Carnet du Bal.* I even saw *Que viva Mexico!*

MG: Did this make you want to be an actor, or a writer?

HP: Just as a plain old moviegoer.

MG: Any favorite among the actors?

HP: I fell in love quite a lot in those days, with people like Veronica Lake. I was crazy about Gene Tierney. Lana Turner. And an English actress called Patricia Roc. It was a long time ago. I was also in on *The Naked City,* Jules Dassin. I thought *The Ox-Bow Incident* was a great film. William Wellman, Henry Fonda, a young Anthony Quinn, and Dana Andrews. I was very pleased when we did *The Last Tycoon* many, many years later; we had a hell of a cast list. De Niro and Robert Mitchum and also Dana Andrews, Ray Milland, and John Carradine!

MG: Any movies coming up?

HP: Not at the moment. [Pause.] I have a certain sense that the kind of way I worked in movies over all these years is narrowing. I suppose I take this from the experience with *The Remains of the Day:* writing a script and then the director getting someone else to write a script. That never happened to me over all this time. My position is: I've always written a screenplay, and that's the screenplay that's been done. The only exception, slightly, was *The Handmaid's Tale,* which I stopped writing, because I was exhausted. I told Volker Schlöndorff to go and get Margaret Atwood to do whatever. What he really did was to get the actors to write a lot of it, although there's still a lot of my stuff in it. That was a bit of a stew, but there was enough of me to still keep my name on it. *The Remains of the Day,* as I told you, is a totally different story.

MG: Did you get paid for The Remains of the Day?

HP: Oh, yes. I did indeed. I had my contractual rights, clear and concrete. Nevertheless, payment or no payment, it's a disappointment. I worked quite a long time at it. But it's all over. I'm not crying about it. I simply never found myself in that tradition, the tradition of many writers being brought in to script a film. The classic Hollywood tradition.

MG: Will you do fewer screenplays or start more projects yourself?

HP: I think that will probably be the thing. But I really still do find film a fascinating craft. It's rather nice for a change to be flexible and on your toes. I have no actual plans, which is great. It's been a hell of a busy year.

A Conversation with Wole Soyinka

James Gibbs

Q: *Has it been proved that drama, because it has a popular base, is a more powerful force for making social analysis and criticism than other art forms?*

S: I think the very property of the theatre, which is one of enactment, lends itself to many interpretive channels and this makes it a more powerful force for social comment than other forms, the novel if you like. The question in a play is constantly being re-examined, re-examined in the light of new information, of new developments in society and of the increasing awareness of the participants in any play. Since theatre, even at the most audience-remote in the West, is still a participant medium—I mean the company cannot go on the stage and act to itself, it has to interact with the audience, so there is always a level of participation. And this interrogates constantly the situation within the place, this permanent question and answer being given in any per-

Originally published in *Literary Half-Yearly* 28, no. 2 (July 1987). Excerpted from *Conversations with Wole Soyinka* (Jackson: University Press of Mississippi, 2001), 76–115.

formance. Of course in societies where the level of participation, of interaction, is even greater the theatre becomes very obviously a tool for social analysis.

Q: What is the ideal number of characters for a play?

S: Well, if you are in the United States of America and you want to write for Broadway, you have a choice of extremes. In other words there are producers who will not look at your play unless it has a cast of thousands. You know, the Hal Prince kind of producer who loves huge spectaculars on stage. On the other hand there are probably even more producers with whom you will score if you can write a play with only two or three characters. In the European and American theatre about half the plays which are enjoying any kind of a successful run have just two or three characters. It's purely an economic thing. It costs them so much to put on a play that only those who have access to bankers and consortiums could actually consider a play with a cast of half a dozen; the others will look asquint unless there are only two or three parts. A form of criticism has even developed—very fascinating to me—in which they looked to see if someone had ever written a play with a cast of more than six—if he had, then he was a renegade and a reactionary. But that's by the way.

Since you and I, however, are not, I think, basically concerned with Broadway or the European theatre, it is very likely that we will continue to write plays which are numerically determined by the theme of the play, the situation. I think what will happen is that you will tend to leave that headache to the director who decides that the play is fascinating enough and, however many or however few characters are in it, will decide to do something about it—because I always insist that between the playwright and the audience stands the director. Plays which have been written for casts of a hundred have been performed successfully sometimes with a cast of ten or fifteen. Something is lost in the process, but other things miraculously are gained. Suddenly there are new perceptions, new precisions, which would have been diffused by the multiplicity of minor roles in the play. Shakespeare's plays today are being performed by casts half the size he ever intended for them. So I would say "Don't worry about the size of the cast when you are writing a play."

But if you are writing for a company—that again is something I have done—in which I have a particular group in mind, a group with which I am working all the time. There's a theme I have in mind and we literally create the play or the sketch together. But that is an instance where you are governed by the company, because you are acting there both as a playwright and as director.

Q: Do you know exactly what will happen in a play when you sit down to write it or do you just have a basic idea?

S: A very good question and one which is answered "yes" and "no." "Yes" there have been plays in which the idea was so compact from beginning to end, everything was set and it followed the pattern in my mind, straight, all the way through. An example is *Death and the King's Horseman*—there was no doubt at all. The same thing with *The Lion and the Jewel.* On the other hand you have plays, like *Madmen and Specialists,* which did not follow the original conception. So . . . it happens both ways.

Q: Should a young playwright try to incorporate music and dance into his play?

S: It is important to make the play organic, do not incorporate music and dance in a contrived way. There is no question at all that any play which succeeds in integrating music, dance, masks and so on is at least one dimension richer than the purely literary form of theatre. And there is no shortage of themes at all in African society which provide the opportunity to indulge in musical drama if that is your forte. The South African theatre is an example of that: a lot of South African plays grew from street music and other areas provide similar examples.

Q: How can the theatre compete with soccer and music for attention?

S: Well, I have to consider that I have a problem here—a very serious problem. This problem has to do with the fact that I come from an advantaged area, one in which people go to see plays. I mean all that one of the folk opera troupes has to do is arrive in the morning, drum through the city, go through the town in a hired lorry with posters on it saying: "We are appearing at so-and-so place tonight" and believe me two hours before the play is due to begin the place is already full. So I have a problem in answering your question.

To move away from that and to keep looking at parallels outside to assure ourselves that some of the problems we are discussing here are not unique, I remember a quarrel I had with Arnold Wesker. Wesker belonged to the bossy Social Reality school which began in the late '50s, towards the '60s, the departure from the old drawing-room drama of Agatha Christie's *The Mousetrap* and so on. I saw Wesker's *The Kitchen,* which is one of the most beautiful plays I have ever seen, it is a strong bit of working-class slice-of-life and shows the pressures which in humdrum employment can build up to an explosion in an unrelieved, desocialized environment. But I began to wonder about this when Wesker began complaining about the working class being apathetic towards his theatre. (He felt, I suppose, he should have been supported because he was dealing with working-class conditions. He was writing the history of the working class movement in England, in plays such as *Chicken Soup with Barley, I'm Talking about Jerusalem* and so on). He sort of felt that the working-class should be flocking to see his plays and I said: "Why the hell should they? This reality is so much part and parcel of their lives that maybe they don't want to see it on the stage." One must make sure that one talks relevantly to his prospective audience and that means relevant in terms, in terms of structure, form, symbols, metaphors. You must be able to engage them in a mutually creative way. They themselves must feel that they are part and parcel of the creative process. But at the same time there is a danger in getting too close, in which case they will say: "Oh, I've lived through *that!*" "I don't want to see *this* as a special event."

Q: What has been your experience of building plays through improvization and how do plays constructed by this means differ from those created by more conventional methods?

S: Well, the plays which have come out of improvization—I always use the term "sketches" because that's really what they are usually, short "sketches"—I find them very rewarding because they are usually directed at a social anomaly, they are meant to challenge the corrupt or repressive authority and that, of course, brings out a level of commitment which is proportionate to the artistic energy which writers bring to their work. So improvization has always been for me a period of intense participation and activity, total involvement, because one not only actually sees the work itself taking shape, but one is reexamining all the time the problems which produce the sketch in the first place. One is, in effect, debating the socio-politics of the situation all the time and, of course, this goes on during informal discussions, and one gets far more educated as a result of this activity. And when we present it before the public there is instant communication, an instant learning-teaching session and, of course, one of the effects of this is that it is highly embarrassing to authority. But it is a different level of creative involvement from sitting down at a typewriter and bashing things out that way.

Q: Do you learn much from your critics?

S: Very, very rarely. I don't think I have ever learnt anything. In fact I stopped reading any criticism of my work for a number of years and only started again when a new pattern of criticism developed from within my own immediate environment. This prompted me to take a look at even what others had been writing for some time. All it did was make me take up my pen and start criticising the critics for ignorance, for basic ignorance as to what theatre of literature is about. In fact there is an on-going battle, a battle royal, right now in African universities on that score.

Q: To what extent do you regard directing a play or the production of a play as an essential part of creating of that play? Is the production a separate part of the process or merely a continuation of the initial impetus?

S: A sensible question and the answer is very simple—for me a play on the page is really cold and dead and my real instinct has always been to see the play fleshed out. I don't feel that the play is completed until I've actually seen it live on the stage. I think I am as much a director as I am a playwright, and when I begin to direct a play I have no respect at all for my text. This has shocked a number of the actors I've worked with. You know actors love their lines. They come and say: "Wole, How can you do this? These are the best lines in the play?" I had this experience most tellingly when I directed *Death and the King's Horseman* at the Goodman Theatre in Chicago. The actors would love these lines and so on, but the lines were just not working for that particular production and so they had to go. They just couldn't believe it. "You can't do this to yourself!" "Oh yes I can!" The two functions, of writer and director, are not really separate. I think I've found that I just look at the text very coldly when I'm directing. It doesn't mean that the lines are useless, but if they are not working for any reason either because of the actor, or the time factor, or something else, say the actual environment. . . . This example was very interesting actually. We were doing *Death and the King's Horseman* in a theatre which was used for Saroyan and Arthur Miller and Eugene O'Neill, the occasional Greek play, one or two modern American playwrights with their very peculiar language—which they call English. I don't know it is! I was working also with black actors who came into the theatre thinking that because they were black therefore they understood the play. So I had to break that down and make them understand that they were just as much strangers to the play as any whites, because this play was from a totally different society. In fact at one time I swore that if I ever met the man or woman who invented the saying that "Black people have a natural sense of rhythm," I was going to decapitate that person immediately, because if there was anything more humbling to those black actors, it was that they could *not* move to the rhythm of the African dances, drums, and so on because they had become so accustomed to the disco culture. For everything which had the slightest bit of subtlety beyond the disco beat, they were lost. Many of them were tone deaf, which they could not believe. They were used to singing all the "yeah, yeah, yeah!" and they had ear-phones clamped to their ears! When I played them the tapes which I had brought from home of some of the songs and said: "You have to learn this now," they weren't into what they thought. But by the time they finished they admitted that they had learned from the experience. They formed themselves into a repertory company and they said they didn't want to go back to whatever they were doing before. Again that was part of the training programme. I just would not settle for their approximations. I felt they really had to break down their bones, get them to learn new auditory habits, hear new sounds, sounds they never knew existed. That meant that even though they spoke "English" they had to learn to read it in a rhythm, that was not British R. P. That is a rhythm I needed for what the language of English is saying in my own language. They had to find a totally new way of saying those lines and, in fact, one famous actress who was playing the lead role had to drop out after two weeks of rehearsal because she could not do it. She had done the classics but she couldn't cope with this! It is an interesting experience working on one's own script if one can divorce oneself from the role of playwright.

Playwrights are a nuisance anyway in the theatre when you are rehearsing. I always lock them out until a week or so to the performance, then their suggestions are welcome. Their advice may not be taken but at least I can afford to listen.

Q: Do you allow those who are directing your plays to take the same unsentimental attitude to your text?

S: Yes. I stay out.

Q: Do you mind if directors change your text?

S: I no longer have any control over the text and I believe that new insights come to a production during rehearsal and also when a play is looked at by somebody else. But, at the same time, I don't believe in undue liberties. I feel free to criticise in the harshest language whatever anybody does with my play—if I agree to see it at all! In the same way as I expect the playwright to chase me around with a club when I've finished with his play, I have to accept full responsibility for what I've done to his play and I don't want him to interfere. If I need clarification, which of course one does from time to time, we'll go out together for a drink and just talk around the subject till I draw out from him—without his knowing—what I really want to know and that's enough. That's all the help I want.

Q: How do you audition actors for a production?

S: Auditioning is very difficult, it is very easy to goof. Whenever possible—I'll let you into the secret: when I have a production on, I find an excuse for somebody to, not necessarily "throw a party," but to have a "function," an occasion at which the potential actors will be at their most relaxed. Let's say, you organize a meeting: "There's going to be a meeting for the play and all whose who are interested . . . " (You can do this sort of thing in a university atmosphere). And before the meeting starts—maybe by "accident"—you reveal that someone is celebrating a birthday, there are going to be drinks around, you invite them to come a little earlier, you watch them when they are unselfconscious, watch them very closely and make notes about their temperaments, the rhythms of their bodies, of how they react in dialogue with other people, that sort of thing. That tells you a lot, I find, about an actor's potential for a role. After that, you build on it; you do a reading, in which sometimes I make people just read the dialogue. And after that you begin the process of really winnowing down the possibilities, you have a few more individual auditions. By the time you have reached that stage you are pretty sure who is getting to do what. I find that I derive most of my information from throwing the actors and actresses into an unselfconscious situation where you can observe without being observed.

Q: What is the best relationship between the actors and the audience?

S: Well, again, that depends very much on the kind of theatre it is. Take Grotowski for instance, this Polish playwright/director, essentially a director, who approaches theatre from an almost monastic point of view. He takes the view that actors should be disciplined like monks and the space relations of the theatre should be such that the audience become almost like mystical voyeurs, peeking on some masonic ritual. He wants the actors to be like organisms under the microscope. He has all sorts of theories about this, essentially that the theatre is a monastic profession, the outsiders are really involved in watching a very private mystery. (Now I don't hold with this view). That is absolutely valid so long as you don't try to apply it to all kinds of theatre and that is why I say that not too much should be made of audience participation, audience involvement. It depends what kind of play it is. What kind of space is available. The proscenium theatre, for instance, I think is a monstrosity. I find I've never been able to work in the proscenium theatre. The kind of theatre which I enjoy working in, the kind of theatre I enjoy *producing* in, is not one which is determined by the proscenium arch. I have seen productions which very clearly belong behind proscenium arches, to the whole idea of looking at the stage as if you were looking through a frame at a picture. The proscenium theatre is appropriate for certain kinds of play.

Then you have celebratory theatres, like Joan Littlewood's theatre, one constant celebration. Well for that you do not attempt to restrain the stage or the audiences in any way. You really want maximum space.

The development of a certain kind of theatre, with which I have never felt the slightest sympathy, which to me was just an expression of American gross self-indulgence and faddism—I think it is called "Liquid Theatre" and it went in different directions like "Theatre of Smell" in which nothing was left any longer to the imagination. If you burn incense on the stage, you've got to make sure that incense is burning in the audience. Things reached the point where the audience was excoriated, was supposed to have become insensitive, to have lost the human touch and therefore the only way to restore that is to have actors clambering over members of the audience. Usually naked! I have always treasured a remark of Kenneth Tynan's during one of these sessions we had. He said: "If I'm sitting down and someone comes climbing over me with her tits bulging I just hope I have a lighted cigarette in my hand to really apply it where it will hurt most!" This kind of excess begins to appeal to the senses instead of to the mind. The theory is that there is no contact between the actor and the audience unless there is *physical* contact—how much more reductionist can you get? This form of theatre went way out on a limb and I am absolutely appalled by that kind of theatre because it oversimplifies the whole business of contact between the audience and the actors.

Then there is the travelling theatre, "folk opera" theatre, which is actually stopped and the audience is appealed to: "Does it seem right to you? What do you think?" If the tradition is worked into the text then there's no problem with it. It is when you take a play from a totally different and incongruous set of cultural circumstances and try to impose this kind of audience participation that you just look like a fool. There are times when I want to sit in the theatre and I don't want anybody to talk to me: "For God's sake just get on with your business. I will extract from it what I need, I will feel satisfied!" I feel that I am being patronized, being talked down to, by the fact that the actors are constantly winking at me, let's put it that way: "Hey, what do you think of that then?" One resents it with certain kinds of plays. On the other hand, in a different kind of play, you don't even wait for the wink, you get up and say: "Hey that's not the way that should go!"

Q: Which very modern playwrights do you regard as most significant and why?

S: That is a difficult question because in fact I went through a couple of years during which whenever I travelled to Europe or America I didn't go to the theatre. One reason was that I found that I had lost the capacity to enjoy theatre for its own sake. I found that I was constantly analysing the production. It was a real hang up and I would be so fed up with myself because I was not submitting myself to the theatrical experience any longer that for a couple of years or so I'd rather go to a musical concert or visit the opera or whatever. Any time I was in the theatre it had become a totally cerebral process. And within the constraints of that it is very difficult for me to say today what kind of playwrights represent for me truly modern theatre. I can, however, talk about a few plays, a few theatrical experiences.

One of my favourite playwrights by the way still is Arden, but that's quite some time ago. I've not seen anything he's done recently.

I loved Ariane Mnouchkine's *1789,* which I saw in Paris a few years ago and which was a festival of revolution, a ritual of revolution, which did not stint on sheer theatricality. Its use of commedia dell'arte, improvizational theatre, audience direct contact and space was really fantastic.

I was fascinated by *Le Regard du Sourd,* by an American Bob Wilson, who has experimented with a kind of theatre which is almost like an animation of paintings. He used to go on for hours and it was largely mythological. His work has been interpreted in terms of Jung. It is difficult to describe and you really have to see it: a slow-motion animation of paintings. His first work in this direction was *Le Regard de Surrealist du Sourd,* translated as *Deafman's Glance,* and it's like getting into the mind of this deaf-mute girl. This playwright was working with a school for the deaf and that is where the idea came from. It was really like an animation of the collective symbols of society seen through the mind, the vision, of this deaf-mute girl. But after that first one I found that he became very self-indulgent and when I went to see his next production I walked out noisily because I thought he was carrying it too far.

The work of Derek Walcott, the Caribbean playwright, fascinates me a lot. He is a poetic playwright who also deals with contemporary sociology. Again talking about the individual in society, he is very much concerned with plotting dramatically his own sensibilities, his own development, in a multi-racial and class conflict ridden society.

Among the British playwrights I have seen Shaffer. I am fascinated by Tom Stoppard's wit, his urbane, intellectual wit and word play, but I derive no real, gutsy, theatrical satisfaction from his work.

I don't think any modern playwright really captivates me, not on the same level as some of the classical playwrights.

Q: What about African playwrights?

S: There is a lot of work going on by African playwrights, especially by the young ones who are very ideologically motivated. In fact I think a lot of the African dramatic genius is being poured into film right now, Ousmane Sembene, for instance, and there are one or two of Ola Balogun's films which are worth mentioning. The young Francophone cineastes seem to be very exciting today and a lot of dramatic talent seems to be siphoned off to the cinema.

Q: Have you been involved with any films?

S: No, that is, I hope that I have not made any movie which is widely distributed. I have been involved in one or two cinema disasters, and I just hope they are not widely distributed!

Q: Do you find the film a more difficult art form than others and would you comment on the state of film producing in Africa?

S: It is more difficult in this sense: it's a far more complicated art which depends very much on the proficiency of a number of people on the technical level. African cinema has suffered from the same kind of colonial imposition as other art forms. Although I must qualify this; it is really not so much an imposition as an acceptance by Africans. The French cinema school, that is, the Francophone cinema school, was the first to start in Africa, and unfortunately it did not concern itself with producing really good faithful pictures which stem from the imagination of the creators. It was more concerned with trying to establish itself as French. In other words, it became or wanted to be a part of the French culture, and it therefore tried to establish in Francophone Africa a kind of French New Wave cinema. It became preoccupied with problems of style and imitativeness instead of getting along with the real business.

By contrast, the Anglophones, when they came into the field, wanted very much to capture what Hollywood had been jettisoning. It is very strange, the contrast between the two. I have sat through hours as a member of the film jury both in Dakar and Tunisia just going through film upon film which either was in the worst Hollywood taste or was a cheap unimaginative pastiche of the French New Wave, such as *Last Year at Marienbad* or *Hiroshima Mon Amour,* but without the kind of historical accumulation which worked on these creators to use that particular form and to make that particular statement. So it was just idiotic. And, unfortunately, the action was no better in the Anglophone simply because the producers attach themselves to some American principle of film producing in which the producer could lift the entire footage and say "O.K., I'm going to get a new editor," or "I don't like the way you are shooting this; I want Americans to be able to understand this film." So by the time he is finished he's gone though about five editors. Stockholm, America, London, back again to America—you know that kind of thing. Simply because the producer and the producing company in West Africa had got themselves enthralled to the monied interests. So there have been difficulties both on the technological level, the commercial details, the amateurishness of some of the techniques, but also some genuine problems. But I don't think the cinema form is alien to the African creative instinct. If we can learn from past mistakes maybe in the next five years we will see an attempt from Africa to obliterate Shaft and Company.

Q: Do playwrights benefit from working with other artists and in other art forms?

S: An artist in any medium shouldn't feel a sense of isolation, he should understand very early and very succinctly that all these various art forms flow into one another. An atmosphere in which we can actually see that, actually see images in the lyric of a song, or the lyric of a play, where he can actually see those images reflected or associated with images in a painting, a sculpture and even hear equivalents in musical compositions which his words might trigger off, is very often useful and *vice versa*. And also he can see that sculpture can inspire a dance, see all these things at work and see how even environmental design speaks to the decorative arts, the plastic arts, one also speaks to the other. I think this is very, very useful so that he doesn't get locked up in a kind of block. Someone was asking me about "writer's block," I told him I experienced it quite often myself, this sort of block very often can be dissolved simply by moving outside of one's own medium to a different matrix of art. That in itself is very often a help. So any kind of atmosphere in which these various art forms can intermingle . . . no force . . . just let them be there, that's all.

Q: What is your advice to anyone contemplating managing a company?

S: First of all, you get yourself a club and a whip—metaphorically speaking. That's the only way you'll ever run a company. Actors, I don't know why, are the laziest beings in the world! Actors do not like discipline and you cannot have an acting company without discipline. I'm not talking about Nigerian actors only, this has been my experience in Europe and America. I think it has to do with a certain confidence in themselves that when the day comes they will be ready. But I am afraid that their work is not superior to the work of the director, the scene designer, the costume maker, the make-up artist and the property makers, and the director must know just what everyone is capable of at every stage. So you have to do a lot of frowning, so to speak, to put a group together and keep them on their toes. I don't give a damn whatever anybody says about democracy in acting companies. It has not worked for me. Actors must know who the director is—it's the only way. Then, of course, you must be totally honest with your group and flog yourself as much as you are ready to flog them.

Q: What are the differences between writing for radio and writing for the stage?

S: Well, briefly, I'll give you one obvious example. You just have to remember that the actors, the action, cannot be seen and therefore your dialogue must be written in such a way so that you do not frustrate your audience, your listeners. By using dialogue the listeners must know that the actors are seeing things which the listeners cannot see. If you don't it is very frustrating for the listener. In other words dialogue must be written in such a way that either it creates the physical objects which are involved in the action or the physical action itself is translated into words. The sound effects can be used also, of course, but they should be at the bottom of the list. What you must do is transfer the physical reality into dialogue. Far more than on the stage, that is essential. You can get away with action on stage. You can involve the audience in the action on stage. But all that has to be transferred to the language of people in between, into dialogue. You can use narration if you like but that is copping out. We should use narration as sparingly as possible, everything has to go into the action between characters.

Q: Do you think narration should be used more in radio plays than in stage plays?

S: Radio plays definitely require narration far more than stage plays. But again I wish always to qualify whatever I say: there are certain forms of theatre, certain specific types of theatre, especially where there is constant rapport with the audience, and in these instances it is part and parcel of the expectation of the audience that the characters will come out and address them directly. In fact a lot of yardage of laughter, of wit, is accumulated by the very means of narrative. It is almost like "narrative counter narrative." What is obvious is introduced in a language which connotes the action and in fact puts the audience in a very receptive frame of mind. So it isn't that narrative is being condemned as such. I am just warning about the fact that it must not be used to replace the skill of the writer, the director, and the actor.

In radio the same thing happens. There will, from time to time, be situations whereby you must use narrative. But even the narrative should be written in a way to enhance the rest of the production, to promote the action, rather than make it very, very static.

> "We are now before the castle of Elsinore, and Hamlet is about to walk the ramparts. It is moonlight—"

And so on and so on. No! Everything I have just said just now can be put into the first two sentences of dialogue in the most natural way. That's what I want to say.

Q: What has been your experience with television?

S: I've written plays specifically for television in Nigeria. I've never directed a television play, although each production that my group has performed in the studio I have had to literally set, set all of the shots, then give it to the technicians to work out what it means in terms of camera. This is for the simple reason that if you don't, all they understand is "close-up, two-shots, wide angle . . ." and they just vary it, 123, 321, 421, and after a few experiences like that I insisted on setting things.

Q: What kinds of theatre forms are there?

S: Theatre forms are constantly being replenished all over the world. There have been, as I said earlier, in the last decade at least twelve theatre forms to the best of my knowledge: from Environmental to Liquid to Living. And each one has very distinct features, both in terms of the material written for it and the method of production, the spatial use and the manipulation of scenes and audiences. For instance, one form employs the concept, that instead of manipulating scenes, you manipulate the audience. You put the scene there and light it. Then you shift the audience. That is to say at the beginning of each scene the audience is told: "Go, over there!" Next one: "Go over there," and so on.

There is no limitation to theatrical forms.

Countercultural Architecture
and Dramatic Structure

David Mamet

I was a student in the turbulent sixties in Vermont at a countercultural college. In that time and place, there flourished something called a school of Countercultural Architecture. Some people back then thought that traditional architecture had been too stifling, and so they designed and built a lot of counterculture buildings. These buildings proved unlivable. Their design didn't begin with the idea of the building's purpose; it began with the idea of how the architect "felt."

As those architects looked at their countercultural buildings over the years, they may have reflected that there's a reason for traditional design. There's a reason that doors are placed in a certain way, there's a reason that sills are made a certain way. All those countercultural buildings may have expressed the intention of the architect, but they didn't serve the purpose of the inhabitants. They all either fell down or are falling down or should be torn down. They're a blot on the land-

Excerpted from "Countercultural Architecture and Dramatic Strucure," from *On Directing Film* by David Mamet, copyright © 1991 by David Mamet. Used by permission of Viking Penguin, a division of Penguin Putnam Inc.

scape and they don't age gracefully and every passing year underscores the je-june folly of those countercultural architects.

I live in a house that is two hundred years old. It was built with an axe, by hand, and without nails. Barring some sort of man-made catastrophe, it will be standing in another two hundred years. It was built with an understanding of, and a respect for, wood, weather, and human domestic requirements.

It's very difficult to shore up something that has been done badly. You'd bet-ter do your planning up front, when you have the time. It's like working with glue. When it sets, you've used up your time. When it's almost set, you then have to make quick decisions under pressure. If you design a chair correctly, you can put all the time into designing it correctly and assemble it at your leisure. In fact, the ancient chairmakers—which is to say chairmakers up until about the turn of the century—used to make their chairs without glue because they correctly understood not only the nature of joints but the nature of woods. They knew which woods would shrink and which would expand with age, so that these woods, when correctly combined, would make the chair stronger over time.

I recognized two things in finishing up my second movie. When you're do-ing the movie, after you finish with the shot list but before you start shooting it, you have a period called "preproduction." In preproduction, you say, "you know what would be a good idea? To really make the audience understand that we're in a garage, what about a sign that says 'garage.'" So you meet with your art department and you talk a lot about signs and you make up a lot of signs. I made two movies and I made up a lot of signs. You never see the signs in a movie—never. You just never see them. They are after-the-fact attempts to shore up that which was not correctly designed.

Another handy but useless "reminder" tool is the process of looping, or ADR (Automatic Dialogue Reading—dialogue recorded and inserted after the movie has been shot), to communicate to the audience information the film lacks. For example, dubbing words into somebody's mouth when we see his back on the screen. To wit: "oh, look, here we go down that staircase that we're trying to get to the bottom of." That never works either. Why? Because all that the audience cares about is *what is the thrust of the scene*—what does the hero want? More precisely, what is the essential aspect of the shot? They aren't there to look at signs, and they won't look at them. You can't force them to look at them. It is the nature of human perception to go to the most interesting thing; just as we know in terms of the dirty joke, the most interesting thing is *what happens next* in the story that you promised the audience you were going to tell them. You can't make them stop and look at that sign. They don't care to indulge you by listening to your looping, so you'd better do your work beforehand.

That work is done in understanding the nature of the materials and using that understanding in the design of the film. That's basically what a film is; it's a design. You know, all these personally felt statements of people who try to put a lot of garbage into the shot and pan around a bunch to show how moved they are by their chosen subject: these are just like countercultural architecture. They may be a personal statement, but they don't serve the turn of the inhabitants or, in this case, the turn of the viewers who would like to know *what happens next.* You tax the audience every time you don't move on to the next essential step of the progression as quickly as possible. You're taxing their good nature. They may indulge you for political reasons—which is what most of modern art is about. Political reasons being, "dammit, I *like* those kinds of bad movies" or "I *like* that kind of countercultural statement. I am one of that group, and I endorse the other members of this group, who appreciate the sort of things this fellow is trying to say." The audience can endorse the triviality of modern art, but they can't like it. I suggest you think about the difference between the way people talk about any performance artist and the way they talk about Cary Grant. And to you lovely enthusiasts who will aver that the purpose of modern art is not to be liked, I respond, "oh, grow up."

The job of the film director is *to tell the story through the juxtaposition of uninflected images*—because that is the essential nature of the medium. It operates best through that juxtaposition, because that's the nature of human perception: to perceive two events, determine a progression, and want to know what happens next.

In a play, the only way you have to convey the action of the plot is through the action of the characters, what they say to each other. With a movie, the action has to be advanced narratively. To advance it through the dialogue is just boring; it is not the proper exploitation of the form. It has to be advanced, showing the audience what's happening, narrating to them the state of mind of the protagonist, which is the worst kind of playwriting.

From what I can see in the writing and directing, film is getting things structured so that it succeeds in spite of itself. You're taking the element of luck out. You also are taking out the elements of feeling and sensitivity, so you're relying absolutely on the structure of the script. The script makes the audience ask what happens next and makes the audience care about the answer to that question.

"Performance art" like drama works, as it's the nature of human perception to order random images in favor of an overriding preconception. Another example of this is neurosis. Neurosis is the ordering of unrelated events or ideas or images in favor of an overriding preconception. "I am," for example, "an unsightly person": that's the overriding preconception. Then, given any two unrelated events I can order them to make them mean *that.* "Oh, yes, I understand. This woman came out of the hall and did not seem to notice me and rushed into the elevator and quickly pushed the button and the elevator closed because I am an unattractive person." That's what neurosis is. It is the attempt of a disordered mind to apply the principle of cause and effect. This same attempt takes place subconsciously in the viewer of a drama.

If the lights go out and the curtain goes up, the overriding idea is "a play is taking place"; "someone is telling me a story." The human brain, understanding that, will take all of the events in the play and form them into a story just as it forms perception into neurosis. It is the nature of human perception to connect unrelated images into a story, because we need to make the world make sense.

If the overriding idea is that *a play is taking place,* then we will form the images that we see, or words that we hear, between the time the curtain goes up and the time the curtain comes down *into* a play whether or not they have been structured as one. Just so with the movie, which is why bad filmmaking can "succeed." It is our nature to want to make sense of these events—we can't help it. The human mind would make sense of them even if they were a random juxtaposition. This being the nature of human perception, the smart dramatist will use it to his advantage and say, "well, if the human mind is going to do all that anyway, why don't *I* do it first? Then I will be going with the flow rather than battling against the tide."

If you aren't telling a story, moving from one image to another, the images have to be more and more "interesting" per se. If you *are* telling a story, then the human mind, as it's working along with you, is perceiving your thrust, both consciously and, more important, subconsciously. The audience members are going to go along with that story and will require neither inducement, in the form of visual extravagance, nor explanation, in the form of narration. *They want to see what's happening next.* Is the guy going to get killed? Is the girl going to kiss him? Will they find the money buried in the old mine?

When the film is correctly designed, the subconscious and the conscious are in alignment, and we *need* to hear what happens next. The audience is ordering the events just as the author did, so we are in touch with both his conscious and his unconscious mind. We have become involved in the story.

If we don't care what happens next, if the film is *not* correctly designed, we may, unconsciously, create our own story in the same way that a neurotic creates his own cause-and-effect rendition of the world around him, but we're no longer interested in the story that we're being told. "Yes, I saw that the girl put the kettle on the fire and then a cat ran out on stage," we might say of "performance art." "Yes, I saw, but I don't quite know where it's going. I'm following it, but I am certainly not going to risk my unconscious well-being by becoming involved." That's when it stops being interesting. So that's where the bad author, like the countercultural architect, has to take up the slack by making each subsequent event *more* diverting than the last—to trick the audience into paying attention.

The end of this is obscenity. Let's really see their genitals, let's really endanger the actor through stunts, let's really set the building on fire. Over the course of a movie, it forces the filmmaker to get more and more bizarre. Over the course of a career, it forces a filmmaker to get more and more outré; over the course of a culture, it forces the culture to degenerate into depravity, which is what we have now.

Interest in a film comes from this: the desire to find out what happens next. The less reality conforms to the neurotic's view, the more bizarre his explanation must become, the end of which development is psychosis—"performance art" or "modern theater" or "modern filmmaking."

The structure of any dramatic form should be a syllogism—which is a logical construct of this form: If A, then B. A play or movie proceeds from a statement: *"if A"* (in which a condition of unrest is created or posited), to a conclusion: *"then B"* (at which time entropy will once again rear its corrective head, and a condition of rest will have been once again achieved).

For example, as we've seen, if a student *needs an extension,* he will pursue a series of actions that will lead him to the extension or to an irrevocable denial of the extension. And then he will be at rest; a condition of entropy will have been achieved. This *entropy* is one of the most interesting aspects of our life as a whole. We are born, certain things happen, and we die. The sexual act is a perfectly good example. Things are called into motion that did not heretofore exist and that demand some form of resolution. Something is called into existence that did not heretofore exist, and then the unrest that this new thing creates has to be resolved, and when it's resolved, the life, the sexual act, the play, is done. That's how you know when it's time to go home.

The guy solved his problem at the whorehouse. The guy lost all his money at the racetrack. The couple was reunited. The bad king died. How do we know this is the end of the story? Because *the rise to power of the bad king* was the problem that we came to see solved. How do we know that *when they kiss* it's the end of the movie? Because it's a movie about the boy not getting the girl. The solution of the problem posited at the beginning of the experience is the end of the story. That's also how we know the scene is over, isn't it?

I said that the scene is the correct unit of study. If you understand the scene, you understand the play or movie. When the problem posited by the scene is over, the scene is over. A lot of times in movies you want to get out of the scene *before* the problem is over and have it answered in the *next* scene, as a matter of fact. Why? So that the audience will follow you. They, you will remember, want to know what happens next.

To get into the scene late and to get out early is to demonstrate respect for your audience. It's very easy to manipulate an audience—to be "better" than the audience—because you've got all the cards. "I don't have to tell you *anything;* I can change the story in midstream! I can be whatever I want. Go to hell!" But listen to the difference between the way people talk about films by Werner Herzog and the way they talk about films by Frank Capra, for example. One of them may or may not understand something or other, but the other understands what it is to tell a story, and he *wants* to tell a story, which is the nature of the dramatic art—to tell a story. That's all it's good for. People have tried for centuries to use drama to change people's lives, to influence, to comment, to express themselves. It doesn't work. It might be nice if it worked for those things, but it doesn't. The only thing the dramatic form is good for is telling a story.

If you want to tell a story, it might be a good idea to understand a little bit about the nature of human perception. Just as, if you want to know how to build a roof, it might be a good idea to understand a little bit about the effects of gravity and the effects of precipitation. If you go up into Vermont and you build a roof with a peak, the snow will fall off. You build a flat roof, the roof will fall down from the weight of the snow—which is what happened to a lot of the countercultural architecture of the 1960s. "There may be a reason people have wanted to hear stories for ten million years," the performance artist says, "but I really don't *care*, because *I have something to say*."

The film business is caught in a spiral of degeneracy because it's run by people who have no compass. And the only thing you can do in the face of this downward force is tell the truth. Anytime anyone tells the truth, that's a counterforce. You cannot hide your objective. No one can hide. Contemporary American films are almost universally sloppy, trivial, and obscene. If your objective is to succeed in the "industry," your work, and your soul, will be exposed to these destructive influences. If you desperately crave acceptance by that industry, you will likely become those things.

The actor cannot hide his objective, neither can the playwright, neither can the film director. If a person's objective is truly—and you don't have to do it humbly, because you'll get humble soon enough—*to understand the nature of the medium,* that objective will be communicated to the audience. How? Magically. I don't know how. Because it will. It just can't be hidden. In addition to what you will or will not learn about the medium through your desire to understand it, that desire *itself* will be manifested.

I carve wood sometimes. It's magical how the wooden object creates itself. One becomes enthralled by and very observant of the grain of the wood, and the piece tells you how to carve it. Sometimes the piece is fighting back against you. If you're honest in making a movie, you'll find that it's often fighting back against you too. It's telling you how to write it. Just as we found in the "got an extension" movie. It's very, very difficult to do these very, very simple problems. They're fighting back against you, these problems, but the mastery of them is the beginning of the mastery of the art of film.

I love making movies. I love writing them and I love directing them. And I don't think film is a lesser form. I do, however, feel absolutely that theater is my real work, and when I'm making movies I sometimes feel as if I'm playing hooky. Still, my work in Hollywood has helped me very much. The good movie has to be written very clearly. The action has to be very clear. You can't take time out to digress to the highways and the byways of what might happen. You've got to tell the story. And I am trying to do this in my plays. I mean I wrote a lot of plays about feeling slices of interesting life. Nothing wrong with that—I just didn't know any better. I'm talking about my earlier plays; *Lakeboat,* for example, and others with those episodic glimpses of humanity. Those were fine, but now I am trying to do something different.

That's because Hollywood and the mass media are flooding the market with trash. The taste and the need for a real theatrical experience, which is an experience in which the audience can come to commune, not so much with the actors but with themselves and what they know to be true, just increase. Everyone's palette has been dulled to an extraordinary degree by the mass media. But that's just the way it is. Television, of course, isn't an art form. It might be, but nobody's figured out how to make it so. It's not even a question of doing good work on television, which happens once in a while. It's that nobody seems to understand the essential nature of the medium. I certainly don't.

Interlude: The Screenwriter as Auteur

Each Film Is My Last

Ingmar Bergman

AN ANT IN THE SNAKESKIN

Artistic creation always manifested itself to me as hunger. I acknowledged it with a certain satisfaction, but during my conscious life I never asked myself what caused this craving. In the last few years the hunger has diminished and been transformed into something else; now I am anxious to find out what the reasons for it were. I have an early childhood memory of my desire to show off achievements: proficiency in drawing, playing ball, the first swimstrokes. I had a strong need to draw the grown-ups' attention to these signs of my presence in the external world. I never felt that people took enough interest in me. When reality was no longer sufficient, I started to invent things; I entertained my friends with tremendous stories of my secret exploits. They were embarrassing lies, which failed hopelessly when confronted with the level-headed scepticism of the world around me. Finally I withdrew, and kept my dream world to myself. A child looking

Reprinted from *Drama Review* 11, no. 1 (Fall 1966): 94–101. Translated by P. E. Burke and Lennart Swahn.

for human contact, obsessed by his imagination, had been quickly transformed into a hurt, cunning, and suspicious daydreamer.

But a daydreamer is no artist except in his dreams.

The need to be heard, to correspond, to live in the warmth of a community, was still there. It grew stronger the lonelier I grew. It goes without saying that film became my means of expression. I made myself understood in a language going beyond words, which failed me; beyond music, which I did not master; beyond painting, which left me indifferent. I was suddenly able to correspond with the world around me in a language spoken literally from soul to soul, in phrases which escaped the control of the intellect in an almost voluptuous way. With the whole stunted hunger of a child I seized upon my medium and for twenty years, tirelessly and in a kind of frenzy, I supplied the world with dreams, intellectual excitement, fantasies, fits of lunacy. My success has been amazing, but at bottom it is an insignificant sequel.

I do not underestimate what I may have achieved. I think that it has been and perhaps still is of importance. But now I can see the past in a new and less romantic light; that is security enough for me. Today my situation is less complicated, less interesting, above all less glamorous than it was. To be completely frank, I experience art (not only film art) as insignificant in our time: art no longer has the power and the possibility to influence the development of our life.

Literature, painting, music, film, and theatre beget and bring forth themselves. New mutations, new combinations arise and are annihilated; the movement seems—seen from the outside—nervously vital. With magnificent zeal the artists project to themselves and to a more and more distracted public picture of a world that no longer cares what they like or think. In a few countries artists are punished, art is considered dangerous and worth stifling and directing. On the whole, however, art is free, shameless, irresponsible; the movement is intense, almost feverish, like a snake's skin full of ants. The snake is long since dead, eaten, deprived of his poison, but the skin is full of meddlesome life.

If I have become one of these ants, I must ask myself if there is any reason to continue my work.

The answer is yes. Although I think that the stage is an old, beloved kept woman, who has seen better days. Although I and many other people find the Wild West more stimulating than Antonioni and Bergman. Although the new music gives us the sense of being suffocated by mathematically rarefied air. Although painting and sculpture, sterilized, decline in their own paralyzing freedom. Although literature has been transformed into a pile of words without any message or dangerous qualities. . . .

I think that people today can dispense with theatre, because they exist in the middle of a drama whose different phases incessantly produce local tragedies. They do not need music, because every minute that are exposed to hurricanes of sound passing beyond endurance. They do not need poetry, because the idea of the universe has transformed them into functional animals, confined to interesting—but from a poetical point of view unusable—problems of metabolic disturbance. Man (as I experience myself and the world around me) has made himself free, terribly and dizzyingly free. Religion and art are kept alive as a conventional politeness toward the past, as a benign, democratic solicitude on behalf of nervous citizens enjoying more and more leisure time. . . .

If I consider all these troubles and still maintain that I want to continue to work in art, there is a simple reason. (I disregard the purely material one.) The reason is *curiosity*. A boundless, insatiable curiosity, that is always new and that pushes me onwards—a curiosity that never leaves me alone and that has completely replaced my craving for community. I feel like a prisoner who, after serving a long term, suddenly is confronted with turbulent life. I note, I observe, I keep my eyes open; everything is unreal, fantastic, frightening, or ridiculous. I catch a flying grain of dust, maybe it is a film—what importance does it have? None at all, but I find it interesting and consequently it is a film. I walk around with the grain of dust that I have caught with my own hands. I am happy or sad. I jostle the other ants, together we accomplish an enormous task. The snake's skin moves.

This and only this is *my* truth. I do not request that it be valid for someone else, and as a consolation for eternity it is of course rather meager. As a basis for artistic activity during some future years it is completely sufficient at least for me. To devote oneself to artistic creation for one's own satisfaction is not always agreeable. But it has one great advantage: the artist lives exactly like every other living creature that only exists for its own sake. This makes a rather numerous brotherhood. . . .

THOU SHALT

Experience should be gained before one reaches forty, a wise man said. After forty it is permissible to comment. The reverse might apply in my case—no one was more certain of his theories and none more willing to elucidate them than I was. No one knew better or could visualize more. Now that I am some-what older I have become rather more cautious. The experience I have gained and which I am now sorting out is of such a kind that I am unwilling to express myself on the art of the filmmaker. . . . The only real contribution the artist can make is his work. Thus I find it rather unseemly to get involved in discussion, even with explanations or excuses.

The fact that the artist remained unknown was a good thing in its time. His relative anonymity was a guarantee against irrelevant outside influences, mate-rial considerations, and the prostitution of his talents. He brought forth his work in spirit and truth as he saw it and left the judgment to the Lord. Thus he lived and died without being more or less important than any other artisan. In such a world flourished natural assurance and invulnerable humility, two qual-ities which are the finest hallmarks of art.

In life today the position of the artist has become more and more precarious; the artist has become a curious figure, a kind of performer or athlete who chases from job to job. His isolation, his now almost holy individualism, his artistic subjectivity can all too easily cause ulcers and neurosis. Exclusiveness becomes a curse which he eulogizes. The unusual is both his pain and his satisfac-tion. . . .

The Script

Often it begins with something very hazy and indefinite—a chance remark or a quick change of phrase, a dim but pleasant event which is not specifically re-lated to the actual situation. It has happened in my theatrical work that I have visualized performers in fresh make-up but in yet-unplayed roles. All in all, split-second impressions that disappear as quickly as they come, forming a brightly colored thread sticking out of the dark sack of the unconscious. If I wind up this thread carefully a complete film will emerge, brought out with pulse-beats and rhythms which are characteristic of just this film. Through these rhythms the picture sequences take on patterns according to the way they were born and mastered by the motive.

The feeling of failure occurs mostly before the writing begins. The dreams turn into cobwebs, the visions fade and become grey and insignificant, the pulse-beat is silent, everything shrinks into tired fancies without strength and reality. But I have decided to make a certain film and the hard work must begin: to transfer rhythms, moods, atmosphere, tensions, sequences, tones, and scents into a readable or at least understandable script.

This is difficult but not impossible.

The vital thing is the dialogue, but dialogue is a sensitive matter which can offer resistance. The written dialogue of the theatre is like a score which is almost incomprehensible to the ordinary person; interpretation demands a technical knack and a certain amount of imagination and feeling. One can write dialogue, but how it should be handled, the rhythms and the tempo, the speed at which it is to be taken, and what is to take place between the lines—all that must be left out, because a script containing so much detail would be unreadable.

I can squeeze directions and locations, characterizations and atmosphere into my film-scripts in understandable terms, but then I come to essentials, by which I mean montage, rhythm and the relation of one picture to the other— the vital "third dimension" without which the film is merely dead, a factory product. Here I cannot use "keys" or show an adequate indication of the tempos of the complexes involved; it is impossible to give a comprehensible idea of what puts life into a work of art. I have often sought a kind of notation which would give me a chance of recording the shades and tones of the ideas and the inner structure of the picture. If I could express myself thus clearly, I could work with the absolute certainty that whenever I liked I could prove the relationship between the rhythm and the continuity of the part and the whole. . . . Let us state once and for all that the film script is a very imperfect *technical* basis for a film.

Film is not the same thing as literature. As often as not the character and substance of the two art forms are in conflict. What it really depends on is hard to define, but it probably has to do with the self-responsive process. The written word is read and assimilated by a conscious act and in connection with the intellect, and little by little it plays on the imagination or feelings. It is completely different with the motion picture. When we see a film in a cinema we are conscious that an illusion has been prepared for us and we relax and accept it with our will and intellect. We prepare the way into our imagination. The sequence of pictures plays directly on our feelings without touching the mind.

There are many reasons why we ought to avoid filming existing literature, but the most important is that the irrational dimension, which is the heart of a literary work, is often untranslatable and that in its turn kills the special dimension of the film. If despite this we wish to translate something literary into filmic terms, we are obliged to make an infinite number of complicated transformations which most often give limited or non-existent results in relation to the efforts expended. I know what I am talking about because I have been subjected to so-called literary judgment. This is about as intelligent as letting a music critic judge an exhibition of paintings or a football reporter criticize a new play. The only reason for everyone believing himself capable of pronouncing a valid judgment on motion pictures is the inability of the film to assert itself as an art form, its need of a definite artistic vocabulary, its extreme youth in relation to the other arts, its obvious ties with economic realities, its direct appeal to the feelings. All this causes film to be regarded with disdain. Its directness of expression makes it suspect in certain eyes, and as a result any and everyone thinks he's competent to say anything he likes, in whatever way he likes, about film art.

I myself have never had ambitions to be an author. I do not wish to write novels, short stories, essays, biographies, or treatises on special subjects. I certainly do not want to write pieces for the theatre. Film-making is what interests me. I want to make films about conditions, tensions, pictures, rhythms, and characters within me which in one way or another interest me. The motion picture and its complicated process of birth are my methods of saying what I want to my fellow men. I find it humiliating for work to be judged as a book when it is a film. Consequently the writing of the script is a difficult period, but useful, as it compels me to prove logically the validity of my ideas. While this is taking place I am caught in a difficult conflict between my need to find a way of filming a complicated situation and my desire for complete simplicity. As I do not intend my work to be solely for my own edification or for the few but for the public in general, the demands of the public are imperative. Sometimes I try a venturous alternative which shows that the public can appreciate the most advanced and complicated developments. . . .

The Studio

I stand in the half-light of the film studio with its noise and crowds, dirt and wretched atmosphere, and I seriously wonder why I am engaged in this most difficult form of artistic creation. The rules are many and burdensome. I must have three minutes of usable film in the can every day. I must keep to the shooting schedule, which is so tight that it excludes almost everything but essentials. I am surrounded by technical equipment which with fiendish cunning tries to sabotage my best intentions. Constantly I am on edge, I am compelled to live the collective life of the studio. Amidst all this must take place a sensitive process which demands quietness, concentration, and confidence.

I mean working with actors and actresses. There are many directors who forget that our work in films begins with the human face. We certainly can become completely absorbed in the aesthetics of montage, we can bring together objects and still life into a wonderful rhythm, we can make nature studies of astounding beauty, but the approach to the human face is without doubt the distinguishing quality of the film. From this we might conclude that the film star is our most expensive instrument and the camera only registers the reactions of this instrument. But in many cases the position and movement of the camera is considered more important than the player, and the picture becomes an end in itself—this can never do anything but destroy illusions and be artistically devastating. In order to give the greatest possible strength to the actor's expression, the camera movement must be simple, free, and completely synchronized with the action. The camera must be a completely objective observer and may only on rare occasions participate in the action. We should realize that the best means of expression the actor has at his command is his *look*. The close-up, if objectively composed, perfectly directed and played, is the most forcible means at the disposal of the film director, while at the same time being the most certain proof of his competence or incompetence. The lack or abundance of close-ups shows in an uncompromising way the nature of the director and the extent of his interest in people.

Simplicity, concentration, full knowledge, technical perfection must be the pillars supporting each scene and sequence. However, they in themselves are not enough. The one most important thing is still lacking: the intimate spark of life, which appears or fails to appear according to its will, crucial and indomitable.

For instance, I know that everything for a scene must be prepared down to the last detail, each branch of the collective organization must know exactly what it is to do. The entire mechanism must be free from fault as a matter of course. These preliminaries may or may not take a long time, but they should not be dragged out and tire those participating. Rehearsals for the "take" must be carried out with technical precision and with everyone knowing exactly what he is to do. Then comes the take. From experience I know that the first take is often the happiest, as it is the most natural. This is because the actors are trying to create something; their creative urge comes from natural identification. The camera registers this inner act of creation, which is hardly perceptible to the untrained eye or ear. I believe it is this which keeps me in films. The development and retention of a sudden burst of life gives me ample reward for the thousands of hours of grey gloom, trial and tribulation. . . .

Morality

Many imagine that the commercial film industry lacks morality or that its morals are so definitely based on immorality that an artistically ethical standpoint cannot be maintained. Our work is assigned to businessmen, who at times regard it with apprehension because it is concerned with something as unreliable as art. If many regard our activity as dubious, I must emphasize that its morality is as good as any and so absolute that it is almost embarrassing. However, I have found that I am like the Englishman in the tropics, who shaves and dresses for dinner every day. He does not do this to please the wild animals but for his own sake. If he gives up his discipline then the jungle has beaten him. I know that I shall have lost to the jungle if I take a weak moral standpoint. I have therefore come to a belief based on three commandments. Briefly I shall give their wording and their meaning. These have become the basis of my activity in the film world.

The first may sound indecent but really is highly moral:

THOU SHALT BE ENTERTAINING AT ALL TIMES

The public who sees my films and thus provides my bread and butter has the right to expect entertainment, a thrill, a joy, a spirited experience. I am responsible for providing that experience. That is the only justification for my activity.

However, this does not mean that I must prostitute my talents, at least not in any and every way, because then I would break the second commandment:

THOU SHALT OBEY THY ARTISTIC CONSCIENCE AT ALL TIMES

This is a very tricky commandment because it obviously forbids me to steal, lie, prostitute my talents, kill, or falsify. However, I will say that I am allowed to falsify if it is artistically justified, I may also lie if it is a beautiful lie, I could also kill my friends or myself or anyone else if it would help my art, it may also be permissible to prostitute my talents if it will further my cause, and I should indeed steal if there were no other way out. If one obeyed artistic conscience to the full in every respect then one would be doing a balancing act on a tight-rope, and could become so dizzy that at any moment one could break one's neck. Then all the prudent and moral bystanders would say, "Look, there lies the thief, the murderer, the lecher, the liar. Serves him right"—never thinking that all means are allowed except those which lead to a fiasco, and that the most dangerous ways are the only ones which are passable, and that compulsion and dizziness are two necessary parts of our activity: that the joy of creation, which is a thing of beauty and joy forever, is bound up with the necessary fear of creation. . . .

In order to strengthen my will so that I do not slip off the narrow path into the ditch, I have a third juicy commandment:

THOU SHALT MAKE EACH FILM AS IF IT WERE THY LAST

Some may imagine that this commandment is an amusing paradox or a point-less aphorism or perhaps simply a beautiful phrase about the complete vanity of everything. However, that is not the case.

It is reality.

In Sweden, film production was halted for all of 1951. During my enforced inactivity I learned that because of commercial complications and through no fault of my own I could be out on the street before I knew it. I do not complain about it, neither am I afraid or bitter; I have only drawn a logical and highly moral conclusion from the situation: *each film is my last.*

For me there is only one loyalty: to the film on which I am working. What comes (or fails to come) after is insignificant and causes neither anxiety nor longing. This gives me assurance and artistic confidence. The material assur-ance is apparently limited but I find artistic integrity infinitely more important, and therefore I follow the principle that *each film is my last.* This gives me strength in another way. I have seen all too many film workers burdened down with anxiety, yet carrying out to the full their necessary duties. Worn out, bored to death and without pleasure they have fulfilled their work. They have suffered humiliation and affronts from producers, critics, and the public without flinch-ing, without giving up, without leaving the profession. With a tired shrug of the shoulders they have made their artistic contributions until they went down or were thrown out.

I do not know when the day might come that I shall be received indifferently by the public, perhaps be disgusted with myself. Tiredness and emptiness will descend upon me like a dirty grey sack and fear will stifle everything. Emptiness will stare me in the face. When this happens I shall put down my tools and leave the scene, of my own free will, without bitterness and without brooding whether or not the work has been useful and truthful from the viewpoint of eternity. Wise and far-sighted men in the Middle Ages used to spend nights in their coffins in order never to forget the tremendous importance of every mo-ment and the transient nature of life itself. Without taking such drastic and un-comfortable measures I harden myself to the seeming futility and the fickle cru-elty of film-making with the earnest conviction that *each film is my last.*

Four **Directing**

Through Theater to Cinema

Sergei Eisenstein

Translated by Jay Leyda and Paya Haskelson

It is interesting to retrace the different paths of today's cinema workers to their creative beginnings, which together compose the multicolored background of the Soviet cinema. In the early 1920s we all
came to the Soviet cinema as something not yet existent. We came
upon no ready-built city; there were no squares, no streets laid out;
not even little crooked lanes and blind alleys, such as we may find in
the cinematropolis of our day. We came like bedouins or gold-seekers
to a place with unimaginably great possibilities, only a small section of
which has even now been developed.

We pitched our tents and dragged into camp our experiences in
varied fields. Private activities, accidental past professions, unguessed
crafts, unsuspected eruditions—all were pooled and went into the
building of something that had, as yet, no written traditions, no exact
stylistic requirements, nor even formulated demands.

Without going too far into the theoretical debris of the specifics of
cinema, I want here to discuss two of its features. These are features of

Excerpted from Sergei Eisenstein, *Film Form* (New York: Harcourt, Brace, 1949).

other arts as well, but the film is particularly accountable to them. *Primo:* photo-fragments of nature are recorded; *secundo:* these fragments are combined in various ways. Thus, the shot (or frame), and thus, montage.

Photography is a system of reproduction to fix real events and elements of actuality. These reproductions, or photo-reflections, may be combined in various ways. Both as reflections and in the manner of their combination, they permit any degree of distortion—either technically unavoidable or deliberately calculated. The results fluctuate from exact naturalistic combinations of visual, interrelated experiences to complete alterations, arrangements unforeseen by nature, and even to abstract formalism, with remnants of reality.

The apparent arbitrariness of matter, in its relation to the *status quo* of nature, is much less arbitrary than it seems. The final order is inevitably determined, consciously or unconsciously, by the social premises of the maker of the film-composition. His class-determined tendency is the basis of what seems to be an arbitrary cinematographic relation to the object placed, or found, before the camera.

We should like to find in this two-fold process (the fragment and its relationships) a hint as to the specifics of cinema, but we cannot deny that this process is to be found in other art mediums, whether close to cinema or not (and which art is not close to cinema?). Nevertheless, it is possible to insist that these features are specific to the film, because film-specifics lie not in the process itself but in the degree to which these features are intensified.

The musician uses a scale of sounds; the painter, a scale of tones; the writer, a row of sounds and words—and these are all taken to an equal degree from nature. But the immutable fragment of actual reality in these cases is narrower and more neutral in meaning, and therefore more flexible in combination, so that when they are put together they lose all visible signs of being combined, appearing as one organic unit. A chord, or even three successive notes, seems to be an organic unit. Why should the combination of three pieces of film in montage be considered as a three-fold collision, as impulses of three successive images?

A blue tone is mixed with a red tone, and the result is thought of as violet, and not as a "double exposure" of red and blue. The same unity of word fragments makes all sorts of expressive variations possible. How easily three shades of meaning can be distinguished in language—for example: "a window without light," "a dark window," and "an unlit window."

Now try to express these various nuances in the composition of the frame. Is it at all possible?

If it is, then what complicated context will be needed in order to string the film-pieces onto the film-thread so that the black shape on the wall will begin to show either as a "dark" or as an "unlit" window? How much wit and ingenuity will be expended in order to reach an effect that words achieve so simply?

The frame is much less independently workable than the word or the sound. Therefore the mutual work of frame and montage is really an enlargement in scale of a process microscopically inherent in all arts. However, in the film this process is raised to such a degree that it seems to acquire a new quality.

The shot, considered as material for the purpose of composition, is more resistant than granite. This resistance is specific to it. The shot's tendency toward complete factual immutability is rooted in its nature. This resistance has largely determined the richness and variety of montage forms and styles—for montage becomes the mightiest means for a really important creative remolding of nature.

Thus the cinema is able, more than any other art, to disclose the process that goes on microscopically in all other arts.

The minimum "distortable" fragment of nature is the shot; ingenuity in its combinations is montage.

Analysis of this problem received the closest attention during the second half-decade of Soviet cinema (1925–1930), an attention often carried to excess. Any infinitesimal alteration of a fact or event before the camera grew, beyond all lawful limit, into whole theories of documentalism. The lawful necessity of combining these fragments of reality grew into montage conceptions which presumed to supplant all other elements of film-expression.

Within normal limits these features enter, as elements, into any style of cinematography. But they are not opposed to nor can they replace other problems—for instance, the problem of *story*.

To return to the double process indicated at the beginning of these notes: if this process is characteristic of cinema, finding its fullest expression during the second stage of Soviet cinema, it will be rewarding to investigate the creative biographies of film-workers of that period, seeing how these features emerged, how they developed in pre-cinema work. All the roads of that period led towards one Rome. I shall try to describe the path that carried me to cinema principles.

Usually my film career is said to have begun with my production of Ostrovsky's play, *Enough Simplicity in Every Sage,* at the Proletcult Theatre (Moscow, March 1923). This is both true and untrue. It is not true if it is based solely on the fact that this production contained a short comic film made especially for it (not separate, but included in the montage plan of the spectacle). It is more nearly true if it is based on the character of the production, for even then the elements of the specifics mentioned above could be detected.

We have agreed that the first sign of a cinema tendency is one showing events with the least distortion, aiming at the factual reality of the fragments.

A search in this direction shows my film tendencies beginning three years earlier, in the production of *The Mexican* (from Jack London's story). Here, my participation brought into the theater "events" themselves—a purely cinematographic element, as distinguished from "reactions to events"—which is a purely theatrical element.

This is the plot: A Mexican revolutionary group needs money for its activities. A boy, a Mexican, offers to find the money. He trains for boxing, and contracts to let the champion beat him for a fraction of the prize. Instead he beats up the champion, winning the entire prize. Now that I am better acquainted with the specifics of the Mexican revolutionary struggle, not to mention the technique of boxing, I would not think of interpreting this material as we did in 1920, let alone using so unconvincing a plot.

The play's climax is the prize-fight. In accordance with the most hallowed Art Theatre traditions, this was to take place backstage (like the bull-fight in *Carmen*), while the actors on stage were to show excitement in the fight only they can see, as well as to portray the various emotions of the persons concerned in the outcome.

My first move (trespassing upon the director's job, since I was there in the official capacity of designer only) was to propose that the fight be brought into view. Moreover I suggested that the scene be staged in the center of the auditorium to re-create the same circumstances under which a real boxing match takes place. Thus we dared the concreteness of factual events. The fight was to be carefully planned in advance but was to be utterly realistic.

The playing of our young worker-actors in the fight scene differed radically from their acting elsewhere in the production. In every other scene, one emotion gave rise to a further emotion (they were working in the Stanislavsky system), which in turn was used as a means to affect the audience; but in the fight scene the audience was excited directly.

While the other scenes influenced the audience through intonation, gestures, and mimicry, our scene employed realistic, even textural means—real fighting, bodies crashing to the ring floor, panting, the shine of sweat on torsos, and finally, the unforgettable smacking of gloves against taut skin and strained muscles. Illusionary scenery gave way to a realistic ring (though not in the center of the hall, thanks to that plague of every theatrical enterprise, the fireman) and extras closed the circle around the ring.

Thus my realization that I had struck new ore, an actual-materialistic element in theater. In *The Sage,* this element appeared on a new and clearer level. The eccentricity of the production exposed this same line, through fantastic contrasts. The tendency developed not only from illusionary acting movement, but from the physical fact of acrobatics. A gesture expands into gymnastics, rage is expressed through a somersault, exaltation through a *salto-mortale,* lyricism on "the mast of death." The grotesque of this style permitted leaps from one type of expression to another, as well as unexpected intertwinings of the two expressions. In a later production, *Listen, Moscow* (summer 1923), these two separate lines of "real doing" and "pictorial imagination" went through a synthesis expressed in a specific technique of acting.

These two principles appeared again in Tretiakov's *Gas Masks* (1923–24), with still sharper irreconcilability, broken so noticeably that had this been a film it would have remained, as we say, "on the shelf."

What was the matter? The conflict between material-practical and fictitious-descriptive principles was somehow patched up in the melodrama, but here they broke up and we failed completely. The cart dropped to pieces, and its driver dropped into the cinema.

This all happened because one day the director had the marvelous idea of producing this play about a gas factory—in a real gas factory.

As we realized later, the real interiors of the factory had nothing to do with our theatrical fiction. At the same time the plastic charm of reality in the factory became so strong that the element of acuality rose with fresh strength—took things into its own hands—and finally had to leave an art where it could not command.

Thereby bringing us to the brink of cinema.

But this is not the end of our adventures with theater work. Having come to the screen, this other tendency flourished, and became known as "typage." This "typage" is just as typical a feature of this cinema period as "montage." And be it known that I do not want to omit the concept of "typage" or "montage" to my own works.

I want to point out that "typage" must be understood as broader than merely a face without make-up, or a substitution of "naturally expressive" types for actors. In my opinion, "typage" included a specific approach to the events embraced by the content of the film. Here again was the method of least interference with the natural course and combinations of events. In concept, from beginning to end, *October* is pure "typage."

A typage tendency may be rooted in theater; growing out of the theater into film, it presents possibilities for excellent stylistic growth, in a broad sense—as an indicator of definite affinities to real life through the camera.[1]

And now let us examine the second feature of film-specifics, the principles of montage. How was this expressed and shaped in my work before joining the cinema?

In the midst of the flood of eccentricity in *The Sage,* including a short film comedy, we can find the first hints of a sharply expressed montage.

The action moves through an elaborate tissue of intrigue. Mamayev sends his nephew, Glumov, to his wife as guardian. Glumov takes liberties beyond his uncle's instructions and his aunt takes the courtship seriously. At the same time Glumov begins to negotiate for a marriage with Mamayev's niece, Turussina, but conceals these intentions from the aunt, Mamayeva. Courting the aunt, Glumov deceives the uncle; flattering the uncle, Glumov arranges with him the deception of the aunt.

Glumov, on a comic plane, echoes the situations, the overwhelming passions, the thunder of finance, that his French prototype, Balzac's Rastignac, experiences. Rastignac's type in Russia was still in the cradle. Money-making was still a sort of child's game between uncles and nephews, aunts and their gallants. It remains in the family, and remains trivial. Hence, the comedy. But the intrigue and entanglements are already present, playing on two fronts at the same time—with both hands—with dual characters . . . and we showed all this with an intertwined montage of two different scenes (of Mamayev giving his instructions, and of Glumov putting them into execution). The surprising intersections of the two dialogues sharpen the characters and the play, quicken the tempo, and multiply the comic possibilities.

For the production of *The Sage* the stage was shaped like a circus arena, edged with a red barrier, and three-quarters surrounded by the audience. The other quarter was hung with a striped curtain, in front of which stood a small raised platform, several steps high. The scene with Mamayev (Shtraukh) took place downstage while the Mamayeva (Yanukova) fragments occurred on the platform. Instead of changing scenes, Glumov (Yezikanov) ran from one scene to the other and back—taking a fragment of dialogue from one scene, interrupting it with a fragment from the other scene—the dialogue thus colliding, creating new meanings and sometimes wordplays. Glumov's leaps acted as *caesurae* between the dialogue fragments.

And the "cutting" increased in tempo. What was most interesting was that the extreme sharpness of the eccentricity was not torn from the context of this part of the play; it never became comical just for comedy's sake, but stuck to its theme, sharpened by its scenic embodiment.

Another distinct film feature at work here was the new meaning acquired by common phrases in a new environment.

Everyone who has had in his hands a piece of film to be edited knows by experience how neutral it remains, even though a part of a planned sequence, until it is joined with another piece, when it suddenly acquires and conveys a sharper and quite different meaning than that planned for it at the time of filming.

This was the foundation of that wise and wicked art of reediting the work of others, the most profound examples of which can be found during the dawn of our cinematography, when all the master film-editors—Esther Schub,[2] the Vassiliyev brothers, Benjamin Boitler, and Birrois—were engaged in reworking ingeniously the films imported after the revolution.

I cannot resist the pleasure of citing here one montage *tour de force* of this sort, executed by Boitler. One film bought from Germany was *Danton*, with Emil Jannings. As released on our screens, this scene was shown: Camille Desmoulins is condemned to the guillotine. Greatly agitated, Danton rushes to Robespierre, who turns aside and slowly wipes away a tear. The sub-title said, approximately, "In the name of freedom I had to sacrifice a friend. . . ." Fine.

But who could have guessed that in the German original, Danton, represented as an idler, a petticoat-chaser, a splendid chap and the only positive figure in the midst of evil characters, that this Danton ran to the evil Robespierre and . . . spat in his face? And that it was this spit that Robespierre wiped from his face with a handkerchief? And that the title indicated Robespierre's hatred of Danton, a hate that in the end of the film motivates the condemnation of Jannings-Danton to the guillotine?!

Two tiny cuts reversed the entire significance of this scene!

Where did my montage experiment in these scenes of *The Sage* come from? There was already an "aroma" of montage in the new "left" cinema, particularly among the documentalists. Our replacement of Glumov's diary in Ostrovsky's text with a short "film-diary" was itself a parody on the first experiments with newsreels.

I think that first and foremost we must give the credit to the basic principles of the circus and the music-hall—for which I had had a passionate love since childhood. Under the influence of the French comedians, and of Chaplin (of whom we had only heard), and the first news of the fox-trot and jazz, this early love thrived.

The music-hall element was obviously needed at the time for the emergence of a "montage" form of thought. Harlequin's parti-colored costume grew and spread, first over the structure of the program, and finally into the method of the whole production.

But the background extended more deeply into tradition. Strangely enough, it was Flaubert who gave us one of the finest examples of cross-montage of dialogues, used with the same intention of expressive sharpening of idea. This is the scene in *Madame Bovary* where Emma and Rodolphe grow more intimate. Two lines of speech are interlaced: the speech of the orator in the square below, and the conversation of the future lovers:

> Monsieur Derozerays got up, beginning another speech . . . praise of the Government took up less space in it; religion and agriculture more. He showed in it the relations of these two, and how they had always contributed to civilization. Rodolphe with Madame Bovary was talking dreams, presentiments, magnetism. Going back to the cradle of society, the orator painted those fierce times when men lived on acorns in the heart of woods. Then they had left off the skins of beasts, had put on cloth, tilled the soil, planted the vine. Was this a good, and in this discovery was there not more of injury than of gain? Monsieur Derozerays set himself this problem. From magnetism little by little Rodolphe had come to affinities, and while the president was citing Cincinnatus and his plough, Diocletian planting his cabbages, and the Emperors of China inaugurating the year by the sowing of seed, the young man was explaining to the young women that these irresistible attractions find their cause in some previous state of experience.
>
> "Thus we," he said, "why did we come to know one another? What chance willed it? It was because across the infinite, like two streams that flow but to unite, our special bents of mind had driven us towards each other."
>
> And he seized her hand; she did not withdraw it.
>
> "For good farming generally!" cried the president.
>
> "Just now, for example, when I went to your house."
>
> "To Monsieur Bizat of Quincampoix."
>
> "Did I know I should accompany you?"

"Seventy francs."

"A hundred times I wished to go; and I followed you—I remained."

"Manures!"

"And I shall remain to-night, to-morrow, all other days, all my life!"

And so on, with the "pieces" developing increasing tension.

As we can see, this is an interweaving of two lines, thematically identical, equally trivial. The matter is sublimated to a monumental triviality, whose climax is reached through a continuation of this cross-cutting and word-play, with the significance always dependent on the juxtaposition of the two lines.

Literature is full of such examples. This method is used with increasing popularity by Flaubert's artistic heirs.

Our pranks in regard to Ostrovsky remained on an "avant garde" level of an indubitable nakedness. But this seed of montage tendencies grew quickly and splendidly in *Patatrac,* which remained a project through lack of an adequate hall and technical possibilities. The production was planned with "chase tempos," quick changes of action, scene intersections, and simultaneous playing of several scenes on a stage that surrounded an auditorium of revolving seats. Another even earlier project attempted to embrace the entire theater building in its composition. This was broken up during rehearsals and later produced by other hands as a purely theatrical conception. It was the Pletnëv play, *Precipice,* which Smishlayev and I worked on, following *The Mexican,* until we disagreed on principles and dissolved our partnership. (When I returned to Proletcult a year later, to do *The Sage,* it was as a director, although I continued to design my own productions.)

Precipice contains a scene where an inventor, thrilled by his new invention, runs, like Archimedes, about the city (or perhaps he was being chased by gangsters—I don't remember exactly). The task was to solve the dynamics of city streets, as well as to show the helplessness of an individual at the mercy of the "big city." (Our mistaken imaginings about Europe naturally led us to the false concept of "urbanism.")

An amusing combination occurred to me, not only to use running scenery—pieces of buildings and details (Meyerhold had not yet worked out, for his *Trust D. E.,* the neutral polished shields, *murs mobiles,* to unify several places of action)—but also, possibly under the demands of shifting scenery, to connect these moving decorations with people. The actors on roller skates carried not only themselves about the stage, but also their "piece of city." Our solution of the problem—the intersection of man and milieu—was undoubtedly influenced by the principles of the cubists. But the "urbanistic" paintings of Picasso were of less importance here than the need to express the dynamics of the city—glimpses of façades, hands, legs, pillars, heads, domes. All of this can be found in Gogol's work, but we did not notice that until Andrei Belyi enlightened us about the special cubism of Gogol. I still remember the four legs of two bankers, supporting the façade of the stock-exchange, with two top-hats crowning the whole. There was also a policeman, sliced and quartered with traffic. Costumes blazing with perspectives of twirling lights, with only great roughed lips visible above. These all remained on paper—and now that even the paper has gone, we may become quite pathetically lyrical in our reminiscences.

These close-ups cut into views of a city become another link in our analysis, a film element that tried to fit itself into the stubborn stage. Here are also elements of double and multiple exposure—"superimposing" images of man onto images of buildings—all an attempt to interrelate man and his milieu in a single complicated display. (The fact that the film *Strike* was full of this sort of complexity proves the "infantile malady of leftism" existing in these first steps of cinema.)

Out of mechanical fusion, from plastic synthesis, the attempt evolves into thematic synthesis. In *Strike,* there is more than a transformation into the technique of the camera. The composition and structure of the film as a whole achieves the effect and sensation of uninterrupted unity between the collective and the milieu that creates the collective. And the organic unity of sailors, battleships, and sea that is shown in plastic and thematic cross-section in *Potemkin* is not by trickery or double-exposure or mechanical intersection, but by the general structure of the composition. But in the theater, the impossibility of the *mise-en-scène* unfolding throughout the auditorium, fusing stage and audience in a developing pattern, was the reason for the concentrated absorption of the *mise-en-scène* problems within the scenic action.

The almost geometrically conventional *mise-en-scène* of *The Sage* and its formal sequel, *Listen, Moscow,* becomes one of the basic elements of expression. The montage intersection eventually became too emphatically exact. The composition singled out groups, shifted the spectator's attention from one point to another, presented close-ups, a hand holding a letter, the play of eyebrows, a glance. The technique of genuine *mise-en-scène* composition was being mastered—and approaching its limits. It was already threatened with becoming the knight's move in chess, the shift of purely plastic contours in the already non-theatrical outlines of detailed drawings.

Sculptural details seen through the frame of the *cadre,* or shot, transitions from shot to shot, appeared to be the logical way out for the threatened hyper-trophy of the *mise-en-scène*. Theoretically it established our dependence on *mise-en-scène* and montage. Pedagogically, it determined, for the future, the ap-proaches to montage and cinema, arrived at through the mastering of theatrical construction and through the art of *mise-en-scène*.[3] Thus was born the concept of *mise-en-cadre*. As the *mise-en-scène* is an interrelation of people in action, so the *mise-en-cadre* is the pictorial composition of mutually dependent *cadres* (shots) in a montage sequence.

In *Gas Masks* we see all the elements of film tendencies meeting. The tur-bines, the factory background, negated the last remnants of make-up and the-atrical costumes, and all elements appeared as independently fused. Theater ac-cessories in the midst of real factory plastics appeared ridiculous. The element of "play" was incompatible with the acrid smell of gas. The pitiful platform kept getting lost among the real platforms of labor activity. In short, the pro-duction was a failure. And we found ourselves in the cinema.

Our first film opus, *Strike* [1924–25], reflected, as in a mirror, in reverse, our production of *Gas Masks*. But the film floundered about in the flotsam of a rank theatricality that had become alien to it.

At the same time, the break with the theater in principle was so sharp that in my "revolt against the theater" I did away with a very vital element of theater—the story.

At that time this seemed natural. We brought collective and mass action onto the screen, in contrast to individualism and the "triangle" drama of the bourgeois cinema. Discarding the individualist conception of the bourgeois hero, our films of this period made an abrupt deviation—insisting on an un-derstanding of the mass as hero.

No screen had ever before reflected an image of collective action. Now the conception of "collectivity" was to be pictured. But our enthusiasm produced a one-sided representation of the masses and the collective; one-sided because collectivism means the maximum development of the individual within the collective, a conception irreconcilably opposed to bourgeois individualism. Our first mass films missed this deeper meaning.

Still, I am sure that for its period this deviation was not only natural but nec-essary. It was important that the screen be first penetrated by the general image, the collective united and propelled by one wish. "Individuality within the col-lective," the deeper meaning, demanded of cinema today, would have found entrance almost impossible if the way had not been cleared by the general con-cept.

In 1924 I wrote, with intense zeal: "Down with the story and the plot!" To-day, the story, which then seemed to be almost "an attack of individualism" upon our revolutionary cinema, returns in a fresh form, to its proper place. In this turn towards the story lies the historical importance of the third half-decade of Soviet cinematography (1930–1935).

And here, as we begin our fourth five-year period of cinema, when abstract dis-cussions of the epigones of the "story" film and the embryones of the "plotless" film are calming down, it is time to take an inventory of our credits and debits.

I consider that besides mastering the elements of filmic diction, the tech-nique of the frame, and the theory of montage, we have another credit to list—the value of profound ties with the traditions and methodology of literature. Not in vain, during this period, was the new concept of film-language born, film-language not as the language of the film-critic, but as an expression of cin-ema thinking, when the cinema was called upon to embody the philosophy and ideology of the victorious proletariat.

Stretching out its hand to the new quality of literature—the dramatics of subject—the cinema cannot forget the tremendous experience of its earlier pe-riods. But the way is not back to them, but forward to the synthesis of all the best that has been done by our silent cinematography, towards a synthesis of these with the demands of today, along the lines of story and Marxist-Leninist ideological analysis. The phase of monumental synthesis in the images of the people of the epoch of socialism—the phase of socialist realism.

NOTES

1. Eisenstein has said that one might define typage as a modern development of the *Comme-dia dell'arte*—with its seven stock figures multiplied into infinity. The relationship lies not in numbers, but in audience conditioning. Upon entrance of Pantalone or the Captain, his mask tells the audience immediately what to expect of this figure. Modern film typage is based on the need for presenting each new figure in our first glimpse of him so sharply and completely that further use of this figure may be as a known element. Thus new, im-mediate conventions are created.—J. L.

2. Schub, long a familiar name to world-documentalists, is known abroad only by the film exhibited in America as *Cannons and Tractors*. The first time Eisenstein ever joined to-gether two pieces of "real film" was while assisting Esther Schub in the re-editing of Lang's *Dr. Mabuse*. This was shortly after the production of *The Sage*. The Vassiliyevs' *Chapayev* establishes their place in cinema history.—J. L.

3. As indicated in "A Course in Treatment," the first two years of Eisenstein's course for di-rectors at the State Cinema Institute emphasize a thorough study of *theater* principles.—J. L.

Class Theatre, Class Film
An Interview with Lindsay Anderson

Kelly Morris

Q: In what way are British films distinct from those of other countries?

Anderson: We haven't had film-makers with the creative independence of directors like Antonioni and Fellini, or Godard and Resnais. This is ceaselessly bemoaned by British bourgeois critics, who want works divorced from the economic and social context that produces them, but it would be impossible to get the money to make such films. On the other hand, British films tend to be less esoteric—we have a strong tradition of social responsibility. This may be related to the rather literary nature of the British cinema—films tend to be produced from novels rather than from original screen plays. Stylistically the British cinema has been slow to follow the more advanced European directors, again partly because of the economic necessity of making films with mass appeal. Also, few technicians in Britain ever see any foreign films. But there is a younger generation of technicians, editors, and cameramen slowly moving in.

Reprinted from *Drama Review* II, no. I (Fall 1966): 122–129.

Q: Many of the films made in England seem to be aimed particularly toward the middle class.

Anderson: This is largely true, and is plainly a comment on the British cultural situation. One likes to think that it's a little less true than ten years ago, when a film with a working class character was really a rarity. I would like to think that *This Sporting Life* is not exactly a bourgeois film; it has been accepted by non-bourgeois audiences. But this country so obstinately remains a class society that the respectable cultural organs have in general—quite unconsciously—fought against taking in the interests and values of the working class. *Saturday Night and Sunday Morning* and *This Sporting Life* were unfavorably received even by "radical" publications such as *The New Statesman*. It's astounding that you still can't make a film in this country in which the principal character is a worker without this being taken as the most interesting thing in the film. The film critics have been writing for years about John Garfield and Humphrey Bogart—equally working class—but those movies have no relevance to our own social situation and do not threaten the position of the bourgeois hero. Now we have apparently radical pictures like *Darling* (significantly popular with New York critics) or *Nothing But the Best,* which appear to be taking a critical attitude towards society, but which are actually respectable, "intelligent," bourgeois assessments of the bourgeois situation. They view from within the situation which they seem to satirize. So they end up as satirical conformist works. They never go to causes, or imply the necessity of a real disruption, a real destruction of the society which has produced them.

Q: Beginning with Look Back in Anger *in the 1950's, there appears to have been a great resurgence in British theatre, led by playwrights such as Harold Pinter, John Osborne, and John Arden. In the same period there seems to have been the rise of the film dealing with working class heroes. Do you think there's any connection between the two?*

Anderson: Well, there was an immediate and direct connection in practical terms. A play, *Look Back in Anger,* a director, Tony Richardson, and a writer, John Osborne, together forced the first penetration into the British cinema of certain ideas and terms. The only reason that Tony Richardson was ever able to become a film director was John Osborne insisting that he direct the film version of *Look Back in Anger.* A little earlier there was *Room at the Top,* which, strictly in terms of its issues, was virtually the first honest film statement of the class situation. Still, it was the kind of situation that might have been seen in numerous Warner Brothers films of the late thirties, starring John Garfield. The crack-up of Britain's old social stratification was reflected first in the theatre. But the class system is more modified than transformed, and the movement of the late fifties hasn't gotten very far. The upper class in Britain is always so clever; it possesses a unique talent for assimilating disturbing elements. The working class actor, for instance, has become fashionable and appears in the Sunday supplements.

Q: How would you distinguish your films from other current British films?

Anderson: My work in cinema doesn't bulk very large. In the fifties, I made documentaries. And from about '57 to about '62 I made no films, and worked in the theatre. This was largely because I wasn't interested in making sponsored films. It's almost impossible to find financing for creative work. Since then I've only made one feature film, *This Sporting Life* in 1963. I just finished making what you might call a featurette of about forty-five minutes, designed as part of a trilogy of Delaney scripts.

Q: What is the relation between film and theatre in your work?

Anderson: Well, I have been told that my work in the theatre is cinematic. I've never been quite sure what that meant. I know that in working in the theatre I'm always very conscious of rhythm and a kind of precise timing, and this is my most uncomfortable obsession when cutting a film. I am slightly at odds with certain contemporary developments which place more emphasis on disintegration than on integration. My tendency is towards a very controlled and rhythmic form. I am not sure if that makes my theatre work "cinematic," or makes my films "theatrical."

Q: About thirty years ago, Eisenstein claimed that film's new developments in cutting, editing, and montage killed the theatre as a performing art. Care to comment?

Anderson: I think economic factors are more important causes of the theatre's apparent decomposition. But I doubt that the theatre is dead, for there are so many very talented people who like doing it, and who can do it in an exciting way. Eisenstein was talking nonsense and probably riding on a wave of enthusiasm. The aesthetics of cinema is very different from the aesthetics of theatre— the enjoyment is different. The theatre remains a place where the author and the actor are more important than the director, while the cinema is ultimately the director's medium. The director has to take the responsibility.

Q: Do you feel that an author can be represented in the theatre with fewer distortions than in a film? Or is it a matter of responsibility for the total experience?

Anderson: The latter. I think that a writer is more likely to be satisfied as a playwright than as a script writer because a film script undergoes a more profound and radical transformation. In my experience a writer is apt to find the film made from his script an agonizing experience. Even if the film is a good one, it is agonizing to see something which he has imagined turned into something else. He is apt to feel a gross sense of deprivation, a helplessness.

Q: In the theatre there appears to be a great problem in the collaboration of directors and playwrights. Is this true for the film writer and director?

Anderson: I've never had disturbing creative divisions between myself and any author whose work I've directed in the theatre. Frankly, playwrights rarely know the difference between a good production and a bad one, they're so delighted by the words. I've worked with Max Frisch twice, and I found that he's perceived exactly what I had been after in directing his plays, and agreed with it. His suggestions have always been marvelously creative, contributing to—without challenging—my fundamental conception. I don't see why there must be a conflict; you're working towards the same end. I certainly can't brook directors who see plays as material in which to advertise their own talent. Likewise, in the cinema, there shouldn't be any problem because the director should—must—choose his collaborator very carefully, and be sure of harmony and understanding.

Q: Over the last ten or twenty years the director has become the major force in the film, while the theatre still relies on fragmented collaboration. Do you feel that more playwright/directors such as Brecht would decidedly improve the nature of our theatre?

Anderson: I don't think the primacy of the film director is any greater than it ever has been. The theory of the *auteur* as coined by the *Cahiers du Cinema* has spread like a virus through the highbrow or would-be-highbrow critical world of the West. The only new thing about this theory has been the touting of second- or third-rate talents by trying to show blinks of attitude or approach in their pictures. So, Howard Hawks is treated as if he were Dostoyevsky. This is ridiculous. I doubt that there's been any development in the theatre because of Brecht as a writer/director. It's very nice if a director can write his own script, or if an author can stage his own plays marvelously. This results in more highly integrated and personal work. It's a fashionable idea but I see no trend towards its realization.

Q: But given the number of contemporary films which seem to be introspective statements by director/authors, don't you feel that the director has emerged or will emerge in a new capacity?

Anderson: Well, this is hardly a new development in the cinema; it simply has developed on a scale that has previously been impossible. For instance, Fellini's *8½* is in the tradition of the French avant-garde film of the early thirties. What is new is a large, educated, international audience which makes such a film economically feasible. The most important stylistic development is the escape from the straight-forward narrative film, previously the basis of the cinema (certainly of the American cinema). We have reached a point where the material of the film can be presented in more interesting, more subjective ways. This increases the kinetic potential of a film.

Q: Do you believe that there is a difference between the two media in the impact of their subject matter on the spectator?

Anderson: In general, the cinema is not as developed an intellectual medium as the theatre. I don't think that the cinema is really a medium for the discussion of ideas, or words. For me the cinema is a poetic medium, while the theatre is less exclusively poetic.

Q: Do you find there are great differences in working with the actors in the theatre as opposed to the film? Do good theatre actors make good film actors or vice versa? And what are some of the problems in this area?

Anderson: I don't sense any difference. Obviously the superficial techniques are different. But the truthfulness and reality which you strive for are exactly the same.

Q: Yes, but there is clearly a need for the hard-core realistic actor in contemporary British films and theatre. How does this affect the grand old traditions of British acting? Do those actors such as Gielgud, Richardson, or Olivier experience great difficulty working with these new movements?

Anderson: I think they do have trouble. They may lack flexibility. Most of them were brought up at a time when the theatre was an even more totally bourgeois preserve. So you do have the extraordinary fact that many of these very accomplished senior actors are totally incapable of playing in anything but a respectable West End accent. They can't put on a northern accent, and that's death today.

Q: How would you account for the fact that there appears to be little or no avant-garde activity in either the film or the theatre in London today?

Anderson: We're living in a society which is making a determined refusal to face reality. Britain today is really a sort of madhouse. The whole life of the nation is built on the most absurd paradox. You've only to switch on the television set and one minute you'll be seeing a politician addressing the nation on the need to face realities and devote ourselves to genuine productivity; the next moment you get a series of commercials bludgeoning you into trying to buy a pile of absolutely useless or trivial products. There is a radical disparity between the reality of that situation and the reality with which this country is attempting to live. One consequence is a great resistance to a more theatrical style of theatre, because we're still stuck with predominantly middle-class audiences which dislike plays that have too deep or uncomfortable a relationship with social truths. This is the great stumbling block to what I think should be the development of theatre.

Q: Then you feel that film and the theatre are in the same relationship to society, in similar situations?

Anderson: Yes, and both are deplorable. At the moment, one hears of all the splendid things that are happening in Britain, from the National Theatre to a certain small group of films. The achievement of these groups is largely fashionable; in relation to what *should* happen, their achievement is very small indeed. The general climate is just as conformist as it ever was, but now it is expressed in shinier terms. The premium on success in Britain has become much stronger. It's no longer fashionable to be an outsider or to retain certain personal standards of integrity. This used to be at least respectable. Not any more.

Miloš Forman, Peter Shaffer, and *Amadeus*

Miloš Forman and Jan Novak

PETER SHAFFER

Back in 1980, when I was in preproduction on *Ragtime,* I came to London for a casting session. My agent, Robby Lantz, happened to have some business there, too, so one night he called me and asked if I'd care to go to the theater with him. I said I'd love to and I didn't even ask what we were going to see. Robby came by in a car to pick me up. On the way to the theater, I finally thought to ask about the play.

"It's a new piece by Peter Shaffer," Robby said.

"Oh, good."

"It's called *Amadeus,* and it's about Mozart and Salieri."

"Oh, shit," I said. I'd seen a number of biographies of composers back in Czechoslovakia. They were a safe subject under Zhdanov and the Stalinists because classical music was too abstract to be politically dangerous. I'd sat through films about Mussorgsky, Glinka, Smetana.

Excerpted from *Turnaround: A Memoir* (New York: Villard, 1994), 257–259, 265–270, 277–279.

They had all bored me profoundly, and here I was, going to a play about not one, but two composers.

If I could have bolted from the car, I'd have made a run for it, but it was too late, so I prepared myself to watch a man in a powdered wig strut about with his head in the clouds where, in these biographies, music always seems to reside.

When the curtain went up, I couldn't have been more surprised. The play could have been about any pair of people connected by a vocation and separated by the deep injustice of supreme talent. I watched Salieri, the king of mediocrity, wrestle with his feelings about a genius. Shaffer's treatment of his envy and admiration, awe and betrayal, had me riveted. Mozart's wonderful music was merely a bonus to a gripping story. When the play ended, I knew that I wanted to film it.

That very evening, Robby took me to see Shaffer, whom I'd never met before, even though we shared the same clever agent. I was crackling with enthusiasm and made a pitch for our collaboration in transferring the play to the screen.

Four weeks later, in New York, Peter and I sat down to talk. I didn't know much about him other than that he was a successful dramatist and that he didn't need me. I explained to Peter that I believed film has its own laws and that to transfer a work from stage to screen, you have to take it apart and reassemble it. Would he be ready to open up his play that way with me? Was he prepared to make that leap of blind faith? He'd used a lot of historical material when he wrote the play, but it was only the point of departure for his story. Now we had to make the play the point of departure for our screenplay.

Peter is a brave man. He said he'd try it.

I think I was lucky, in that Peter had had most of his plays transferred to the screen and had been disappointed with every one of the movies. He had even written the screenplay for *Equus* himself and he still wasn't pleased with the result, so he was ready to be as ruthless with his darling as he had to be.

We didn't actually sit down to write the screenplay for another year and a half because I still had to shoot and finish *Ragtime,* which turned out to be fortuitous because although the play had been a huge success on the stage, when my lawyer and friend Bruce Ramer shopped it around Hollywood, no one showed any interest in it. The project had four strikes against it: It was a costume movie; it was about classical music; it dealt with the past in a remote corner of Europe that no one gave a damn about; and it was an expensive proposition. The only producer who even considered the project was Ray Stark. And even he was merely talking about recording a stage production of the play on film. Peter and

I finally wound up sitting down to work under the auspices of an independent producer—my old collaborator Saul Zaentz.

When we started to pick the play apart for the screenplay, Peter's courage never wavered. We took four months, and turned the play inside out. One of the challenges was to find a satisfying narrative frame for the story. We wound up with the simple conceit of Salieri's confession, which sets up the dramatic action of the film in flashbacks. We came up with the idea through a simple chain of deductions: an old composer had attempted suicide, which nowadays would bring a psychiatrist into the picture, but what would have happened in the eighteenth century? They would have rushed a priest to the old man, which was perfect for our story because a man of God made a fitting foil to the blasphemous Salieri, who is railing at the Creator for his whimsical distribution of talent.

Once we had the structure, everything else quickly fell into place: we made the priest a young man mouthing platitudes, a fellow mediocrity and a musical layman who had never heard of the old composer because Salieri had been forgotten even while he was alive, another reason for his self-annihilating rage. In screenwriting, it's the simplicity that usually takes all the sweat.

I'd never worked with flashbacks before and never really cared for them, but I didn't mind using this narrative strategy in *Amadeus* since we had Mozart's music to whisk us through the transitions. And in purely technical terms, the flashback structure lets you pack the story with more detail and incident than linear narration.

Peter approached the work with gut-wrenching humility. He wrote many different versions of scenes that had worked splendidly in the theater but which would not have withstood the sharper scrutiny of the cinema. He added wonderful new moments, and, in the end he produced a superb screenplay.

MOZART IN HOLLYWOOD

Peter Shaffer had once worked for the music publisher Boosey and Hawkes, so he had a knowledge of music, but he was unable to draw on it in his play. Music interferes with the spoken word onstage. This is a matter of simple practicality—they both compete for the attention of the ear. In film, however, the image has a far greater weight than the word, and music mates with images with the greatest of ease, multiplying the power of both, so we were able to restore the genius of Mozart that was left out of the play. In fact, we thought of the music as the third character in our film.

In hindsight, this was our shrewdest decision. I discovered in the cutting room that Mozart's music not only worked magic on the audience, it even had the power to narrate parts of our story. Mozart's notes became as important as the words of our script or the images of our story. I didn't know enough about classical music to choose my musical collaborators, so I asked Czech piano virtuoso Ivan Moravec whom he would recommend as having the greatest practical knowledge and feel for the eighteenth century. He suggested Sir Neville Marriner or Sir Colin Davis.

Neville Marriner happened to be a friend of Peter Shaffer's, so Saul Zaentz arranged for us to meet with him first. Neville had a layover in New York on his way to Minnesota, where he was conductor and musical director of the Minnesota Symphony Orchestra, so Saul, Peter, and I met him in a conference room at Kennedy Airport. The knighted conductor had an hour between flights and seemed leery of us. We made our pitch, and he considered it warily. Perhaps he saw us as Hollywood corruptors of his art.

"I would do it under one condition," he finally said.

"Which is?"

"Not a single note of Mozart's music can be altered in the film."

We shook hands on it, and, in the end, not a single bar of Mozart's music in the film had been touched.

Next I hired Twyla Tharp to choreograph our opera sequences. It never crossed my mind to use anyone else, and Twyla soon left on a casting mission to Prague. She was going to bring the nucleus of her troupe from New York for *Amadeus,* but she needed to find more dancers. Part of her mission was to look for opera singers to act in our operatic excerpts. We didn't need them to sing because Marriner was going to record the sound with different voices in London beforehand, but I wanted real opera singers onstage.

In most movies, the musical score is the last thing added to the film, but for *Amadeus,* where the music was as important as it is in musicals, we had to have it on tape beforehand. We would then play it on location and choreograph our action to this score.

Twyla left for Prague while I was still casting the film in New York. A few days later, her angry phone call woke me up at three o'clock in the morning.

"Miloš, I'm quitting this project! I've had enough of Prague and all these maestros here! I'm leaving!" She got me at the right time. I was too sleepy and disoriented to yell back at her or get insulted or do anything else I might have done if I had my normal working energy, so luckily I didn't shoot myself in the foot. As I lay on the bed with the receiver by my ear, I was overcome by a deep sadness.

"*Say something*, dammit, Miloš!" she said. I didn't know what to tell her. I was feeling so depressed that I didn't want to utter another word in my life.

"Why aren't you saying anything? Hello? Miloš? Are you there?"

"What do you want me to tell you, Twyla? If you're leaving us, what can I do?" Now Twyla was nearly in tears, and somehow, tenderly, she talked her frustration out of her system.

What happened was that when she arrived in Prague, she was taken to the National Theater to see the best dancers and opera singers in the country. They were all dismissive of her. They acted as if they were doing her a favor by talking to her. She had never come across a bigger crowd of prima donnas in her life. In Czechoslovakia, once you get into the National Theater, you have a sinecure for life. People begin to call you "maestro," and anything you do for the mere mortals after that is a huge favor. You certainly never take another artistic risk.

Twyla hadn't come to Prague looking for favors. She was used to working hard and living for her work. She wasn't about to massage egos of second-rate artists whom she couldn't respect.

When she told me the problem, I called a friend in Prague, Jan Schmidt, and asked him to take Twyla to the city operetta, where the dancers were still used to working hard and the heads had yet to swell. We needed professionals, not "artists." Twyla ended up being very happy with her Czech dancers. And she did an absolutely outstanding job on the film.

Mirek Ondříček was, of course, my cinematographer again, and it was his suggestion to consider a Prague costume designer. He thought that a local artist would have a greater feeling for the time and place of our story and that Dóda Pištěk, one of the best painters of his generation, was my best bet. I vaguely knew this bald, athletic man, but when I went to dinner with him, I discovered his rapid-fire wit and unusual sensibility. Dóda was humming with nervous energy and had an immense, almost childlike, playfulness that made for a wonderful asset on a film location, so I offered him the job.

Dóda had designed the costumes for over a hundred Czech movies, but he was very excited to have the resources of an American production behind him. For the first time in a long career, he was able to use craftsmen and materials that would have been too costly for any of his Barrandov budgets. The downside was that this meant he'd have no excuses to fall back on if something went wrong. But Dóda relished the chance to show what he could do. He bought his fabrics in London and had his costumes sewn in Italy. They looked absolutely splendid.

I never considered anyone but Josef Svoboda to design the opera sets. This old collaborator of mine from *Laterna Magica* had become one of the top set designers of Europe. He jetted from one opera house to another, but he managed to squeeze us into his crowded schedule and gave me witty and imaginative sets.

Once again, I saw over a thousand actors during the casting process. *Amadeus* had been a huge stage success and the parts of Mozart and Salieri were rightly considered plum roles in Hollywood, so Robby received a lot of feelers and offers from agents of famous actors.

One night he called me from Los Angeles.

"Something totally unbelievable has just happened, Miloš," he said. He had just had lunch with a high-level executive of a major Hollywood studio. The studio would underwrite our film, he proposed, if we cast Walter Matthau as Mozart.

"Walter is a Mozart freak. He knows every last note Mozart ever scribbled," said the executive.

"Yes, well," Robby replied evenly. "But do you realize that Mozart was this blond young man who died at thirty-five?"

There was a short silence.

"Yes, *I* know!" the executive quickly recovered. "But Robby! Who knows that in America?!"

I later learned that Matthau had in fact wanted to play Salieri, a very legitimate notion; but his request got scrambled in the brain of the executive, who couldn't imagine that, in a movie called *Amadeus,* a star of Matthau's stature could possibly want to play some never-heard-of character named Salieri.

I'd already made up my mind, however, not to be moved by the entreaties of powerful agents or friends or by any pressure from the studios. I'd stubbornly follow my instincts and fill the principal parts with unfamiliar actors.

Mozart's face isn't commonly known, which was good for our film. It gave me a blank spot in the audience's consciousness to draw on, so I had a chance to make them believe from the very first shot that they'd just discovered the man. If I were to cast a star in the part I'd throw that chance away. And if the famous Mozart was played by an unknown actor, then the forgotten Salieri certainly couldn't be portrayed by a film star because that would pull the initial attention toward the wrong character and undercut the delicate transfer of emotion between the screen and the audience.

In the end, I found my Mozart in Tom Hulce, my Salieri in F. Murray Abraham, my Constance, Mozart's wife, in Meg Tilly, and my emperor in Jeffrey Jones. And so in the winter of 1981, I moved from New York to Prague and started preproduction.

Tom Hulce had to learn to play the piano for the role. He had never played before, but he put in several hours a day at the keyboard for weeks on end, and, according to Neville Marriner, his fingers never hit a wrong note in the film. He also had to invent Mozart's shrill giggle, which Peter had employed to great dramatic effect in the play and which had its genesis in a tiny aside in a letter by an aristocratic gossip who wrote of her shock upon hearing the harsh squawking that issued from the lips of Mozart. When this man who had composed such divine music laughed, she said, he seemed more animal than human. I'd seen six or seven productions of the play and every actor who played Mozart invented his own laugh, so I left Hulce alone. He tried out all sorts of sounds until he struck on a wild, high-pitched giggle that was perfectly pitched to his personality.

Our two principals also had to learn how to conduct an eighteenth-century orchestra, which was a problem because no one knows how this was done two hundred years ago. I asked my old friend Zdeněk Mahler, who has an intimate knowledge of music, to comb the historical record for clues, and he found that no one used batons in the eighteenth century. Finally, though, it was Marriner who gave us the look of period conducting. He videotaped himself conducting all the bits of motivated music in *Amadeus* the way he thought it had been done in Mozart's time. Hulce and Abraham prepared by copying his movements.

Prague and its surroundings provided us with nearly all the locations we needed, except for the interiors of our imperial palace. Only the Hradčany Castle's halls shone with the splendor I was looking for, but it was the domicile of the president, and Communist Party chairman Husák certainly wasn't about to rent out his abode to an American movie company. I'd begun to reconcile myself to someplace in Vienna when someone told me to check out the residency of the Prague archbishop, which still belonged to the Catholic Church.

In this wonderfully preserved palace I found precisely what I had been looking for, so our Barrandov go-betweens approached its occupant, the aged Cardinal František Tomášek, and asked if he'd be willing to loan it to us. They brought back a depressing reply: "The cardinal considers all film to be the instrument of the devil."

The quote rang with such medieval pathos that I became suspicious. I'd been away from Prague for ten years, but I still had a lot of friends there and this effective network soon brought me a more plausible explanation of why the cardinal had turned us down: the Catholic Church was closely watched by the Communists, and State Security had an agent serving as the cardinal's secretary. It was this man who had turned Tomášek against our film. He told the old churchman that we were atheists, that we wanted to film naked women in his palace, that we were out to mock him and to desecrate his residency.

Once I understood more clearly what had happened, I searched for a way to approach the cardinal directly. We didn't move in the same circles, but a friend of another friend knew a carpenter who was just then fixing Tomášek's study, so he saw him every day.

The cardinal became furious when the carpenter repeated his putative quote about the devil. He had never said any such thing; he recognized it as the voice of our go-betweens throwing a little extra Marxist creativity into the message, so he immediately invited me to come see him.

"See what I've had to deal with here for the last thirty years?" he complained.

Tomášek, as it turned out, loved Mozart's music, and was very friendly. I described our film to him, and he granted us permission to use his palace on the spot.

We began shooting on schedule, and everything went smoothly until Meg Tilly got into a pickup game of soccer on a Prague street and tore the ligaments in one of her ankles. We hadn't shot any of her scenes yet, but I had to recast the role of Constanze while the production was rolling.

A few days after Tilly's injury, on a Friday evening, Saul and I flew to Paris and then took the Concorde to New York. We saw fifty actresses on Saturday, did callbacks on Sunday, and narrowed the choice down to two women. We just couldn't make up our minds, so we flew both of them back to Prague for more screen tests.

I was back on the set on Monday, so we didn't miss a day of production. That evening, we looked at the screen tests and I made a gut decision to go with Elizabeth Berridge. She only had a couple of days to prepare for the role between her costume-fitting sessions, but it was all she needed. Mozart's wife had been the daughter of a concierge, and Elizabeth gave us a tart, earthy, wonderful Constanze. And, in the end, she fell in love in Prague and married one of our Czech technicians.

ENTER MOZART

In the fall of 1982, I moved back to Fantasy Records in Berkeley, a place of wonderful memories. I edited *Amadeus* there in that strange and familiar mood in which you hope for the best and prepare for the worst.

One of the hardest things in filmmaking is cutting scenes that are otherwise good but retard the flow of emotion or throw off the film's rhythm. When I edited *Amadeus,* I had to drop three scenes—two big and one small—with the late Kenneth McMillan, an actor whom I liked enormously. He had played the fire chief in *Ragtime,* and in *Amadeus,* he was a rich man whose daughter took piano lessons from our irresponsible genius. Kenneth had great comedic timing and I loved watching him work these light scenes, but when I saw the rough cut of the entire film, these episodes caused the story to drag. It was painful, but I had to admit that McMillan's character had no dramatic purpose.

The editing process always reveals things that slipped by during the film's shooting. I had come to know and love Mozart when I wrote the screenplay with Shaffer. Still, I somehow managed to underestimate the sheer magic of his art. In the editing room, every time I focused on Mozart, he grew bigger. For example, one of the most memorable moments in Shaffer's play occurs at the end of the first act: Constanze comes to Salieri to ask for his help. Wolfgang Amadeus is monumentally impractical, and the Mozarts are broke again. Perhaps the court composer, such an influential person, would be kind enough to pass on some commissions to Mozart.

"He really works hard," says Constanze, showing Salieri a thick stack of Mozart's compositions to prove it. Salieri realizes that she has brought the originals of Mozart's work, and he is eager to have a look at these transcriptions of the volcanic stream of Mozart's creativity. What he sees nearly flattens him: Mozart's first drafts look as neat as other composers' polished presentations. There are hardly any corrections. Even the note sheets reveal the vigor of Mozart's genius, and this realization stabs straight into the heart of Salieri's inferiority. Now he desperately wants to cuckold Mozart, to better him in something, to strike back at him in any way he can.

As the curtain is about to fall, Salieri tells Constanze that he will help her husband, but only if she comes to see him, alone, at night. Constanze seems desperate enough to do anything to save her family from financial ruin, so in the theater I couldn't wait for the second act to begin. Would Constanze go to Salieri? Would she submit to him? Does she have something up her sleeve? Would she stop herself in time?

The curtain goes up and Constanze accepts Salieri's terms. She goes to his room and offers herself to him, but Salieri doesn't take her. He is content to humiliate her and throw her out.

I wanted to retain the juicy drama of this episode. Both F. Murray Abraham and Elizabeth Berridge relished the drama of Salieri's exploitation of Constanze and acted it beautifully. I edited the footage and it looked just fine, but when I added the music, I realized that its power completely changed the scene. As I watched the close-up of Salieri's face while he rifled through Mozart's drafts and heard the four or five celestial motifs from the very compositions that Salieri is examining, as I heard the range of instrumentation, heard the richness of emotion and mood and invention, I was as overwhelmed by Mozart's genius as Salieri was. And once I felt the grand power of that music, I didn't need to see anything more because no sexual betrayal, no mundane humiliation could ever touch this greatness. I would never have believed it, but the music suddenly flattened the fine, titillating scene of high drama into a petty, anticlimactic redundancy.

In the final cut, Salieri skims the drafts, hears the corresponding cadenzas, and is overwhelmed. He has no thoughts of seduction, revenge, cuckolding, humiliation. He has just received the final proof of his own mediocrity. He drops the sheets on the floor, stepping on them as he flees the room, the woman, the music, the spirit of Mozart. And there the scene ends.

When the reviews came out, not a few music critics got violently upset over the liberties we had taken with the historical facts of Mozart's life. I thought their objections pedantic and their passion complimentary. Our film had never purported to be a factual biography of an obscure relationship. It was clearly a historical fantasy, a dramatic construct, a meditation on possibilities past, a playful story.

Moviegoers responded to our film differently. *Amadeus* was and continues to be a money-maker.

In the spring of 1985, *Amadeus* was nominated for eleven Oscars, with Tom Hulce and F. Murray Abraham vying for the same prize in the Best Actor category. It won eight of them, but my biggest reward came at the end of every screening I saw. All over the world, entire audiences sat glued to their seats right through the six minutes of end titles, listening to Mozart's divine music.

Shakespeare in the Cinema
A Film Directors' Symposium

It is almost always necessary to make cuts and other changes in the text when cinematically adapting a Shakespeare play. What is your own philosophy or strategy for making cuts, for updating antiquarian or obscure words, or for rewriting or rearranging scenes?

Peter Brook: Common sense.

Sir Peter Hall: This is why I prefer Shakespeare in a foreign language. The best Shakespeare films to me—such as Kurosawa's *Throne of Blood* and *Ran* and the Solzhenitsyn *Hamlet*—are those that take his themes and characters and ignore his text. I think Shakespeare's text is essentially theatrical and it's dependent on an imaginative make-believe between the audience and the actor, live at the particular moment that they're doing it. I don't like Shakespeare on the screen, any more than I like opera on the screen, because I think both of them are imaginative artificialities. Therefore if you do Shakespeare, of course

---

Reprinted from *Cineaste* 24, no. 1 (1998): 48–55, with permission of Gary Crowdus, *Cineaste* magazine.

you have to cut it, butcher it, and you wouldn't do that to Mozart or to Wagner. Even the best Shakespeare film is as far away from Shakespeare as a reproduction postcard is from a painting. It's better to do it than not do it, but don't kid yourself that it's Shakespeare.

Richard Loncraine: If you're making a Shakespeare film for a contemporary audience, you have to make sure that they don't get bored. Shakespeare wrote *Richard III* about 400 years ago, when people were used to words. They didn't have much visual stimulus—there was no set design, there was no television, there was no cinema obviously, so words were crucial. In our telling of the story, we have everything from special effects, to scored music, and exciting imagery. We can communicate with pictures an awful lot of what Shakespeare expressed with words. Ian McKellen and I worked very closely together on the film. Ian was largely responsible for cutting the text and I was largely responsible for the imagery and styling and the communication of ideas that weren't in the play. The opening of the film, for example, where we see a tank coming through a wall, up until the point where the king is shot, was all from two previous Shakespeare plays. An audience at the time, when Shakespeare wrote the plays, would have known about this prehistory, but you can't expect a modern cinema audience to have any understanding of that, apart from the fact that they've gone out for an evening's entertainment.

I do believe that you can cut the text. Shakespeare's plays were almost never put on in their full-text form; *Richard III* runs four-and-a-half hours, which is more than most people can deal with. We made a very strong decision not to *write* any Shakespeare text because, otherwise, why bother? You might as well find something else. So you can change the text, and you can also move text around—it's a strong Shakespearean tradition to take a scene or a line of dialog and move it. Shakespeare did it all the time.

Baz Luhrmann: Our philosophy in adapting *Romeo and Juliet* for the screen was to reveal Shakespeare's lyrical, romantic, sweet, sexy, musical, violent, rude, rough, rowdy, rambunctious storytelling through his richly invented language. Consequently, our specific strategy was to avoid changing or adding words. We were adamant that we should maintain the colour and taste of the actual words even to the extent of the "thee" and "thou."

Setting the story in the contemporary world of urban gangs allowed us to put Shakespeare's inventive usage to work as a dexterous and ornate street rap. This game allowed us to justify all words even when the actual meaning was not immediately apparent. For example, in a contemporary film a character in a gang may say something is "Bad" when in fact the meaning is "Good." In a similar fashion Tybalt says to Mercutio "thou consortest with Romeo" with "consortest" bearing a sexual inference. Therefore, we see that if the intention behind the word is clear then the meaning will be too.

Where we took significant liberty was in restructuring and cutting. We felt it was important to serve Shakespeare's ultimate goal of strong storytelling. He had to arrest the attention of a very noisy, disparate, savage yet honest audience not unlike at your local cinema. To facilitate this he used all the devices at his disposal, the clash of low brow comedy with high tragedy, the use of popular song (pop music) etc. Similarly, we developed a specific cinematic language for *Romeo and Juliet* that transformed all of these devices into cinematic equivalents in order to achieve the same goal with our noisy, disparate, savage yet honest audience.

Trevor Nunn: In my view, *Twelfth Night* is as near a perfect work for the theater as any that one can nominate. It's exquisite, as perfect as *The Marriage of Figaro* is in opera, or as perfect as *Some Like It Hot* is as a movie. It is that fine and balanced, it has perfect equipoise. So one tampers with it at one's peril. I did several things I'm sure would mortify some scholars. I introduced a prologue, because it was discovered that audiences were having difficulty in orientating themselves, and trying to discover exactly who these twins were. I thought it was a good idea to provide an extra sense that Feste is an observer and to some extent a teller of tales, especially because of the content of his final song, and so I liked the idea of Feste having some introductory material that gave us a context. I tried to make that before the credits, so that as it were William Shakespeare's play started after the credits. I also did a certain amount of transposition, partly because I wanted to clarify narrative, and, in one all-important area, to emphasize ironic counterpoint. I fought to keep as much of the text as possible, and I lost some of the battles, but we retained about sixty-five percent of Shakespeare's text and I think that compares favorably with a lot of recent Shakespeare films where one is down to forty or even thirty percent of the original text. That strikes me as almost a contradiction in terms, that you're doing a great work by Shakespeare, but you're not prepared to include his language.

Oliver Parker: I don't have a strategy regarding cuts. I'm sure it would vary according to the particular piece and my vision of it. In the case of *Othello*, it was my intention to make a film that was fast-moving, vibrant, and accessible to a modern audience. Cuts and changes are therefore inevitable (the play uncut can run up to four hours).

To present the plays in their entirety would be a disservice to Shakespeare. I'm sure if he were alive today, he'd be radically reworking the text for a new medium, and would most likely want to direct it. His plays are colossal things, open to infinite interpretation. With *Othello,* I was moved and inspired to take a particular course and the alterations to the text came about as a direct result. I'm interested in remaining true to the spirit, not to the text, of plays.

Roman Polanski: I'm definitely not for rewriting scenes, unless there's really a possibility of making them clearer by some minute change. There is so much literature written by so many scholars that, in certain cases, they have it all ready for you. If a change helps the clarity and does not spoil the verse, you may in some cases do that. I don't recall us doing it. I say "us" because I was lucky to have such an illustrious collaborator as Ken Tynan, someone who was very comfortable with the subject. I very often relied on his judgment when such decisions were to be made.

Cuts definitely have to be made, just because of length. You may also rearrange the text sometimes, film it in a different sequence, without harming the play—in fact, you can sometimes help it. The plays were written for the stage and had to take into account the rigidity of that format. The stage just doesn't allow you to tell your story in the way you would necessarily want to tell it, whereas the film allows you to tell it in any way. If there is some kind of retrospective narration, for example, you can use a flashback, which you cannot on the stage.

So we played a lot with the text, but it was not just some kind of frivolous sloppiness, it was most often based on research. We studied whatever there was on *Macbeth* and tried to apply the ideas of various scholars by adapting the text in such a way that it would be clearer, easier to understand for the audience, and yet would not harm the beauty of the verse.

Franco Zeffirelli: Anything created in another medium, like a novel or a play, has to accept certain rules when it migrates into the formidable medium of cinema—the length of the film, the language of images, and so on. I cannot think of one novel or play that has been transposed entirely—apart from an exception like Branagh's *Hamlet*—because otherwise your film would last five hours. Adaptation is therefore inevitable, a necessity that no one can escape. Not just cutting obscure lines, which is automatic, because, if the audience doesn't understand the dialog, you must cut it or find other solutions. You must also deal with the redundance of verbal illustration, which is not necessary in cinema, and also the subplots. Subplots are all right on the stage, or when reading, but in films, subplots interfere all the time and they're very difficult to deal with.

Should the actors in a Shakespearean film be classically trained stage actors, prefer-
ably with previous experience in Shakespeare's plays, or do you believe that any good
actor, with proper direction, can perform Shakespearean roles?

Peter Brook: Yes and/or no. A *really* good actor is all that's needed.

Sir Peter Hall: Yes, but they have to learn the technique, which is as particular and specific as learning to fence or to dance or to sing a song. You have to breathe in a certain place, you have to phrase in a certain place. Shakespeare tells you when to go fast, when to go slow, when to pause, when to come in on cue, which words to emphasize; he doesn't tell you *why,* that's the actor's choice. but the score is very, very detailed, indeed.

Richard Loncraine: Yes, I think any actor can perform in Shakespeare. Kristin Scott-Thomas had never done any Shakespeare before and I think she held her head up remarkably well in playing Lady Anne. Iambic pentameter is obviously the classic Shakespearean problem in terms of text. Ian McKellen feels that if you do it properly, it's the natural rhythm of breathing, and, in our film of *Richard III,* everyone spoke in iambic pentameter, correctly, and it certainly didn't get in the way there. If it becomes monotonous and you start talking/like this/because it's/the way/the rhythm/has to be/eventually you'll/start to/nod off. I don't think Shakespeare intended it to be that way. So, yes, I think anyone can deal with Shakespeare as an actor. In the end they must be entertaining and charismatic. Academic training is probably a hindrance rather than a help.

Baz Luhrmann: I am always surprised by how many people relate to the nine-teenth-century notion of Shakespeare or the 1930s fashion of Received Pronun-ciation as the so-called "classical style." We spent a year researching the Eliza-bethan stage, focusing on the linguistic work of Anthony Burgess and holding discussions with people like Sir Peter Hall. It became clear that Received Pro-nunciation, that is, the round vowel sounds of Olivier and Gielgud or "Voice Beautiful" as it is known, is a relatively new fashion.

It is fair to say that if the Elizabethan actor were to perform for us today both his sound and style of acting would quite likely shock our notion of "Classical." The sound of his language would be more guttural with a heavy rolled "r." As Anthony Burgess pointed out it was closer to the sound of the American accent than "Voice Beautiful." Regardless of an actor's formal training, or the lack of it, the simple answer is whatever makes a particular production at a particular moment in time work for that particular audience is "right."

Trevor Nunn: I was very fortunate because I had ten days to rehearse with the actors before we started shooting. Most of the actors in our film of *Twelfth Night* were immensely experienced in classical work, particularly in Shakespeare. Mel Smith, a renowned English comedian, was inexperienced in Shakespeare, but he was very responsive, very interested in direction, and in analyzing the text, and in any hints I could give him about how best it should be spoken. Helena (Bonham Carter) had not done a Shakespeare play before, but she and I had worked together before on *Lady Jane,* which had to do with renaissance society, and we'd read a number of texts together on that occasion, so I felt she was fairly well qualified. She needed a great deal of encouragement and detailed work, but then Helena loves to work hard. So I think there can be any number of cases where actors, like Helena or Mel, haven't any Shakespeare experience, but they were prepared to do the work and they were working with someone sufficiently knowledgeable or experienced to be able to provide the background and to help them.

I don't think an ad hoc approach to Shakespeare is in any way defensible. When you gather a group of people together and set them off on a Shakespeare text, naturally they will all have different ideas, such as, "I think I have to be rhetorical, I have to make the verse line very bold," or, "Oh no, I think it should be very naturalistic, I think it should be very thrown away," or "I think you have to breathe at the end of every line," or "I think that you have to obey Shakespeare's punctuation," or "I think that you have to obey the capital letters." There are God knows how many theories, some of them sensible, some of them completely daft, but you're bound to get people with all of those different ideas gathered together in a room. So not only does clear arbitration have to happen, and in many cases clear instruction, but textual analysis has to be done in considerable detail, or it just isn't going to be possible for actors under the prevailing conditions of film production—you know, you're in the trailer, doing make-up, or waiting for the weather, and suddenly you're on, and you have to deliver. If you're not prepared, you're not going to have any opportunity on the set to have insights into alternative meanings, to begin to adjust inflection, to discover that rhythmically you're all wrong, that the important thing is that the line is an irregular line and not a regular line, because that's the effect that Shakespeare is after. You can't do that on set.

Oliver Parker: Certainly, it is important to be at ease with the language, and for some actors, training is invaluable. However, my priority was to cast great film actors who can bring the characters to life on screen. Sometimes, what is appropriate for stage can be dangerous for film. As an experienced theater actor myself, I have sometimes sensed in myself a responsibility to "deliver" beautiful verse, to convey its many meanings to the detriment of the character.

Roman Polanski: I think that any actor can indeed perform Shakespeare, but in talking about my concrete experience, I worked with English actors and almost all actors in England have had theatrical training. At some time in their lives they went on the road and played Shakespeare, and I would say that all of those I worked with on *Macbeth* had some kind of Shakespearean experience. But any good actor can say the text.

Franco Zeffirelli: What's needed is proper direction and the proper talent. I've experienced the full range of actors and actresses playing in my films, from the two little "green" actors playing Romeo and Juliet—he was a Cockney boy and she was fourteen—but I pulled out of them what I was looking for—youth, innocence, and passion. The words were conquered practically one by one, through the painstaking efforts of voice coaches and the actors themselves. On the other hand, I've used the most illustrious, experienced actors, like Richard Burton, so every case presents its own problems, its own advantages.

What is your view of the proper presentation of Shakespeare's verse in a film? Should it be delivered differently on screen than on the stage? Do you attempt to preserve the poetic and musical quality of the blank verse, or do you think it's more important for the actors to achieve a more naturalistic delivery that will not seem so alien to the ears of contemporary moviegoers, most of whom are not theatregoers?

Peter Brook: Neither. If the actor is intimately close and sensitive to the life of the thought and feeling in each word and line, the result *inevitably* has a true rhythm and music.

Sir Peter Hall: The verse has to be underplayed. One of the problems about Shakespeare on screen is that he wrote for an intimate theater, in which one could both shout and whisper, and that vocal range is part of the Shakespeare experience. If you shout in a film you look like an old ham. So half the Shakespeare dynamic range vocally goes out the window as soon as you put it on screen.

As for the musical quality of the blank verse, those are external judgements.

I don't think that you can speak poetically or speak musically. You can speak with sense, with wit, and with a concrete imagination, and if you don't you're a rotten old Shakespearean ham. I detect at the back of your questions a feeling that film acting needs to be real whereas Shakespeare acting needs to be false, and that is not true.

Baz Luhrmann: One of the great things about Shakespeare's text is its musicality and rhythm. The fact is the actor learns so much about what they are doing and saying from the rhythm itself. I do believe that this rhythm should, where possible, be maintained. As far as the way in which it's delivered, again it is whatever works for a particular situation. There is no reason why an actor cannot deliver the line in a natural style while maintaining the underlying meter.

Trevor Nunn: It seems to me that the camera requires work of actors that is quite fundamentally untheatrical and unstylized. It requires actors to be as truthful as is conceivably possible. The camera is associated with eavesdropping on the real event. Consequently, what is said in front of the camera needs to convey to the cinema audience the sense that it has not been written, that the language of the screen is being invented by the character in the situation spontaneously at that moment. We must not be aware of the writer. The challenge that I gave to the actors was that every syllable of that text had to be in order, as written, every pentameter, and in some cases half-line pentameters, had to be accurately learned and observed, *but* it was essential that I should remain unaware of a writer. I wanted that sense that it was being spoken in real situations and being invented by the characters.

That's more possible with *Twelfth Night* than in many texts, because a lot of the play is in prose and therefore the imperative for the rhythmic line is less obvious. The play breaks into verse at key moments of high romance, of deep feeling, but a lot of it was written at a time when Shakespeare himself was exploring the possibilities of real speech, overheard speech, and slang. In addition to retaining as much of the text as possible, my aim was to keep it very tightly on the leash as far as its accuracy is concerned, and *yet* encouraging every conceivable foible of naturalistic delivery was the task that I set the actors. Indeed, I said to them, if at any point I feel you are reciting something by a great writer, then it's going to be cut, start again.

Oliver Parker: Shakespeare's verse is a gift to the actor. It contains great insights into the character and is an astonishing channel for emotions. Iambic pentameters have a rhythm very close to normal speech. On screen there is the opportunity to make it sound even more natural, to be even more intimate. At the same time, I find the language stylistically liberating. It challenges you to find an equivalent cinematic style.

My preference is to see a balance; to try to establish the real world of the film where the characters sound convincingly natural, but without being bound by naturalism, and where you can then take creative leaps in filmmaking reflecting the creative spirit in the verse.

Roman Polanski: Definitely. You cannot use stage techniques, whether it's Shakespeare or any other author. I think the theatrical way of delivering lines grates on the ear. I live in France, where there's an entirely different tradition in the theater, one that has more to do with Racine than with Shakespeare, and I've had at times to sit through a French play performed in the traditional way and, to me, it's completely unbearable. But in England I don't have this feeling, I enjoy it. English actors have a way of saying Shakespeare's verse in such a way that it sounds pretty naturalistic, and yet it does not break the musical quality of the blank verse.

Franco Zeffirelli: I have a strong experience in opera, and you could pose the same question about singers, who have to sing so that both the passion and meaning of what they're singing is communicated to the audience. It's important to respect the musicality in verse, so if somebody speaks in a poetic form, you have to respect certain rules. But what matters in the end is to make that verse, those lines, become real and touch the hearts and minds of a contemporary audience. If it's something composed or written centuries ago, of course, you use the aura of that period in the language, but in the end you have to communicate with a contemporary audience. They don't come for an academic exercise. The author's intention was to get to their heart, their mind, so we must try to achieve the same purpose.

Do cinematic techniques offer new possibilities for exploring and presenting Shakespeare (such as dealing with subtext)? Do you believe that a film version of a Shakespeare play demands a more fully developed interpretation of the play on the part of the film director than a stage presentation does?

Peter Brook: Yes.

Sir Peter Hall: No, I don't. I think the advantage of Shakespeare on the screen, which I regard as minimal, is that you can get closer, you can see more of the internal workings of the actor. But if you do your work properly in the theater, you can do it just as well in the theater. But surely the point is that nothing happens on a Shakespearean stage, unless it's said. Everything happens on the screen without it being said. Cinema is not a verbal medium, so it doesn't need Shakespeare's text in the same way.

Richard Loncraine: I concur with the idea that, if Shakespeare were alive today, he'd be writing movies and television. He was obviously a man of the moment, and he was not adverse to commerciality. Several of the characters in *Richard III* were put in because they were related to the manager of the theater in which they first performed the play, so he wasn't above selling out. He did it bloody well. His idea of being commercial was to use every technique available—fireworks, cannon, whatever was at his disposal, and I think a modern filmmaker should use every technique available. Every generation will have its Shakespeare plays. The *Richard III* that McKellen and I did was one version. You could make another one a week later, it would be just as valid and possibly just as good. Shakespeare wrote about humanity, about things we all know about—soap opera, if you like. That's what makes soap opera work today, you care about the characters. I think Shakespeare had rather too many characters in most of his plays for a modern audience, but otherwise he wrote about things as accessible today as they were four hundred years ago.

Baz Luhrmann: I don't believe the demands on the stage director are more or less great than that of the film director. Having worked in both film and theater, I have found the interpretation of a text needs equal thought and development regardless of the medium. Obviously when cinematic language can replace stage convention it may help the telling; however, this is not specific to Shakespeare.

Trevor Nunn: I entirely agree that a cinematic rendering of Shakespeare requires, first of all, a great deal of highly developed visual imagination and inventiveness, often beyond anything that Shakespeare delineated in the text, such as changing location, breaking scenes into smaller units, or setting them in unusual places that allow some sort of heightened perception. I think this is very important and unquestionably this is the business of cinema. You're right to stress the issue of interpretation, because there's very little point in making a film of Shakespeare if what one says, going into it, is "I just want to give an honest account of this text for people who maybe have not read it before," when clearly cinema works, at its best, because of strong directorial concept—however headstrong, however personal—it works through personal vision. Shakespeare is very fruitful territory for personal vision because the plays mean such different things to different people. They also mean different things at different times in history. In our fast-changing world, Shakespeare's plays often change in meaning from decade to decade, sometimes even from year to year.

I think in recent years the films that have worked have had very bold intentions and very refreshing intentions, the major example being Baz Luhrmann's film of *Romeo and Juliet.* It didn't score particularly high marks with me for the amount of text that managed to survive, or in many cases the decisions that were taken about what that text actually meant, how it was learned or how it was phrased. All of that pales into insignificance, however, when you consider that the director achieved a *completely* personal vision that contained urgency and immediacy and anger and relevance, all of which really did address itself to a youthful audience which responded. So I think there's great value in it as a film, but I don't think of it as being the total solution. I certainly don't think of *Twelfth Night* as being the total solution, either, because although we got a number of things right, we didn't find a context that was sufficiently exciting for the wider audience.

Oliver Parker: Having done *Othello* on stage, I was very excited to approach and explore the piece cinematically. Suddenly it was possible to evoke the period and setting more fully, at the same time as you could move right up close to the characters, even to visualize, to illustrate their thoughts. Verbal exposition can be encapsulated within a few images. New energy can be found by intercutting scenes by juxtaposing images. The text can be probed by the image to underscore or even undermine it.

In the case of *Othello,* I was inspired by the verbal imagery and themes to pursue visual ones. The elements, for example, play a large part in the text. The passions are tidal, deep and uncontrollable as the ocean. How great to be able to start on the Grand Canal and end with a funeral at sea. Iago is nearly drowned and Desdemona bathes before she meets her fate. Iago toys with his satanic image, literally playing with fire. Light and dark fight it out on screen. We descend from the bright Cyprus sky to the pitch black bedroom where Othello blows out the final candle before he murders his wife.

I wouldn't say that a film version requires a more fully developed interpretation. Development in both film and theater can be infinite. Film, though, obviously needs more adaptation.

Roman Polanski: Definitely. Cinema gives you infinite possibilities. As I said earlier, Shakespeare was limited by the stage, and if he were living today he would write the same stuff in a different way. It's like the great composers who in each epoch produced music for the available instruments. Shakespeare wonderfully understood the demands of his audiences and, if he woke up today and saw a good cinematic adaptation of his play, he would be delighted.

Franco Zeffirelli: The camera must be at the service of the text, and sometimes the words take on much more powerful or subtle meanings through the camera. In *Hamlet,* we did the "To be or not to be" soliloquy—a very intimate, agonizing series of reflections—in a crypt, as if it were a dialog between a man and himself and his audience, or the world rather, and the camera did a splendid job of realizing that. The film medium gives rise to an innumerable variety of such possibilities.

Is it possible for film versions of Shakespeare to be too visual, too realistic? Do you prefer to utilize fully the cinema's capacity for verisimilitude, or do you prefer to maintain a certain abstraction in the sets and decor? Why?

Peter Brook: Too much information clogs the brain. Too rich food creates indigestion. Simplicity is not a style, nor a virtue—simply a necessity.

Sir Peter Hall: I don't think abstraction in the cinema means anything. The act of filming is already an abstraction, so if you abstract an abstraction . . . well, let me put it this way, a bare stage and three actors acting *Julius Caesar* can make me believe it's ancient Rome. Bring a camera in and then put it up on the screen and the audience would say, "That's not ancient Rome, that's three actors on a bare stage." Cinema is visual, it is about images. I liked Baz Luhrmann's film of *Romeo and Juliet,* I just wish they hadn't spoken, because they couldn't.

Richard Loncraine: No. You cannot upstage Shakespeare. I think the plays can use any technique that makes them more accessible and entertaining. If it works, do it. I consider myself very lucky in that I had the privilege of discovering Shakespeare for myself. I was taught Shakespeare rather badly at a British private school and came away feeling that Shakespeare was not for me. I turned to the arts, I became an art student, a sculptor, and it wasn't until my middle forties that I realized that it wasn't Shakespeare, but me, who had the problem. I had dismissed things like Shakespeare, opera, and ballet as not for me, but in my middle years I've realized that I was the one at fault. Most Shakespeare directors are buffs, they're Shakespearean scholars, they've either played it on stage or they've directed it at university, they're well informed. I knew *nothing* about Shakespeare, I was a complete novice, so I approached it as a man in the street. When I directed *Richard III,* I insisted on knowing exactly what was going on in every scene. I wouldn't let one word go by. Before we started, I often had to ask Ian, "What does this sentence mean? I don't understand it." By the time we came to shoot the film, I obviously knew quite a lot about the play and I knew the text backwards. I still would clarify to the other actors that we all had to have the balls to say, "We're a bit confused here. Does anyone know what's going on?," because they've very complicated scenes. I think there should be an honesty about directing Shakespeare.

Baz Luhrmann: Is it possible to do a film version of Shakespeare that is "too visual, too realistic"? Too much for whom? The concept that there is a set of Shakespearean rules with a foreword by the great man himself, with chapter headings such as "too visual," "too realistic," "over-abstraction, under-abstraction: the use of cryptic symbolism in the minimalist style" is not only ludicrous but irrelevant.

Little factual information about Shakespeare has survived. However, we do get the sense that he liked to "pack the house;" was big on laughter; big on tears; loved the pun, the bawdy gag, the odd song, and a spectacular "blood and guts" sword fight. Above all he would delight, amaze, and captivate with words while managing at the same time to draw a curtain back and reveal the human condition. In any case I think in any film, whether Shakespeare or not, the visual language has to reveal, support, and clarify the storytelling.

Trevor Nunn: For *Twelfth Night,* I delighted in embracing that capacity for verisimilitude. It was wonderful to be able to have Olivia's household as a place where you could imagine how strong that father's influence had been, how stricken the household was with the unexpected death of the brother, and how it had lurched towards stasis, that it could almost not run as a household because of Olivia's grief and waywardness, and therefore the house had become dependent on Malvolio. The scale of the house, the number of servants, and the workforce needed to keep the place running, somehow gave extraordinary authority and credibility to Malvolio. So there's a whole set of circumstances which can be presented only because of cinematic verisimilitude that provide layers of, first of all, credibility and, finally, of tragic meaning to Malvolio's story.

I also liked the challenge of saying, "If Viola is going to present herself as a boy in Orsino's court, what sort of court is it?" I reached the conclusion that there were no women there, it was like a military academy, that again it was a place where his father had had a very strong influence and this young nobleman was also slightly out of control, that the military authority for the area had no strong leadership anymore. I liked the idea of Viola having to pass a whole number of tests before anybody was going to really buy the story. I enjoyed the challenge of saying we've got to believe in Orsino's belief in the boy, because then a real miracle can happen at the end, because the work is so overwhelmingly about gender. Shakespeare constructs the story so that, for very believable reasons, Viola has to become her brother. It's a way of keeping him alive, even though she's accepted the fact that he's dead, because by becoming him she can stop hating herself for being the one who was saved, and she can somehow imagine that she's keeping him alive in this world, and trying to behave as he would behave. All of that becomes very credible when you turn the requirements of cinematic naturalism on it.

Oliver Parker: Film cannot be too visual, though I think you can be too literal. I believe the poetry, the stylization should be embraced and reflected in the film. Otherwise, why do Shakespeare in the first place? At the same time, I find it exciting and invaluable to utilize verisimilitude, to ground the story in reality. It's just that if you're too grounded, you lose the metaphorical dimension.

Roman Polanski: I don't believe that you can make a movie with theatrical, abstract sets, it's impossible. I can't stand them. I'm a fan of Orson Welles, but for me his *Macbeth* is unbearable—it's set in some kind of limbo with bad plumbing. On the other hand, you can create a world which while being realistic is also somehow—I don't know whether I can use the word theatrical, because in the context it sounds pejorative—but it is, in fact. I'm making movies today largely because the first films that greatly impressed me, that made me truly love the cinema, had this quality of creating a specific world different from reality. Olivier's movies, particularly *Hamlet,* was my beloved film when I was about fourteen or fifteen. I saw it innumerable times. What seduced me the most was that world he managed to create, which was something like a fairy tale. So I do believe that you can create this type of reality. But it doesn't always work.

A good example, although it's not exactly Shakespeare, is a film adaptation of an opera, like Losey's *Don Giovanni,* a film which I find hard to stand. If you use such conventional material as an opera, it has to be cinematically re-created in an equally conventional world. You can't have characters sing on green grass,

Fig. 9. Jon Finch in *Macbeth* (1971), adapted by Kenneth Tynan from the play by William Shakespeare (1606), which translated well both to the politically charged atmosphere of America at the time and to the personally afflicted life of its director, Roman Polanski. Directed by Roman Polanski. Courtesy of Billy Rose Theatre Collection, The New York Public Library for the Performing Arts, Astor, Lenox and Tilden Foundations.

in a totally realistic setting, and then suddenly go into some Italian theatrical decor with forced perspective. He mixed those two things and they clash; it just doesn't work.

Franco Zeffirelli: I don't think it's necessary to modernize Shakespeare's plays and there's no advantage in losing the splendor and vitality of those stories in their own historical settings. I've done this sort of thing on the stage. I did *Much Ado About Nothing* at the National Theatre, with a fantastic cast, and it was an experiment which worked very well. Setting it in an equivalent, more recent setting made the play more enjoyable for a contemporary audience, but when you do *Hamlet,* you can't set *Hamlet* in the court of the Austrian Emperors, because it speaks best when it's set in its own cultural background and historical setting.

Is it important for a director of a Shakespearean film to be knowledgeable about the history, the culture, and the cosmology of the Elizabethan world in which Shakespeare wrote his plays?

Peter Brook: Enough not to be thought a moron, but not so much as to forget that it has to make sense *now*.

Sir Peter Hall: I think it helps, but it's much more important for him to have an imaginative response to Shakespeare's images. I don't mean his verbal images, but the image of the whole play.

Baz Luhrmann: As with any story, if you don't understand the world in which the text was generated and if you don't have an absolute, totally, and utterly thorough understanding of the history, culture, and cosmology of everything about that world, then you are interpreting the text in a vacuum.

Trevor Nunn: I was taught as a young teenager by a teacher, with whom I had something bordering on idolatry, who read Shakespeare plays with us and who expanded the texts. So, from that age, I've been consumed with a desire to find out more about Shakespeare, to learn everything about his language, his vocabulary, his slang, the words he invented, the dramaturgy that he invented, things that didn't exist before Shakespeare. I can't think of starting on any of the plays without wanting to consult all of that background knowledge, and that's regardless of saying, "I concluded that I want to change the imagery of the play and set it in the nineteenth century." I did a production of *Timon of Athens* that was set in 1995, but that doesn't alter the extent to which the play needs to be researched. Every particle of its original intention needs to be understood because surely the intention of the contemporary production is to find ways of releasing the original intention more potently to an audience in our own age. I might need to represent the work differently in order to do that, but I must know everything about its original force, if I'm going to undertake that. I don't believe that one can ever say that ignorance is bliss.

Oliver Parker: Important, yes. Essential, no. It depends on the particular vision of the director and how close it is to the original play.

Roman Polanski: *[Laughs]* I've read an interview with Billy Wilder where they ask him, because Billy cowrote most of his scripts, whether he believes that a director should know how to write. And he said, "No, I don't think so, but it helps if he can read." You can quote this, it's answer enough. I mean, how can you deal with such material if you're not well read, if you have no knowledge of that period.

Franco Zeffirelli: I think it's essential, for Shakespeare, or for any great author you're dealing with. You study a lot about him, what came before, what happened around him. When I directed the Brontë film *Jane Eyre,* I was totally immersed in the cultural and social problems of England at that time. You had to do that to know the correct procedures. You can't just jump in and expect to know how a character behaves in a historical context without knowing that historical context.

What is your view of filming historically updated versions of Shakespeare's plays as opposed to period presentations?

Peter Brook: Very delicate question. The meaning must be vivid, direct, and alive today. But both modern and antiquated externals can block as much as help.

Sir Peter Hall: Well, none of us know what "period" means, anymore than we know what "update" means. Shakespeare put chimney pots and clocks in Rome; it didn't bother him, he didn't know they didn't have them. I think every Shakespeare play or film has to have its own visual world, and if it makes you think, "Daddy, why are they talking about swords?," when actually all they've got is pistols, then it's rubbish. But you can't be period accurate, that's antiquarian and boring.

Richard Loncraine: I think both are valid, both have their place. It was not my idea to set *Richard III* in the Thirties—that was decided by Richard Eyre, who directed it as a stage play, with Ian McKellen. I never saw the stage play, so I've no idea what it was like, but I believe we took the idea and ran with it, and extended it on, which is what I'd hoped we would do. I think setting *Richard III* in the fascist era was certainly a valid interpretation and I decided to make a world that wasn't England, because I felt that that was going to be confusing. We had period language that was written four hundred years ago and I didn't want the language to clash with the imagery by setting it in a period or a place that was known. Setting it in an unknown time and place—you weren't in London, you weren't in Strasbourg, you weren't in New York, you were somewhere in this movie—I think helped to blur the lines between four-hundred-year-old language and the more contemporary imagery. Shakespeare never performed his plays in period costume, they were played in whatever actors turned up on the day in, so Shakespeare obviously didn't think it was that important, and neither do I.

Baz Luhrmann: Having directed Shakespeare in theater, opera, and film, it's never been a question of, is there a right or a wrong method. One must simply address an audience at a particular moment in time and attempt to reveal the greater richness of the particular idea or story. Whether you do an unbelievably accurate Elizabethan version, performed on a bare stage, in the middle of the day to four thousand mostly drunk punters with the female roles played by adolescent boys in drag and spoken in a virtually incomprehensible accent, or any other interpretation, it is correct if it reveals the heart of the story and engages and awakens the audience to the material.

Trevor Nunn: I'm all in favor of people taking a different approach to visual imagery in contemporary production, be it in the theater or in the cinema. Often what happens when strong conceptual lines are taken with Shakespeare is that things come alive in very unexpected ways and that's much more commendable than the inept version that sets out to take the play at face value. Ian McKellen's approach to *Richard III* as a sort of twentieth-century rise of a fascist party, for example, has insights attached to it.

Oliver Parker: I respect the desire to update the plays, especially when the intention is to connect with a wider audience. I don't think, though, that it necessarily makes it more relevant. Sometimes it seems just a gimmick. But when it's done wittily and thoroughly, it can be terrific. Baz Luhrmann's *Romeo + Juliet* is a case in point. I found it passionate and poignant and hugely accessible.

Roman Polanski: I absolutely hate those updated versions. I'm allergic to them. I think that Shakespeare can indeed be played like jazz—you know, there are no other directions than "enter" and "exit" or "is slain" or whatever— so you can act it and stage it any way you want, but what's the point of updating it? That's a cacophony. If filmmakers fear Shakespeare is antiquated, then leave him alone, they should look for different material. If you accept certain conventions, and the convention of the language is one of them, then you have to find adequate elements to express it. You just can't dress people in contemporary clothes or, what's worse, shift it to some other period. What's the point of throwing it into the nineteenth century?

Franco Zeffirelli: As I've said, I don't think dressing the characters in modern costumes has any advantage. When I did *Romeo and Juliet,* I did it period, but after a few minutes the audience forgot that the story took place in Verona four or five hundred years ago, and that people were dressed in a certain way. They were engaged immediately through their identification with characters they came to love. When you have the power of a character that surpasses contemporary dressing up and other references, I don't think you need to make that effort. Actually, it might misfire. The Luhrmann film didn't update the play, it just made a big joke out of it. But apparently the pseudo-culture of young people today wouldn't have digested the play unless you dressed it up that way, with all those fun and games.

We have to help young people face the past with honesty, courage, and greed, because we learn so much from the past. We live in very dry, very poor times, and we have to go back to when our garden was full of flowers and marvelous fruits, because today our poor plants are sterile, they don't produce anything. Children do learn from the past, because only if you know the past can you properly contemplate the present and the future. When you look at the head of David by Michelangelo, that's beyond time, it's an emotion that will last forever. Art has the tremendous advantage of defeating time. François Mitterand, when he opened the Musée d'Orsay, said, "When I look at a work of art, I understand that man can defeat death."

Producing a Shakespearean film is usually referred to as "popularizing" Shakespeare for a mass moviegoing audience. What is your view? What sort of compromises does such "popularization" involve?

Peter Brook: None willingly.

Sir Peter Hall: The fact that a lot of people are aware of *Romeo and Juliet* because of Baz's film doesn't mean, when they go to see the play of *Romeo and Juliet,* that they won't be woefully disappointed, because it's nothing like the film. I think that popularization is valuable but we shouldn't kid ourselves that it's the real thing. I'm a purist because I believe that a great artist deserves to be respected and not cut to hell.

I've spent about forty-five years of my life doing Shakespeare, including dozens of Shakespeare productions on the stage. This is what I passionately believe. When I did my film of *A Midsummer Night's Dream,* I thought it would be interesting to use the camera as an attempt to get closer to the text. That was the avowed intention of that film, which some people liked very much and others didn't. But that was bending film towards the text. I cut very, very little of it and I deliberately didn't make it, as it were, filmic. I made it verbal and I think it's probably the best spoken version of the play that you could find. Reinhardt's film is better as a piece of film. I was trying to expose the play on film, not adapt the play into a film.

I've seen all the new Shakespeare films and, as I say, I'd sooner they were done than not. I'm sure they're interesting some people and they're keeping Shakespeare alive in some sense, but I don't think the cinema can get up and take a bow and say, "We do Shakespeare," because by its own confession it can't. It can't have the full text, it can't actually use the text in the right way. It's a popularizing reproduction, but, as for myself, I wouldn't ever go to the cinema for Shakespeare.

Richard Loncraine: Shakespeare didn't write plays to be stuck in drawers or that no one went to see, he wrote them for a mass audience. He had no amplification, so with more than about five hundred people, no one could hear what the hell was going on, but if Shakespeare could have had loudspeakers he would have played to audiences in the thousands. Compromise by doing Shakespeare on film? Not at all. I think it's probably a strength. There are certainly things you have to adapt. In *Richard III,* Richard doesn't even get killed on stage. He's killed off stage and someone comes in and says, "The king is dead." Well, you certainly can't do that with a film audience, they would tear you apart. So Shakespeare certainly has to be adapted for the screen, but if you respect the man's writing and you approach it as if he is the one doing the adapting—I mean, try to think of what Shakespeare would have done—you probably won't go far wrong.

Baz Luhrmann: It is almost embarrassing to me when people start talking about Shakespeare as if his intention was not to be popular or as if he was a storyteller, playwright, poet and actor who was not interested in the widest possible audience. Do we think Shakespeare would be turning in his grave because he beat Sylvester Stallone at the opening weekend of *Romeo and Juliet?* I don't think so.

Are we trying to say that a man who had to play to 4,000 punters a day and to every kind of person from the street sweeper to the Queen of England wouldn't be interested in being successful in the multiplexes? At what time was Shakespeare only interested in playing to a small elite? I don't understand that notion. It seems the antithesis of everything Shakespeare stood for is to treat his text as high culture.

Trevor Nunn: There is this pressure, partly from film production companies and partly one's own knowledge and instincts. You want your film to play to the widest possible audience, and yet you want to be able to hold your head up amongst Shakespeare scholars and not to have to say, "I deliberately abandoned all my beliefs for that period of time," or "I wittingly vulgarized this bit of material for commercial considerations."

Shakespeare was an extraordinary example of a writer who discovered the going form. There was this huge creative energy in him, a sheer appetite for creation, and he chose the theater. He didn't choose prose, he didn't choose long narrative poetry, he chose the theater because it seemed to him to be the going form, where the excitement was. That was where people who could write were suddenly congregating, and where there was this huge burst of activity. I think the going form changes from age to age, and it's not an accident that in the nineteenth century, it was the novel, and the greatest writers became novelists and the less great writers continued to struggle with the theater. There's obviously a sense in which the cinema is now the going form, and I'm convinced that, were he alive today, Shakespeare would be gravitating towards cinema. He would want to be an auteur, he would want to be in charge of everything, and one suspects that he would have done it wonderfully.

Oliver Parker: I applaud the desire to popularize Shakespeare, to introduce him to a mass audience to prove the stories, characters, and language can be extremely entertaining and accessible. What makes him such a genius is the many layers to his work—his ability to be insightful, moving, and profound, while entertaining at the same time. Given that so many people now regard him as the province of academics, I think it is important to reclaim him as a popular artist. I don't think this need debase him. The point is to encourage people into their seats, and, as he was a shareholder in the Globe Theatre, I'm sure he would sympathize.

Roman Polanski: Whether you refer to it this way or not, it's a fact, not a matter of opinion. Certainly more people have seen Olivier's film of *Hamlet* than have seen theatrical productions of it. Whether a film adaptation of Shakespeare requires compromises depends on the standing of a director who can oppose the influence of the habitual committee that is asking him to make it for the lowest common denominator. When I shot *Macbeth*, I didn't compromise in any way. Whatever changes we made were based on research, and, as for the illustration, you can illustrate certain things in such a way that you do not need to replace antiquated words, because they become clear by the visual context or through acting.

Franco Zeffirelli: There is a preconceived attitude—Shakespeare, oh my God!—but there is also a big reward when you present a classical story straightforward, and you don't try to be literally modern with it, because people will respond. You must do everything possible to grab the audience, but convincing the audience that they are revisiting a great classic under the proper conditions is an effort we should make. With my films I've tried to return Shakespeare to the popular audience that he originally wrote for. Juliet Capulet and Romeo Montague in Verona expressed themselves more nobly, more fully, than young people do today. But what's more important is that the essence of man, what man is and what he needs, has not changed since the stone age. We cry and laugh at the same anguishes and the same jokes.

Are you encouraged by the present vogue for Shakespearean films? Will such a trend make it easier for you to make another Shakespearean film? Do you have a Shakespeare play in mind that you would like to film?

Peter Brook: Yes. No. No.

Sir Peter Hall: No, I don't think so. Shakespeare never makes sufficient money to really interest the moguls. There are always little spurts and little false dawns, but I don't really think the situation has changed. The biggest problem we've had in Britain, and probably it's so in America, too, is that that dreadful BBC series has completely buggered the proper filming or videotaping of Shakespeare for years and years and years. Almost none of them were worth watching. They combined all the things that I think is in the background of your questions—awful historicism, awful ham acting, and the wrong kind of respect for the text. The backlog is not promising.

I would love to make a film of *The Merchant of Venice* in Venice, with Dustin Hoffman. I nearly did, because I did it with him on the stage, on the West End and Broadway. While I would like to make another Shakespeare film, I'm sure to try again would mean doing a bastard version, cut to bits, and I wouldn't want to do that.

Richard Loncraine: Shakespeare tends to go in bursts, and we have had a big one recently. The film business, as a money-making operation, has never been an easy marriage of art and commerce, but if a Shakespeare film makes money, as the recent *Romeo and Juliet* did, then it will encourage studios to make other Shakespeare films. Certainly the copyright isn't a problem. *Richard III* was not a financially successful movie, though it made its money back. It was creatively successful almost everywhere in the world, and I hope it will encourage young filmmakers to turn to Shakespeare. It's certainly made me discover Shakespeare. I would love to direct another Shakespeare film, but not until I've made a contemporary movie. I'm very interested in doing *The Merchant of Venice* and McKellen and I are certainly discussing that.

Baz Luhrmann: When I was young I was mostly exposed to bad productions and found Shakespeare impenetrable. Then one day I experienced the stage production of *Twelfth Night* by Neil Armfield and suddenly a curtain was pulled back. Shakespeare's storytelling was suddenly relevant and I realized what I'd been missing out on. In answering your question, it is encouraging that many different directors are taking on the responsibility of revealing the richness of these plays to audiences who, like myself, may have missed out, while at the same time reawakening old fans through fresh tellings.

Concerning *Romeo and Juliet,* I expect my interpretation to be written off as "old hat" one day soon and replaced by a new cinema version. Maybe it will be a very accurate Elizabethan interpretation—who knows? What is really important is, as Benjamin Britten once said, if a story is true then there will be many different productions in many different places and it will go on and on. My own view is that truly great story telling defies time, geography, and the so-called rules of right and wrong; the proof of its worth is that it lives on.

Trevor Nunn: I'm completely delighted by the vogue in Shakespeare films. I'm slightly worried that the huge hit was the one that in many ways encouraged producers to believe that what you have to do is to cut the text to within an inch of its life and concentrate on narrative, because I think it would be sad if all Shakespeare films followed that formula. I yearn to go to somebody's Shakespeare film where it's especially long, it says we really are going to do the whole text, and it still works.

I'm not going to be making a Shakespeare film for a while because I've taken on the responsibility of a huge theater company, but, yes, I would love to do another one. There are several titles I would think of. I was beaten to the punch on *Othello.* I did a television version of which we're very proud, with Ian McKellen as Iago. I think we got a lot out of it. *Troilus and Cressida* would make a wonderful film, but people would cut the text to smithereens because the text is very hard, very difficult.

Fig. 10. *King Lear* (1971), directed by Grigori Kozintsev. In keeping with the concerns of the Soviet Union of the time, Kozintsev's adaptation reflects a concern for the poor people most affected by Lear's division of his kingdom. Courtesy of Billy Rose Theatre Collection, The New York Public Library for the Performing Arts, Astor, Lenox and Tilden Foundations.

Oliver Parker: Of course, the current interest in Shakespeare can only be good. There is not, however, an endless reservoir of plays and many of the great ones have recently been done. *Measure for Measure* is a notable exception.

Roman Polanski: I suffered so much because of that film. It's very difficult to put a film together, to get the financing, and since *Macbeth* was not financially successful, I really sort of said that's it. I don't know if there's really a vogue. I think they're just short of subjects and are trying to dig them up wherever they can.

I would love to do another Shakespeare film. I would do it exactly the same way I did *Macbeth,* though, by just telling the story in the way I think the author intended, except that he did not have at his disposal the present means of production. Today you have all these visual effects which can facilitate certain scenes, which before required so much money and effort, but which you can do now with the help of computers, like all those magical things in *A Midsummer Night's Dream.*

Franco Zeffirelli: Well, in a way I think I've contributed enough to the cause of reviving Shakespeare and bringing him to the attention of a mass audience. Nevertheless, I do have three or four ideas, one or two of which would be very surprising—I won't mention the titles because others will snatch them—but for now I'm trying to tell other stories.

A Conversation with Julie Taymor

Stephen Pizzello

In theatrical circles, director/designer Julie Taymor is renowned as an adventurous and highly imaginative artist with a flair for mind-bending visuals. Her stage productions have garnered considerable acclaim; most recently, she earned two Tony Awards (direction and costume design) for her Broadway rendition of *The Lion King*.

In 1996, Taymor directed *Juan Darien* at the Lincoln Center's Beaumont Theater, and saw the fruits of her labor produce five Tony nominations, including one for Best Director. Some of her other theater credits include *Juan Darien—A Carnival Mass* (which earned two Obies and numerous other awards), *The Green Bird*, *The Flying Dutchman*, *Salome*, *The Magic Flute*, *The Tempest*, *The Taming of the Shrew*, *The Transposed Heads,* and *Liberty's Taken.*

Taymor directed her first opera when she took on Stravinsky's *Oedipus Rex* in 1992 for the Saito Kinen Orchestra in Japan, with Seiji Ozawa conducting. Her film version of the live production (shot by

Reprinted from *American Cinematographer* 81, no. 2 (February 2002): 64–73. Reprinted with permission of *American Cinematographer* © 2000, 2002.

cinematographer Bobby Bukowski) premiered at the Sundance Film Festival and won the Jury Award at the Montreal Festival of Films on Art. After the picture was broadcast internationally in 1993, Taymor won an Emmy Award and the 1994 International Classical Music Award for Best Opera Production.

She also gained filmmaking experience by writing and directing *Fool's Fire*, an hour-long adaptation of Edgar Allan Poe's *Hopfrog* that was also shot by Bukowski. Produced by American Playhouse, it premiered at the (pre-Sundance) American Film Festival in Park City, and aired on PBS in March of 1992. An experimental blend of 35mm footage and high-definition video, *Fool's Fire* went on to win the Best Drama Award at the Tokyo International Electronic Cinema Festival.

Taymor's production of Shakespeare's *Titus Andronicus* was produced off-Broadway by Theater for a New Audience in the spring of 1994. She subsequently adapted the play into a film script, and kept her unique interpretation intact on the screen with the help of top-flight collaborators, including cinematographer Luciano Tovoli, ASC, AIC, two-time Oscar-winning costume designer Milena Canonero (*Chariots of Fire, Barry Lyndon*), production designer Dante Ferretti (a five-time Oscar nominee whose credits include *The Adventures of Baron Munchausen, The Age of Innocence, Interview With the Vampire,* and *Kundun*), and composer Elliot Goldenthal (a two-time Oscar nominee for his work on *Interview With the Vampire* and *Michael Collins*).

Taymor discussed *Titus* with *AC* during a recent visit to Los Angeles.

American Cinematographer: *Have you always been interested in film as a creative medium?*

Taymor: Yes, but because I grew up doing theater, I was always busy with that. I never put aside the time to shift over to film, although I did do some Super 8 work and two-dimensional animation as a teenager. I eventually took a summer film course at New York University, and later on I participated in both the theater and film labs at the Sundance Institute. My first big film project was *Fool's Fire,* which was televised on the PBS series *American Playhouse.* Unfortunately, that was only an hour-long film, so it couldn't be categorized as either a short film or a feature. It went to festivals and won awards, but not many people got to see it. *Fool's Fire* was experimental in nature, but very much controlled within a studio.

Titus therefore wasn't my first time working with cameras, but it was my first real feature film on location. It was very different than working within theatrical limitations or entirely within a studio.

How did you get your motion-picture version of Titus Andronicus *off the ground?*

Taymor: I'd done the play off-Broadway, and I decided to write a script adapted from Shakespeare's original text. Ellen and Robbie Little from the Overseas Film Group [who eventually would serve as executive producers of the film, along with Stephen K. Bannon] optioned the screenplay. We then went through the process of casting actors, and when Anthony Hopkins signed on to star, all of that became much easier. It was still hard to get enough money, but that's always difficult—especially when you're dealing with one of Shakespeare's tragedies, as opposed to a comedy like *A Midsummer Night's Dream* or *Much Ado About Nothing.* However, [producer] Jody Patton of Clear Blue Sky liked the screenplay very much, and she'd seen a PBS behind-the-scenes show about my work on *The Tempest* [for the stage]. She'd enjoyed that, and my Broadway version of *The Lion King* was just beginning to bloom, so she and Paul Allen decided to back *Titus.*

The film's budget should have been bigger when we started, but at a certain point you have to just start working with what you have. Once everyone began seeing dailies, we got some more money for the CGI shots and other postproduction work.

What led you to select Titus Andronicus *as your first feature-film project?*

Taymor: I've had other offers, but I've always loved *Titus Andronicus.* I felt that it was the most contemporary and accessible of Shakespeare's plays, and I also thought it had the most to say about the violence that's taking place in the world right now. It's a very powerful play, and I knew it could be a movie.

Frankly, I think Shakespeare should be given some kind of Lifetime Achievement Aware for Screenwriting. His plays *are* screenplays, because there's no scenery in them; he doesn't place those types of limitations on the reader's imagination. They're not like modern plays, which often have two or three characters sitting around in living rooms or kitchens. Plays like that are so boring—they lack the vision and scope of Shakespeare. He doesn't include specific settings, so if you're adapting one of his plays, you can envision anything you want. As an artist, I find it very exciting to be able to add my own ideas, such as staging a key scene with Titus in a bathtub. There's nothing in the play that says Titus is sitting in a tub, or that Rape, Revenge, and Murder visit him in the guise of animals. I'm very dedicated to Shakespeare's intent, but I've also taken some artistic license with the material. For example, Titus's grandson is a minor character in the original play, but I wanted to expand his role a bit to show the scope of the story through his eyes.

In both the play and the film, you've melded various eras into a unique, timeless, and rather surreal setting. The costumes, production design, and other visual elements combine both classical and modern Western aesthetics. What inspired you to adopt that creative strategy?

Taymor: That idea is introduced in the first scene, in which the young boy is shown sitting at a kitchen table and playing with toys representing both modern superheroes and classical soldiers. From there he enters this kind of time-warp that transports him into an ancient coliseum, where Titus and his soldiers are returning from their victorious battle with the Goths.

I had talked everything over with my wonderful Italian collaborators, and we really worked on how we could unify this world that's actually a collision of various worlds. By introducing that concept in the first scene, we could then combine tanks, chariots, motorcycles, horses, and Etruscan armor in the following sequence. All of that was extremely plotted out, because I had spent four years working on *Titus*. I'd done it as a play, so I had already been through that rigorous discipline of "reducing" things. As a theater director, you have to be very strict about getting things down to their essence. I also work as a theatrical designer, and I'm always striving to find the simplest and most essential way to create a scene. Before *The Lion King,* my productions didn't have huge budgets, and I think that gave me discipline as a director.

What were some of your specific visual influences in terms of the material?

Taymor: In the theater version, everything was much more black-and-white, and one of the strongest influences was the work of [still photographer] Joel Peter Witkin. In both the play and film, I wanted that sense of defamed, deflowered elegance. When you go to Rome, you see graffiti on these beautiful monuments. The symbol of Titus is really a great sculpture from antiquity with a broken hand and a broken foot. In his photography, Witkin often defiles various masterpieces, but they're still beautiful in the end. *Titus* is a dark tale, but it's also very moving—there's exquisite beauty in the ugliness and the torture. The play could be treated as a big, Grand Guignol comic book, but I think the poetry of the story is too rich and too deep to take that approach.

In Playing With Fire, *a book about your work, you've cited both Fellini and Kurosawa as influences.*

Taymor: I think Kurosawa's *Ran* and Orson Welles's *Chimes of Midnight* are the best screen interpretations of Shakespeare's work. I've always loved Kurosawa; I spent a year in Paris [at age 16, studying mime at L'École de Mime Jacques LeCoq,] and when I used to go to the Cinémathèque to see films, Kurosawa classics like *Rashomon* and *The Seven Samurai* were among the first that I watched there.

With Fellini, I'm not as drawn to his *entire* sensibility. Oddly enough, I'm not that into *8½* or his other movies that deal with male-female relationships, but I love *Nights of Cabiria* and *Amarcord*. I'm a caricaturist, and so was Fellini. I also sculpt and make masks, and I think I share Fellini's love of the human face, as well as his interest in puppets, clowns, the carnival, and the theater.

The film seems to have a very strict color scheme. Was that by design?

Taymor: Yes. The costumes became a difficult challenge, because we were trying to limit our color palette in that respect. We'd limited our palette in the theatrical production as well, because when you're covering such a great span of time, you have to find a [visual] way to glue it all together. My instructions to [costume designer] Milena Canonero were that everything should be either metallic, black, white, red, or blue, with no other colors except for the green of the grass if necessary. Originally, I wanted to drain the colors, and we experimented with various lab processes. But when we shot the film, it was so beautiful and rich that we decided against using desaturation.

How did you determine the individual costumes for the various characters?

Taymor: Costumes convey character, and various periods evoke certain feelings in the viewer. In *Titus,* each character spoke to me in a different way. Lavinia is therefore dressed like a lady from the 1950s, with her little short gloves and veil. She's the beautiful girl you want to defile, the jewel of Rome, and I thought of Grace Kelly as the archetype. We put Lavinia quite literally on a pedestal, like Degas's ballerina. In the play we used an actual pedestal, but that was too literal for the film, so we changed it to a tree stump.

Tamora, on the other hand was more of the 1930s and '40s. She's more androgynous, so we put her in a sleek metal gown with her hair slicked back. Meanwhile, Titus's clothing goes from black to grey to white as the story progresses, from armor to a sweater to a bathrobe to a chef's outfit. He gets lighter and lighter. When he's in the sweater, he's like an uncle from the 1960s—his armor has been pierced, and he's been violated. He ends up seemingly stripped of all his power, sitting naked in a bathtub.

Transforming Titus *into a feature film allowed you go "open up" the play on a larger canvas. How did that additional freedom impact your directorial instincts?*

Taymor: Well, I've never directed an entire army of extras before! I particularly remember going to the location of the Goth camp, which was at this fabulous quarry. It was really daunting, but after we set up all of the tents and soldiers, I just began working my way through it. Camera movement came fairly naturally to me, because I tend to think in very visual terms. We created shot lists ahead of time, but we didn't use many storyboards. Once we went to a given location, I could visualize things, and Luciano and I would sit together and plot things out beforehand. I do like to pre-edit [in my mind], and on this picture I also had a great editor, Françoise Bonnet. I don't do tons of coverage, because I don't believe in it—to me, shooting a lot of coverage means that you don't have a clear idea of what you're after. It's good to have coverage if you have to make cuts for length, or if you're dealing with action scenes.

In fact, some scenes in the film were staged exactly as they were in the play, such as the sequence in which the heads of Titus's sons are brought to him in a wagon. We shot that scene from behind Titus and the other characters who are with him, so that when his shoulders begin shaking, you think he's crying—until he turns around and you see that he's actually laughing. In that situation, there was really no need for additional coverage or close-ups. The scene was preconceived to produce a particular effect.

In the theater, you don't get to edit, so the transitions—how you move from one scene to the next—are very important, because they all happen right in front of the audience's eyes. In movies, you can cut, which creates a lot of possibilities. However, I think those options can be even more exciting if you have a clear, preconceived idea in your mind. I generally don't like to "discover things" at the editing stage, but still, I must say that Françoise managed to come up with some very surprising and exciting ideas.

What were some of the key problems you faced on a larger-scale film project?

Taymor: Well, the biggest problems were getting the permissions to use certain locations, and dealing with the weather. The logistics were the real torture for me. We began shooting in October, and it would get dark at three o'clock in the afternoon while we were shooting an enormous scene in a forest. We were fighting the sun or the rain all the time. During the scene at the crossroads, we wanted gray skies, and they'd be there for a moment and then go away again. I never had to confront those types of problems on my previous film projects, which were both shot indoors.

I much preferred shooting on Dante Ferretti's sets, which were just magnificent and very imaginative. His work on this film is really an example of beautiful and truly *conceptual* production design. He was the one who introduced me to E.U.R., Mussolini's government center, which is known as the "square coliseum" [and serves as the exterior of the Emperor's palace in the film]. In our desire to blend eras, that building really served as the perfect link to the past; it's a "modern" structure, but Mussolini was trying to recreate the grandeur of the Roman Empire when he built it.

What led you to hire Luciano Tovoli as your cinematographer?

Taymor: When I started the film, he wasn't available, but I decided to make a change [regarding the cinematographer's position] during production, and he was available at that point. Luciano has done great work, and I love the crystalline quality of his photography. He understands depth of field in a way that's very exciting. When we were on the set, I'd sometimes think he was using too much light, but he'd always say, "Don't worry, Julie, it will give us tremendous range." And it did—his approach to the lighting gave the picture extraordinary depth and clarity.

How involved did you get with the lighting and composition?

Taymor: I was certainly very involved with those aspects of the shoot. Since I come from the theater, where there's no natural light, I'm used to creating stylized lighting. I think Luciano was a bit surprised by how much I knew about it. He was aware that I didn't have a lot of experience making films, but I do enjoy playing with lighting effects, and I think he was pleased about that. I understand and love the art of lighting, and I also realize that it takes time to set everything up. Sometimes that setup time can be debilitating for the director and the actors, but if you're trying to tell the story through lighting and imagery, the wait is well worth it. With a cinematographer like Luciano, you know you're going to get beautiful results, and I think I gave him a big more freedom than he's had on some of his other projects. I felt that I was able to tap into his talents, and I gave him the space he needed. I had some great artists around me on this project, and I let them do their jobs.

As far as the framing was concerned, we shot the film in the Super 35 format, and since I'm a painter and a visual artist, every single shot was carefully composed. There wasn't one shot in the film where I didn't know what was going to appear in a given corner or background. Luciano has a beautiful humility and openness, and he's so comfortable in his own experience that he can work well with a newcomer and appreciate new ideas.

In the play, you used intermittent, haiku-like images, which you dubbed "Penny Arcade Nightmares," to reveal the inner landscapes of the characters' minds. In the film, these interludes were shot against bluescreen and then composited digitally. What made you opt for that approach?

Taymor: The Penny Arcade Nightmares were composited by Kyle Cooper [of the Los Angeles-based visual design firm Imaginary Forces], who has done some striking title sequences for various films, including *Seven*. I knew I was going to do those sequences digitally ahead of time. If we'd done them optically, it would have been really frustrating. I've done some compositing on high-definition video, but I didn't want a video look. Kyle understood my desire to lend those sequences a surreal, handmade look that was a bit funky; I didn't want them to be *slick*. I wanted to keep that same raw quality that we'd lent the Penny Arcade Nightmares in the stage version. We provided Kyle with the raw footage for the sequences, and he put them together based on my descriptions of what I wanted to see. It was an interesting collaboration.

You also used Mad Cow's Time-Slice system during the film's climactic banquet sequence to heighten the key moment by "freezing" it. The use of similar camera-array systems has become very popular in television commercials and feature films such as The Matrix. *Did you simply feel as if that instant in the story required a special kind of technological spotlight, so to speak?*

Taymor: Well, I initially intended to use that technique three times during the banquet scene, but that seemed a bit excessive, as well as expensive and time-consuming. I decided that if I was going to use it, I should do it to highlight the final act [of violence] that the child sees. I think in that regard, it worked as the climax of the film. I actually hadn't seen *The Matrix* or all of those commercials before we did it. I've seen them since then, of course, but I think we used the technique as more than just an effect—to me, all effects have to have an underlying meaning that relates to the film's narrative content.

We shot that sequence without the effect as well, but I think you need to stop that moment to highlight the way we create art out of violence, or masterpieces out of torture. The banquet sequence really plays with the way an audience perceives violence.

Your personal interpretation of Shakespeare's work is often categorized as completely original, but Shakespeare himself often cribbed from other sources. How would you assess your work on Titus *in that regard?*

Taymor: I'm a person of this day and age, so my approach to the material is quite naturally influenced by all of the movies, plays, books, and paintings I've absorbed. You can't run away from all of that; it's how you twist and turn those influences that makes the work interesting.

For example, in *Titus* we have a huge orgy sequence in the palace featuring visual elements that will certainly recall Fellini's *Satyricon,* because both scenes involve orgies set in ancient Rome. But at the same time, the sequence in *Titus* is really nothing like the orgy scenes in *Satyricon.* Fellini's version is much more formalized and theatrical.

In the same vein, if you're shooting military marches and you do it well, on some level it's going to look like the work of [German Third Reich filmmaker] Leni Riefenstahl. It's not as if we consciously set out to copy that style.

In my opinion, "originality" is a very dumb concept—it's very "late 20th Century." None of Shakespeare's stories are original. You can read passages written by Plutarch that have the exact same lines, and watch Shakespeare's genius as he twists the language and makes it deep and poetic. It's how an artist assembles his or her influences into a whole piece that really matters.

Interlude: The Actor as Director A Trip to Don Quixoteland: Conversations with Orson Welles

Juan Cobos, Miguel Rubio, and J. A. Pruneda

Q: One of the constants of your work is the struggle for liberty and the defense of the individual.

Welles: A struggle for dignity. I absolutely disagree with those works of art, those novels, those films that, these days, speak about despair. I do not think that an artist may take total despair as a subject: we are too close to it in daily life. This genre of subject can be utilized only when life is less dangerous and more clearly affirmative.

Q: In the transposition of The Trial *to the cinema, there is a fundamental change; in Kafka's book, K's character is more passive than in the film.*

Welles: I made him more active, properly speaking. I do not believe that passive characters are appropriate to drama. I have nothing against Antonioni, for example, but, in order to interest me, the characters must do something, from a dramatic point of view, you understand.

Reprinted from "A Trip to Don Quixoteland: Conversations with Orson Welles," by Juan Cobos, Miguel Rubio, and J. A. Pruneda, trans. Rose Kaplin, *Cahiers du Cinéma* 5 (1966): 34–47.

Q: Was The Trial *an old project?*

Welles: I once said that a good film could be drawn from the novel, but I myself didn't think of doing it. A man came to see me and told me he believed he could find money so that I could make a film in France. He gave me a list of films and asked that I choose. And from that list of fifteen films I chose the one that, I believe, was the best: *The Trial.* Since I couldn't do a film written by myself, I chose Kafka.

Q: What films do you really want to do?

Welles: Mine. I have drawers full of scenarios written by me.

Q: What is astonishing in your work is this continual effort to bring solutions to the problems posed by directing.

Welles: The cinema is still very young and it would be completely ridiculous to not succeed in finding new things for it. If only I could make more films! Do you know what happened with *The Trial?* Two weeks before our departure from Paris for Yugoslavia, we were told that there would be no possibility of having a single set built there because the producer had already made another film in Yugoslavia and hadn't paid his debts. That's why it was necessary to utilize that abandoned station. I had planned a completely different film.

Everything was invented at the last minute because physically my film had an entirely different conception. It was based on an absence of sets. And this gigantism I have been reproached for is, in part, due to the fact that the only set I possessed was that old abandoned station. An empty railroad station is immense! The production, as I had sketched it, comprised sets that gradually disappeared. The number of realistic elements were to become fewer and fewer and the public would become aware of it, to the point where the scene would be reduced to free space as if everything had dissolved.

Q: The movement of the actors and the camera in relation to each other in your films is very beautiful.

Welles: That is a visual obsession. I believe, thinking about my films, that they are based not so much on pursuit as on a search. If we are looking for something, the labyrinth is the most favorable location for the search. I do not know why, but my films are all for the most part a physical search.

Q: You reflect about your work a great deal.

Welles: Never *a posteriori*. I think about each of my films when I am preparing for them. I do an enormous sketch when starting. What is marvelous about the cinema, what makes it superior to the theatre, is that it has many elements that may conquer us but may also enrich us, offer us a life impossible anywhere else. The cinema should always be the discovery of something. I believe that the cinema should be essentially poetic; that is why, during the shooting and not during the preparation, I try to plunge myself into a poetic development, which differs from narrative development and dramatic development. But, in reality, I am a man of ideas; yes, above all else—I am even more a man of ideas than a moralist, I suppose.

Q: Do you believe it is possible to have a form of tragedy without melodrama?

Welles: Yes, but that is very difficult. For any *auteur* who comes out of the Anglo-Saxon tradition, it is very difficult. Shakespeare never arrived at it. It is possible, but up to the present no one has succeeded. In my cultural tradition, tragedy cannot escape from melodrama. We may always draw from tragic elements and perhaps even the grandeur of tragedy but melodrama is always inherent to the Anglo-Saxon cultural universe. There's no doubt about it.

Q: Is it correct that your films never correspond to what you were thinking of doing before starting them? Because of producers, etc.

Welles: No, in reality, in what concerns me, creation, I must say that I am constantly changing. At the beginning, I have a basic notion of what the final aspect of the film will be, more or less. But each day, at every moment, one deviates or modifies because of the expression in an actress's eyes or the position of the sun. I am not in the habit of preparing a film and then setting myself to make it. I prepare a film but I have no intention of making *this* film. The preparation serves to liberate me, so that I may work in my fashion; thinking of bits of film and of the result they will give; and there are parts that deceive me because I haven't conceived them in a complete enough way. I do not know what word to use, because I am afraid of pompous words when I talk about making a film. The degree of concentration I utilize in a world that I create, whether this be for thirty seconds or for two hours, is very high; that is why, when I am shooting, I have a lot of trouble sleeping. This is not because I am pre-occupied but because, for me, this world has so much reality that closing my eyes is not sufficient to make it disappear. It represents a terrible intensity of feeling. If I shoot in a royal location I sense and I see this site in so violent a way that, now, when I see these places again, they are similar to tombs, completely dead. There are spots in the world that are, to my eyes, cadavers; that is because I have already shot there—for me, they are completely finished. Jean Renoir said something that seems to be related to that: "We should remind people that a field of wheat painted by Van Gogh can arouse a stronger emotion than a field of wheat in nature." It is important to recall that art surpasses reality. Film becomes another reality. Apropos, I admire Renoir's work very much even though mine doesn't please him at all. We are good friends and, truthfully, one of the things I regret is that he doesn't like his films for the same reason I do. His films appear marvelous to me because what I admire most in an *auteur* is authentic sensitivity. I attach no importance to whether or not a film is a technical SUCCESS: moreover, films that lack this genre of sensitivity may not be judged on the same level with technical or aesthetic knowingness. But the cinema, the true cinema, is a poetic expression and Renoir is one of the rare poets. Like Ford, it is in his style. Ford is a poet. A comedian. Not for women, of course, but for men.

Q: Apart from Ford and Renoir, who are the cineastes *you admire?*

Welles: Always the same ones; I believe that on this point I am not very original. The one who pleases me most of all is Griffith. I think he is the best director in the history of the cinema. The best, much better than Eisenstein. And, for all that, I admire Eisenstein very much.

Q: In your films, one has the sensation that real space is never respected: it seems not to interest you.

Welles: The fact that I make no use of it doesn't in the least signify that it doesn't please me. In other terms, there are many elements of the cinematographic language that I do not utilize, but that is not because I have something against them. It seems to me that the field of action in which I have my experiences is one that is least known, and my duty is to explore it. But that does not mean to say that it is, for me, the best and only—or that I deviate from a normal conception of space, in relation to the camera. I believe that the artist should explore his means of expression.

In reality, the cinema, with the exception of a few little tricks that don't go very far, has not advanced for more than thirty years. The only changes are with respect to the subject of films. I see that there are directors, full of future, sensitive, who explore new themes, but I see no one who attacks form, the manner of saying things. That seems to interest no one. They resemble each other very much in terms of style.

Q: *You must work very quickly. In twenty-five years of cinema, you have made ten films, you have acted in thirty, you have made a series of very long programs for television, you have acted and directed in the theatre, you have done narrations for other films and, in addition, you have written thirty scenarios. Each of them must have taken you more than six months.*

Welles: Several of them even longer. There are those that took me two years but that is because I set them aside from time to time in order to do something else and picked them up again afterwards. But it is also true that I write very rapidly.

Q: *You write them completely, with dialogue?*

Welles: I always begin with the dialogue. And I do not understand how one dares to write action before dialogue. It's a very strange conception. I know that in theory the word is secondary in cinema but the secret of my work is that everything is based on the word. I do not make silent films. I must begin with what the characters say. I must know what they say before seeing them do what they do.

Q: *However, in your films the visual part is essential.*

Welles: Yes, but I couldn't arrive at it without the solidity of the word taken as a basis for constructing the images. What happens is that when the visual components are shot the words are obscured. The most classical example is *Lady From Shanghai*. The scene in the aquarium was so gripping visually that no one heard what was being said. And what was said was, for all that, the marrow of the film. The subject was so tedious that I said to myself, "This calls for something beautiful to look at." Assuredly, the scene was very beautiful. The first ten minutes of the film did not please me at all. When I think of them I have the impression it wasn't me that made them. They resemble any Hollywood film.

Q: *How do you work with actors?*

Welles: I give them a great deal of freedom and, at the same time, the feeling of precision. It's a strange combination. In other words, physically, and in the way they develop, I demand the precision of ballet. But their way of acting comes directly from their own ideas as much as from mine. When the camera begins to roll, I do not improvise visually. In this realm, everything is prepared. But I work very freely with the actors. I try to make their life pleasant.

Q: *Your cinema is essentially dynamic.*

Welles: I believe that the cinema should be dynamic although I suppose any artist will defend his own style. For me, the cinema is a slice of life in movement that is projected on a screen; it is not a frame. I do not believe in the cinema unless there is movement on the screen. This is why I am not in agreement with certain directors, whom, however, I admire, who content themselves with a static cinema. For me, these are dead images. I hear the noise of the projector behind me, and when I see these long, long walks along streets, I am always waiting to hear the director's voice saying, "Cut!"

The only director who does not move either his camera or his actors very much, and in whom I believe, is John Ford. He succeeds in making me believe in his films even though there is little movement in them. But with the others I always have the impression that they are desperately trying to make Art. However, they should be making drama and drama should be full of life. The cinema, for me, is essentially a dramatic medium, not a literary one.

Q: That is why your mise-en-scène is lively: it is the meeting of two movements, that of the actors and that of the camera. Out of this flows an anguish that reflects modern life very well.

Welles: I believe that that corresponds to my vision of the world; it reflects that sort of vertigo, uncertainty, lack of stability, that *melange* of movement and tension that is our universe. And the cinema should express that. Since cinema has the pretension of being an art, it should be, above all, film, and not the sequel to another, more literary, medium of expression.

Q: Herman G. Weinberg said, while speaking of Mr. Arkadin, *"In Orson Welles' films, the spectator may not sit back in his seat and relax, on the contrary he must meet the film at least half-way in order to decipher what is happening, practically every second; if not, everything is lost."*

Welles: All my films are like that. There are certain *cineastes*, excellent ones, who present everything so explicitly, so clearly, that in spite of the great visual power contained in their films one follows them effortlessly—I refer only to the narrative thread. I am fully aware that, in my films, I demand a very specific interest on the part of the public. Without that attention, it is lost.

Q: Lady From Shanghai *is a story that, filmed by another director, would more likely have been based on sexual questions.*

Welles: You mean that another director would have made it more obvious. I do not like to show sex on the screen crudely. Not because of morality or puritanism; my objection is of a purely aesthetic order. In my opinion, there are two things that can absolutely not be carried to the screen: the realistic presentation of the sexual act and praying to God. I never believe an actor or actress who pretends to be completely involved in the sexual act if it is too literal, just as I can never believe an actor who wants to make me believe he is praying. These are two things that, for me, immediately evoke the presence of a projector and a white screen, the existence of a series of technicians and a director who is saying, "Good. Cut." And I imagine them in the process of preparing for the next shot. As for those who adopt a mystical stance and look fervently at the spotlights.

For all that, my illusion almost never ends when I see a film. While filming, I think of someone like myself: I utilize all of my knowledge in order to force this person to want to see the film with the greatest interest, I want him to believe what is there on the screen; this means that one should create a real world there. I place my dramatic vision of a character in the world . . . if not, the film is something dead. What there is on the screen is nothing but shadows. Something even more dead than words.

Q: *Do you like comedy?*

Welles: I have written at least five scenarios for comedy and in the theatre I have done more comedies than dramas. Comedy fills me with enthusiasm but I have never succeeded in getting a film producer to let me make one. One of the best things I did for television was a program in the genre of comedy. For example, I like Hawks' comedies very much. I even wrote about twenty-five minutes of one of them. It was called, *I Was a Male War Bride.* The scenarist fell ill and I wrote almost a third of the film.

Q: *Have you written scenarios of comedies with the intentions of making them?*

Welles: I believe the best of my comedies is "Operation Cinderella." It tells of the occupation of a small Italian town (which was previously occupied by the Saracens, the Moors, the Normans and, during the last war, by the English and, finally, the Americans) by a Hollywood film company . . . and this new occupation unfolds exactly like a military operation. The lives of all the inhabitants of the town are changed during the shooting of the film. It's a gross farce. I want very much to do a comedy for the cinema.

In a certain sense, *Quixote* is a comedy, and I put a lot of comedy in all of my films but it is a genre of comedy that—and I regret to tell you this because it is a weakness—is understood only by Americans, to the exclusion of spectators in other countries, whatever they may be. There are scenes that, seen in other countries, awake not the slightest smile and that, seen by Americans, immediately appear in a comic vein. *The Trial* is full of humor, but the Americans are the only ones to understand its amusing side. This is where my nationality comes through: my farces are not universal enough. Many are the arguments I've had with actors due to the fact that scenes are posed in absolute forms of comedy and only at the last five minutes do I change them into drama. This is my method of working: showing the amusing side of things and not showing the sad side until the last possible second.

Q: There is a kinship between your work and the works of certain authors of the modern theatre, like Beckett, Ionesco, and others . . . what is called the theatre of the absurd.

Welles: Perhaps, but I would eliminate Ionesco because I do not admire him. When I directed *Rhinoceros* in London, with Laurence Olivier in the principal role, as we repeated the work from day to day it pleased me less. I believe that there is nothing inside it. Nothing at all. This kind of theatre comes out of all types of expression, all types of art of a certain epoch, is thus forged by the same world as my films. The things this theatre is composed of are the same composed in my films, without this theatre's being in my cinema or without my cinema's being in this theatre. It is a trait of our times. There is where the coincidence comes from.

Q: There are two types of artists: for example, Velasquez and Goya; one disappears from the picture, the other is present in it; on the other hand you have Van Gogh and Cezanne . . .

Welles: I see what you mean. It's very clear.

Q: It seems to me that you are on the Goya side.

Welles: Doubtless. But I very much prefer Velasquez. There's no comparison between one and the other, as far as being artists is concerned. As I prefer Cezanne to Van Gogh.

Q: And between Tolstoy and Dostoievsky?

Welles: I prefer Tolstoy.

Q: But as an artist . . .

Welles: Yes, as an artist. But I deny that, for I do not correspond to my tastes. I know what I'm doing and when I recognize it in other works my interest is diminished. The things that resemble me the least are the things that interest me the most. For me Velasquez is the Shakespeare of painters and, for all that, he has nothing in common with my way of working.

Q: What do you think of what is called modern cinema?

Welles: I like certain young French *cineastes,* much more than the Italians.

Q: Did you like L'Année dernière à Marienbad?

Welles: No. I know that this film pleased you; not me. I held on up to the fourth reel and after that I left at a run. It reminded me too much of *Vogue* magazine.

Q: How do you see the development of the cinema?

Welles: I don't see it. I rarely go to the movies. There are two kinds of writers, the writer who reads everything of interest that is published, exchanges letters with other writers, and others who absolutely do not read their contemporaries. I am among the latter. I go to the movies very rarely and this is not because I don't like it, it is because it procures me no enjoyment at all. I do not think I am very intelligent about films. There are works that I know to be good but which I cannot stand.

Q: It was said that you were going to make "Crime and Punishment"; what became of this project?

Welles: Someone wanted me to do it. I thought about it, but I like the book too much. In the end, I decided that I could do nothing and the idea of being content to illustrate it did not please me at all. I don't mean to say by that that the subject was beneath me, what I mean is that I could bring nothing to it. I could only give it actors and images and, when I can only do that, the cinema does not interest me. I believe you must say something new about a book, otherwise it is better not to touch it.

Aside from that, I consider it to be a very difficult work, because, in my opinion, it is not completely comprehensible outside of its own time and country. The psychology of this man and this constable are so Russian, so nineteenth-century Russian, that one could never find them elsewhere; I believe that the public would not be able to follow it all the way.

Q: There is, in Dostoievsky, an analysis of justice, of the world, that is very close to yours.

Welles: Perhaps too close. My contribution would most likely be limited. The only thing I could do is to direct. I like to make films in which I can express myself as *auteur* sooner than as interpreter. I do not share Kafka's point of view in *The Trial.* I believe that he is a good writer, but Kafka is not the extraordinary genius that people today see him as. That is why I was not concerned about excessive fidelity and could make a film by Welles. If I could make four films a year, I would surely do "Crime and Punishment." But as it costs me a great deal to convince producers I try to choose what I film very carefully.

Q: With you, one seems to find, at the same time, the Brechtian tendency and the Stanislavski tendency.

Welles: All I can say is that I did my apprenticeship in Stanislavski's orbit; I worked with his actors and found them very easy to direct. I do not allude to "Method" actors; that's something else altogether. But Stanislavski was marvelous. As for Brecht, he was a great friend to me. We worked together on "Galileo Galilei." In reality he wrote it for me. Not for me to act in, but in order for me to direct it.

Q: How was Brecht?

Welles: Terribly nice. He had an extraordinary brain. One could see very well that he had been educated by the Jesuits. He had the type of disciplined brain characterized by Jesuit education. Instinctively, he was more of an anarchist than a Marxist, but he believed himself a perfect Marxist. When I said to him one day, while we were talking about "Galileo," that he had written a perfectly anti-communist work, he became nearly aggressive. I answered him, "But this Church you describe has to be Stalin and not the Pope, at this time. You have made something resolutely anti-Soviet!"

Q: What relationship do you see between your work as a film director and as a theatre director?

Welles: My relationships with these two *milieux* are very different. I believe that they are not in intimate rapport, one with the other. Perhaps in me, as a man, that relationship exists, but technical solutions are so different for each of them that, in my spirit, I establish absolutely no relationship between these two mediums.

In the theatre, I do not belong to what has succeeded in becoming the Brechtian idea of theatre; that particularly withdrawn form has never been appropriate to my character. But I have always made a terrible effort to recall to the public, at each instant, that it is in a theatre. I have never tried to bring it into the scene, I have rather tried to bring the scene to it. And that is the opposite of the cinema.

Q: *Perhaps there is a relationship in the way the actors are handled.*

Welles: In the theatre there are 1,500 cameras rolling at the same time—in the cinema there is only one. That changes the whole aesthetic for the director.

Q: *Did Huston's* Moby Dick, *on which you worked, please you?*

Welles: The novel pleases me very much, but it doesn't please me as a novel so much as a drama. There are two very different things in the novel: that sort of pseudo-biblical element that is not very good, and also that curious nineteenth-century American element, of the apocalyptical genre, that can be rendered very well in the cinema.

Q: *In the scene you acted in the film—did you make any suggestions as to the way of handling it?*

Welles: All we did was discuss the way in which it would be shot. You know that my discourse is very long. It goes on throughout a full reel, and we never repeated it. I arrived on the set already made-up and dressed. I got up on the platform and we shot it in one take. We did it using only one camera angle. And that is one of Huston's merits, because another director would have said, "Let's do it from another angle and see what we get." He said, "Good," and my role in the film ended right there!

Q: *You said one day that you have had a great deal of difficulty finding the money to make your films, that you have spent more time struggling to get this money than working as an artist. How is this battle at this time?*

Welles: More bitter than ever. Worse than ever. Very difficult. I have already said that I do not work enough. I am frustrated, do you understand? And I believe that my work shows that I do not do enough filming. My cinema is perhaps too explosive, because I wait too long before I speak. It's terrible. I have bought little cameras in order to make a film if I can find the money. I will shoot it in 16 mm. The cinema is a *metier* . . . nothing can compare to the cinema. The cinema belongs to our times. It is "the thing" to do. During the shooting of

The Trial, I spent marvelous days. It was an amusement, happiness. You cannot imagine what I felt.

When I make a film or at the time of my theatrical premieres, the critics habitually say, "This work is not as good as the one of three years ago." And if I look for the criticism of that one, three years back, I find an unfavorable review that says that that isn't as good as what I did three years earlier. And so it goes. I admit that experiences can be false but I believe that it is also false to want to be fashionable. If one is fashionable for the greatest part of one's career, one will produce second-class work. Perhaps by chance one will arrive at being a success but this means that one is a follower and not an innovator. An artist should lead, blaze trails.

What is serious is that in countries where English is spoken, the role played by criticism concerning serious works of cinema is very important. Given the fact that one cannot make films in competition with Doris Day, what is said by reviews such as *Sight and Sound* is the only reference.

Things are going particularly badly in my own country. *Touch of Evil* never had a first-run, never had the usual presentation to the press and was not the object of any critical writing in either the weeklies, the reviews, or the daily papers. It was considered to be too bad. When the representative from Universal wanted to exhibit it at the Brussels Fair in 1958, he was told that it wasn't a good enough film for a festival. He answered that, in any case, it must be put on the program. It went unnoticed and was sent back. The film took the *grand prix,* but it was no less sent back.

Q: Do you consider yourself a moralist?

Welles: Yes, but against morality. Most of the time that may appear paradoxical, but the things I love in painting, in music, in literature, represent only my penchant for what is my opposite. And moralists bore me very much. However, I'm afraid I am one of them!

Q: In what concerns you, it is not so much a question of a moralist's attitude but rather an ethic that you adopt in the face of the world.

Welles: My two Shakespearean films are made from an ethical point of view. I believe I have never made a film without having a solid ethical point of view about its story. Morally speaking, there is no ambiguity in what I do.

Q: But an ambiguous point of view is necessary. These days, the world is made that way.

Welles: But that is the way the world appears to us. It is not a true ambiguity: it's like a larger screen. A kind of a moral cinemascope. I believe it is necessary to give all the characters their best arguments, in order that they may defend themselves, including those I disagree with. To them as well, I give the best defensive arguments I can imagine. I offer them the same possibility for expression as I would a sympathetic character.

That's what gives this impression of ambiguity: my being chivalrous to people whose behavior I do not approve of. The characters are ambiguous but the significance of the work is not. I do not want to resemble the majority of Americans, who are demagogs and rhetoricians. This is one of America's great weaknesses, and rhetoric is one of the greatest weaknesses of American artists; above all, those of my generation. Miller, for example, is terribly rhetorical.

Q: What is the problem in America?

Welles: If I speak to you of the things that are wrong it won't be the obvious ones; those are similar to what is wrong in France, in Italy, or in Spain; we know them all. In American art the problem, or better, one of the problems, is the betrayal of the Left by the Left, self-betrayal. In one sense, by stupidity, by orthodoxy and because of slogans; in another, by simple betrayal. We are very few in our generation who have not betrayed our position, who have not given other people's names . . .

That is terrible. It can never be undone. I don't know how one starts over after a similar betrayal that, however, differs enormously from this, for example: a Frenchman who collaborated with the gestapo in order to save his wife's life— that is another genre of collaboration. What is so bad about the American Left is that it betrayed in order to save its swimming pools. There was no American Right in my generation. Intellectually it didn't exist. There were only Leftists and they mutually betrayed each other. The Left was not destroyed by McCarthy: it demolished itself, ceding to a new generation of Nihilists. That's what happened.

You can't call it "Fascism." I believe that the term "Fascism" should only be utilized in order to define a quite precise political attitude. It would be necessary to find a new word in order to define what is happening in America. Fascism must be born out of chaos. And America is not, as I know it, in chaos. The social structure is not in a state of dissolution. No, it doesn't correspond at all to the true definition of Fascism. I believe it is two simple, obvious things: the technological society is not accustomed to living with its own tools. That's what counts. We speak of them, we use them but we don't know how to live with them. The other thing is the prestige of the people responsible for the technological society. In this society the men who direct and the savants who represent technique do not leave room for the artist who favors the human being. In reality, they utilize him only for decoration.

Q: As an artist and as a member of a certain generation, do you feel isolated?

Welles: I have always felt isolated. I believe that any good artist feels isolated. And I must think that I am a good artist, for otherwise I would not be able to work and I beg your pardon for taking the liberty of believing this; if someone wants to direct a film, he must think that he is good. A good artist should be isolated. If he isn't isolated, something is wrong.

Q: These days, it would be impossible to present the Mercury Theatre.

Welles: Completely impossible for financial reasons. The Mercury Theatre was possible only because I was earning three thousand dollars a week on the radio and spending two thousand to sustain the theatre. At that time, it was still cheap to sustain a theatre. Plus I had formidable actors. And what was most exciting about this Mercury Theatre was that it was a theatre on Broadway, not "off." Today, one might have a theatre off-Broadway, but that's another thing.

What characterized the Mercury Theatre was that it was next door to another where they were doing a musical comedy, near a commercial theatre, it was in the theatre center. Part of the neighboring bill of fare was the Group Theatre which was the official theatre of the Left: we were in contact without having an official relationship; we were of the same generation, although not on the same path. The whole thing gave the New York of that time an extraordinary vitality. The quality of actors and that of spectators is no longer what it was in those marvelous years. The best theatre should be in the center of everything.

Q: Does that explain your permanent battle to remain in the milieu of the cinema and not outside of the industry?

Welles: I may be rejected, but as for me, I always want to be right in the center. If I am isolated, it is because I am obliged to be, for such is not my intention. I am always aiming for the center: I fail, but that is what I try to attain.

Q: Are you thinking of returning to Hollywood?

Welles: Not at the moment. But who knows what may change at the next instant? . . . I am dying to work there because of the technicians, who are marvelous. They truly represent a director's dream.

Q: A certain anti-Fascist attitude can be found in your films . . .

Welles: There is more than one French intellectual who believes that I am a Fascist . . . it's idiotic, but that's what they write. What happens with these French intellectuals is that they take my physical aspect as an actor for my idea as an *auteur.* As an actor I always play a certain type of role: Kings, great men, etc. This is not because I think them to be the only persons in the world who are worth the trouble. My physical aspect does not permit me to play other roles. No one would believe a defenseless, humble person played by me. But they take this to be a projection of my own personality. I hope that the great majority at least considers it obvious that I am anti-Fascist.

True Fascism is always confused with Futurism's early fascistic mystique. By this I make allusion to the first generation of Italian Fascism, which was a way of speaking that disappeared as soon as the true Fascism imposed itself, because it was an idiotic romanticism, like that of d'Annunzio and others. That is what disappeared. And that is what the French critics are talking about.

Q: What will your Falstaff *be like?*

Welles: I don't know . . . I hope it will be good. All I can say is that from the visual point of view, it will be very modest and, I hope, at the same time satisfying and correct. But as I see it, it is essentially a human story and I hope that a good number of stupid cinema people will feel deceived. That is because, as I just said, I consider that this film should be very modest from the visual point of view. Which doesn't mean it will be visually non-existent but rather that it will not be loud on this level. It concerns a story about 3 or 4 people and these should, therefore, dominate completely. I believe I shall use more close-ups. This will really be a film completely in the service of the actors.

Q: You are often accused of being egocentric. When you appear as an actor in your films, it is said that the camera is, above all, in the service of your personal exhibition. For example, in Touch of Evil *the shooting angle moves from a general shot to a close-up in order to catch your first appearance on getting out of the car.*

Welles: Yes, but that is the story, the subject. I wouldn't act a role if it was not felt as dominating the whole story. I do not think it is just to say that I utilize the camera to my profit and not to the profit of the other actors. It's not true. Although they will say it even more about *Falstaff* but it is precisely because in the film I am playing Falstaff, not Hotspur.

Fig. 11. Jeanne Moreau and Orson Welles in *Falstaff* (1966). Based on several history plays and one comedy by William Shakespeare. Directed by Orson Welles. Courtesy of Billy Rose Theatre Collection, The New York Public Library for the Performing Arts, Astor, Lenox and Tilden Foundations.

At this time I think and rethink, above all, of the world in which the story unfolds, of the appearance of the film. The number of sets I will be able to build will be so restrained that the film will have to be resolutely anti-Baroque. It will have to have numerous rather formal general shots, like what one may see at eye level, wall frescoes. It is a big problem creating a world in period costumes. In this genre, it is difficult to get a feeling of real life; few films arrive at it. I believe this is due to the fact that one has not concretized, in all its details, before starting to work, the universe presupposed by such a film.

Falstaff should be very plain on the visual level because above all it is a very real human story, very comprehensible and very adaptable to modern tragedy. And nothing should come between the story and the dialogue. The visual part of this story should exist as a background, as something secondary. Everything of importance in the film should be found on the faces; on these faces that whole universe I was speaking of should be found. I imagine that it will be "the" film of my life in terms of close-ups. Theoretically, I am against close-ups of all types, although I consider few theories as given and am for remaining very free.

I am resolutely against close-ups, but I am convinced that this story requires them.

Q: *Why this objection to close-ups?*

Welles: I find it marvelous that the public may choose, with its eyes, what it wants to see of a shot. I don't like to force it, and the use of the close-up amounts to forcing it: you can see nothing else. In *Kane,* for example, you must have seen that there were very few close-ups, hardly any. There are perhaps six in the whole film. But a story like *Falstaff* demands them, because the moment we step back and separate ourselves from the faces, we see the people in period costumes and many actors in the foreground. The closer we are to the face the more universal it becomes; *Falstaff* is a somber comedy, the story of the betrayal of friendship.

What pleases me in *Falstaff* is that the project has interested me as an actor although I am rarely interested in something for the cinema in terms of being an actor. I am happy when I do not perform. And *Falstaff* is one of the rare things that I wish to achieve as an actor. There are only two stories I wish to do as an actor that I have written. In *The Trial* I absolutely did not want to perform and, if I did it, it is because of not having found an actor who could take the part. All those we asked refused.

Q: *At the beginning you said you would play the part of the priest . . .*

Welles: I shot it, but, as we hadn't found an actor for the role of the lawyer, I cut the sequences in which I appeared as a priest and started shooting again. *Falstaff* is an actor's film. Not only my role but all the others are favorable for showing a good actor's worth. My *Othello* is more successful in the theatre than on film. We shall see what happens with *Falstaff,* which is the best role that Shakespeare ever wrote. It is a character as great as Don Quixote. If Shakespeare had done nothing but that magnificent creation, it would suffice to make him immortal. I wrote the scenario under the inspiration of three works in which he appears, one other in which he is spoken of, and complete it with things found in still another. Thus, I worked with five of Shakespeare's works. But, naturally, I wrote a story about Falstaff, about his friendship with the prince and his repugnance when the prince becomes King. I have great hopes for this film.

Q: *What do you think of the American cinema, as seen from Europe?*

Welles: I am surprised by the tendency of the serious critics to find elements of value only among the American directors of action films, while they find none in the American directors of historical films. Lubitsch, for example, is a giant. But he doesn't correspond to the taste of cinema aesthetes. Why? I know nothing about it. Besides, it doesn't interest me. But Lubitsch's talent and originality are stupefying.

Q: And Von Sternberg?

Welles: Admirable! He is the greatest exotic director of all time and one of the great lights.

Q: Let's talk about other directors. What do you think of Arthur Penn? Have you seen The Left-Handed Gun?

Welles: I saw it first on television and then as cinema. It was better on television, more brutal, and beyond that I believe that at that time Penn had more experience directing for television and so handled it better, but for cinema this experience went against him. I believe him to be a good theatre director, an admirable director of actresses—a very rare thing: very few *cineastes* possess that quality.

I have seen nothing by the most recent generation, except for a sampling of the avante-garde. Among those whom I would call "younger generation" Kubrick appears to me to be a giant.

Q: But, for example, The Killing *was more or less a copy of* The Asphalt Jungle?

Welles: Yes, but *The Killing* was better. The problem of imitation leaves me indifferent, above all if the imitator succeeds in surpassing the model. For me, Kubrick is a better director than Huston. I haven't seen *Lolita* but I believe that Kubrick can do everything. He is a great director who has not yet made his great film. What I see in him is a talent not possessed by the great directors of the generation immediately preceding his, I mean Ray, Aldrich, etc. Perhaps this is because his temperament comes closer to mine.

Q: And those of the older generation? Wyler, for example? and Hitchcock?

Welles: Hitchcock is an extraordinary director; William Wyler a brilliant producer.

Q: How do you make this distinction between two men who are both called directors?

Welles: A producer doesn't make anything. He chooses the story, works on it with the scenarist, has a say in the distribution and, in the old sense of the term American producer, even decides on the camera angles, what sequences will be used. What is more, he defines the final form of the film. In reality, he is a sort of director's boss.

Wyler is this man. Only he's his own boss. His work, however, is better as boss than as director, given the fact that in that role he spends his clearest moments waiting, with the camera, for something to happen. He says nothing. He waits, as the producer waits in his office. He looks at twenty impeccable shots, seeking the one that has something, and usually he knows how to choose the best one. As a director he is good but as a producer he is extraordinary.

Q: According to you, the role of director consists in making something happen?

Welles: I do not like to set up very strict rules, but in the Hollywood system, the director has one job. In other systems he has another job. I am against absolute rules because even in the case of America we find marvelous films achieved under the absolute tyranny of the production system. There are even films much respected by film societies that weren't made by directors but by producers and scenarists. . . . Under the American system, no one is capable of saying whether a film was or was not directed by a director.

Five **Acting**

Remarks on the Actor

Siegfried Kracauer

The film actor occupies a unique position at the junction of staged and unstaged life. That he differs considerably from the stage actor was already recognized in the primitive days when Réjane and Sarah Bernhardt played theater before the camera; the camera let them down pitilessly. What was wrong with their acting, the very acting which all theatergoers raved about?

Stage actor and screen actor differ from each other in two ways. The first difference concerns the qualities they must possess to meet the demands of their media. The second difference bears on the functions they must assume in theatrical plays and film narratives respectively.

QUALITIES

How can the stage actor's contribution to his role be defined in terms of the cinema? To be sure, like the film actor, he must draw on his na-

Excerpted from Siegfried Kracauer, *Theory of Film* (New York: Oxford University Press, 1960), 93–101.

ture in the widest sense of the word to render the character he is supposed to represent; and since his projective powers are rarely unlimited, a measure of type-casting is indispensable for the stage also. But here the similarities end. Due to the conditions of the theater, the stage actor is not in a position directly to convey to the audience the many, often imperceptible details that make up the physical side of his impersonation; these details cannot cross the unbridgeable distance between stage and spectator. The physical existence of the stage performer is incommunicable. Hence the necessity for the stage actor to evoke in the audience a mental image of his character. This he achieves by means of the theatrical devices at his disposal—a fitting make-up, appropriate gestures and voice inflections, etc.

Significantly, when film critics compare the screen actor with the stage actor, they usually speak of the latter's exaggerations, overstatements, amplifications.[1] In fact, his mask is as "unnatural" as his behavior, for otherwise he would not be able to create the illusion of naturalness. Instead of drawing a true-to-life portrait which would be ineffective on the stage, he works with suggestions calculated to make the spectators believe that they are in the presence of his character. Under the impact of these suggestions they visualize what is actually not given them. Of course, the play itself supports the actor's conjurer efforts. The situations in which he appears and the verbal references to his motives and fears and desires help the audience to complement his own definitions so that the image he projects gains in scope and depth. Thus he may attain a magic semblance of life. Yet life itself, this flow of subtle modes of being, eludes the stage. Is it even aspired to in genuine theater?

Emphasis on Being

Leonard Lyons reports the following studio incident in his newspaper column: Fredric March, the well-known screen and stage actor, was making a movie scene and the director interrupted him. "Sorry, I did it again," the star apologized. "I keep forgetting—this is a movie and I mustn't act."[2]

If this is not the whole truth about film acting it is at least an essential part of it. Whenever old films are shown at the New York Museum of Modern Art, the spectators invariably feel exhilarated over expressions and poses which strike them as being theatrical. Their laughter indicates that they expect film characters to behave in a natural way. Audience sensibilities have long since been conditioned to the motion picture camera's preference for nature in the raw. And since the regular use of close-ups invites the spectator to look for minute changes of a character's appearance and bearing, the actor is all the more obliged to relinquish those "unnatural" surplus movements and stylizations he would need on the stage to externalize his impersonation. "The slightest exaggeration of gesture and manner of speaking," says René Clair, "is captured by the merciless mechanism and amplified by the projection of the film."[3] What the actor tries to impart—the physical existence of a character—is overwhelmingly present on the screen. The camera really isolates a fleeting glance, an inadvertent shrug of the shoulder. This accounts for Hitchcock's insistence on "negative acting, the ability to express words by doing nothing."[4] "I mustn't act," as Fredric March put it. To be more precise, the film actor must act as if he did not act at all but were a real-life person caught in the act by the camera. He must seem to *be* his character.[5] He is in a sense a photographer's model.

Casualness

This implies something infinitely subtle. Any genuinely photographic portrait tends to sustain the impression of unstaged reality; and much as it concentrates on the typical features of a face, these features still affect us as being elicited from spontaneous self-revelations. There is, and should be, something fragmentary and fortuitous about photographic portraits. Accordingly, the film actor must seem to be his character in such a way that all his expressions, gestures, and poses point beyond themselves to the diffuse contexts out of which they arise. They must breathe a certain casualness marking them as fragments of an inexhaustible texture.

Many a great film maker has been aware that this texture reaches into the deep layers of the mind. René Clair observes that with screen actors spontaneity counts all the more, since they have to atomize their role in the process of acting;[6] and Pudovkin says that, when working with them, he "looked for those small details and shades of expression which . . . reflect the inner psychology of man."[7] Both value projections of the unconscious. What they want to get at, Hanns Sachs, a film-minded disciple of Freud's, spells out in psychoanalytical terms: he requests the film actor to advance the narrative by embodying "such psychic events as are before or beyond speech . . . above all those . . . unnoticed ineptitudes of behavior described by Freud as symptomatic actions."[8]

The film actor's performance, then, is true to the medium only if it does not assume the airs of a self-sufficient achievement but impresses us as an incident—one of many possible incidents—of his character's unstaged material existence. Only then is the life he renders truly cinematic. When movie critics sometimes blame an actor for overacting his part, they do not necessarily mean that he acts theatrically; rather, they wish to express the feeling that his acting is, somehow, too purposeful, that it lacks that fringe of indeterminacy or indefiniteness which is characteristic of photography.

Physique

For this reason the film actor is less independent of his physique than the stage actor, whose face never fills the whole field of vision. The camera not only bares theatrical make-up but reveals the delicate interplay between physical and psychological traits, outer movements and inner changes. Since most of these correspondences materialize unconsciously, it is very difficult for the actor to stage them to the satisfaction of an audience which, being in a position to check all pertinent visual data, is wary of anything that interferes with a character's naturalness. Eisenstein's 1939 claim that film actors should exert "self-control . . . to the millimeter of movement"[9] sounds chimerical; it testifies to his ever-increasing and rather uncinematic concern for art in the traditional sense, art which completely consumes the given raw material. Possessed with formative aspirations, he forgot that even the most arduous "self-control" cannot produce the effect of involuntary reflex actions. Hence the common recourse to actors whose physical appearance, as it presents itself on the screen, fits into the plot—whereby it is understood that their appearance is in a measure symptomatic of their nature, their whole way of being. "I choose actors exclusively for their physique," declares Rossellini.[10] His dictum makes it quite clear that, because of their indebtedness to photography, film productions depend much more than theatrical productions on casting according to physical aspects.

FUNCTIONS

From the viewpoint of cinema the functions of the stage actor are determined by the fact that the theater exhausts itself in representing interhuman relations. The action of the stage play flows through its characters; what they are saying and doing makes up the content of the play—in fact, it is the play itself. Stage characters are the carriers of all the meanings a theatrical plot involves. This is confirmed by the world about them: even realistic settings must be adjusted to stage conditions and, hence, are limited in their illusionary power. It may be doubted whether they are intended at all to evoke reality as something imbued with meanings of its own. As a rule, the theater acknowledges the need for stylization.* Realistic or not, stage settings are primarily designed to bear out the characters and their interplay; the idea behind them is not to achieve full authenticity—unattainable anyway on the stage—but to echo and enhance the human entanglements conveyed to us by acting and dialogue. Stage imagery serves as a foil for stage acting. Man is indeed the absolute measure of this universe, which hinges on him. And he is its smallest unit. Each character represents an insoluble entity on the stage; you cannot watch his face or his hands without relating them to his whole appearance, physically and psychologically.

Object Among Objects

The cinema in this sense is not exclusively human. Its subject matter is the infinite flux of visible phenomena—those ever-changing patterns of physical existence whose flow may include human manifestations but need not climax in them.

In consequence, the film actor is not necessarily the hub of the narrative, the carrier of all its meanings. Cinematic action is always likely to pass through regions which, should they contain human beings at all, yet involve them only in an accessory, unspecified way. Many a film summons the weird presence of furniture in an abandoned apartment; when you then see or hear someone enter, it is for a transient moment the sensation of human interference in general that strikes you most. In such cases the actor represents the species rather than a well-defined individual. Nor is the whole of his being any longer sacrosanct. Parts of his body may fuse with parts of his environment into a significant configuration which suddenly stands out among the passing images of physical life. Who would not remember shots picturing an ensemble of neon lights, lingering shadows, and some human face?

This decomposition of the actor's wholeness corresponds to the piecemeal manner in which he supplies the elements from which eventually his role is built. "The film actor," says Pudovkin, "is deprived of a consciousness of the uninterrupted development of the action in his work. The organic connection between the consecutive parts of his work, as a result of which the distinct whole image is created, is not for him. The whole image of the actor is only to be conceived as a future appearance on the screen, subsequent to the editing of the director."[11]

---

* In his *Stage to Screen*, Vardac submits that the realistic excesses of the nineteenth-century theater anticipated the cinema. To the extent that the theater then tried to defy stage conditions, he argues, it was already pregnant with the new, still unborn medium.

Fig. 12. Eric Bogosian in *Talk Radio* (1988), adapted by Eric Bogosian and Oliver Stone from the play by Eric Bogosian (1985). Directed by Oliver Stone. On the stage, Bogosian made his reputation with the virtuosity of his one-man shows. Stone was able to control Bogosian's power so that it played on the screen, resulting in one of this performer's most compelling screen-acting appearances. Courtesy of Billy Rose Theatre Collection, The New York Public Library for the Performing Arts, Astor, Lenox and Tilden Foundations.

"I mustn't act"—Fredric March is right in a sense he himself may not have envisaged. Screen actors are raw material;[12] and they are often made to appear within contexts discounting them as personalities, as actors. Whenever they are utilized this way, utter restraint is their main virtue. Objects among objects, they must not even exhibit their nature but, as Barjavel remarks, "remain, as much as possible, below the natural."[13]

TYPES

The Non-Actor

Considering the significance of the screen character's unstaged nature and his function as raw material, it is understandable that many film makers have felt tempted to rely on non-actors for their narrative. Flaherty calls children and animals the finest of all film material because of their spontaneous actions.[14] And Epstein says: "No set, no costume can have the aspect, the cast of truth. No professional faking can produce the admirable technical gestures of a topman or a fisherman. A smile of kindness, a cry of rage are as difficult to imitate as a rainbow in the sky or the turbulent ocean."[15] Eager for genuine smiles and cries, G. W. Pabst created them artificially when shooting a carousal of anti-Bolshevist soldiery for his silent film, *The Love of Jeanne Ney:* he herded together a hundred-odd Russian ex-officers, provided them with vodka and women, and then photographed the ensuing orgy.[16]

There are periods in which non-actors seem to be the last word of a national cinema. The Russians cultivated them in their revolutionary era, and so did the Italians after their escape from Fascist domination. Tracing the origins of Italian neorealism to the immediate postwar period, Chiaromonte observes: "Movie directors lived in the streets and on the roads then, like everybody else. They saw what everybody else saw. They had no studios and big installations with which to fake what they had seen, and they had little money. Hence they had to improvise, using real streets for their exteriors, and real people in the way of stars."[17] When history is made in the streets, the streets tend to move onto the screen.* For all their differences in ideology and technique, *Potemkin* and *Paisan* have this "street" quality in common; they feature environmental situations rather than private affairs, episodes involving society at large rather than stories centering upon an individual conflict. In other words, they show a tendency toward documentary.

Practically all story films availing themselves of non-actors follow this pattern. Without exception they have a documentary touch. Think of such story films as *The Quiet One, Los Olvidados,* or the De Sica films, *The Bicycle Thief* and *Umberto D.:* in all of them the emphasis is on the world about us; their protagonists are not so much particular individuals as types representative of whole groups of people. These narratives serve to dramatize social conditions in general. The preference for real people on the screen and the documentary approach seem to be closely interrelated.

The reason is this: it is precisely the task of portraying wide areas of actual reality, social or otherwise, which calls for "typage"—the recourse to people who are part and parcel of that reality and can be considered typical of it. As Rotha puts it: "'Typage' . . . represents the least artificial organisation of reality."[18] It is not accidental that film directors devoted to the rendering of larger segments

---

* A notable exception was the German cinema after World War I: it shunned outer reality, withdrawing into a shell. See Kracauer, *From Caligari to Hitler,* pp. 58–60.

of actual life are inclined to condemn the professional actor for "faking." Like Epstein, who turns against "professional faking," Rossellini is said to believe that actors "fake emotions."[19] This predilection for non-actors goes hand in hand with a vital interest in social patterns rather than individual destinies. Buñuel's *Los Olvidados* highlights the incredible callousness of despondent juveniles; the great De Sica films focus on the plight of the unemployed and the misery of old age insufficiently provided for. Non-actors are chosen because of their authentic looks and behavior. Their major virtue is to figure in a narrative which explores the reality they help constitute but does not culminate in their lives themselves.

The Hollywood Star

In institutionalizing stars, Hollywood has found a way of tapping natural attractiveness as if it were oil. Aside from economic expediency, though, the star system may well cater to inner needs common to many people in this country. This system provides variegated models of conduct, thus helping, however obliquely, pattern human relationships in a culture not yet old enough to have peopled its firmament with stars that offer comfort or threaten the trespasser— stars not to be mistaken for Hollywood's.

The typical Hollywood star resembles the non-actor in that he acts out a standing character identical with his own or at least developed from it, frequently with the aid of make-up and publicity experts. As with any real-life figure on the screen, his presence in a film points beyond the film. He affects the audience not just because of his fitness for this or that role but for being, or seeming to be, a particular kind of person—a person who exists independently of any part he enacts in a universe outside the cinema which the audience believes to be reality or wishfully substitutes for it. The Hollywood star imposes the screen image of his physique, the real or a stylized one, and all that this physique implies and connotes on every role he creates. And he uses his acting talent, if any, exclusively to feature the individual he is or appears to be, no matter for the rest whether his self-portrayal exhausts itself in a few stereotyped characteristics or brings out various potentialities of his underlying nature. The late Humphrey Bogart invariably drew on Humphrey Bogart whether he impersonated a sailor, a private "eye," or a night club owner.

But why is any one chosen for stardom while others are not? Evidently, something about the gait of the star, the form of his face, his manner of reacting and speaking, ingratiates itself so deeply with the masses of moviegoers that they want to see him again and again, often for a considerable stretch of time. It is logical that the roles of a star should be made to order. The spell he casts over the audience cannot be explained unless one assumes that his screen appearance satisfies widespread desires of the moment—desires connected, somehow, with the patterns of living he represents or suggests.

The Professional Actor

Discussing the uses of professional actors and non-actors, Mr. Bernard Miles, himself an English actor, declares that the latter prove satisfactory only in documentary films. In them, says he, "non-actors achieve all, or at any rate most, that the very best professional actors could achieve in the same circumstances. But this is only because most of these pictures avoid the implications of human action, or, where they do present it, present it in such a fragmentary way as never to put to the test the training and natural qualities which differentiate an actor from a non-actor." Documentary, he concludes, "has never faced up to the problem of sustained characterization."[20]

Be this as it may, the majority of feature films does raise this problem. And challenged to help solve it, the non-actor is likely to forfeit his naturalness. He becomes paralyzed before the camera, as Rossellini observes;[21] and the task of restoring him to his true nature is often impossible to fulfill. There are exceptions, of course. In both his *Bicycle Thief* and *Umberto D.*, Vittorio De Sica—of whom they say in Italy that he "could lure even a sack of potatoes into acting"[22]—succeeds in making people who never acted before portray coherent human beings. Old Umberto D., a rounded-out character with a wide range of emotions and reactions, is all the more memorable since his whole past seems to come alive in his intensely touching presence. But one should keep in mind that the Italians are blessed with mimetic gifts and have a knack of expressive gestures. Incidentally, while producing *The Men*, a film about paraplegic veterans, director Fred Zinnemann found that people who have undergone a powerful emotional experience are particularly fit to re-enact themselves.[23]

As a rule, however, sustained characterization calls for professional actors. Indeed, many stars are. Paradoxically enough, the over-strained non-actor tends to behave like a bad actor, whereas an actor who capitalizes on his given being may manage to appear as a candid non-actor, thus achieving a second state of innocence. He is both the player and the instrument; and the quality of this instrument—his natural self as it has grown in real life—counts as much as his talent in playing it. Think of Raimu. Aware that the screen actor depends upon the non-actor in him, a discerning film critic once said of James Cagney that he "can coax or shove a director until a scene from a dreamy script becomes a scene from life as Cagney remembered it."[24]

Only few actors are able to metamorphose their own nature, including those incidental fluctuations which are the essence of cinematic life. Here Paul Muni comes to mind—not to forget Lon Chaney and Walter Huston. When watching Charles Laughton or Werner Krauss in different roles, one gets the feeling that they even change their height along with their parts. Instead of appearing as they are on the screen, such protean actors actually disappear in screen characters who seem to have no common denominator.

NOTES

1. See, for instance, Lindgren, *The Art of the Film,* pp. 156–57; Barbaro, "Le cinéma sans acteurs," in *Le Rôle intellectuel du cinéma,* p. 227; Barjavel, *Cinéma total . . . ,* p. 81.
2. Quoted by Lyons, "The Lyons Den," *New York Post,* June 5, 1950.
3. Clair, *Réflexion faite,* p. 187.
4. "Film Crasher Hitchcock," *Cue,* May 19, 1951.
5. Cf. Barjavel, op. cit. pp. 84–85.
6. Clair, op. cit. p. 187.
7. Quoted by Rotha, *Documentary Film,* p. 143, from Pudovkin, "Acting—The Cinema *v.* the Theatre," *The Criterion,* vol. VIII, no. 1.
8. Sachs, "Film Psychology," *Close Up,* Nov. 1928, vol. III, no. 5:9.
9. Eisenstein, *Film Form,* p. 192.
10. Rossellini, "Dix ans de cinéma (I)," *Cahiers du cinéma,* Aug.–Sept. 1955, vol. IX, no. 50:9. See also Balázs, *Der sichtbare Mensch,* pp. 55–56.
11. Pudovkin, *Film Technique and Film Acting,* part I, p. 109.
12. Cf. Cooke, *Douglas Fairbanks,* p. 6.
13. Barjavel, *Cinéma total . . . ,* p. 81.
14. Cited by Rotha, *Documentary Film,* p. 149. See also Rotha, *The Film Till Now,* p. 363.
15. Quoted by Marie Epstein, "Biographical Notes," in Bachmann, ed., *Jean Epstein, 1897–1953; Cinemages,* no. 2:8.
16. See Kracauer, *From Caligari to Hitler,* p. 175.
17. Chiaromonte, "Rome Letter: Italian Movies," *Partisan Review,* June 1944, vol. XVI, no. 6:628.
18. Rotha, *Documentary Film,* p. 148. See also Nicholl, *Film and Theatre,* p. 172.
19. Reynolds, *Leave It to the People,* p. 147.
20. Miles, "Are Actors Necessary?" *Documentary News Letter,* April 1941, vol. 2, no. 4:71.
21. Rossellini, "Dix ans de cinéma (I)," *Cahiers du cinéma,* Aug.–Sept. 1955, vol. IX, no. 50:9.
22. Chiaromonte, op. cit. p. 623.
23. Zinnemann, "On Using Non-Actors in Pictures," *The New York Times,* Jan. 8, 1950.
24. Ferguson, "Life Goes to the Pictures," *films,* Spring 1940, vol. 1, no. 2:22.

WORKS CITED

Bachmann, Gideon, ed., *Jean Epstein, 1897–1953; Cinemages* (New York, 1955), no. 2. A Jean Epstein memorial issue.

Balázs, Béla, *Der sichtbare Mensch, oder die Kultur des Films,* Wien/Leipzig, 1924.

Barbaro, Umberto, "Le cinéma sans acteurs," in *Le Rôle intellectuel du cinéma,* Paris, 1937, pp. 225–34. [Published by the Institut de Coopération Intellectuelle, Société des Nations.]

Bardèche, Maurice, and Brasillach, Robert, *The History of Motion Pictures,* New York, 1938. Translated and edited by Iris Barry.

Barjavel, René, *Cinéma total: Essai sur les formes futures du cinéma,* Paris, 1944.

Chiaromonte, Nicola, "Rome Letter: Italian Movies," *Partisan Review* (New York, June 1949), vol. XVI, no. 6:621–30.

Clair, René, *Réflexion faite: Notes pour servir à l'histoire de l'art cinématographique de 1920 à 1950,* Paris, 1951.

Cooke, Alistair, *Douglas Fairbanks: The Making of a Screen Character,* New York, 1940.

Eisenstein, Sergei M., *Film Form: Essays in Film Theory,* New York, 1949. Edited and translated by Jay Leyda.

Ferguson, Otis, "Life Goes to the Pictures," *films* (New York, Spring 1940), vol. I, no. 2:19–29.

"Film Crasher Hitchcock," *Cue* (New York), May 19, 1951.

Kracauer, Siegfried, *From Caligari to Hitler,* Princeton, 1947.

Lindgren, Ernest, *The Art of the Film,* London, 1948.

Lyons, Leonard, "The Lyons Den," *New York Post,* June 5, 1950.

Miles, Bernard, "Are Actors Necessary?" *Documentary News Letter* (London, April 1941), vol. 2, no. 4:70–74.

Pudovkin, V. I., *Film Technique and Film Acting,* New York, 1949. Part I: Film Technique; part II: Film Acting. Translated by Ivor Montagu.

Reynolds, Quentin, *Leave It to the People,* New York, 1948.

Rossellini, Roberto, "Dix ans de cinéma (I)," *Cahiers du cinéma* (Paris, Aug.–Sept. 1955), vol. IX, no. 50:3–9.

Rotha, Paul, *The Film Till Now.* With an additional section, "The Film Since Then," by Richard Griffith. New York, 1950.

———, *Documentary Film.* With contributions by Sinclair Road and Richard Griffith. London, 1952.

Sachs, Hanns, "Film Psychology," *Close Up* (Territet, Switzerland, Nov. 1928), vol. III, no. 5:8–15.

Zinnemann, Fred, "On Using Non-Actors in Pictures," *The New York Times,* Jan. 8, 1950.

Interview with Elia Kazan

Michel Ciment

You started in theater. How did that happen?

Kazan: The thing that brought me into the theater was, oddly
enough, films by Eisenstein and Dovzhenko that I saw in the early
thirties. They made a profound impression on me. So before I was
ever in the theater I wanted above all to be a film director.

It was impossible in those days, or I felt it was, to say, "I'm going to
be a film director," and start becoming one. So when I got a chance to
go with The Group Theatre I jumped at it. There I met two men,
Harold Clurman and Lee Strasberg, who did the same thing that the
Eisenstein and Dovzhenko films did: made me feel that the performing arts, theater and film, can be as meaningful as the drama of living
itself. And they made the theater, which was at that time in New York
just a way to kill time, seem relevant to the social events of the time.

I was taken into The Group Theatre, was a stage manager for a

Excerpted from *Kazan on Kazan* (New York: Viking, 1974), 34–52, 66–72, 174–
177.

while, then an actor. But always in the back of my head what I *finally* wanted was to be a film director. During my early years with The Group Theatre I did make a couple of documentary films, one with a man named Ralph Steiner. He and I and another actor went out to the city dump, and improvised a two-reel comedy that was great fun to do.

The Group Theatre broke with the English tradition in the American Theatre.

It was exactly the opposite to the then British tradition. The then British tradition was an imitation of behaviour. That is, a person would study the external manifestations of a certain experience or emotion and imitate them. The Group actors would induce the actual emotion within themselves and then judge or try to control what came out of it. We would get ourselves *into* the state of the actor of the role rather than imitate the externals of the role. In that sense, we were diametric. More than that, the English acting of the twenties and the thirties imitated other performances so it was even once more removed. That's why the Group and the Actors' Studio had such an influence up to five or six years ago on the young British actors. Tony Richardson and the Royal Court were influenced by the production of *Streetcar* and *Death of a Salesman* and so was John Osborne. Their productions were also looking for a natural rather than a theatrical movement, for an ensemble rather than a star feeling, everything being subordinated to the projection of a theme rather than entertainment. I think the Group Theatre was the greatest influence on the world theatre since the great Russians of the twenties.

How did you direct plays in those days?

I tried to put myself in the author's shoes. I used to try to say: "I'm now speaking for this author." Each author is different. I said to myself: "I'm doing *Tea and Sympathy* by Robert Anderson—this should be like a Chopin prelude, light, delicate, without overstressing" or "I'm doing a play by Tennessee Williams: he's morally ambivalent, he admires the people who destroy him, he doubts himself, he is afraid of certain people and yet he is drawn to them. I must see life like he sees it." When I did a play by Arthur Miller, I said to myself: "This man deals in ethical absolutes (at least he did through the plays I directed), he is absolutely certain where he stands on issues. He is certain maybe because he is afraid of facing ambivalences, but I must not introduce ambivalences. I must keep it clear, forceful. I must save up force for the last part because he makes a final summation statement at the end of every play." And so on, and so on. In other words, I tried to think and feel like the author so that the play would be in the scale and in the mood, in the tempo and feeling of each writer. I tried to *be* the author, I was many men but none of them was myself. That's why I like my films so much more than I do my plays although I was accorded much more absolute praise when I did plays. My films are my own face, they have my faults and my characteristics.

1947 was an important year: a play you directed won the Pulitzer Prize, you got the Academy Award for Gentleman's Agreement *and you started the Actors' Studio. Was there an evolution in your ideas about acting between the end of the Group Theatre and the founding of the Actors' Studio, and why did you found it?*

The Group Theatre had meant a lot to me and I missed it personally and professionally. I missed the fact that there was training going on, that the tradition of the Group had stopped functioning. I missed it, not as a memory or as something of the past, but as a place where I could find new actors, where I could work myself on things of an experimental nature. I was right to miss it because out of the first classes of the Actors' Studio came people like Julie Harris, Karl Malden, Kim Hunter, Marlon Brando, Jimmy Dean, Pat Hingle, and so on. It was like a farm where I was raising new products that I would use, but also deeper than that: I'd started as an actor and my craft up to that time was based on acting. It was important to me that it be kept going. It was started as a small, modest group. There wasn't much to it, just two classes; I taught one and Bob Lewis the other. I said to myself: "I have to make a whole generation of actors." And we did that. I took the basic exercises of the Stanislavsky method—developing the senses, developing imagination, developing spontaneity, developing the force of the actor and, above all, arousing his emotional resources. I had taken those classes myself from Clurman and Strasberg in my time. I had taught downtown at the New Theatre League, the Communist Theatre. So I'd had quite a bit of experience teaching by then.

Everybody came to the doors of the Actors' Studio. I used to be one of the three judges, with Strasberg and Crawford; we used to judge the auditions of aspiring actors every two months or so. I used to know all the kids. They would perform a short scene from a play. We were always interested to see what plays they preferred. They varied through the years. At the beginning they were usually plays by Clifford Odets, then they became plays by Tennessee Williams and Arthur Miller, then five or six years later they were plays by Edward Albee and Harold Pinter. You could tell what was in young people's minds by the plays they submitted themselves in. I liked the Actors' Studio a lot. It had no goal except to give the actors a place to work. It gave a lot of people much happiness, much friendship, acceptance, a sense of being safe and wanted, and training. The actor's position in our theatre is a very bad one, very humiliating; what the Actors' Studio did just humanly was a wonderful thing.

This went on from about 1947, and I was satisfied with it, right through 1952, 1953, 1954 when I did *On the Waterfront.* I was teaching both classes then— I had the older class later. I tried to continue with these people. And I had people like Anthony Quinn, Rod Steiger, Marlon Brando, Shelley Winters—and whenever that cocker James Dean came around, I had him too. But I knew by this time that teaching was not for me, that I didn't have the patience or the stability for it. I liked that the Studio existed but I would shrink from totally committing myself to it. I liked to wander around the world and the country and do a lot of different things. The whole thing in my life then was multiplicity. Fifteen years later it became singleness, that is to write and film about the stuff that deeply interests me and has affected my life. Then I was both a free soul and wanted to be tied down and have a home. The Actors' Studio was my artistic home. It was also like a moral burden on me, in the sense that it was up to me to continue what the Group Theatre had given me.

So I was looking around for someone who was by nature a teacher, and I knew who I had in mind: Lee Strasberg. It took me a long time to get Strasberg involved; he hesitated, he backed off, he qualified, he did everything in the world to try and get out of it. I just persisted. About that time I was beginning to collaborate on the preparation of scripts like *Face in the Crowd, Splendor in the Grass,* and so on. I was directing plays and movies both, in those years; I didn't have time to go teach, and didn't have much interest in it after a while. I wasn't a particularly good teacher. I would be very good some days and then on other days I would find the work tedious and get through it as best I could. Strasberg—it fits him perfectly, he's a superb teacher. I think he's a very fine man. He's very criticised by many of my friends but I admire him a great deal. The Actors' Studio and he became synonymous, which is the way I wanted it. The Actors' Studio and this kind of acting have become the central tradition of American acting. Now, not only all these actors have become famous, but they have followers. I quit the Actors' Studio at a good time because it was becoming something I didn't want it to be. At a certain time, after Strasberg was in there and it became his place and not mine, I kept pulling back, and though he kept holding me over the years, slowly and slowly I withdrew. When I saw that he was happy there and comfortable and secure and wealthy, I left. He always wanted to make it a producing thing, to make a theatre of it. I was never interested in that idea. But as a training ground it was of great value.

Your feeling for collaboration must come from the Group Theatre.

There's a fundamental difference: I think there should be collaboration, but under my thumb! I think people should collaborate with *me*. I think any art is, finally, the expression of one maniac. That's me. I get people who help me, but I'm the centre of it. The whole damn thing in the Actors' Studio, by the time I left it, was that everybody had a voice, and everybody was equal, and everybody knew how they should do things. That's fine for a school, but it has nothing to do with art. Art is the overwhelmingly strong impression that one obsessed visionary puts on his work. It's important that the people who collaborate with you are able to see things as you do, but also that they're willing to ask you what you want and try to give it to you. When I have people I like, it's enormously pleasurable. And I like being contradicted because it helps the work, so long as I can, at a point, say: "That's it." But I think a lot of other directors don't allow contradiction because they're afraid. They're not certain enough of themselves. If you're certain of yourself, you can hear all the other voices; if you are not certain of yourself, you're anxious, and you don't want everybody to talk. If you don't let anybody express himself, that's bad too. With actors, I allow a tremendous amount of initiative. I always set the goal of each day first; I tell them what I want that day. The good actors have often surprised me by giving me my goal, my result, through means I didn't anticipate. That's the best way.

There's a period in the rehearsal of a play which hasn't quite got a parallel in a film: after you rehearse a play for about ten days or so, you begin to want something to happen against you. You want actors to take the play over, to make it theirs, to eliminate you. If you've rehearsed it well, the actors are on the track, and doing the things you want, but they've also pushed you to the back. In the first days of rehearsal you're up on the stage with the actors: by the end of the first week you sit in the first, second, or third row; about the tenth day you begin to move back; and in the second week you're sitting in the back row. You let them run without interjecting any criticism. After a play opened, I disappeared.

Don't you think there was a particular kind of relationship between the Russian school of acting and some American trends?

I think that Stanislavsky was particularly suited to be adopted by the American theatre. For instance, in Chekhov, whom he staged a lot, there is the use of silence, a surface realism and strong feelings working underneath, which is very close to O'Neill. And today the new directors on the stage oppose theatre to drama, theatre being the gestures, the silence, the choreography, etc., and drama being the written text. Before the Group, O'Neill brought in Freud, the interest in inner conflicts, the demon and the angel in the same person. Stanislavsky was also peculiarly suited to us because he emphasised not the heroic man but the hero in every man. That Russian idea of the profound soul of the inconspicuous person also fits the American temperament. We have not got the burden that everybody should be noble, or behave heroically, that the English used to have. We helped them get out of it.

For you the Method was not a theory but a practical objective.

The Method is more than a system for actors. It is a method for training actors and not a few handy rules. This training leads to the second aspect which the Method represents—how to rehearse a play:

—there must be a permanent company that stays together with basic training and several productions,

—this company must be trained in the same way and have the same social and artistic ideals,

—the rehearsal of the play must take several months to do and be at one stage freely improvisational and at all times the work of an ensemble.

One aspect of the Method is a way of controlling and using the unconscious; so that things are not just impulsive, they must be structured. We were very oppressively aware in New York how unfortunate and quick our rehearsal period was. Most plays are rehearsed in two and a half weeks because the third week you are in the scenery. You are trying on costumes, you are not really rehearsing.

Did you use the "as if" method as a stimulus?

That's not a way I like. It means that for instance when you talk to so-and-so it is as if you are talking to your mother and so on. At the beginning I used it because it is a neat, handy device. But the more genuine thing is the true situation. Many of these tricks were debasements of the Method, reducing it to a series of easy rules. Americans like handy rules, quick solutions.

The idea with the Method was to consider the play like the trunk of a tree with the branches coming out and you had a branch that led you to another branch and slowly you came to the first climax of the play which contained the theme. The idea was that if you performed all the tasks on the way you would be able to perform the task at the end. We used to refer to it as the spine with all the vertebrae coming off it. So when I was preparing films I also tried to capture in a phrase what the essential task was, to sum it up in one sentence.

The Method also gave me a way of getting the psychology clear, of charting the progress of a character through a film. Tennessee Williams did not agree with me—he said I was exaggerating, that it came from my Communist days when we thought people would become clearer and better with time. He thought people went on behaving the same way all their lives. He has a tragic view of life which is not mine; I would agree with him only in the sense that I believe our characters are our fates.

There's a basic element in the Stanislavsky system that has always helped me a lot in directing actors in the movies. The key word, if I had to pick one, is "to want." We used to say in the theatre: "What are you on stage *for?* What do you walk on stage to get? What do you want?" I always asked that of actors; what they're in the scene to obtain, to achieve. The asset of that is that all my actors come on strong, they're all alive, they're all dynamic—no matter how quiet. The danger of the thing may be a frenzied feeling to my work, which is unrelieved and monotonous. In my later works I try to allow myself to rely more on quieter effects. Another thing in the Stanislavsky system that I always stress a lot when I direct actors is what happened just before the scene. I not only talk about it, I sometimes improvise it. By the time the scene starts, they're fully in it, not just saying lines they've been given. Sometimes I do a scene that's unrelated to the scene in the script, something that happened, say, a day before, but that motivates the scene, so the actor knows what he's bringing into the scene that he plays. All these things are cinematic in that they take the reliance off the dialogue, off the spoken word and put it on activity, inner activity, desire, objects, partners—partners being the people you play with. All this can be photographed: the movement to achieve something can be photographed, what you are trying to achieve—the object—can be photographed, the partner and your relationship to him can be photographed. The lines are put into what I think is their proper place, into a secondary position. That's more or less the way I try to work. Another thing I've tried to stress is a basic simplicity; that is, listening to the person who's talking to you, and talking to him, not declaiming. I initially and immediately try to break down any declamatory, old-fashioned theatrical remnants in the style of the performer. And very often, when I've worked with a performer and then I don't see him for a while, and he appears in someone else's picture, I realise he's gone back to over-theatricalism.

How do you cast?

The problem is that the basic channel of the role must flow through the actor. He has to have the role in him somewhere. He must have experienced it to some extent. That's why I don't cast by reading. I take the actor for a walk or I take him to dinner or I watch him when he doesn't notice it and I try to find what is inside him. I am known for casting "on instinct," which is not the correct word because I have studied the actor carefully, even if quickly. Sometimes I make very rapid decisions but I never cast by looks because looks are false. And I don't believe in heroes anyway, so good looks don't mean anything to me.

An actress who played a leading role in a play I cast because her husband, whom she had divorced, had told me all about her sex habits. She was a very proper girl when you looked at her but I knew what she really was, so that's how she got cast. I know a lot about the personal lives of actors. At the Actors' Studio I knew the actors not only as technicians but as people. The material of my profession is the lives the actors have led up till now.

How do you rehearse?

I slowly begin to rehearse the next scene without rehearsing it; I lead them up to it without saying: "Now, let's siddown, come on, everybody." I mean I don't act like a boss: we're collaborators. In their dressing-rooms, I start talking to them about the next scene, the moments in it, what happens in it, and what happens before it, particularly. It's very important, that you re-establish what happens before it. So before you know it, we're rehearsing. I've always got to have the actors ready at the same time the scenery's ready. If they can do their work and if they can be ready—so that when the crew sees, or the other actors see the scene, they see it in some sort of shape—they feel protected. If they know that I've approved of what they've done, they feel protected too. That's very important, to get them over their shyness and uncertainties, privately, beforehand.

Another thing I do is—I throw them little new problems as they go along— little changes—I revise the thing for them. A performance is like a little flame, it's about to go out, you throw some more kerosene or gasoline on it, so it comes up again. You know what the source of the scene is, in the actor, so you keep it revived by the little things you say.

Your actors used to be more flamboyant—it seems they're more relaxed now.

Right, they're more relaxed, less showy, less affected. But what gets better now is my themes. They used to see my pictures and they'd say: "Ah, what a great performance Karl Malden gives, wasn't Kim Hunter wonderful?" But the play or the film was a platform, where these set pieces, these showpieces were performed. Now I want the basic theme of the thing to come out.

I was also, in those days, in the theatre particularly, protecting scripts that I felt were weak. I avoid doing that now, I trust myself and the material more. I say that even if it's a little boring, even if it's a little slow, that's what I'm talking about. I don't want you to watch how flashy this performance is, I want you to think about what's really going on. Sometimes it's not even bad to do it that way—a little boring, a little slower—it's not bad. I never did it till about ten years ago. Somebody just sits on a porch, in the front yard there's a cow. Or Kirk Douglas' mother is just sitting with her hands folded in a hospital waiting-room, she doesn't move, she doesn't say anything, she's not crying, she's just sitting there and you feel—I photograph through a window—how lonely she is, right? She doesn't say: "Oh God, I'm lonely!" Nothing. You let the audience work. That's another thing I'm still trying to learn, which is to let the audience feel, don't tell the audience what they should feel, let them find it, trust them to. It took me many years to get this.

In a sense, would you say that the natural outlet of the Method would be the cinema?

There's a lot of truth in that, but I don't agree with it completely. The camera looks into the people, so the need for life to be there is important; but the wonderful thing about the movies is that there are so many other elements: the *plastic* elements, the dance, the movement, the *visual* elements, the composition, the *oral* elements, the music of city sounds, of country sounds. And the element of nature, the effect of nature on experience, the relationship between the experience and the act, the experience and the environment, the wind, rain and snow, dawn and dusk, the whole thing!

What was your problem in using the Method in films?

Everybody's problem is his talent, not his faults. My problem is that I can always make things forceful. I used to make every scene GO GO GO! mounting to a climax, and if I had sixty minutes in a picture there were sixty climaxes, *ready?* CLIMAX! all right, rest a minute—CLIMAX! That was what I used to do. And it's easy to do, you know, make somebody shout, or grab somebody by the neck or throw somebody out, or slam a door, or open a window, or hit somebody with a hammer, or eat something quick in disgust—it's easy to do. It's bullshit! Bullshit! So you see what I mean, the problem of a man is his virtues, not his faults. It was my facility, my experience, my knowledgeability I had to watch out for.

How did you come to work in Hollywood?

In 1944 I began to get offers from the companies, particularly Warners and Fox, both of whom did more contemporary, down-to-earth subjects. I was offered *A Tree Grows in Brooklyn* and *A Letter to Uncle* by Clifford Odets. Jerry Wald wanted me at Warners and Louis B. Lighton at Fox. I read *A Tree* and saw in it material I knew something about, the streets of New York and the lives of the working class. I met Lighton and liked him immediately. I thought he was most honest and I signed up with him. But I had nothing whatever to do with the script. I didn't write one word of it and this is true for the next few films too. The first draft was done by Tess Slesinger and Frank Davis, whom I have never met. Lighton added to it and made it better. I think I enlarged *Tree* a bit by encouraging Lighton to put in a little more of the immigration theme than he otherwise would have because it meant something to me.

How did you use the setting in that first film?

This was the beginning of something that was a catastrophe on *Sea of Grass*. I was naïve and I didn't expect the scenery would overwhelm me that way. The scenery in *A Tree* was rather good, but there was something essentially false. If we had shot in New York on the East side, it would have been truer to life. But much worse than the scenery—the rooms were too clean, too nice, too much the work of the property man—were the hairdressing and costumes. They looked like magazine illustrations. The only truly correct thing on the visual side of *A Tree* was the face of the little girl, Peggy Ann Garner. Because her father was overseas in the war, because her mother had problems, because she herself was going through a lot of pains and uncertainties, Peggy's face was drawn and pale and worried. It looked exactly right. She was not pretty at all, or cute or picturesque, only true. It was also my idea not to have any background music but just source music—the sound of an organ-grinder and so on. But my luck on this film was to have this congenial, affectionate, mutually trusting relationship with Lighton.

Did you direct actors differently from in the theatre?

No; I directed actors the same way: I read first, and worked slowly and built each scene very carefully. Actually the movement of the scenes is not bad. What I would do differently is the interpretations of the characters. I have nothing against this picture, but I was not sure of myself, the whole thing was a mystery to me.

. . .

A Streetcar Named Desire *is your only experience of making a film from a stage play.*

First, I must say that I had a very great resistance to doing it. It's very hard to become involved in something a second time. I did it for an extremely personal reason, which is that I feel closer to Williams personally than to any other playwright I've worked with. Possibly it's the nature of his talent—it's so vulnerable, so naked—it's more naked than anyone else's. I wanted to protect him, to look after him. Not that he's a weak man—he's an extremely strong man, very strong-minded. But when he asked me repeatedly to make the film of *Streetcar,* I finally said I'd do it.

I thought, 'Well, that's a stage play, I think it's the best play I've ever done. It ranks with O'Neill's best plays, as the best America has ever had. I must try to find visual equivalents for the verbal poetry that it has.' I engaged a screenwriter and we began to "open it up" from the point of view of time, and from the point of view of where the events occurred, to work backwards into Blanche's past. We had scenes from before the start of the present play, designed to show the circumstances under which Blanche left her home community. We tried to show that she was sort of a refugee in the New Orleans scene. We worked fairly hard for four or five months. Then I read this script and I thought, well, we've done a pretty good job on it. Then I put it away and got involved in doing some other things, casting. I reread it a week later and I thought it was awful—it had lost the best qualities of Williams' work. Even as story-telling it was bad, because the strength of *Streetcar* is its compression. And I suddenly made a very radical decision—right or wrong, it was radical—I suddenly decided, I'm going to just shoot the play. And I'll even put most of it in the apartment. Most of it happens in Williams' imagination, I'm not going to pretend it takes place actually on the streets of present-day New Orleans. There *is* a streetcar named Daisy Rae—"desire"—but it has more symbolic reality than actual reality, and I said: I'm not going to *show* her in the streetcar named Desire, that would just be a visual joke, whereas if she talks about it, it comes out fragrant, weighted with her emotions. So I photographed my production of his masterpiece—and I do think it's a masterpiece—almost precisely as he had written it for the stage.

Once I decided on that, I started to work on the *mise en scène* and the décor. I said to Richard Day, who was my art director: "This community is a very damp community, very hot, like New York was last week—and the walls perspire! I want to see actual water coming out of the walls. I want the walls to be crumbling. I want the walls themselves to be *rotten,* and I want the environment to be a picturisation of decay." But actually you don't photograph that. In this kind of production where you have people talking all the time, you photograph the people talking. I told him: "That's a swell job you did, Dick"—but I thought "Well, a little of it will show, but not very much." And again I went back to photographing a stage production. Now I don't think I would've done that with any other play I've done; I wouldn't have done it with *Death of a Salesman,* and I liked it a lot. I would have moved that around a lot. But Williams relied on me, he wanted his play done a certain way, he didn't want his words broken into.

The other big decision I had to make was who to put in the film. In those days I didn't have casting or cutting rights—these came later with *On the Waterfront,* because Spiegel was in a bad position. From then on I've always had those rights, but I didn't have them then, so it was a matter of discussion between the producer, a guy named Charlie Feldman, a nice, agreeable but not very strong man, and myself. I urged that we use the original cast, and he would not go for it. Finally, after much hassling, we came to an agreement that we would have one movie star in it. Brando was not a star in those days, his first picture had not come out yet—a picture with Kramer, about paraplegics. Feldman wanted Vivien Leigh, and finally I agreed, with the understanding that I could have all the rest of the cast I had had in New York, which was in the spirit of sticking as much as possible to the original stage production.

Didn't you make some changes, towards the end?

I think the end of the stage play is better than the end of the film. It's not, to me, as dramatic as the other. I've always felt, about Williams, that there is a residing ambivalence in everything he does; which means that very often you can look at events and know they can either go one way or the other. They're not like they are in Miller, "this is *it.*" When you watch Williams' plays, you have the same feeling that you have in life, that you cannot anticipate what will happen next.

What did bother me a lot was a thing I had no control over at that time: the censorship cuts made to satisfy what was then the Breen Office. There was a big controversy about that, and finally it was cut behind my back, after I'd left. It was a small cut, of 40 seconds; but I felt very badly about it, and I still do, because it was a wonderful scene Kim Hunter had when she was responding to Brando calling her from the bottom of the stairs. They said it was a moment of orgasm, which only shows that the priests who are the censors don't know anything about orgasm, don't know anything about any kind of relationship between the sexes. It was nothing, it was just that she was excited by him, she was excited by his need for her, she heard his voice desiring her, and she responded to it. That's all it was, it was a perfectly natural thing. I think that cut hurt the picture a tiny bit. Backward elements within the organisation of the Catholic Church were determined to keep a certain amount of power for their censoring organisation. And they did make themselves felt in *A Streetcar Named Desire*. There was a particular priest, whose name I've forgotten, who met with us and made several requests for changes. These were disguised; he made a point of saying: "These are not requests for changes, I'm only telling you what bothers us and what would make us give this picture a C rating if they were not somehow met." It was quite a clear threat. But I fought very hard on this, because I had very strong grounds, because the play had been acclaimed. The changes were finally made without notifying me. I found out after Warner had agreed to make them. I had no legal ground to stand on, all I could do was write an article in the *New York Times*. And the villain of the article was Jack Warner, who had gone behind my back. I said everything, naming names, just like I do with everything. I named who did what, I named the priests, and I said what I thought of them. The interesting thing is, I thought Jack Warner would be hurt by it, but he was not. I realise you can't hurt these people, you can't insult them, because they can say they don't think less of themselves for it! You say, "You did a very underhand thing," and they say, "Sure, I did. I do underhand things all the time." And you can see it doesn't hurt at all. Anyway—they won.

The main problem I had with that production was that Vivien Leigh—whom I was very fond of, I still think of her tenderly—had played the part in England, under the direction of her husband, Laurence Olivier. He is a fine theatre artist, but still, what he saw in the play was something an Englishman would see from a distance, and was not what *I* saw in the play. She kept telling me, the first week, "When Larry and I did it in London—" and I had to keep saying, "But you aren't doing it with Larry now, you're doing it with me." It took several weeks to break her down. So, in my opinion, the first two or three reels of the picture are not too good. Then, somewhere around the second or third reel, she and I got together, got an understanding; and she became enthusiastic about what I was saying to her. And we became very close—and I really loved her. I think the last half of *Streetcar* was excellent, and I was really awfully glad she got an Oscar, I think she deserved it.

The blues piano music was changed into an orchestra.

I don't think in the theatre we ever had the blues piano the way it's described in the script—I think we had a small jazz ensemble playing blues. Blues is the national emotional music of the blacks in this country, and the effect was a poetic wedding of the feeling of pain and isolation the blacks had in the community, and the way the pseudo-aristocratic whites felt. There was nothing changed about that in the picture and Williams wouldn't have allowed it if he thought it was wrong. He liked the music. It was by Alex North, but the vocabulary of the music was all blues.

In Williams, contradictions lead to tragedy, whereas in your work they are lively, they lead to dialectic.

Williams once made a remark to me, that stuck in my mind: "There should always be an area in a dramatic character that you don't understand. There should always be an area of mystery, in human characters." In his notes Dostoievsky says of Prince Myshkin: "The Prince should be everywhere mysterious. He should be unexplained." Williams too tries not to explain, whereas in my training as an actor we had to justify the way everybody behaved, we had to explain to ourselves the reasons, so we could recreate the experience out of which that behaviour came . . . And then Williams criticised some of my work with other people; he said: "People don't change as much as you have them change." I didn't say anything; I thought they did. But I realised there was a difference between the way he and I approached life. I think he is closer to the feeling of death moving in on him. Somebody once said that you couldn't do good work in dramatic form until you had included the possibility of your own death. He lived with this, he lived with death all the time, he was brought up in it.

Let me make a parallel. Blanche Dubois, the woman, *is* Williams. Blanche Dubois comes into a house where someone is going to murder her. The interesting part of it is that Blanche Dubois-Williams is *attracted* to the person who's going to murder her. That's what makes the play deep. I think one of the best things I did for the play was to cast Brando in it—Brando has the vulgarity, the cruelty, the sadism—and at the same time he has something terribly attractive about him. So you can understand a woman *playing* affectionately with an animal that's going to kill her. So she at once wants him to rape her, and knows he will kill her. She protests how vulgar and corrupted he is, but she also finds that vulgarity and corruption attractive. Harold Clurman directed the road version of the play, and he saw the play as almost symbolic, as though Blanche represented Culture that was dying, Culture being devoured by the aggressive, cruel forces around it in American life. He saw Blanche as a heroine. I didn't; I saw Blanche as Williams, an ambivalent figure who is attracted to the harshness and

Fig. 13. Marlon Brando and Vivien Leigh in *A Streetcar Named Desire* (1951), adapted by
Oscar Saul from the play by Tennessee Williams (1947). Everyone in the cast except Vivien
Leigh had performed in the original Broadway production of *Streetcar*. Directed by Elia
Kazan. Courtesy of Billy Rose Theatre Collection, The New York Public Library for the
Performing Arts, Astor, Lenox and Tilden Foundations.

vulgarity around him at the same time that he fears it, because it threatens his
life.

Thinking about that helped me clarify for myself my own feeling about the
ambiguity in character. I saw this attraction/repulsion, fear/love thing all
around me. I see it all the time—I tell you, I see it in marriages, in love-con-
nections between people where there's resentment at the same time as there's
love. It isn't only that I'm attracted to it as an artist—it is the *truth* for me, and
I think that when you don't have that in a work, the work suffers, not in regard
to subtlety only, but suffers in regard to truth-telling. As I began more and more
to assert my own view of life, I expressed these contradictory impulses in my
films.

. . .

You've always liked to work with a homogeneous group.

Ideally, what should happen in every film is a complete unit. That's another thing I do; I've always used certain people—Karl Malden, Pat Hingle, Marlon Brando, Julie Harris, Lee Remick, Eli Wallach, Burl Ives, Kim Hunter, Jo Van Fleet, Paul Mann, Mike Strong, in film after film and play after play. I know them, I understand their limitations, and they trust me. I think basically they're honest, simple people without glamour. The men are not trying to show off how strong they are and the girls how pretty they are and all that nonsense. They're there to play human beings. It's the same with composers; I use the same composers over and over. The best way would be if they'd write the music while I was shooting the picture, if they watched rehearsals, met the actors, and not only read the script but knew how it was being directed and how it was being performed—if they hung around with me. That's the way I'd like it.

I used the same costume-designer in 85% of my films, a woman named Anna Hill Johnstone, who is one of the greatest collaborators I've ever had, in the sense that she completely tunes herself to me; she's so honest that there's never any sense in her costumes that she's trying to make a striking effect of her own, or get notices. The costumes and the scenery should not be noticed. The totality should be noticed—but not the direction, or the performances, or anything else. Anyway, Anna Hill Johnstone is the essence of that. For a film of a "low order" like *Waterfront* or *America America,* she goes to the Salvation Army and gets all these old clothes that these bums leave there. She buys forty, fifty dresses of this kind and has them fumigated. In *On the Waterfront* she threw them on the floor and had the actors come in, and they picked what fitted them. The clothes all looked like they'd been worn. But when we made *The Arrangement,* I wanted an apron for Deborah Kerr and it cost 350 dollars! The worst of it was that when it was on her, it didn't look as if she'd picked it herself and used it many times, or washed it.

What do you think are the most important stages in film-making?

George Stevens said a film was one-third writing and preparation, one-third shooting, and one-third editing and scoring. That makes a lot of sense but it's never been the way I really felt. For me a film is half conceptual, the core of it— you get into what the events mean, what you're trying to express. I feel that that's the most important stage in a film. Then you work out the rest—it's just work. But if you are careless with the first stage, you make something which is flaccid at its centre. I like the audience to feel something is being said to them. I like them to be puzzled and disturbed.

Eisenstein had an idea of the tension in a shot which I always remembered.

He gave an example of a pile of wood, and a man sitting with an axe in his hand. The man was not active, and the wood was waiting to be cut. There was a tension in that: you'd say, why isn't he cutting it? When is he going to cut it? Is it too much for him? And so on. The shot itself had a tension, a conflict in it. That's conception too. It isn't a matter of getting a shot of the pile of wood and a shot of the man; the whole thing is one shot. There was a time when I staged just like I do in the theatre, all medium-shot and people walking around. Hitchcock said scornfully of that kind of picture that it's just photographs of lips moving. He made fun of it. Later, when I began to study films, I saw his was a correct view. I began to cut and cut and cut. Well, now I do something in between. I try not to overstress now.

Many directors work with film more than I do in the way of cutting. Though up to now I've been there every minute, though I know cutting is essential and central and a very creative process, I'm on top of it, but I don't do as much with it. George Stevens sits there himself and runs it back and forth, takes out this much here and adds that much there. Many old-time directors shoot more angles than I do, and then they make their picture in the cutting-room. I tend to make it more on the "floor." I'm very clear about what I want. I know it when I've got it, because I used to be an actor. I don't have a lot of set-ups, maybe seven or eight a day. I don't rely on miracles in the cutting-room. I shoot more economically now than I used to, with an idea of where the cuts should be. At the end of every day I tell the cutter the way I think it should go together. I say, you're free to experiment, but I want you to know my intention and try to work it out my way first.

My angles are plain, none of them are very tricky. When you have spectacular angles you notice them and not what's happening. There were a lot of cutters who influenced me, who taught me: Harmon Jones on *Panic,* David Weisbart on *Streetcar,* Dede Allen on *America America,* who is as good a cutter as there is. *The Visitors* was cut by a very sensitive man with excellent taste, who also photographed the picture, Nick Proferes. He's comparatively inexperienced, but very gifted. He cuts right to the heart of things.

The theatre is increasingly foreign to you.

I can't even read plays now. They don't seem to be in the rhythm of this time. Shakespeare is more contemporary than the plays that are being written today. He leaps from here to there, he goes to climaxes, and the figures are big-sized.

I am a person that moves. I think of life as moving—as a struggle, an escape, and a pursuit. Cinema is more compatible with this than the theatre. I have dreams, when I'm asleep, of working in the theatre again. I spent thirty-two years in the theatre, you know—but when I actually get up in the morning and I face life, I think of novels and films.

The Rules of the Game is the film which is the closest to my ideal on the screen. The highest form of art is when there's no formalistic "genre" difference between the comedy, the farce, the tragedy, the social meaning, the symbolism. It's one piece. That's what I've been trying to do all my life, really. It's the way I view life. My films are not comedies, but there's a lot of fun in them; they're not tragedies, because there's a sense that life goes on, they don't collapse at the end in despair. *The Rules of the Game* has everything in it, but it's all one. Renoir is a big enough man so that he finds people at once tragic, very funny, ridiculous, beautiful, sensitive, insensitive, cruel, generous, foolish, heroic. And he uses nature a lot—the environment that we live in. He doesn't just move in front of scenery; he lives *in* an environment which is putting its imprint, its impression and its force on him. And I believe in that too.

Acting Stage vs. Screen

Leo Braudy

Acting in Europe and America has been historically defined by the varying interplay of the heightened and the normal, the theatrical and the nonchalant, in the conception of the role. Until the Renaissance, there was little attempt to place any special value on the absorption of the rhythm, themes, and gestures of everyday life into drama or acting style. Aristotle had taught that the most intense feelings possible in drama were those in tragedy, when the characters and the acting style were on a much higher plane than the normal life of the audience. Everyday life, where the characters and the way they behave tend to be on the same or lower social levels than the audience, was primarily a source of stylized comedy. The stage was raised above the audience in part because the characters and their impersonators were not to be considered as individually as the audience might assess each other. In Greek, Roman, and medieval society, actors therefore tended to por-

tray beings purer than the audience, the somber figures of myth and the carica-
tures of comedy—a division of acting labor not unlike that of the silent screen.

Shakespeare helped make an enormous change in this relation between the
audience and the actors by elaborating the analogies possible between the
world and the stage. He began the European theater's effort to absorb and reflect the life of the audience as much as to bring the audience out of itself into
another world. Comedy could therefore become more serious because it was no
longer necessary to involve emotions lower than the grand style of tragedy.
More intimate theaters and better lighting permitted a more nuanced acting
style. By the mid-eighteenth century David Garrick had become the first to attempt historical authenticity in costuming, once again asserting the need to
ground the play and the style of acting in some possible and plausible setting
rather than a special world of theater. The "fourth wall" theories of the latter
nineteenth century further defined theatrical space and dramatic acting as an
extension of the world of the audience. Stylized acting did not disappear, of
course. The broader styles remained in opera, ballet, and popular comedy, as
well as revivals of classics, symbolic and proletarian drama, and the experiments
with ritual theater from the end of World War Two to the present.

Acting on stage had necessarily developed a tradition of naturalness as well.
In the eighteenth century Diderot had argued that the paradox of acting is that
an actor must be cold and tranquil in order to project emotion. Actors who play
from the soul, he said, are mediocre and uneven. We are not moved by the man
of violence, but by the man who possesses himself. In the early twentieth century, Konstantin Stanislavsky turned Diderot's view of the actor self-possessed
in passion into a whole style. He rejected theories of acting based on imitation
and emphasized instead an actor's inner life as the source of energy and authenticity for his characterizations. More "mechanical" and expressionist styles of
stage acting implicitly attacked Stanislavsky's methods by their emphasis on the
intensity of emotion and the visual coherence of the stage ensemble. Minglings
of the two traditions produced such hybrids as the Group Theater, in which the
interplay between ensemble and individual produced a thematic tension often
missing from Eisenstein's productions, whether on stage or in film. Elia Kazan's
film style, for example, with its mixture of expressionistic, closed directorial
style and open, naturalistic acting, is a direct descendant of this tradition.*

* Diderot's *Paradoxe sur le comédien* was not published until 1830, although it was written in
  the late 1760s. A later printing in 1902 may have had an influence on Stanislavsky's theories.

Our ability to learn what films can tell us about human character has suffered not only from preconceptions derived from the novel of psychological realism, but also from assumptions about acting that are drawn from the stage. We know much better what our attitude should be toward characters in fiction and drama. Unlike those forms, films emphasize acting and character, often at the expense of forms and language. Films add what is impossible in the group situation of the stage or the omniscient world of the novel: a sense of the mystery inside character, the strange core of connection with the face and body the audience comes to know so well, the sense of an individuality that can never be totally expressed in words or action. The stage cannot have this effect because the audience is constantly aware of the actor's impersonation. Character in film generally is more like character as we perceive it everyday than it is in any other representational art. The heightened style of silent film acting could be considered an extension of stage acting, but the more personal style allowed by sound film paradoxically both increased the appeal of films and lowered their intellectual status. The artistic was the timeless, Garbo not Dietrich, Valentino not Gable.

But character in sound film especially was not so much deficient as it was elusive. Films can be less didactic about character because the film frame is less confining than the fictional narrative or the theatrical proscenium. Sound films especially can explore the tension between the "real person" playing the role and the image projected on the screen. The line between film actor and part is much more difficult to draw than that between stage actor and role, and the social dimension of "role" contrasts appropriately with the personal dimension of "part." Film acting is less impersonation than personation, part of personality but not identifiable with it. "Can Ingrid Bergman commit murder?" ask the advertisements for *Murder on the Orient Express* (Sidney Lumet, 1975); the casual substitution of actress for character crudely makes an assertion that better films explore more subtly. Unlike the stage actor, the film actor cannot get over the footlights. Although this technical necessity may seem to make him less "real" than the stage actor, it makes his relation to the character he plays much more real. Audiences demand to hear more about the private life of the film actor than the stage actor because film creates character by tantalizing the audience with the promise of the secret self, always just out of the grasp of final articulation and meaning. The other life of a stage character is the real life of the person who plays him. But the other life of a film character is the continuity in other films of the career of the actor who plays him. In plays the unrevealed self tends to be a reduced, meaner version of the displayed self; in films it is almost always a complex enhancement. Within the film a character may have a limited meaning. But the actor who plays him can potentially be a presence larger than that one part, at once more intimate and more distant than is ever possible on stage.*

Film preserves a performance that is superior to the script, whereas stage performances and plays are separate realities, with the performance often considered second best. The stage actor is performing a role: he may be the best, one of the best, the only, or one of many to play that role. But the role and its potentials will exist long after he has ceased to play it, to be interested in it, to be alive. The film actor does not so much perform a role as he creates a kind of life, playing between his characterization in a particular film and his potential escape from that character, outside the film and perhaps into other films. The stage actor memorizes an entire role in proper order, putting it on like a costume, while the film actor learns his part in pieces, often out of chronological order, using his personality as a kind of armature, or as painters will let canvas show through to become part of the total effect. If the movie is remade and another actor plays the part, there is little sense of the competition between actors that characterizes revivals on stage. "Revival" is a stage word and "remake" is a film word. Hamlet remains beyond Booth's or Olivier's or Gielgud's performance, but Alan Ladd as Gatsby and Robert Redford as Gatsby exist in different worlds.

Filmmaking is a discontinuous process, in which the order of filming is influenced more by economics than by aesthetics. Film actors must therefore either have stronger personalities than stage actors or draw upon the resources of personality much more than stage actors do. Strong film actors can never do anything out of character. Their presence defines their character and the audience is always ready for them to reveal more. Even though studio heads like Louis Mayer forced actors and actresses to appear "in character" offscreen as well, we sense and accept potential and variety from the greatest movie actors, while we may reject less flamboyant fictional characters as "unreal" or refer to the woodenness of stage characterization. Continuity in stage acting is thematic continuity: "Watch in happiness someone whom you will soon see in sorrow" is one of the fatalistic possibilities. But the discontinuities of film act-

---

* In these remarks, I am obviously talking not so much about the craft of acting as about the effects of acting on the audience. I would hope, however, that what I say has implications for craft and method as well, at least in terms of a test of effectiveness beyond the pleasures of theory.

ing allow the actor to concentrate on every moment as if it were the only reality that existed. No matter how conventionalized the plot, the film actor can disregard its clichés and trust instead to the force and continuity of his projected personality to satisfy beyond the more obvious forms of theme and incident. Because he must present his play in straightforward time, a stage director will work with the actor to get a "line" or a "concept" of the character that will permeate every scene. But movie acting, bound in time to the shooting schedule and the editing table, must use what is left out as well as what is expressed. The greatest difference between a film and a stage version of the same work is less in the "opening" of space that films usually emphasize than in the different sense of the inner life of the characters we get. . . .

Movies therefore stand between the strongly social emphasis of theater and the strongly individual emphasis of novels, incorporating elements of both. At a play we are always outside the group, at the footlights. But at a film we move between inside and outside, individual and social perspectives. Movie acting can therefore include stage acting better than stage acting can include movie acting. George C. Scott, for example, is essentially a stage actor who also can come across very well in film. When he was making *Patton* (Franklin Schaffner, 1970), he insisted that he repeat his entire first speech eight times to allow for the different camera angles; he refused to repeat only the sections that corresponded to the rephotographing. His sense of the character was therefore what I have been describing as a stage sense of character, in which the continuity is linear and spelled out. The performance is excellent and effective, but Scott's way of doing it tells us nothing of the differences in stage and film acting. It may have a touch of the New York stage actor's almost traditional hostility to films. At best, it is only another example of the way a newer art can more comfortably embrace the methods of an older art than the other way around. In fact, virtuosity in films tends to be a characteristic of second leads or medium minor characters, not stars, and the Academy Awards perpetuate the stage-derived standards by giving so many awards to actors and actresses cast against type, that is, for stage-style "virtuosity."

The film actor emphasizes display, while the stage actor explores disguise. But stage acting is still popularly considered to be superior to film acting. An actor who does a good job disappears into his role, while the bad (read "film") actor is only playing himself. The true actor, the professional craftsman, may use his own experience to strengthen his interpretation. But the audience should always feel that he has properly distanced and understood that experience; it is another tool in his professional workchest. The false actor, the ama-

Fig. 14. *You Can't Take It with You* (1938), adapted by Robert Riskin from the play by George S. Kaufman and Moss Hart (1936). Lionel Barrymore came from a famous stage-acting family, and his film performances—"theatrical" in the sense that they are bold and large—display the dominance of craft over personality. Directed by Frank Capra. Courtesy of Billy Rose Theatre Collection, The New York Public Library for the Performing Arts, Astor, Lenox and Tilden Foundations.

teur actor, the film actor, on the other hand, works on his self-image, carries it from part to part, constantly projecting the same thing—"himself." Such a belief is rooted in an accurate perception; but it is a false interpretation of that perception. The stage actor does project a sense of holding back, of discipline and understanding, the influence of head over feelings, while the film actor projects effortlessness, nonchalance, immediacy, the seemingly unpremeditated response. Thus, when stage actors attack film actors, they attack in some puritanical way the lack of perceptible hard work, obvious professional craft, in the film actor's performance. Like many nonprofessionals in their audience, such stage actors assume that naïveté, spontaneity, "being yourself," are self-images that anyone in front of a camera can achieve. A frequent Actors Studio exercise, for example, is "Private Moment," in which the student is asked to act out before the group something he or she ordinarily does alone that would be very embarrassing if someone happened to see. Private self-indulgences and private games are thereby mined for their exposable, group potential. But the concentration of film, its ability to isolate the individual, makes every moment that way, and so the problem of the film actor may be to scale down intimacy rather than discover and exaggerate it.

How do we know the "themselves" film actors play except through the residue of their playing? How much do film actors, as opposed to stage actors, model their offscreen selves to continue or contrast with their screen images? To accuse an actor of "playing himself" implies that we have seen and compared the "real" and "false" selves of the actor and reached a conclusion. Film acting deposits a residual self that snowballs from film to film, creating an image with which the actor, the scriptwriter, and the director can play as they wish. Donald Richie has recorded that the Japanese director Yasujiro Ozu said: "I could no more write, not knowing who the actor was to be, than an artist could paint, not knowing what color he was using." Ozu's remark indicates how a director takes advantage of a previously developed image in order to create a better film. But the stage actor in a sense ceases to exist from play to play; we experience only the accumulation of his talent, his versatility. In our minds the stage actor stays within the architectures he has inhabited, while the film actor exists in between as well, forever immediate to our minds and eyes, escaping the momentary enclosures that the individual films have placed around him.

"Playing yourself" involves one's interpretation of what is most successful and appealing in one's own nature and then heightening it. Film actors play their roles the way we play ourselves in the world. Audiences may now get sustenance from films and from film acting because they no longer are so interested in the social possibilities of the self that has been the metaphysic of stage acting since Shakespeare and the Renaissance, the place of role-playing in the life of the audience. The Shakespearean films of Laurence Olivier and Orson Welles clearly express the contrast. The tendency in stage acting is to subordinate oneself to the character, while the great film actor is generally more important than the character he plays. Our sense of Olivier, in his Shakespearean roles is one of distance and disguise: the purified patriotism of Henry V, in which all the play's negative hints about his character have been removed; the blond wig he uses to play Hamlet, so that, as he has said, no one will associate him with the part; the bent back, twisted fingers, and long black hair of Richard III. But Welles assimilates the roles to himself. Costume for Welles is less a disguise than a generation from within and so he presented it in various television appearances of the 1950s, gradually making up for his part while he explained the play to the audience, until he turned full face into the camera and spoke the lines. In theater we experience the gap between actor and role as expertise; in film it may be described as a kind of self-irony. The great stage actor combats the superiority of the text, its preexistence, by choosing his roles: Olivier will play Hamlet; Olivier will play a music-hall comic. The great film actor, assured that his image absorbs and makes real the script, may allow himself to be cast in unpromising roles, if only for visibility. In the audience we feel Welles's character to be part of his role, whereas we perceive not Olivier's character but his intelligence and his ability to immerse himself in a role. Olivier is putting on a great performance, but Welles feels superior enough to the Shakespearean text to cut, reorganize, and invent. Olivier is a great interpreter; Welles is an equal combatant. For both, Shakespeare is like a genre, similar to the western, that offers materials for a contemporary statement. But Olivier sticks closely to the language and form of the play itself. We judge Olivier finally by Shakespeare, but we judge Welles by other films. Both choose those Shakespearean plays that emphasize a central character. But Olivier's willingness to allow Shakespeare the last word frees him for the more assertive political roles, whereas Welles stays with the more domestic or even isolated figures of Macbeth and Othello. Olivier began his Shakespearean film career with the heroic self-confidence of Henry V, while Welles, at least for the moment, has ended his with Falstaff—the choice of the ironic imagination of film over the theatrical assertion of social power.

These distinctions between stage acting and film acting are, of course, not absolute but points on a slippery continuum. Marlon Brando's career, for example, is a constant conflict between his desire to be versatile—to do different kinds of films, use different accents, wear different costumes—and the demand of his audience that he elaborate his residual cinematic personality. Brando tries to get into his roles, and often sinks them in the process, while Cary Grant pumps them up like a balloon and watches them float off into the sky. The main trouble that Chaplin has in *A Countess from Hong Kong* (1967) is taking two actors (Brando and Sophia Loren), whose own sense of their craft emphasizes naturalistic, historically defined character, and placing them within a film world where they would best exist as masks and stereotypes. Their efforts to ground their characters destroy the film. It may be funny if Chaplin or Cary Grant vomited out a porthole, but it's not funny when Brando does it. Brando can be funny in films only as a counterpoint to our sense of "Brando," for example in *Bedtime Story* (Ralph Levy, 1964). When he is acting someone else, the ironic sense of self-image that is natural to a film actor does not exist. We share Cary Grant's sense of distance from his roles, whether they are comic, melodramatic, or whatever, because it corresponds to our sense of personal distance from our daily roles in life. The sense of "putting it on" that we get from Brando's greatest roles—*A Streetcar Named Desire, Viva Zapata!, The Wild One, On the Waterfront*—stands in paradoxical relation to Method theories of submergence in the role. Brando's willingness to cooperate with Bernardo Bertolucci in the commentary on and mockery of his screen image that forms so much of the interest of *Last Tango in Paris* may indicate that he no longer holds to the theatrical definition of great acting. His progenitor role in *The Godfather* seems to have released him to create the paradox of the self-revealed inner life of a screen image elaborated by *Last Tango*. In the films of the 1970s, character, and therefore acting as well, has taken on the central importance in film. And the stage actor in film finds that his virtuosity is more a parlor trick than a technique of emotional and artistic power. Films make us fall in love with, admire, even hate human beings who may actually in the moment we watch them be dead and dust. But that is the grandeur of films as well: the preservation of human transience, the significance not so much of social roles as of fragile, fleeting feelings.

A Conversation with Sam Waterston

Joanmarie Kalterie

Sam Waterston was born in Cambridge, Massachusetts on November 15, 1940. He attended Brook School, where his father taught languages, Groton Academy, and Yale University. As an undergraduate, he joined the Yale Dramat, an extra-curricular group, and the experience of playing Lucky in their production of *Waiting for Godot* confirmed his desire to become a professional actor. He spent a season in summer stock with the Wellesley 20 Group, which included Rosemary Harris and Ellis Rabb, and during a junior year in Paris, he became involved with the American Actors Workshop headed by John Berry (who left this country due to blacklisting in the McCarthy era).

Not long after graduating from college, Mr. Waterston made his New York stage debut when he took over the role of Jonathan in Arthur Kopit's *Oh Dad, Poor Dad, Mama's Hung You in the Closet and I'm Feelin' so Sad.* He played Silvius in *As You Like It,* replaced Roddy Maude-Roxby as Colin in *The Knack,* played Prince Hal in *Henry IV,*

Reprinted from *Actors on Acting: Performing in Theatre and Film Today* (New York: Sterling, 1979), 141–67.

Tom Lewis in *The Trial of the Catonsville Nine,* and Laertes in *Hamlet* with Stacy Keach in the title role. During this period, he played a wide range of characters, including a pregnant homosexual in *Spitting Image,* but his breakthrough as a leading man came in 1972 when he appeared as Benedick in *Much Ado about Nothing.*

As Mr. Waterston explains it, he had just come back from California after working in a few short-running plays, was broke, and had no prospects. A telephone call from Joseph Papp reversed his luck and led to the role which Mel Gussow of *The New York Times* would call "a superb comic performance," and which would win him the Drama Critics Circle Award, the Drama Desk Award, and an Obie.

Among the stage roles which followed have been those of Prospero in *The Tempest;* Torvald Helmer in *A Doll's House* (with Liv Ullmann in the role of Nora); Vladimir in *Waiting for Godot;* and *Hamlet* himself. He received an Emmy nomination as Tom Wingfield opposite Katherine Hepburn as Amanda in the television production of *The Glass Menagerie.* In films, he has played Nick Carraway, the narrator of *The Great Gatsby;* a comic Indian in Frank Perry's contemporary Western, *Rancho Deluxe;* and has appeared in Woody Allen's first serious drama, *Interiors.*

Mr. Waterston is tall and angular, resembling somewhat of a cross between Tony Perkins and Jean-Pierre Léaud. He has bemused, sometimes quizzical dark eyes and a gentlemanly manner.

For this talk, which was held at my home, Mr. Waterston arrived formally dressed in a tie and jacket, but he soon removed the jacket, loosened the tie— and looked relieved to do so. As we talked, he was sitting in a large armchair, alternately leaning forward on the edge of the seat, and sinking back with his legs up, drawing his knees to his chest when he laughed. He was anxious to avoid too much abstract analysis of acting, and though the more specific technical processes, he admitted, are endlessly fascinating to him, he was puzzled why anyone else, particularly a non-actor, would find them even interesting. Rather than inflate his accomplishments, his impulses—and quite sincerely—were consistently to cut them to scale.

Mr. Waterston has one son from a previous marriage. His present wife, Lynn Woodruff, is a model, and the two live in an apartment in Manhattan.

I understand that your father was an English and foreign-language teacher with an interest in the theatre. In fact, your first stage appearance was as a page in a produc-

tion of Antigone *that he directed. Do you think his interest in drama had much to do with your motivations to become an actor?*

I'm sure it did. He is English and was an amateur actor when he was in college at Oxford. He was a contemporary of a lot of people who are growing old in the theatre in England now—like Gielgud and Redgrave—and he knew some of them. So, he's had a life-long interest in the theatre, and I'm sure that had something to do with my own. As you say, the first play I was ever in was a play that he directed.

What was it about your earliest experiences with acting that excited you? Do you remember?

That's a hard question to answer, because I think that your reasons for being in a business or a craft or an art change over the years. And then when you look at them in retrospect, you apply your more recent thinking to the distant past. I know that when I was in high school, I liked acting *very* much but I was in a school that didn't particularly encourage it. They prepared people for business or public service or the clergy more than the theatre, and they put on just one play a year. But the basic motivation to become an actor—for me and maybe for others—is partly a love of fantasy worlds, and partly a kind of ego reinforcement that you don't find elsewhere. I don't know which of those motivations matters most, but I think the impulse to act alternates between those two things, and one is more respectable, I suppose, than the other.

You played Lucky in Waiting for Godot *at Yale, didn't you? I understand that was a turning-point experience for you.*

Yes, it was. There were two things about it that were wonderful. One was that I had a revelation such as Stanislavsky describes coming to people when they are doing a play. I had a revelation in the last performance of that play that ignited the whole character and illuminated it in a great flash right while I was standing on the stage. And then that illumination *worked* . . . instantaneously! That was the first thing that was very exciting. The other aspect of it was the way it worked, which was . . .

. . . that it got a response from your audience?

Yes, but it was more than that. It was like an ecstatic experience. I'm not sure that I'm using that word right, but the only other time I've had an experience like that was when I was skiing once, a year or so later. I'd skied all my life, but never for a long time at a stretch. And then I went skiing when I was a student in Europe. I went to Austria for three weeks, and I skied every day, all day long. I actually began to get pretty good. Towards the end of the time, I was skiing parallel down the mountain, and I was going about sixty miles an hour. (I was probably going twelve, but it felt like sixty.) Everything was just working perfectly, and I wasn't thinking about it any more and suddenly, I had a sense of taking off. It was like flight. And the same thing happened when I was doing that play.

As I was doing the speech, I was thinking things that were brand new. I had never thought of the character in the way that it came to me to think of it at that moment. All the thought processes were changed, and I had the sensation that every single one of them was being communicated explicitly to the audience. Now, I realize you could delude yourself about that one, but I had some corroboration. When I wanted the audience to laugh, they laughed; when I wanted them to be silent, they were absolutely silent; they interrupted the speech in the middle at the point where I had designed a break, and applauded. So, I had reason to believe that what I felt was real. I felt that I had finger-tip control over the audience. And that's the ego trip of it. But then there was another sensation of incredible communication, which neither I nor they were really responsible for. It was just taking place in the air between us. It wasn't really my fault, or to my credit, that I had figured out what to do—it just came to me! It was like a group experience . . . with me standing there, of course, and everybody watching.

It's interesting that you compare that acting experience to athletics. I can see where they would be very similar in seeking a coordination between the body and the mind. But, could you tell me what the nature of your revelation was? What was it that connected you to your character?

Oh, it was very simple, and I'm not sure it would ever work again. In fact, I just redid *Waiting for Godot . . .*

. . . and you played another character.

Yes, I played another character. And I never told anyone. I sort of *hinted* to the guy who was playing the part of Lucky that I had had this idea, but you know, it's another person. And I was also afraid that I would tell it to him, and he'd try it and then he'd say, "Oh, that's no good; it doesn't really work; it's not exactly right."

But it was really quite simple: we were only scheduled to do five performances of the play, and I had had a very hard time learning the part. It was specifically mapped out, though I wasn't responsible for all the mapping by any means. It was very much given to me by the director. I would sing it here, and go fast there, and make this a unit, and take a break there, and not breathe after this word . . .

Very technical points?

Yes. And I got very good at that. But I always felt that there was some essence that I hadn't gotten yet. The review in the Yale *Daily News* had said I was too smart for the part, and that bugged the hell out of me. So I was thinking about all these things when I was on the stage carrying the bags, waiting for my turn to speak. I kept thinking over and over again that this was the last performance, that I wasn't going to get another chance to do it again, that I hadn't gotten it right yet, and would I ever get it right, and if I didn't get it right tonight, I'd never get another opportunity. . . . Over and over, round and round, the same thoughts. And just then as Pozzo said, "Speak, pig," I thought: I never am going to say this again, I am never, I am never going to speak again, I'm never going to speak again, I, Lucky, am never going to speak again, so I have to say everything that I know right now! And, of course, that's exactly the situation of the character. Lucky never does speak again. And it fits very neatly. So it just took off.

Your experience exactly coincided with the character's . . .

Yes! And the flash of light was that it coincided. It was exciting!

And it verified the observations of Stanislavsky.

Yes, he says that happens every so often. But, you know, it doesn't happen so very often.

Did you study at the Actors Studio where the teaching, as I understand it, draws very much upon Stanislavsky?

I was an observer at the Actors Studio for a while. But I didn't study there, I did a couple of plays there once, yet I never became a member. I did an audition from the play that I had performed and they said, "That's fine, but now you have to do something from another piece of material." I thought, who needs this? It was very small-minded of me, really. I'm sorry I didn't, in a way. I think it's probably the best gym in town.

You think that's the value of it—to have a place where you can work out, act out, and experiment?

Well, I do know that when people aren't working in the theatre, they have an opportunity there to exercise with very good people. And that has to be good.

What do you think about the value of drama school in general?

Just any old drama school? I think it would very much depend on who it was, and what the school was.

What I'm asking, really, is whether it's important to know the history of the theatre, the literature of the theatre, to have some intellectual terms for thinking and talking about what you do.

I, myself, never went to drama school. I took some courses at the Yale Drama School, but I don't know what it would be like to spend three or four years studying theatre. Acting is a function, however, and the risk that you run by just going out into the world and getting jobs without any training is that you don't have any foundation. Someday, inspiration is bound to fail you, and then so will your body and your voice and your technique for approaching a part. You have to acquire those skills solidly and a drama school sounds like a good place to do it. But I think that carries a liability, too. Because it's a school situation, you're not actually putting the ideas you learn to work, and the possibility arises of applying your intelligence in the wrong way. Just as when you go to college, the possibility arises of learning an absolutely specious and completely invalid way of looking at any given subject. Now, I don't know how you get around that problem, but the facility of analysis and the kind of arrogant attitude which you learn in school are just bankrupt when you have to actually stand on the stage and represent somebody.

Knowing what you know now about the profession of acting, would you go about your training any differently than you have done?

Well, the best teaching I ever had, in any discipline at all, has always been from a great teacher, not from a great place. I went to Yale and in all the disciplines that I studied, there were only three or four teachers in my whole experience there that really enlightened me at all about what we were reading, or studying, or talking about. I think that you have to go look for teachers, whatever you study, because a great teacher for one person is a lousy teacher for another.

You've said that John Berry, whom you worked with in Paris at the American Cultural Center, was a very good teacher.

Yes, he is a great teacher. And he was teaching a course because he had an interest in doing it. He wasn't making any money from it. He was energetic, colorful, tough, and extremely generous emotionally. He was always experimenting with us. But he also taught me the rudiments of approaching a part.

Which were . . . ?

. . . which were based on Stanislavsky and [Michael] Chekhov: dividing your work up into beats; figuring out what your intentions are; getting on a rail and riding it; having little checkpoints so that if you're off the rail, you can get back on; and throwing away all the work when you perform.

What do you mean by checkpoints?

If your own feelings get awakened while you're working, they could lead you anywhere, and so you need to have little landmarks for yourself so that the monitor inside you can say, "Oh, yeah. That's all right. Keep on doing what you want, you just passed the third-mile marker and you're still on the right street." But if you get to the place where the third-mile marker is supposed to be, and you're not where you're supposed to be, then you know that you've got to find it.

You mean where you're supposed to be in terms of the internal emotions?

Well, I'm not talking about blocking, which would be the physical positioning; I am really talking about internal sign posts. For instance, if you get to a certain point in a scene where you're supposed to be ragingly angry at the person who's on stage with you, and you find yourself feeling other things, then that doesn't necessarily mean that anything's wrong because you may be able to justify it; but you've got to make sense out of it somehow.

What would be your first step in the preparation of a role? What's the first thing you do upon being cast?

It's something that I wish I could avoid doing, but that I do automatically, and that is, I figure it out. Then I spend a long time correcting all the mistakes that I made by going ahead and figuring it out.

Figuring it out?

It's the facile analysis that I was talking about before. It's easy to figure things out, and it may be perfectly valid, but it doesn't have anything to do with acting. You can give a very intelligent reading that way without busting it open, without having it breathe. But you find out that you're wrong soon enough; the director tells you so; scenes don't work. And then if you're lucky, things get radically corrected. Finally, with all you've absorbed from what you've figured out and from what's been pouring into you during the rehearsals, you achieve a third state—just doing it without thinking about it.

Rosemary Harris said that it took her four years to forget the things she learned in drama school, but that she was very glad to have gone there, because now that she had forgotten them, she could put them easily and readily to use. So I think that I do that in a sort of mini-way. When I do a part, I work it out the way you would work out a thesis. And then, since that is demonstrably inadequate, I throw it out. But some things remain. And then, of course, I do all the detail work: figuring out what I intend to achieve by everything that I say and do. I try to find verbs for all the things that I'm doing and avoid adjectives.

Why avoid adjectives?

This is a technical point, but it's a useful tool. The nice thing about verbs is that they are not qualities, they're actions—as opposed to adjectives, which are not actions, but qualities. For instance, if I say to myself, "I must get you to allow me to take that chair home with me," and if I make those stakes very high, and if you continued to refuse and I have a whole set of circumstances about who you are and what I have been led to believe you are going to do, then that may make me mad. If that's what I'm trying to achieve, that will be good. But if I say to myself, "I am now going to be mad," or "I'm going to do this angrily," then it doesn't lead inside anywhere—it just stays superficial.

So you root your emotions in actions rather than conjuring them from thin air.

Yeah, but insofar as any of this becomes an intellectual crutch, insofar as this leads you to say, "I am now doing the correct thing, I am doing this methodically," then I think it's bad. What you really want it to do ultimately is to release you into simple behavior. This last time that we did *Waiting for Godot*, Walter Asmus, the director, didn't want to hear, think, or talk about these things. He occasionally accommodated us by talking when he realized that we were just paralyzed without it. He attempted then, in a spirit of international accord, to make us feel better about ourselves by saying, "Sure, we could talk about these things if you want to." But, in fact, what he wanted to do was to have us stand in certain places, talk in certain ways, go faster or slower, and really, that was it. There wasn't anything secret behind it. There was something in the form of the play that he thought was absolutely communicative, and it was plenty, more than enough, better without anything else. Once we got over our automatic resistance to it, the dread of going out on stage bare, then it flipped into the ultimate state that we wanted. Because what you aim for, no matter how you get to it, is to be out there naked, doing something well-formed, in which you are just there.

So this method of not talking about the play and not analyzing its meaning did, in fact, work?

I don't know if it worked for other people, but it worked for me. I felt like it was some of the best work I had ever done. It was certainly very good for me as an actor at this point in my life to have somebody tell me that all the things that I held dear were not important, and that I would still be all right without them. Because along with all the certitudes you acquire, you carry along a lot of junk. It makes you think: "I can't do this unless . . . and unless this, unless that. . . ." And maybe the truth is that you can do with a lot less than you think.

So you're saying that what the actor really strives for is to have all his analysis and technique seep into his subconscious or unconscious mind?

Yeah, and then I think it depends on who the person is. All this stuff would apply not at all to somebody who responded viscerally from the start, who responded in an unfiltered way without the interference of thinking. That person might find the encouragement to think and analyze very useful. But since it's my automatic response, it's also my enemy. Being analytical is the capacity that one learns in school, but it's important to remember that what you are doing to impress the professors, you are ultimately doing to yourself, because it becomes a habit. If you're writing a paper on the history of art, for example, you have the capacity to make talk about the structure and emotional content of Picasso, and to make it sound very good, and for it to be on a certain level, perfectly adequate—but it doesn't have anything to do with the making of the painting.

It has to do with the appreciation of the painting.

Well, it does have something to do with the appreciation of a painting, yes, and that's why professors like to see people write that way. But it won't help you paint. And when I work on a part, all that analysis tends to lead me away: it blinds me to the character.

For instance, when I was working on the role of Torvald, the male-chauvinist husband of *A Doll's House,* I completely figured the guy out. But it took an audience to tell me that I didn't like him and that I was standing away from him and saying: "I don't want any of you to be confused about this. I am actually not at all like this, so let's all participate in stomping all over this guy." I walked on the stage in Philadelphia, and the audience saw that I thought Torvald was a figure of fun, and they made fun of him. Then within five or ten minutes, they began to wonder what the hell they were doing in the theatre. If he was so ridiculous, why did Nora marry him in the first place? What was the price? So then, I inched closer; I made him like people in my family. Finally, I had to say: I am he, he is me. I see how I could do what he does and now I'm going to do it. Dislike me, but believe that it's a real person that you're looking at and not just a piece of cardboard. And when his wife Nora leaves him, it costs him like it would cost you or me. Not: "Ah, finally! The first seeds of Women's Liberation have been planted. The men are going to get it." I had seen all the implications of the play, the historical context of the drama and all of that, but it was leading me off into brain-food. It's satisfying to an audience to see something clearly structured, but what they really want to know is *you*. All they really want to see is *you*. Because you and they are all people and they want to see people.

You're showing them aspects of themselves.

"A mirror up to nature."

Speaking of Hamlet, *I was wondering if we could talk a little about the Joseph Papp production that you did in Central Park. That's the role, I suppose, that every actor yearns to do. Did you consciously try to bring something unique to it? Did you make an effort to interpret the role in any new way?*

No, because my entire theory about Shakespeare is that it's right there and that you should do it simply. Now, I don't think that my Hamlet was very simple, but then I don't think that the material is simple. I think that Shakespeare is most satisfying when a context is found that makes the material accessible and that makes it possible to just do it. I'm not sure we ever really did successfully find a context that made him accessible. The one that we did in the Park was done as a military state and everybody was in uniform, very buttoned up. It did make it accessible, but it also had an unfortunate effect of burying a lot of personalities in monochromatic uniforms so that the individuality of these people, like Polonius, for example, was a little bit lost. Hamlet's problem was also a little plain: he's in a repressive state, so naturally he'd be very upset. Everybody was dressed in grey, and every male had a version of the same uniform. It was very, very severe. But that's the production. The pleasure of doing it is something else entirely, and I think it would be just as pleasant to do it in a trash can.

Does the context of a Shakespearean play greatly affect your conception of the character, or is the context more for the benefit of the audience?

The context is just as important, if not more so, to the audience because an actor's got to make a context for himself whether there is one or not. Two contexts that I thought worked very well and in favor of the plays were the contexts of *Much Ado about Nothing* and *The Tempest*. *Much Ado* was set in turn-of-the-century America, and so it certainly couldn't have been anything that Shakespeare ever thought of, but the minute the audience saw where they were, they knew something about the play. They understood what the people were doing in a way that no behavior on the part of the actors could have communicated. So the context fed the actors, but it fed the audience, too. And it was very nice because the circuit kept going on and reinforcing itself.

Do you think then, that Shakespeare is best done for Americans in an American context?

I don't know. *The Tempest* was done on a beach. The whole stage was filled with sand. It had a little hill on one side and another little hill going across the back. Then there was a scrim. It was like a set for *Waiting for Godot* almost. Prospero and Miranda and Caliban and Ariel were barefoot; Prospero had on a pair of tattered old pants and a Sufi jacket; Miranda wore a dress that had seen better times; and Caliban was a mess. But they were all perfectly at home on this sand. Then the people who were ship-wrecked came on stage in their gigantic Italian Renaissance costumes, with huge sleeves and big high-heeled shoes and they couldn't walk. Well, it spoke volumes. And as they became used to the island (those that eventually did), they shed some of their clothes and began to be able to navigate better. It reinforced one of the threads of the play very nicely. There was nothing about it that said it was in an American context, but there was also nothing about it that said, "These clothes are being worn so that you will understand that the setting is long ago and far away and that you are having a cultural experience as opposed to an immediate one." The people who were wearing the distancing clothes were deliberately made to be seen as incapable of functioning properly there, so there was a relationship that the audience could have to those clothes that *wasn't* distancing.

When Stacy Keach played Hamlet, he apparently studied a great deal of the criticism that had been written by Shakespearean scholars. Did you find it helpful to do the same?

I read a lot of criticism, yes, but I never read anything that talked about the part in the way that I conceived it. But the most enlightening stuff came from people saying, "This is what this sentence means." I got that habit from one of those three or four terrific professors that I had at Yale, who used to have fun telling us about productions of various Shakespeare plays that he had seen where interpretations of parts had been founded on the misinterpretations of sentences. Whole scenes were done wrong because somebody thought that a word meant "angry" when it really meant "blessed."

I think it was Shaw who said, with Shakespeare, one should "play on the lines and within the lines, but never between the lines."

Yes, I think that's true. Because of the experience of working with Walter Asmus on *Waiting for Godot,* I would like to do some Shakespeare that is *very* strictly conceived, with very, very strict attention to the structures that are in the play. I think Shaw's statement is absolutely correct, because the life of the play is in the lines. If you stop to act in between them, everybody loses the thread; they don't get carried on the words. But the audience has to get used to listening in that way, listening without always checking with themselves to see if they're keeping up; they have to get used to just letting the words flow the way they let images flow when they watch a movie. They don't go, "Am I seeing all that's there?"

I once read something by Gielgud where he said that classics don't demand the same imagination of the actor because, for instance, there is no such thing as the life of the character before the play begins; there is no life except in the play. Do you find that you create Shakespearean characters differently than more contemporary ones for that reason?

My professor used to say that all the time, too. He used to say, "Iago is just bad. He's bad, that's it! You can't go asking yourself what his mother did to him." Yet, you have to be rooted in something. You have to find a door into the heart and mind of the character so that you can come out on stage and just be bad. But it can't just be hot air, because that way, you can't get in it. How can you get in— being bad? You can't. And so I think that interpreting Shakespearean characters is somewhat the same as in other plays where you have to find something that ignites you and yet will be appropriate to the text. The off-stage life of other plays is of no use unless it enlightens what's happening on the stage. You can't figure out little, tricky revelations that you do with behavior, that don't have a textual base, and try to slide an interpretation of the part past the lines.

Is that something you can do with more contemporary material?

You can, but I don't think it would be desirable there either. But you can, because contemporary plays lean more heavily on behavior, that kind of how-does-he-pick-up-the-glass kind of behavior.

What part does personal experience play in the creation of a Shakespearean role? Do you draw on that?

You draw on what you've got. Lots of people have said that everything that you're ever going to be able to use creatively in your life, you've experienced by the age of six, or the age of three, or the age of eleven. But those early experiences in your life are the food for your work. They are.

Is it a matter of consciously trying to link your psyche to Hamlet's?

It's what we were talking about before. Being able to safely fly—that's what you try to get. As opposed to flying something, you want to fly! It's not flying a toy plane and saying, "Look at the wonderful way in which I manipulate the controls," although there is a whole school of acting that is epitomized by Olivier, which is largely admiration for the magnificent employment of techniques that he uses. But, in the end, what makes that kind of acting exciting is that Olivier is personally exciting, and with all that jazz on another person, it wouldn't be half as interesting. Because he has a dynamic presence, the flying of this toy plane that he does becomes very interesting. His performance is something that you actively admire. I do think that the reason he is thought, among his contemporaries, to be the greatest actor in England, has much to do with the fact that you can look at his performance and do to it what you can do, as we were discussing before, with a Picasso painting. You can say, "He drew this line here, and look how he did it. Then he balanced it with that there, and look how he did that. Lo and behold, this is how he constructed it, and isn't it admirable!"

Do you think that English actors, in general, are still more outwardly mannered than inwardly motivated?

That may be true, but I'm not sure whether we should talk about acting in these ways at all. These things that we are discussing are just the tools of the trade. You can't really talk about acting because acting is a person. There is no such thing, maybe, as acting: there are only actors, and they all devise techniques that they hope will make it easier for them to get God's gift out. Sometimes their techniques work against them and sometimes they work for them; but they're God-given gifts nonetheless.

The thing that everybody wants to see is an actual person going through an actual experience, and whether his voice has a sixteen-note range or a two-note range doesn't matter a damn because he communicates how he communicates. So it's an intellectual exercise to talk about it at all. You do it, that's it.

Do you think that acting then is a matter of inspiration?

No, I think it's even simpler. I think it has to do with some kind of visibility. People can see you. Part of it is just given to you by the fact that all the lights are turned out, and there is nothing else to look at. Then there are obviously grades of difference between people; some you want to watch more than others. And the actor's visibility can be focused by tricks and devices and techniques and staging and close-ups and editing and all kinds of things. It can be made to seem much stronger than it is. You can do a lot with a little and so on. But ultimately, it is either there or not.

Do you find that your creation of a role is different if it's for the stage rather than for film?

Yes, I guess that it is different in myriad ways, but not fundamentally. Basically, I think that you've got to get into the character, try to understand him, figure out what he means by everything he says, and try to make it all matter a lot. Trying to make it matter a lot is terribly important. Everybody's visibility is increased greatly in proportion to how much their work matters to them. You see that happen all the time in life. There's a crowd of totally anonymous people, and somebody wants something very badly; that person doesn't have to raise his voice, but he starts to glow, and he becomes interesting. This is a factor in films and theatre equally. You don't have to be so concerned about focus and communication and being seen in a film, however, because the director will either take care of it or he won't.

Personality, I suppose, is another word for this quality of "being visible." Yet it's the reason many actors object to doing film work; they say movies call more for being a personality than for being an actor.

Personal mannerisms don't work any better in the movies than they do in the theatre. But the person, the person-ness or personality of the actor is what makes people want to go to see him. Audiences wanted to see Barbra Streisand in the theatre for the same reasons that they want to see Barbra Streisand in the movies. Because, "By golly, there's somebody!"

Which of the two—movies or theatre—do you prefer?

Hmmm. Well, I do prefer them equally. I'm sure that my life would be very different if they both paid equal amounts of money. I'm sure that the theatre would be very different, and it might be both better and worse. When you talk about the theatre and the movies, you have to talk about them as they are today in the United States, and that has to do with economics. The theatre is pathetically underfunded. Pathetically! Because of that, it makes it unfairly difficult to do good work. I mean, a competitive atmosphere is very good for all artists. Not having it come easy is good too; it makes for "muscle." But I think that it's gone too far. The economics of handiwork in this country, of all kinds of handiwork, is under a terrible strain. There's just totally unfair competition from mechanized things, and some balance has to be found if the quality of the handiwork is going to be maintained.

But I love acting in the theatre; I love it. And I love acting in the movies, too. Of course, the pleasures of acting in the movies are very odd, like doing the same thing twenty-three times in a row and altering it not at all, or only a teeny-weeny bit. And as Alan Bates said, "Movies photograph thought." I loved that; I think that it's true. And total release from any concern about pitching your performance, projecting it, is nice. It has forced the theatre to change, too, because people want to be able to see directly in the theatre now as well.

What makes a director a good director for you to work with?

Having a very particular vision.

Are movies entirely a director's medium?

I don't know if I mean that. Even today, the actors that you see in films stick in your head much more powerfully than the directors or the screenwriters do. Their image is before you; they are the vessel that communicates. So it's an actor's medium, because you can't do without them; but I think finally, it's a collaborative medium. In terms of will, the will belongs to the director. But then I think acting's a passive thing anyway. When you get completely high from it, and it is the best that it is, you are in the grips of passion. I don't mean scenery-eating passion; I mean that things are passing through you. You are a pipe in a channel.

Does it bother your sense of a character to shoot out of sequence?

I think that it depends on the material. I've never done a film that was like a play (where the emotional tension is built verbally) that wasn't really shot in continuity. If I had I'm sure my performance would have suffered. *The Glass Menagerie,* for instance, was pretty much shot in sequence. You need to know what you did before; you need to know what temperature was reached in the scene that preceded so the one that follows can follow. *The Great Gatsby* was shot entirely out of sequence and the only thing that was dislocating about that was one situation where the prelude to a scene was shot in Newport, and then months later, a scene that took place on the other side of the door was shot. When a unit like that one is not filmed together, that's bad. As long as you're shooting the whole lump, however, it's not too bad. It's not bad at all, in fact, because it releases you from another thing that you imagine is needed when it's not. Playwrights do an awful lot for you: they structure things. Some actors think that they have to do all the structuring or else they haven't done their job. Yet in a very important sense, a lot of it is already done; and an actor just does as he's told.

So shooting out of sequence does have the advantage of leaving you with just the moment?

Yes. This is a time when the director has to be the judge. He has to see the picture as a conductor hears the music; he has to know if on this given day, when you are shooting the scene, you're talking too fast or too slow, or your motor's not running at the speed that's going to be needed when it gets put in the context of the entire film. Obviously, not everything can be remedied by cutting.

We were talking before about the economics of movies. For The Great Gatsby, *David Merrick invested about seven million dollars in the production. Did acting in such a huge Hollywood enterprise make you feel pressured?*

It wasn't a pressure on me! I felt delighted. I thought: "They're doing all this for us! They're building this house just for me!" It was the most expensive film that I had ever worked on before or since. And it was wonderful, it really was. Very impressive how good these people are in all their various little, tiny jobs: the guy that makes the walls look old, for instance. There are so many tremendously able people. When they have that much money, they are all there and it's quite awesome. It was fun, it was exciting. It was like being a little boy and thinking, "I better stay awake and be good."

Do you enjoy watching your performances in the movies or on TV?

When I first saw myself on film, I was just horrified and now when I see myself, it's like watching home movies; it reminds me of where we were when we shot it. But I can't watch a film and tell if it's any good or not because I can't focus on what's actually happening on the screen. I keep having tangential thoughts—about what the weather was like, for instance. I can't tell whether I'm doing a good job or not, because what I really register is whether I thought so when I shot it. I always remember that explicitly. If I thought I did it well at the time, I almost invariably think it is good when I see it. And if I wasn't pleased, I almost invariably think it is bad. But all this has no relation to the truth of whether it is, in fact, good or bad.

Do you generally feel a little bit of dissatisfaction with your work?

Yes, it is kind of chronic . . . and a waste of time for me. If it weren't so chronic, maybe it wouldn't be such a waste of time.

Maybe it's the thing that keeps you going, that keeps you aspiring for a better performance.

Maybe, but I think that it's not worth much. It gives me lots of adrenaline and it makes me want to work hard out of fear, but it's something that I don't think the audience is interested in. They want you in the most direct serving that you can give them, and your preoccupation with whether or not you played it right is absolutely, totally a boring subject to them; it's an interference in terms of communication.

So your self-consciousness as an actor . . .

. . . is totally useless, except sometimes it fits the character and then you luck out. What usually happens to me is that I go through the rehearsal period and I get to the dress rehearsal, and I say, "This is absolutely hopeless and we're all going to be destroyed by this. It's all your fault, I don't know why I'm here tonight. I think I should quit." Then somebody says, "Pull yourself together," and I say, "All right, I'll go on, but it's going to be terrible," and from then on, I'm fine. I've released myself from all that worry.

Do you find comedy more difficult than serious drama?

I guess the serious stuff is more difficult. For the experience of something serious in the theatre to be really satisfying, the hold on the audience can never be let go. So it requires a much more perfect collaboration amongst all the people who are doing it, and a more thorough wholeness of the concept.

There's more freedom for you in comedy?

No, but it's easier to be bad in something serious than it is in a comedy. You often see in reviews, for example, that people say, "This is not an entirely satisfying evening, but there are some very funny things in it." You don't see that written about a serious play: "This is not an entirely satisfying evening but there are some very sad things in it." A serious drama has bitten off something bigger.

Comedy can be taken in parts and you can enjoy the parts without necessarily enjoying the whole.

Yes, because you laugh. You can't laugh and then tell yourself, "I had an awful time." But serious things require more focus. Of course, comedies can fall apart on a lot of laughs, too, and the audience can come out feeling sort of stale, as if they smoked too much, or as if they've been had. But in terms of difficulty, I think it's probably harder to do serious things.

Do you find then that serious things are ultimately more satisfying to do?

No, because acting is a lot of fun. It's game-playing, that's what it is. And when I say that serious things are harder than comedies, it's balanced equally by the fact that the details of comedy are a lot more difficult than the details of serious work. In comedy, if the details don't work, they don't work, and there's a real accurate way of telling if they're failing. So timing and playing the exact right note that releases the laugh, all that's tremendously tricky. When I replaced an actor in *The Knack,* I had an awful time. There were certain laughs which came absolutely naturally to him; his control over them was very smooth. Yet I couldn't get them at all; the harder I tried, the more impossible it became.

Did you work out a happy ending? Did you finally get "the knack"?

I got different laughs. I was a different person. So, it was bound to work out that way. But at the time, I thought I was terrible.

Is acting ever easy for you, or do you feel that each part is sort of a struggle?

There's an interesting struggle and a wasted struggle. But that's part of the fun because the struggle is to get your imagination around somebody else. The character is like you, but different from you—or maybe very different from you. How are you going to bring yourself to bear, bend yourself to fit him?

That's the pleasure of it. In fact, a great portion of the pleasure of acting is rehearsing.

Is that the point in the whole process of a performance that you most enjoy—the rehearsal?

The experiences vary, but I would say I most enjoy the first two-thirds of the rehearsal, and then the run after the first two or three weeks. They are the greatest fun. The last third of the rehearsal is the most painful, but it's often the most productive; the pressure's on and things sometimes come very fast. I had a wonderful time rehearsing a play in seven days once. We did *Rosencrantz and Guildenstern Are Dead* at Williamstown and the pressure was on the whole time. There wasn't a second to indulge in any of this stupid struggle because solutions *had* to be found. And I loved it.

When you're performing, do you find that you have new and deeper insights into the character; does your conception keep growing, or does it reach a sort of plateau?

New and different insights. The play changes, the shape of things changes. If it's a comedy, the laughs move around, the scenes shift. I don't think the audience notices too much. The surprises and the differences that are fascinating to us are, in reality, quite small. Again, one forgets that the playwright has done an awful lot of work. After a certain performance, you may think, "Aw, the whole thing went out the window." But the play still said all the same words, the structure was still there, it still presented the same characters, and was played by the same actors.

Do you find yourself getting bored after a long run?

Yes, but it goes in cycles. I think this is true for a lot of people. The play sags and then you think, "I can't face this any more," and then something new comes along, the thing changes, you change a little bit, and everything seems to pick up—at least for a while.

Is there any particular method you have to make a performance seem very fresh, when in fact you're a bit tired?

Fear is a good tool!

Are you nervous before you go on?

Not always. Critics bother me a lot. I don't like them. I don't think that they apply the right criteria, and again I think it's this business of analysis. I don't know how there could be a good critic because I really think that a good critic would be an appreciator. And I don't know how anybody could be expected to appreciate the things that they see when they have to see so much. No one should be obliged to go to the theatre that often. Once you do, your ability to respond changes. More and more of your visceral and intuitive responses get put to sleep, and your brain gets fancier.

How about good reviews—do they increase your self-consciousness?

Oh, the truth about reviews is that you hate the bad ones and you love the good ones. That's the truth for me. There's not too much point, in my own life, in looking any further than that. I don't think that critics are interested in the same things. Criticism, at least over the period that I have witnessed it, has always been preoccupied with everything except what was going on. It's either preoccupied with the past or terrified of missing the innovative. Critics are not able to just look. That's why it took such a long time for criticism to catch up with the movies.

Yes, in the old days, movies were not considered worthy of a critic's attention.

The cinema was so plainly just something that was going on, that people were going to see, that they were loving, and that was making buckets of money. There was no history of movie acting to compare people's performances to, so they just said, "This is not art." Movie criticism, when the movies were booming, was like TV criticism is today. The general attitude goes, "It's pleasant, but we know the whole medium is sort of polluted anyway, so we're only talking about different varieties of garbage." And now the critics look back at all those films they ignored and they say, "Oh my, *auteurs,* cinema this, cinema that." They apply fancy words to it, and they make themselves great. It's all very classic. I dislike critics. I know some people that don't read them at all, but I can't bring myself to do that. I want to be flattered.

You are at the point in your career where you can choose your roles. Is there anything specific that you look for in a part?

I think it is an exaggeration to say that I can choose my roles. I am a working actor now just as I always was. In the sense that I can choose my roles now, I've always chosen them. I haven't done anything that was absolutely awful unless I had to. I was on a television interview with Henry Fonda and he said that he was always worried about what he was going to do next. One would think that he was in a position to choose his roles. But it's not so. There's one important dividing line in the profession of acting, and that is between those who can generate work on their own, who can find financing for their own projects, and those who can't. Those who can, get to choose; and those who can't, choose among either a large or small number of possibilities.

Let's say you were offered several roles for the same set period of time. What would it be that would make you want to do one over the other? Is there anything in particular that you look for?

There are three elements. One is trying to guess whether it will be good, bad, or indifferent as far as your career is concerned. There's the money, and then there's the intrinsic interest of the thing itself. I have been lucky throughout my career in that if something has been very, very interesting, I've been able to do it somehow. I've escaped by the hair of my chin not having to turn something interesting down because I had to make money, because I had to drive a taxicab just to pay the bills; that's never quite happened.

I imagine that playing Prince Hal in Henry IV, Part I *would be fun because he's rather a guiltless character. Do you tend to take on the characteristics of a role you play?*

I think that's one of the good-bad things, the sugar-coated nasties about being in the theatre. You delude yourself into thinking that you possess the qualities of the person that you're portraying, but you can't go very far without finding that you're kidding yourself.

The best example of that was when we did *The Trial of the Catonsville Nine*. It's a play about the Berrigan brothers and others who were on trial for protesting the war in Vietnam. We held discussions after the play was over with the audience, and they were frequently skeptical or hostile toward the position of the people in the play. The characters, of course, are real historical figures, they were contemporaries of ours, and we all developed strong sympathies for them. Soon, we began talking to the audience as if we had their credentials! There was a period there where we would actually say to the audience, "How can you sit there doing nothing?" Yet, in fact, we were being paid perfectly handsome salaries for performing on Broadway in a play for which we were receiving critical acclaim, making a decent living, and furthering our careers. And the characters we portrayed were out paying with their lives for what they felt! When I did Hamlet, a similar delusion occurred. I started saying to myself, "Boy, how smart I am! Look at what I'm thinking!"

When you did The Trial of the Catonsville Nine, *though, did you feel it was important to make a political statement against the war? Do you care if what you do has a social message?*

By the time we did that play in New York, I knew hardly anybody who was in favor of the continuation of the war in Vietnam, so I have to say that it was not a difficult position for any of us to take, although we were all certain that we were being watched. It was a lot less "real" than it was "theatre." However, it doesn't much matter what we thought because the play remained. The fact that we were for it or against it didn't matter because the play did its good by itself. But your question is, do I think the theatre should have social significance?

Not whether the theatre should or should not, but whether that's important to you in terms of the particular work you choose to do.

The theatre's social impact is contained within what it is; it shows people to themselves and that is its social impact—period. That's not the only thing that it does, of course; it has a lot to do with the world of the imagination and opening people's horizons and getting people to think and feel about things. The theatre has certainly been the instrument of a number of different social institutions and it works well as a support for religion or for a political system or for different social consciousnesses; it's a good propagandizing instrument. But I don't think that's what it's fundamentally about. The importance that the theatre has in our culture now has a lot to do with the fact that it's a handicraft. And it isn't about things, it's about people. It's something that people are doing in front of people, and I think that is a gigantic social service in itself. We're finding this out in the way that these cities of ours are going to pieces—solutions to social problems require *personal* engagement; they cannot be even benevolently designed.

Systems don't work without a lot of personal involvement. That's why we were wrong when we were doing *The Trial of the Catonsville Nine* to feel as we did. The most eloquent person in that play was the guy who spoke the least. He was a priest who had returned from South America where he'd been thrown out for helping some poor peons try to organize a little cooperative somewhere in the mountains to feed themselves. He went to a dinner party soon thereafter and some people said, "We're going to pour blood on some draft files in Catonsville, Maryland, tomorrow. Who's for this and who's against it? It's about the war in Vietnam." Well, he hadn't had anything to do with the war in Vietnam, but at the time, it was just a yes or no situation. He did not do terribly much analysis, but he committed very much of his life. And if my work has any social value, it will be because I have devoted my life to something that is humane. I don't do it with the same motive that he did, so I'm not saying that we're comparable in any way, but he was willing to act, to commit himself personally, whatever it brought. To me, he was the most powerful personality of all those in the play.

So the existence of theatre is a great social benefit in itself, and you don't feel it's necessary to make explicit political messages.

I think that the things Norman Lear has put on television have probably had some good impact. It's very difficult to figure out what their impact has been, but it certainly has been something. And it is not idle of him to have thought that, with this gigantically powerful instrument, he might be able, while he was entertaining people and making his own living and giving lots of other people jobs, to do something positive about major problems that face our society— like racism and prejudice, the liberation of women and all the other issues that he has said it's okay to talk about on TV. He certainly does that and television is certainly a great place to open a forum. But whether you could directly, with a play, create a revolution—I just don't think so. On the other hand, I don't think that it makes the theatre impure to espouse such a position.

You've called yourself a "fact actor." What do you mean by that?

I mean that I try to exercise a certain amount of restraint: I try to remember that the play speaks, and that my job is to let the play speak for itself. What I'd like to do in the future is be more clear, more blunt. I have more to do in terms of the simplicity and directness of my acting. The great thing about the theatre is doing it.

Statements

Judi Dench, Fiona Shaw, and Brenda Fricker

JUDI DENCH

The Method: Don't Call It Theatre

I've seen a lot at the Actors Studio, and I think that is too introverted for me, much too introverted. I mean, I think that's fine if you haven't got an audience, and you're doing it in a way for yourself. I remember going to the Studio and seeing something, and I couldn't hear it. I just couldn't hear it. I thought "Well, it's fine for them. That's a really private class, it's got nothing to do with me, or anybody else sitting here." None of us could hear. So I don't know what that's got to do with acting. That's got to do, maybe, with self-examination, but it's not to do with telling the story of a great dramatist. Or maybe not such a great dramatist—and trying to be the sieve for that writer—in order to tell an audience that story. If it's for yourself, then it's fine, but that's not what I think the business is about. I don't think it is for ourselves, I

Excerpted from *In the Company of Actors,* by Carole Zucker (London: A & C Black, 1999), 49–50, 157–159, 61–62.

think it's very much to do with our commitment and our communication with other people, that's what I understand it to be. British actors act from the guts, but they go about it in a different way.

I once did a film, *Saigon—Year of the Cat,* with a very famous American actor in it, Frederic Forrest, and he wouldn't say any of the lines that were written. And they were written by a very considerable dramatist, David Hare. He was an absolute sweet man to work with, but he would not say David Hare's lines. And it was very difficult. I was fine, because it didn't affect me so much, because I can adapt very quickly to something. It affected a lot of other people, not least of all David Hare and Stephen Frears, the director. And we can all do that; I've improvised an entire film, called *Four in the Morning,* which won the Critics Award at Cannes, a very long time ago now, and that was fine. But if you're actually going to do a film that is written by somebody, if you're going to do Shakespeare, you must do Shakespeare, or you must do David Hare, or you must do Chekhov, or you must do Strindberg, or Miller, or whatever, unless you want to do your own thing, which is fine, but then don't call it theatre.

FIONA SHAW

On Styles of Acting, the Method, and Shakespeare

I've nothing against Method acting, I believe in whatever produces the event that occurs in front of my eyes. Except where it's not totally achieved, and that's usually the luck of the person who is applying it. So, for instance, who are the great Method actors we've got? You've got Brando or De Niro, obviously, Harvey Keitel. They're very similar, all three of them, you see. It suits their personality. But I don't think they represent an enormous spectrum of mankind. There are tricks with all styles of acting. And the Method was a moment of reaction against what was seen as an untrue style. You see, the great French style of acting was about pretense, because it came from the court. It was about dressing up, and masks and pretending. So, somebody who was in the court of Louis XIV, trying to be the beggar, would do some sort of gesture toward pretending to be a beggar. Now, this was seen as false, but its nature was false, and it was meant to be false. I am the courtier, so I could never be a beggar. It was about the dance of falseness, about disguise: underneath this beggar is in fact a courtier. The Shakespearean style in England was much more robust, really. It was for Henry V, "O for a muse of fire . . . ," it was people coming and saying:

"I won't give you a whole biography about me, but picture this: 'O for a muse of fire . . . '" Othello would come out and talk to you. Much nearer to what was later to be called Method. It was about being. It was about the fusion of emotional consequence with intellectual thought, fabulous intellectual thought due to a particular quirk of Elizabethan language.

By the time we hit the twentieth century, you have a country, America. I'm now going to precís into something very unworthy of America. You have a culture that, due to its multinational mix—which is why it was called a melting-pot when it was formed—had a tendency towards the noun. People stopped using the filigree language of the eighteenth or nineteenth century, because people would come from all over the world going: "coffee," or "pizza," or "work," "car," "money." (Laughs) The fineries of the inherited courtier behaviour: "Would it be possible for me to interest you in a cup of coffee?" just had no place for a moment. This produced an imagination of an immense sad loss, of distant inheritance, which is captured fantastically in the twentieth century film world of people unable to reply, unable to speak. So, instead they used these tiny words, and they broke up what they were saying. They invented this thing of broken thought. And broken thought is often what is mistaken for Method acting; which is, you are speaking, and half-way through your thought, another thought comes in, which is hidden from the listener. Now, this has subsequently bubbled up into the biggest trick of Method acting. So that anybody who . . . stops . . . halfway through a line . . . .

The style of the Elizabethan language is merely that while you said, "To be or not to be, that is the question," you were genuinely trying to communicate, "To be or not to be, that is the question," not "To be . . . or not to be . . . that is the question." You weren't trying to say: "I am more important than what I am saying," you were saying, "What I am saying is more important than me."

I don't believe the rather school-marmish reply to Shakespeare, I don't believe that when Hamlet says: "To be or not to be. That is the question," he's really thinking about how to go to bed with his mother or something. Because the energy needed to communicate to the audience, "To be or not to be" should take the entire concentration of that actor to really make you hear it—the actual force of intellectual power to be able to thread that thought right through to the end of that speech. There is no energy left to be going, "But what I really want to say is, how am I going to kill Claudius?"

When you deconstruct language as we have done—I would say that when God died, the end of God by Nietzsche at the end of the nineteenth century, resulted in the preoccupation of drama changing from being about describing or coming to terms with the world outside you, to being about the *inability* to come to terms with the world inside you. By lowering language, by using much fewer words: our books are smaller, our vocabulary's smaller; by losing faith in the fact that we were in dialogue with the universe/God/audience, we're suddenly thrown back into a world where there is no God/audience/universe, so we've begun to implode into our inner world of chaos. And because of that, a few little dribbles that come out of our mouths: "The horror, the horror . . . " in *Apocalypse Now* replaces the great text of *Macbeth*. Now they just say, "the horror, the horror," and that is full of what's called subtext, because of the enormous gaps between these tiny utterances and our emotional experience. This new language we've developed, is a sort of debris language. It's a language of: "Did you go to the movie?" "Yeah." "How was it?" "Great!" You sense that the person really wants to go up to bed, or wants a coffee, or a drink. You sense other things because what's being delivered to you is not valuable. I do believe that we are trying to apply these subtextual discoveries—this notion that when people speak, they're thinking about something else—to earlier plays. But as soon as you get back before the nineteenth century, it doesn't really function in that way. This is not to mean that there isn't psychology in Shakespeare. It's full of psychology because we're full of psychological baggage. But it's very hard to name your own. I find more and more the people in the rehearsal room who tell each other about their psychological baggage, are missing the entire point. The point is you can't see your own. You can talk about it, but don't see your own.

I think psychology is a tool. I think learning iambic pentameter is a tool. None of these things need be oppressions or totalities. They're so evidently not. But, again, maybe this is a bit like what Sartre would say: "Destiny is history," isn't it? You could look back at the moment before you die, and say: "I see, so that's the way my life went." But how can we describe that in advance? In fact, it becomes very obvious why your life went like this when you look back. When you look forward, it could be anything. So, when you say: "Well, because I'm doing this, I'm sure my character would do this," is to reduce the possibility of that person, because we are built in contradiction. The really fantastic thing about Shakespeare is his obsession with antithesis—the antithesis being so total—that even "the cat is dead, or the cat is not dead," you get it within the line: "To be, or not to be," I mean, that's only half a line. "That is the question." Three separate thoughts, two of them opposites, all in the same verse line, before you even get: "Whether 'tis nobler in the mind to suffer the slings and arrows of outrageous fortune / or take arms against a sea of troubles, and by opposing, end them / To die. To sleep." This endless balance—we live somewhere in that, I think. I just did *Richard II,* two years ago, and you get this fantastic sense in Richard II of somebody—again, now I'm standing over the play, and I hope this isn't an interpretation—who is both loved and is destroyed by his cousin; and who both loves and wishes to destroy his cousin. Well, you'd think: either you want to destroy him or you don't, but no, people are like that. How many of us love our mothers more than anyone else in the world, and the person you most want to murder in the world is your mother? It is precisely this contradiction in which I think we all really live, and I think the great healing power of theatre—or the potential of theatre—is that by looking at other people's troubles and contradictions, you don't feel so bad about your own. It has a fantastic healing power to see other people making mistakes, to watch Macbeth get steeped so deep in blood that he goes on. To watch him do that, to watch him go on murdering, to know that it could be you, allows you to forgive other people's sins and your own. A bit Catholic, isn't? (Laughs)

BRENDA FRICKER

Stage and Film Acting

I've just finished a play in the theatre, at the Gate, called *The Weeping of Angels,* by Joe O'Connor. It's been seven years since I've been on the stage, so I was a nervous wreck the first night. I was playing this eighty year old nun. It's set in the future; it's about the last three nuns in Ireland, after all the convents are gone. It's happening as we speak, people aren't joining up, or getting vocations or whatever you call it. I found that very hard, that one. We did an awful lot of rewriting on it. It's hard to put your head into that kind of water, and particularly in theatre, where you really can't stop, you have to keep going. But again, if you have a good writer, there shouldn't be any difficulty, it should be written clearly enough to see.

The only difference, really, between stage and film, is the immediacy of it. Technically, the audience is a member of the cast, which you don't have in filming. The connection there is lovely, and the buzz you get from a good night; the buzz you get from working with good actors, and the flow of just starting and finishing is wonderful. And it is different; I'd forgotten things like about how you can manipulate audiences. I got a really rowdy crowd in one night, and I had this eight-minute speech coming up, which is a beautiful love speech, and I thought, how am I going to control them? They're going to laugh at all the bits; when I say "his tongue was in my mouth," they're going to go "ewwww," and I got them. I got them! I don't know what I did, I don't know how I did it, but I got them to shut up. That was a great feeling. I went down to the bar and had three pints of Guinness to celebrate, immediately. It was really great. It's instinctual, I don't know what you do, I don't know how you make them listen. Maybe it's the writing, maybe those words are good enough to get them into it.

I like film because it's a different discipline; it's a different controlling of disciplines, and containing energies in a different way. You're always asked about the hanging around on a movie shoot, how you do that. That's why they spend money on decent trailers, and have people looking after us, so you can be comfortable, and conserve your energy when you're in front of the camera. I mean, the people behind the camera work a lot harder, and they don't have nice trailers to sit in, which sometimes gets my conscience moving. But it is only different forms of discipline, I think: movies, television, the stage. Just using your head in a different way, that's all.

But I hate the camera. I'm constantly getting directors saying "Lift your head up, Brenda, we can't see your face." The first time I saw myself on screen I felt like everybody else. I wouldn't look. But again, Barry, when he was working, got a lot of stuff that I had done, and made me sit down and go through it technically, and I used to watch him editing, I used to see rushes of his stuff, so he taught me a hell of a lot, technically. Rushes don't worry me now. In fact, I usually find that I'm not looking at myself at all, I'm looking at something else in the rushes. Because you can't do anything about it then anyways, it's too late. I think vanity has something to do with it, and I'm not particularly vain. If you are somebody who wants to look pretty all the time, then it might disturb you. If I don't like something I will ask for another take. If I think I won't get it, I'll say "fuck" in the middle of a line, so they'll have to go again, they'll have to cut.

I'm always saying to directors when they want to do close-ups. "Why? Why do you have to do close-ups, it's a form of terrorism." Because sometimes you have some of those wonderful directors, with big, wide shots, and you can relax, and you can choose to look where *you* want, and not where *they* want you to look, you know. But you get these in-house styles and, I get very dissatisfied with the way people shoot things, just far too much of the camera trying to do it.

As Glenda Jackson says, if a film is two hours long, and you get five minutes right, you're winning, because it's just so hard. But sometimes you think "That wasn't too bad, that was lovely, yeah." You do get it right sometimes, that's kind of an accident, and it's quite nice.

Afterword: The Artist as Visionary
Scenarios and Arguments

Antonin Artaud

Q: What sort of films do you like?

A: I like all sorts of films. But no real motion pictures have ever been made. I think we can accept only one sort of film; the kind where every effective means of sensual stimulation is used. Motion pictures involve a complete reversal of our scale of values, a complete revolution in sight, logic, and perspective. Films are more ebullient than phosphorous and more captivating than love. Why do we insist on perpetually using themes which neutralize the effectiveness of film because they belong to the theatre?

Q: What sort of films would you like to see made?

A: I demand weird, fantastic films; philosophically speaking, poetic films and psychic films. Nothing I have said excludes either psychology or love, nor does it mean jettisoning any of our human feelings.

Excerpted from *Drama Review* II, no. I (Fall 1966): 166–167, trans. Victor Corti. Originally published in *Oeuvres Complètes*, vol. 3 (Guillimard, 1961).

But it does mean films in which those things which make up the heart and mind are ground down and then remixed, as this will endow them with un-discovered cinematographic features. Motion pictures call for exaggerated subjects and detailed psychology. They require repetition, emphasis, after-thoughts. Aspects of the human soul. We are all cruel in films. Therefore this art's rhythm and speed give it an unparalleled, powerful formula, and its char-acteristic detachment from life and illusory appearances require precise screen-ing and the incarnation of different elements. For this reason they require extraordinary themes, climacteric degrees in the soul, and a visionary atmo-sphere.

Motion pictures are a remarkable stimulant. They work directly on the brain cells. When this art's exhilaration has been blended in the right proportions, it will leave the theatre far behind and we will relegate the latter to the attic of our memories. Theatre already involves trickery. We patronize it far more to see the actors than the works they perform—in any case it is they first and foremost who work on us. But the actors are only a living symbol in motion pictures. They are the whole stage, the author's thoughts, the sequence of events. For this reason we never give them a second thought. Chaplin plays Chaplin, Pickford plays Pickford, and Fairbanks plays Fairbanks. They are the film. We could not visualize it without them. Yet while they appear in the foreground, they do not obscure anything else. That is why they do not exist, and nothing comes be-tween the work and us. Motion pictures have a poisonously harmless and direct quality; they get right under our skin like a morphine injection. For this reason, a film's subject matter must not be inferior to the film's active potential—and must spring from fantasy.

Bibliography

Aicken, Frederick. "Shakespeare on the Screen." *Screen Education* 211 (Sept.–Oct. 1963): 33–35.

Allen, Jeanne. "Copyright Protection in Theatre, Vaudeville, and Early Cinema." *Screen* 21, no. 2 (Summer 1980): 79–91.

Allen, Robert C. *Vaudeville and Film, 1895–1915: A Study in Media Interaction.* New York: Arno, 1980.

Alpert, Hollis. "Film and Theatre." *The Dreams and the Dreamers: Adventures of a Professional Movie Goer.* New York: Macmillan, 1962. 233–251.

———. "Movies Are Better than the Stage." *Saturday Review* (23 July 1955): 5–6, 31–32.

Anderegg, Michael. *Orson Welles, Shakespeare, and Popular Culture.* New York: Columbia University Press, 1999.

———. "Shakespeare on Film in the Classroom." *Literature/Film Quarterly* 4, no. 2 (1976): 165–175.

Anderson, R. "What Is to Become of the Theater?" *Illustrated World* 24 (1916): 660–665.

Andrew, Dudley. "Adaptation." *Concepts in Film Theory,* 96–106. Oxford: Oxford University Press, 1984.

Andrews, Cyril Bruyn. *The Theatre, the Cinema, and Ourselves.* London: Clarence House, 1947.

Arnheim, Rudolf. "A New Laocoön: Artistic Composites and the Talking Film." 1938. *Film as Art*. Berkeley: University of California Press, 1957. 199–230.

Atkinson, E. J. R. *Key to the Adaptation of the Best of Shakespeare's Plays to the Stage—Cinema Interaction Process for the Production of Drama*. New York: Knickerbocker, 1920.

Aycock, Wendy, and Michael Schoenecke. *Film and Literature: A Comparative Approach to Adaptation*. Lubbock: Texas Tech University Press, 1988.

Aylesworth, Thomas G. *Broadway to Hollywood*. New York: Bison Books, 1985.

Bacon, Henry. *Continuity and Transformation: The Influence of Literature and Drama on Cinema as a Process of Cultural Continuity and Renewal*. Helsinki, Finland: Suomalainen Tiedeakatemia, 1994.

Balàzs, Béla. *Theory of the Film, Character and Growth of a New Art*. Trans. Edith Bone. 1953. New York: Dover, 1970. (See Ch. 3, "A New Form—Language," and Ch. 20, "The Script.")

Ball, Robert Hamilton. "The Shakespeare Film as Record." *Shakespeare Quarterly* 3, no. 3 (July 1952): 227–236.

———. "Shakespeare in One Reel." *Hollywood Quarterly Journal of Film, Radio, and Television* 8 (1953–1954): 139–149.

———. *Shakespeare on Silent Film: A Strange Eventful History*. London: George Allen and Unwin, 1968.

———. "On Shakespeare Filmography." *Literature/Film Quarterly* 1, no. 4 (Fall 1973): 299–306.

Barber, Lester E. "This Rough Magic: Shakespeare on Film." *Literature/Film Quarterly* 1, no. 4 (Fall 1973): 372–376.

Baskin, Ellen, and Mandy Hicken, comp. *Enser's Filmed Books and Plays: A List of Books and Plays from Which Films Have Been Made, 1928–1991*. 1968. Rev. ed. Aldershot, Hants (England): Ashgate, 1993.

Bauer, L. V. "The Movies Tackle Literature." *American Mercury* 14 (1928): 288–294.

Bazin, André. "Theater and Cinema." *What Is Cinema?* Vol. 1. Ed. and trans. Hugh Gray. Berkeley: University of California Press, 1967. 76–124.

Beja, Morris. *Film and Literature: An Introduction*. New York: Longman, 1979.

Belsey, Catherine. "Shakespeare and Film: A Question of Perspective." *Literature/Film Quarterly* 11, no. 3 (1983): 152–158.

Beman, Lamar T. *Selected Articles on Censorship of the Theatre and Moving Pictures*. New York: H. W. Wilson, 1931.

Benedek, Laslo. "Play into Picture." *Sight and Sound* 22 (Autumn 1952): 82–84, 96.

Benjamin, Walter. "The Work of Art in the Age of Mechanical Reproduction." 1935. *Illuminations*. Trans. Harry Zohn. Ed. Hannah Arendt. New York: Schocken, 1969. 217–251.

Bentley, Eric. *The Playwright as Thinker*. New York: Harcourt, 1946. 8–16.

Berchtold, W. E. "Grand Opera Goes to Hollywood." *North American Review* 239 (1935): 138–146.

Bingham, Robert. "Movies: The Shakespeare Boom." *The Reporter* (17 Nov. 1955): 34–37.

Block, R. "Not Theatre, Not Literature, Not Painting." *Dial* 88 (1924): 472–473.

Blum, Richard. *American Film Acting: The Stanislavsky Heritage*. Ann Arbor, Mich.: UMI Research Press, 1984.

Boose, Lynda E., and Richard Burt, eds. *Shakespeare, the Movie: Popularizing the Plays on Film, TV, and Video.* New York: Routledge, 1997.

Braudy, Leo. "The Freedom of Theatre." *Jean Renoir: The World of His Films.* New York: Doubleday, 1972. 65–103.

Brecht, Bertolt. "The Film, the Novel, and Epic Theatre." *Brecht on Theatre.* Ed. and trans. John Willett. New York: Hill and Wang, 1964. 47–50.

Brewer, Gay. *David Mamet and Film.* Jefferson, N.C.: McFarland, 1993.

Brewster, Ben, and Lea Jacobs. *Theatre to Cinema: Stage Pictorialism and the Early Feature Film.* New York: Oxford University Press, 1997.

Brode, Douglas. *Shakespeare in the Movies: From the Silent Era to "Shakespeare in Love."* New York: Oxford University Press, 2000.

Brook, Peter. "Finding Shakespeare on Film: Interview with Geoffrey Reeves." *Film Theory and Criticism.* Ed. Gerald Mast and Marshall Cohen. New York: Oxford University Press, 1974. 316–321.

———. "Shakespeare on Three Screens." *Sight and Sound* 34 (Spring 1965): 66–70.

Brown, John Russell, ed. *Drama and Theatre, with Radio, Film, and Television.* London: Routledge and Kegan Paul, 1971.

Buchman, Lorne M. *Still in Movement: Shakespeare on Screen.* New York: Oxford University Press, 1991.

Buhler, Stephen M. *Shakespeare in the Cinema: Ocular Proof.* Albany: State University of New York Press, 2002.

———. "Text, Eyes, and Videotape: Screening Shakespeare Scripts." *Shakespeare Quarterly* 46, no. 2 (Summer 1995): 236–244.

Bulman, James C., and H. R. Coursen, eds. *Shakespeare on Television: An Anthology of Essays and Reviews.* Hanover, N.H.: University Press of New England, 1988.

Burnett, Mark Thornton, and Ramona Wray, eds. *Shakespeare, Film, Fin de Siècle.* New York: St. Martin's, 2000.

Camp, Gerald M. "Shakespeare on Film." *Journal of Aesthetic Education* 3, no. 1 (Jan. 1969): 107–120.

Carter, Huntly. "Cinema and Theatre: The Diabolical Difference." *English Review* 55 (1932): 313–320.

———. *The New Theatre and Cinema of Soviet Russia.* 1924. New York: Arno, 1970.

Cartmell, Deborah. *Interpreting Shakespeare on Screen.* New York: St. Martin's, 2000.

Cartmell, Deborah, and Imelda Whelehan, eds. *Adaptations: From Text to Screen, Screen to Text.* New York: Routledge, 1999.

Ciment, Michael. *Kazan on Kazan.* New York: Viking Press, 1974.

Clair, René. "From Theatre to Cinema." *Reflections on the Cinema.* Trans. Vera Traill. London: William Kimber, 1953. 107–113.

Clayton, B. "Shakespeare and the Talkies." *English Review* 49 (1929): 739–752.

Clayton, Thomas. "Aristotle on the Shakespearean Film; or, Damn Thee, William, Thou Art Translated." *Literature/Film Quarterly* 2 (1974): 183–189.

Cohn, Ruby. *Modern Shakespeare Offshoots.* Princeton, N.J.: Princeton University Press, 1976.

Collick, John. *Shakespeare, Cinema, and Society.* Manchester, England: Manchester University Press, 1989.

Collier, Jo Leslie. *From Wagner to Murnau: The Tranposition of Romanticism from Stage to Screen.* Ann Arbor, Mich.: UMI Research Press, 1988.

Collignon, Jean, et al. "Theater and Talking Pictures in France." *Yale French Studies* 5 (1950): 34–40.

Combs, Richard, and Raymond Durgnat. "Shakespeare on Film." *Film Comment* 37, no. 4 (July/Aug. 2001): 56–61.

Condon, Frank. "Over the Bridge to the Movies." *The Saturday Evening Post* 214 (16 Jan. 1932): 31–48.

Corrigan, Timothy. *Film and Literature: An Introduction and Reader.* Upper Saddle River, N.J.: Prentice-Hall, 1999.

Costello, Donald P. *The Serpent's Eye: Shaw and the Cinema.* South Bend, Ind.: University of Notre Dame Press, 1965.

Costello, Tom, ed. *International Guide to Literature on Film.* London: Bowker-Saur, 1994.

Coursen, Herbert R. *Shakespeare: The Two Traditions.* Rutherford, N.J.: Fairleigh Dickinson University Press, 1999.

———. *Shakespeare in Production: Whose History?* Athens: Ohio University Press, 1996.

———. *Shakespearean Performance as Interpretation.* Newark: University of Delaware Press, 1992.

———. *Teaching Shakespeare with Film and Television: A Guide.* Westport, Conn.: Greenwood Press, 1997.

———. *Watching Shakespeare on Television.* Cranbury, N.J.: Fairleigh Dickinson University Press, 1993.

Crowdus, Gary. "Words, Words, Words: Recent Shakespearean Films." *Cineaste* 23, no. 4 (Fall 1998): 13–19.

Crowl, Samuel. *Shakespeare Observed: Studies in Performance on Stage and Screen.* Athens: Ohio University Press, 1992.

Cubitt, Sean. *Videography: Video Media as Art and Culture.* New York: St. Martin's, 1993.

Daniels, Robert L. *Laurence Olivier: Theater and Cinema.* New York: A. S. Barnes, 1980.

Davies, Anthony. *Filming Shakespeare's Plays: The Adaptations of Laurence Olivier, Orson Welles, Peter Brook, and Akira Kurosawa.* Cambridge: Cambridge University Press, 1988.

———. "Shakespeare and the Media of Film, Radio, and Television: A Retrospect." *Shakespeare Survey* 39 (1987): 1–11.

Davies, Anthony, and Stanley Wells, eds. *Shakespeare and the Moving Image: The Plays on Film and Television.* Cambridge: Cambridge University Press, 1994.

Dehn, Paul. "The Filming of Shakespeare." *Talking of Shakespeare.* Ed. John Garrett. London: Hodder & Stoughton, 1954. 49–72.

Dench, Ernest A. *Playwriting for the Cinema.* London: A & C Black, 1914.

Dick, Bernard F. *Hellman in Hollywood.* Rutherford, N.J.: Fairleigh Dickinson University Press, 1982.

Disher, M. W. "Classics into Films." *Fortnightly Review* 130 (1928): 784–792.

Donaldson, Peter S. *Shakespearean Films/Shakespearean Directors.* Boston: Unwin Hyman, 1990.

The Drama Review 11, no. 1 (Fall 1966). Special issue, "Film and Theatre."

Druxman, Michael B. *The Musical: From Broadway to Hollywood.* New York: A. S. Barnes, 1980.

Dukes, Ashley. "English Scene: Chiefly about Screenwriting." *Theatre Arts Monthly* 18 (1934): 822–829.

Durgnat, Raymond. "Canned Theatre Comes Alive." *Films,* 1, no. 11 (1981): 10–14.

———. "The Mongrel Muse." *Films and Feelings.* London: Faber and Faber, 1967. 19–30.

Dworkin, Martin S. "'Stay, Illusion!' Having Words about Shakespeare on Screen." *Wascana Review* 2 (1976): 83–93; and *Journal of Aesthetic Education* 11, no. 1 (1977): 151–161. First appeared in the *Literary Tabloid* 1, no. 5 (Oct. 1975).

Eckert, Charles W., ed. *Focus on Shakespearean Films.* Englewood Cliffs, N.J.: Prentice-Hall, 1972.

Eidsvik, Charles. *Cineliteracy: Film among the Arts.* New York: Random House, 1978.

———. "Perception and Convention in Acting for Theatre and Film." *Post Script: Essays in Film and the Humanities* 8, no. 2 (1989): 21–35.

Eisenstein, Sergei. *Film Form: Essays in Film Theory.* 1949. Ed. and trans. Jay Leyda. New York: Meridian Books, 1957.

Ellis, John. "The Literary Adaptation: An Introduction." *Screen* 23, no. 1 (May–June 1982): 3–5.

Erskine, Thomas L., and James M. Welsh, eds. *Video Versions: Film Adaptations of Plays on Video.* Westport, Conn.: Greenwood Press, 2000.

Esslin, Martin. *The Field of Drama: How the Signs of Drama Create Meaning on Stage and Screen.* London and New York: Methuen, 1987.

Feist, Gene. "Stage and Film Acting: The Growing Dichotomy." *National Forum* 70, no. 3 (Summer 1990): 19–20.

Felheim, Marvin. "Criticism and the Films of Shakespeare's Plays." *Comparative Drama* 9 (1975): 147–155.

"Film Adaptations of Shakespeare's Works." Editorial. *Cineaste* 24, no. 1 (Winter 1998): 1.

Foreman, Carl, and Tyrone Guthrie. "Debate: Movies versus Theatre." *New York Times Magazine* (29 April 1962): 10–11, 43, 45–46, 48, 50, 53.

Frye, Northrop. "Specific Forms of Drama." *Anatomy of Criticism,* 282–292. New York: Athenaeum, 1965.

Fuegi, John. "Explorations in No Man's Land: Shakespeare's Poetry as Theatrical Film." *Shakespeare Quarterly* 23 (1972): 37–49.

Fulton, A. R. *Motion Pictures: The Development of an Art from Silent Films to the Age of Television.* Norman: University of Oklahoma Press, 1960. (See esp. Ch. 12, "From Play to Film.")

Gable, Josephine Dillon. *Modern Acting: A Guide for Stage, Screen, and Radio.* New York: Prentice-Hall, 1940.

Gerdes, Peter R. "Film and/or Theatre: Some Introductory Comments." *Australian Journal of Screen Theory* 7 (1980): 4–17.

Gielgud, John, and John Miller. *Shakespeare: Hit or Miss?* London: Sidgwick and Jackson, 1991.

Gies, M. "Directing Actors: The Method Approach." *Filmmakers* 13 (Aug. 1980): 24–30.

Gifford, Denis. *Books and Plays in Films, 1886–1915: Literary, Theatrical, and Artistic Sources of the First Twenty Years of Motion Pictures.* Jefferson, N.C.: McFarland, 1991.

Gilman, Richard. "About Nothing—with Precision." *Common and Uncommon Masks.* New York: Random House, 1971. 30–37.

Goble, Alan, ed. *The Complete Index to Literary Sources in Film.* New Providence, N.J.: Bowker, 1999.

Godfrey, Lionel. "It Wasn't Like That in the Play." *Films and Filming* (Aug. 1967): 4–8.

Goodwin, James. "Literature and Film: A Review of Criticism." *Quarterly Review of Film Studies* 6, no. 2 (Spring 1979): 227–246.

Grady, Hugh. *Modernist Shakespeare.* Oxford: Clarendon Press, 1991.

Griffin, Alice. "Shakespeare through the Camera's Eye." *Shakespeare Quarterly* 17 (1966): 383–387. See also earlier articles in same, 4 (1953): 331–336; 6 (1955): 63–66; 7 (1956): 235–240.

Gunning, Tom. "The Cinema of Attractions: Early Film, Its Spectator, and the Avant-Garde." *Wide Angle* 8, no. 3–4 (Fall 1986): 63–70.

———. "D. W. Griffith: Historical Figure, Film Director, and Ideological Shadow." In *D. W. Griffith and the Origins of American Narrative Film.* Urbana: University of Illinois Press, 1991. 32–56.

———. "Filmed Narrative and the Theatrical Ideal: Griffith and the *film d'art.*" Ed. P. Guibbert. *Les premiers ans du cinéma français.* Perpignan, France: L'Institut Jean Vigo, 1985. 123–129.

Handke, Peter. "Theater und Film: Das Elend des Vergleichens" (Theater and Film: The Misery of Comparison). In *Prosa, Gedichte, Theaterstücke, Hörspiele, Aufsätze.* Frankfurt: Suhrkamp Verlag, 1969. 314–326. Translated in *Theater and Film: The Misery of Comparison.* Trans. Donald Nordberg. Englewood Cliffs, N.J.: Prentice-Hall, 1974. 165–175.

Hannon, William M. *The Photodrama: Its Place among the Fine Arts.* New Orleans: Ruskin, 1915.

Hapgood, Robert. "Shakespeare on Film and Television." *The Cambridge Companion to Shakespeare Studies.* Ed. Stanley Wells. Cambridge: Cambridge University Press, 1986, 273–286.

Hardison, O. B. "Shakespeare on Film: The Developing Canon." *Proceedings of the Comparative Literature Symposium* 12 (1981): 131–145.

Harrington, John. *Film and/as Literature.* Englewood Cliffs, N.J.: Prentice-Hall, 1977.

Hatchuel, Sarah. *Companion to the Shakespearean Films of Kenneth Branagh.* Winnipeg, Canada: Blizzard, 1999.

Hawkes, Terence, ed. *Alternative Shakespeares.* Vol. 2. London: Routledge, 1996.

Hayman, Ronald. "Shakespeare on the Screen." *Times Literary Supplement* 26 (Sept. 1968): 1081–1082.

Hennedy, Hugh. "Shakespeare on the Screen." *Commonweal* 95 (1971): 134–135.

Herring, Robert. "Shakespeare on the Screen." *Life and Letters Today* 16, no. 7 (1937): 125–130.

Herzog, Charlotte. "The Movie Palace and the Theatrical Sources of its Architectural Style." *Cinema Journal* 20, no. 2 (Spring 1981): 15–37.

Hitchcock, A. M. "The Relation of the Picture Play to Literature." *English Journal* 4 (1915): 292–298.

Hodgdon, Barbara. "Shakespeare on Film: Taking Another Look." *The Shakespeare Newsletter* 26 (1976): 26.

———. *The Shakespeare Trade: Performances and Appropriations.* Philadelphia: University of Pennsylvania Press, 1998.

Holderness, Graham. "Radical Potentiality and Institutional Closure: Shakespeare in Film and Television." *Political Shakespeare.* Ed. J. Dollimore and A. Sinfield. Manchester, England: Jonathon and Alan, 1985. 182–201.

———. *Shakespeare Recycled: The Making of Historical Drama.* Hertfordshire, England: Harvester Wheatsheaf, 1992.

———. "Shakespeare Rewound." *Shakespeare Survey* 45 (1993): 63–74.

———. *Visual Shakespeare: Essays in Film and Television.* Hatfield, U.K.: University of Hertfordshire Press, 2002.

Homan, Sidney R. "A Cinema for Shakespeare." *Literature/Film Quarterly* 4, no. 2 (Spring 1976): 176–186.

———. "Criticism for the Filmed Shakespeare." *Literature/Film Quarterly* 5, no.4 (1977): 282–290.

Hooker, B. "Shakespeare and the Movies." *Century Magazine* 93 (1916): 298–330.

Horton, Andrew S., and Joan Margretta, eds. *Modern European Filmmakers and the Art of Adaptation.* New York: Frederick Ungar, 1981.

Howlett, Kathy M. *Framing Shakespeare on Film.* Athens: Ohio University Press, 2000.

Hughes, Glenn. "Making the Film Pay for the Theatre." *Theatre Arts Monthly* 16 (1932): 561–565.

Hulfish, D. S. *The Motion Picture: Its Making and Its Theatre.* Chicago: Electricity Magazine Corporation, 1909.

Hurt, James, ed. *Focus on Film and Theatre.* Englewood Cliffs, N.J.: Prentice-Hall, 1974.

Hurtgen, Charles. "The Operatic Character of Background Music in Film Adaptations of Shakespeare." *Shakespeare Quarterly* 20, no. 1 (Winter 1969): 53–64.

Jackson, Peter. "Shakespeare: Stage versus Screen." *Plays and Players* 6 (Dec. 1958): 8–9.

Jackson, Russell, ed. *The Cambridge Companion to Shakespeare on Film.* Cambridge: Cambridge University Press, 2000.

Jenkins, Henry. *What Made Pistachio Nuts? Early Sound Comedy and the Vaudeville Aesthetic.* New York: Columbia University Press, 1992.

Jones, Henry Arthur. "The Dramatist and the Photoplay." *Mentor* 9 (1921): 29.

Jorgens, Jack J. "The Cinematic Bard." *The Washingtonian* (May 1976): 272–277.

———. *Shakespeare on Film.* Bloomington: Indiana University Press, 1977.

———. "Shakespeare on Film and Television." *William Shakespeare: His World, His Work, His Influence.* Ed. John F. Andrews. New York: Scribner's, 1985, 681–703.

Kalter, Joanmarie, ed. *Actors on Acting: Performing in Theatre and Film Today.* New York: Sterling, 1979.

Kauffmann, Stanley. "Melodrama and Farce: A Note on a Fusion in Film." *Melodrama.* Ed. Daniel Gerould. New York: New York Literary Forum, 1980. 169–172.

————. "Notes on Theater-and-Film." *Performance* 1, no. 4 (Sept.–Oct. 1972): 104–109. Reprinted in Kauffmann's *Living Images*. New York: Harper & Row, 1975. 353–362.

Kazan, Elia. Interview in *Directors at Work: Interviews with American Film-Makers*. Eds. Bernard R. Kantor, Irwin R. Blacker, and Anne Kramer. New York: Funk and Wagnalls, 1970. 149–173.

Kelly, F. M. *Shakespearean Costume for Stage and Screen*. London: A & C Black, 1970.

Kennedy, Dennis. *Looking at Shakespeare: A Visual History of Twentieth-Century Performance*. Cambridge: Cambridge University Press, 1993.

Kermode, Frank. "Shakespeare in the Movies." *Film Theory and Criticism*. Ed. Gerald Mast and Marshall Cohen. New York: Oxford University Press, 1974. 322–332.

Kerr, Heather, Robin Eaden, and Madge Mitton, eds. *Shakespeare: World Views*. Newark: University of Delaware Press, 1996.

Kitchin, Laurence. "Shakespeare on the Screen." *Shakespeare Survey* 18 (1965): 70–74.

Knopf, Robert. *The Theater and Cinema of Buster Keaton*. Princeton, N.J.: Princeton University Press, 1999.

Knowles, Dorothy. *The Censor, the Drama, and the Film, 1900–1934*. London: Unwin Brothers, 1934.

Kracauer, Siegfried. "The Theatrical Story" and "Remarks on the Actor." *Theory of Film: The Redemption of Physical Reality*. New York: Oxford University Press, 1960. 93–101, 215–231.

Kreuger, Miles, ed. *The Movie Musical: From Vitaphone to 42nd Street*. New York: Dover Publications, 1975.

Krows, A. E. "Literature and the Motion Picture." *Annals of the American Academy of Political and Social Science* 128 (1926): 70–73.

Langman, Larry. *Writers of the American Screen: A Guide to Film Adaptations of American and Foreign Literary Works*. New York: Garland, 1986.

Lawson, John Howard. "Theatre." *Film: The Creative Process*. New York: Hill and Wang, 1964. 187–194.

Leech, Clifford. "Dialogue for Stage and Screen." *Penguin Film Review* 6 (April 1948): 97–103.

Lehmann, Courtney. *Shakespeare Remains: Theatre to Film, Early to Postmodern*. Ithaca, N.Y.: Cornell University Press, 2002.

Leonard, William Torbert. *Theatre: Stage to Screen to Television*. 2 vols. Metuchen, N.J.: Scarecrow Press, 1981.

Lillich, Meredith. "Shakespeare on the Screen." *Films in Review* (June–July 1956): 247–260.

Linden, George. "The Staged World." *Reflections on the Screen*, 2–29. Belmont, Calif.: Wadsworth, 1970.

Lindsay, Vachel. "Thirty Differences between the Photoplays and the Stage." In *The Art of the Moving Picture*. New York: MacMillan, 1916. Reprint, New York: Liveright, 1970. 179–198.

Lippmann, Max, ed. *Shakespeare in Film*. Wiesbaden, Germany: Saaten Verlag, 1964.

Literature/Film Quarterly. Special issues on Drama into Film or Shakespeare on Film: 1, no. 4 (1973); 4, no. 2 (1976); 5, no. 4 (1977); 11, no. 3 (1983); 14, no. 4 (1986); 19, no. 1 (1991); 20, no.4 (1992); 22, no. 2 (1994); 25, no. 2 (1997); 28, no. 2 (2000); 29, no. 2 (2001); 30, no. 3 (2002).

London, Todd. "Shakespeare in a Strange Land" (on Theater and Motion Picture Versions of Shakespeare's works). *American Theatre* 15, no. 6 (July–Aug. 1998): 22–24, 63–66.

Loving, Pierre. "Is the Play Vanishing?" *Drama* 12 (1922): 311–312.

Lusardi, James P., and June Schlueter, eds. *Shakespeare Bulletin* (incorporating *Shakespeare on Film Newsletter* since 1992). Easton, Penn.: English Department, Lafayette College.

MacKinnon, Kenneth. *Greek Tragedy into Film*. Rutherford, N.J.: Fairleigh Dickinson University Press, 1986.

Manvell, Roger. *Shakespeare and the Film*. New York: A. S. Barnes, 1979.

———. "Shakespeare as a Scriptwriter." *World Review* (May 1952): 56–59.

———, ed. "Shakespeare on the Screen." Special issue of the *Journal of the Society of Film and Television Arts* 37 (Autumn 1969).

———. *Theater and Film: A Comparative Study of the Two Forms of Dramatic Art, and of the Problems of Adaptation of Stage Plays into Films*. Rutherford, N.J.: Fairleigh Dickinson University Press, 1979.

Marble, A. L. "The Movies and Appreciation of Drama." *Photo-Era* 64 (1930): 163–164.

Marill, Alvin H. *More Theatre: Stage to Screen to Television*. Metuchen, N.J.: Scarecrow Press, 1993.

Marder, Louis. "The Shakespeare Film: Facts and Problems." *The Shakespeare Newsletter* 23 (1973): 42, 49.

Marowitz, Charles. *Recycling Shakespeare*. New York: Applause, 1991.

Marsden, Jean I., ed. *The Appropriations of Shakespeare: Post-Renaissance Reconstructions of the Works and the Myth*. London: Harvester Wheatsheaf, 1991.

Mason, James. "Stage vs. Screen." *Films and Filming* 1, no. 2 (Nov. 1954): 5; 1, no . 3 (Dec. 1954): 7.

Mast, Gerald. *Can't Help Singin': The American Musical on Stage and Screen*. New York: Overlook Press, 1987.

Matthews, Brander. "Are the Movies a Menace to the Drama?" *North American Review* 205 (1917): 447–454.

McAuliffe, Jody, ed. *Plays, Movies, and Critics*. Durham, N.C.: Duke University Press, 1993.

McCrindle, Joseph F., ed. *Behind the Scenes: Theater and Film Interviews*. New York: Holt, Rinehart, & Winston, 1971.

McDonald, Keiko. *Japanese Classical Theater in Films*. Rutherford, N.J.: Fairleigh Dickinson University Press, 1994.

McDonald, Neil. "The Relationship between Shakespeare's Stage-craft and Modern Film Technique." *Australian Journal of Screen Theory* 7 (1980): 18–33.

———. "Shakespeare on Film." *McGraw-Hill Encyclopedia of World Drama*. Vol. 4. 2nd ed. Ed. Stanley Hochman. New York: McGraw-Hill, 1984. 411–427.

McDonald, Russ, ed. *Shakespeare Reread: The Texts in New Contexts*. Ithaca, N.Y.: Cornell University Press, 1994.

McDonnell, Patricia. *On the Edge of Your Seat: Popular Theater and Film in Early Twentieth-Century American Art*. New Haven, Conn.: Yale University Press, 2002.

McDougal, Stuart Y. *Made into Movies: From Literature to Film*. New York: Holt, Rinehart, & Winston, 1985.

McKernan, Luke, and Olwen Terris, eds. *Walking Shadows: Shakespeare in the National Film and Television Archive*. London: British Film Institute, 1994.

McLean, Andrew M. *Shakespeare: Annotated Bibliographies and Media Guide for Teachers*. Urbana, Ill.: National Council of Teachers of English, 1980.

Merritt, Russell. "Rescued from a Perilous Nest: D. W. Griffith's Escape from Theatre into Film." *Cinema Journal* 21, no. 1 (Fall 1981): 2–30.

Millard, Barbara C. "Shakespeare on Film: Towards an Audience Perceived and Perceiving." *Literature/Film Quarterly* 5, no. 4 (Fall 1977): 352–357.

Morris, Peter, ed. *Shakespeare on Film*. Ottawa: Canadian Film Institute, 1972.

————. "Shakespeare on Film." *Films in Review* 24 (1973): 132–163.

Münsterberg, Hugo. "The Means of the Photoplay." *The Film: A Psychological Study*. 1916, as *The Photoplay: A Psychological Study*. New York: Dover, 1970. 73–82.

Murray, Edward. *The Cinematic Imagination: Writers and the Motion Pictures*. New York: Frederick Ungar, 1972.

Musser, Charles. *The Emergence of Cinema: The American Screen to 1907*. New York: Charles Scribner's Sons, 1990.

Naremore, James, ed. *Film Adaptation*. New Brunswick, N.J.: Rutgers University Press, 2000.

Nathan, George Jean. "The Play Is Still the Thing." *Forum* 86 (1931): 36–39.

Nichols, Bill, ed. *Movies and Methods*. Berkeley: University of California Press, 1976.

Nichols, Nina Da Vinci, and Jana O'Keefe Bazzoni. *Pirandello and Film*. Lincoln: University of Nebraska Press, 1995.

Nicoll, Allardyce. *Film and Theatre*. New York: Thomas Y. Crowell, 1936. Reprint, New York: Arno, 1972.

Olivier, Laurence. "Filming Shakespeare." *Journal of the British Film Academy* (Autumn 1955): n.p.

Orlandello, John. *O'Neill on Film*. Rutherford, N.J.: Fairleigh Dickinson University Press, 1982.

Ornstein, Robert. "Interpreting Shakespeare: The Dramatic Text and the Film." *University of Dayton Review* 14, no. 1 (1979–80): 55–61.

Orr, Christopher. "The Discourse on Adaptation." *Wide Angle* 6, no. 2 (1984): 72–76.

Osborne, Laurie E. "Mixing Media in Shakespeare: Animating Tales and Colliding Modes of Production." *Post Script* 17, no. 2 (Winter–Spring 1998): 73–89.

Panofsky, Erwin. "Style and Medium in the Motion Pictures." *Critique* 1, no. 3 (Jan.–Feb. 1947): 5–18 and 27–28. Reprinted in *Film Theory and Criticism*. 5th ed. Eds. Gerald Mast and Marshall Cohen. New York: Oxford University Press, 1999. 279–292. Also in Talbot, Daniel, ed. *Film: An Anthology*. Berkeley: University of California Press, 1970. 15–32.

Parker, Barry M. *The Folger Shakespeare Filmography: A Directory of Feature Films Based on the Works of William Shakespeare*. Washington, D.C.: Folger Shakespeare Library, 1979.

Pearson, Roberta E., and William Uricchio. "How Many Times Shall Caesar Bleed in Sport: Shakespeare and the Cultural Debate About Moving Pictures." *Screen* 31, no. 3 (Autumn 1990): 252, 258.

Pendleton, Thomas A. "Shakespeare . . . with Additional Dialog." *Cineaste* 24, no. 1 (1998): 62–66.

Phillips, Gene D. *The Films of Tennessee Williams*. Philadelphia: Art Alliance, 1980.

Phillips, James E. "Shakespeare as Screen Writer." *Hollywood Quarterly Journal of Film, Radio, and Television* 8 (1953–1954): 125–130.

Pilkington, Ace G. *Screening Shakespeare from "Richard II" to "Henry V."* Newark: University of Delaware Press, 1991.

Pizzello, Stephen. "From Stage to Screen: Interview with Julie Taymor." *American Cinematogapher* 81, no. 2 (Feb. 2000): 64–73.

Playfair, Nigel. "Theatre and the Films." *English Review* 52 (1931): 336–341.

Potter, Henry C., George Roy Hill, and Gene Saks. "Stage to Film." *Action* 3, no. 5 (1968): 12–14.

Pudovkin, V. I. *Film Acting*. Ed. and trans. Ivor Montagu. 1929 and 1933. Hackensack, N.J.: Wehman Brothers, 1968. See esp. "The Theatre and the Cinema," pp. 229–239.

———. *Film Technique*. Ed. and trans. Ivor Montagu. Hackensack, N.J.: Wehman Brothers, 1968. See esp. "The Peculiarities of Film Material," pp. 79–121.

———. "Stanislavsky's System in the Cinema." Trans. T. Shebunina. *Sight and Sound* 22, no. 3 (Jan.–March 1953): 115–118, 147–148.

Raynor, Henry. "Shakespeare Filmed." *Sight and Sound* 22 (1952): 10–15.

Reddington, John. "Film, Play, and Idea." *Literature/Film Quarterly* 1, no. 4 (1973): 367–371.

Richmond, Hugh M. "The Synergistic Use of Shakespearean Film and Video-tape." *Literature/Film Quarterly* 5, no. 4 (1977): 362–364.

Robinson, W. R., ed. *Man and the Movies*. Baton Rouge: Louisiana State University Press, 1967.

Roemer, Michael. "Shakespeare on Film: A Filmmaker's View." *The Shakespeare Newsletter* 26 (1976): 26.

Ross, T. J. "Shakespeare among the Nations: The Tragedies in the International Cinema." *Literary Review* 22 (1979): 381–382.

Rothwell, Kenneth S. *A History of Shakespeare on Screen: A Century of Film and Television*. Cambridge: Cambridge University Press, 1999.

———. "Appreciating Shakespeare on Film." *Literature/Film Quarterly* 5, no. 4 (1977): 365–367.

Rothwell, Kenneth S., and Bernice W. Kliman, eds. *Shakespeare on Film Newsletter*. Published from 1976 to 1992. Subsequently incorporated into *Shakespeare Bulletin*.

Rothwell, Kenneth S., and Annabelle Henkin Melzer. *Shakespeare on Screen: An International Filmography and Videography*. New York: Neal-Schuman, 1990.

Rubin, Martin. *Showstoppers: Busby Berkeley and the Tradition of Spectacle*. New York: Columbia Press, 1993.

Rumens, S. "The Step from Stage to Screen." *Film Making* 14 (Sept. 1976): 35–37.

Seldes, Gilbert. "The Plot and the Picture." *New Republic* 43, 563 (Sept. 16, 1925): 97–98.

———. *The Seven Lively Arts*. New York: Harper and Brothers, 1924. Reprint, Mineola, N.Y.: Dover, 2001.

"Shakespeare in the Cinema: A Film Directors' Symposium." *Cineaste* 24, no. 1 (Winter 1998): 48–55.

"Shakespeare on Film: A Selected Checklist." *Literature/Film Quarterly* 4, no. 2 (Spring 1976): 191–193.

Shakespeare Quarterly. Special issue, "Screen Shakespeare." 53, no. 2 (Summer 2002). Ed. Barbara Hodgdon.

Shaughnessy, Robert, ed. *Shakespeare on Film.* New York: St. Martin's, 1998.

Shaw, Bernard, and Archibald Henderson. "Drama, the Theatre, and the Films." *Fortnightly Review* 122 (1924): 289–302. Reprinted in *Table-Talk of G. B. S.*. New York: Harper, 1925. 53–65.

Shelley, Frank. *Stage and Screen.* London: Pendulum, 1946.

Silviria, Dale. *Laurence Olivier and the Art of Filmmaking.* Rutherford, N.J.: Fairleigh Dickinson University Press, 1985.

Simon, Scott. "The Classic Western According to Shakespeare." *Literature/Film Quarterly* 24, no. 2 (1996): 114–127.

Sinyard, Neil. *Filming Literature: The Art of Adaptation.* London: St. Martin's, 1986.

Skovmand, Michael, ed. *Screen Shakespeare.* Aarhus, Denmark: Aarhus University Press, 1994.

Sontag, Susan. "Film and Theatre." *Film Theory and Criticism.* 4th ed. Ed. Gerald Mast and Marshall Cohen. New York: Oxford University Press, 1992. 363–374. Also from *Styles of Radical Will.* New York: Farrar, Straus and Giroux, 1960. 99–122.

Starks, Lisa S., and Courtney Lehmann. *The Reel Shakespeare.* Madison, N.J.: Fairleigh Dickinson University Press, 2002.

Staton, Shirley F. "Shakespeare Redivivus: Supplementary Techniques for Teaching Shakespeare." *Literature/Film Quarterly* 5, no. 4 (1977): 358–361.

Styan, J. L. *The Shakespeare Revolution: Criticism and Performance in the Twentieth Century.* London: Cambridge University Press, 1977.

———. "Sight and Space: The Perception of Shakespeare on Stage and Screen." *Shakespeare, Pattern of Excelling Nature.* Ed. David Bevington and Jay L. Halio. Newark: University of Delaware Press, 1978. 198–209.

Syberberg, Hans-Jürgen. "Theater and Film, or Adolphe Appia and Me." Trans. Bert Cardullo. *Film Criticism* 24, no. 2 (Winter 1999–2000): 55–65.

Taylor, Gary. *Reinventing Shakespeare.* New York: Weidenfeld and Nicholson, 1989.

Taylor, John Russell. "Shakespeare in Film, Radio, and Television." *Shakespeare: A Celebration, 1564–1964.* Ed. T. J. B. Spencer. Baltimore: Penguin Books, 1964. 97–113.

Thorp, Margaret Farrand. "Shakespeare and the Movies." *Shakespeare Quarterly* 9, no. 3 (Summer 1958): 357–366.

Tibbetts, John C. *The American Theatrical Film: Stages in Development.* Bowling Green, Ohio: Bowling Green State University Popular Press, 1985.

Tibbetts, John, and James M. Welsh, eds. *The Encyclopedia of Stage Plays into Film.* New York: Facts on File, 2001.

Toles, George E., ed. *Film/Literature.* Winnipeg: University of Manitoba Press, 1983.

Törnqvist, Egil. *Transposing Drama: Studies in Representation.* New York: St. Martin's, 1991.

———. *Between Stage and Screen: Ingmar Bergman Directs.* Amsterdam, Holland: Amsterdam University Press, 1995.

"Tough Acts" (Film Adaptations of William Shakespeare's Plays). Editorial. *Sight and Sound* 7, no. 2 (Feb. 1997): 3.

Tucker, Nicholas. "Shakespeare and Film Technique." *Screen Education* (Sept.–Oct.1963): 36–41.

Vardac, A. Nicholas. *Stage to Screen: Theatrical Method from Garrick to Griffith.* Cambridge: Harvard University Press, 1949. Reprint, *Stage to Screen: Theatrical Origins of Early Film, David Garrick to D. W. Griffith.* New York: Benjamin Blom, 1968; New York: Da Capo, 1987.

Viera, Maria. "Using Theatrical Acting Techniques in the Production of Short Films." *Journal of Film and Video* 46, no. 4 (Winter 1995): 13–23.

Von Sternberg, Josef. "Acting in Film and Theatre." *Film Culture* 1, no. 5–6 (Winter 1955): 1–4, 27–29.

Walker, Robert Matthew. *From Broadway to Hollywood: The Musical and the Cinema.* London: Sanctuary Publishing, 1996.

Waller, Gregory A. *The Stage/Screen Debate: A Study in Popular Aesthetics.* New York: Garland, 1983.

Welsh, James M. "Shakespeare with—and without—Words." *Literature/Film Quarterly* 1, no. 1 (1973): 84–88.

Welsh, James M., and Richard Vela. *Shakespeare into Film.* New York: Checkmark, 2002.

Williams, D. P. "Cinema Technique and the Theatre." *Nineteenth Century* 110 (1931): 602–612.

Williams, Raymond, and Michael Orrom. *Preface to Film.* London: Film Drama, 1954.

Willis, Susan. *The BBC Shakespeare Plays: Making the Televised Canon.* Chapel Hill: University of North Carolina Press, 1991.

Willson, Robert F., ed. *Shakespeare Entering the Maze.* New York: Peter Lang, 1995.

———. *Shakespeare in Hollywood, 1929–1956.* Madison, N.J.: Fairleigh Dickinson University Press, 2000.

Wyatt, E. V. "The Stage and the Screen." *Catholic World* 135 (1932): 718–720.

Yacowar, Maurice. *Tennessee Williams and Film.* New York: Frederick Ungar, 1977.

Youngblood, Gene. "Intermedia Theatre." *Expanded Cinema.* New York: E. P. Dutton, 1970. 365–386.

Zilboorg, G. "Art and the Cinema." *Drama* 12 (1922): 352.

Zuber-Skerritt, O., ed. *The Languages of Theatre: Problems in the Translation and Transposition of Drama.* Oxford: Pergamon, 1980.

Zucker, Carole. *In the Company of Actors: Reflections on the Craft of Acting.* London: A & C Black, 1999.

Select Filmography

Thousands of plays have been adapted to the screen over the past one hundred years. What follows, therefore, is not intended to be comprehensive or judgmental. Rather, I have endeavored to suggest one hundred or so films that would be fruitful to examine in light of the essays included, and the ideas treated, in this book.

All My Sons (1948). Adapted by Chester Erskine from the play by Arthur Miller (1947). Directed by Irving Reis. With Edward G. Robinson and Burt Lancaster.

Amadeus (1984). Adapted by Peter Shaffer from his play (1979). Directed by Miloš Forman. With F. Murray Abraham and Tom Hulce.

American Buffalo (1997). Adapted by David Mamet from his play (1975). Directed by Michael Corrente. With Dustin Hoffman and Dennis Franz.

As You Like It (1936). Adapted by Robert J. Cullen and Carl Mayer; treatment suggested by James M. Barrie, from the play by William Shakespeare (1599). Directed by Paul Czinner. With Laurence Olivier and Elizabeth Bergner.

The Balcony (1963). Adapted by Ben Maddow from the play by Jean Genêt (1956). Directed by Joseph Losey. With Shelley Winters and Peter Falk.

The Beggar's Opera (1952). Adapted by Dennis Cannan and Christopher Fry from the play by John Gay (1727). Directed by Peter Brook. With Laurence Olivier and Stanley Holloway.

Bent (1997). Adapted by Martin Sherman from his play (1980). Directed by Sean Mathias. With Clive Owen and Ian McKellen.

Betrayal (1983). Adapted by Harold Pinter from his play (1978). Directed by David Jones. With Jeremy Irons and Ben Kingsley.

Blithe Spirit (1945). Adapted by Noel Coward from his play (1941). Directed by David Lean. With Rex Harrison and Constance Cummings.

Bodas de Sangre (1981). Adapted by Alfredo Manas from the play *Blood Wedding (Bodas de Sangre)*, by Federico García Lorca (1933). Directed by Carlos Saura. With Antonio Gades and Cristina Hoyes.

Boesman and Lena (2000). Adapted by John Berry from the play by Athol Fugard (1969). Directed by John Berry. With Danny Glover and Angela Bassett.

Breaker Morant (1980). Adapted by John Hardy and David Stevens from the play by Kenneth G. Ross (1978). Directed by Bruce Beresford. With Edward Woodward and Jack Thompson.

Brief Encounter (1945). Adapted by David Lean and Ronald Neame from the play *Still Life* by Noel Coward (1936). Directed by David Lean. With Trevor Howard and Celia Johnson.

The Browning Version (1994). Adapted by Ronald Harwood from the play by Terence Rattigan (1948). Directed by Mike Figgis. With Albert Finney and Greta Scacchi.

Butley (1973). Adapted by Simon Gray from his play (1971). Directed by Harold Pinter. With Alan Bates and Jessica Tandy.

Cabaret (1972). Adapted by Jay Presson Allen from the play by Joe Masterhoff (1966), itself based on the play *I Am a Camera* (1951), by John Van Druten, and the writings of Christopher Isherwood. Directed by Bob Fosse. With Liza Minnelli and Michael York.

Carousel (1956). Adapted by Phoebe and Henry Ephron from the Rogers and Hammerstein musical play and the English adaptation by Benjamin F. Glazer of the play *Liliom,* by Ferenc Molnar (1908). Directed by Henry King. With Gordon MacRae and Shirley Jones.

Cat on a Hot Tin Roof (1958). Adapted by Richard Brooks and James Poe from the play by Tennessee Williams (1955). Directed by Richard Brooks. With Elizabeth Taylor and Paul Newman.

Chicago (2002). Adapted by Bill Condon from the musical by Bob Fosse and Fred Ebb (1975). Original music by John Kandor and Fred Ebb. Directed by Rob Marshall. With Renée Zellweger, Catherine Zeta-Jones, and Richard Gere.

Children of a Lesser God (1986). Adapted by Mark Medoff and Hesper Anderson from the play by Mark Medoff (1980). Directed by Randa Haines. With William Hurt and Marlee Matlin.

The Children's Hour (1961). Adapted by John Michael Hayes and Lillian Hellman from the play by Lillian Hellman (1934). Directed by William Wyler. With Audrey Hepburn and Shirley MacLaine.

Chimes at Midnight (Falstaff) (1965). Directed and adapted by Orson Welles from the plays *Henry IV, Parts I & II* (1597–1598), *Henry V* (1598–1599), *Richard II* (1595–1596), and *The Merry Wives of Windsor* (1600–1601), by William Shakespeare (with additional narration based upon Raphael Holinshed's *Chronicles of England*, 1577). With Orson Welles and John Gielgud.

Come Back, Little Sheba (1952). Adapted by Ketti Frings from the play by William Inge (1949). Directed by Daniel Mann. With Burt Lancaster and Shirley Booth.

The Connection (1962). Adapted by Jack Gelber from his play (1959). Directed by Shirley Clarke. With William Redfield and Roscoe Lee Browne.

The Crucible (1996). Adapted by Arthur Miller from his play (1953). Directed by Nicholas Hytner. With Daniel Day-Lewis and Winona Ryder.

Cyrano de Bergerac (1990). Adapted by Jean-Paul Rappeneau and Jean-Claude Carrière from an English translation by Anthony Burgess of the play by Edmond Rostand (1897). Directed by Jean-Paul Rappeneau. With Gérard Depardieu and Anne Brochet.

Dangerous Liaisons (1988). Adapted by Christopher Hampton from his play *Les Liaisons dangereuses* (1985), itself based on the novel *Les Liaisons dangereuses,* by Choderlos de Laclos (1782). Directed by Stephen Frears. With Glenn Close and John Malkovich.

A Delicate Balance (1973). Adapted by Edward Albee from his play (1966). Directed by Tony Richardson. With Katharine Hepburn and Paul Scofield.

Doctor Faustus (1967). Adapted by Nevill Coghill from the play by Christopher Marlowe (1589). Directed by Richard Burton and Nevill Coghill. With Nevil Coghill and Richard Burton.

A Doll's House (1973). Directed and adapted by Joseph Losey from the play by Henrik Ibsen (1879). With Jane Fonda and Trevor Howard.

The Dresser (1983). Adapted by Ronald Harwood and Peter Yates from the play by Ronald Harwood (1980). Directed by Peter Yates. With Albert Finney and Tom Courtenay.

Driving Miss Daisy (1990). Adapted by Alfred Uhry from his play (1987). Directed by Bruce Beresford. With Jessica Tandy and Morgan Freeman.

Edward II (1992). Adapted by Derek Jarman, Ken Butler, Steve Clark-Hall, Stephen McBride, and Antony Root from the play by Christopher Marlowe (1592). Directed by Derek Jarman. With Steven Waddington and Kevin Collins.

The Elephant Man (1980). Adapted by Christopher DeVore, Eric Bergren, and David Lynch from the play by Bernard Pomerance (1979). Directed by David Lynch. With Anthony Hopkins and John Hurt.

The Emperor Jones (1933). Adapted by DuBose Heyward from the play by Eugene O'Neill (1920). Directed by Dudley Murphy. With Paul Robeson and Dudley Digges.

The Entertainer (1960). Adapted by John Osborne and Nigel Kneale from the play by John Osborne (1957). Directed by Tony Richardson. With Laurence Olivier and Joan Plowright.

Fool for Love (1985). Adapted by Sam Shepard from his play (1983). Directed by Robert Altman. With Sam Shepard and Kim Basinger.

A Funny Thing Happened on the Way to the Forum (1966). Adapted by Melvin Frank and Michael Pertwee from the musical play by Burt Shevelove and Larry Gelbart (1962), with score and lyrics by Stephen Sondheim. Directed by Richard Lester. With Zero Mostel and Buster Keaton.

The Glass Menagerie (1987). From the play by Tennessee Williams (1944). Directed by Paul Newman. With Joanne Woodward and John Malkovich.

Glengarry Glen Ross (1992). Adapted by David Mamet from his play (1984). Directed by James Foley. With Al Pacino and Jack Lemmon.

Golden Boy (1939). Adapted by Lewis Meltzer, Daniel Taradash, Sarah Y. Mason, and Victor Heerman from the play by Clifford Odets (1937). Directed by Rouben Mamoulian. With William Holden and Barbara Stanwyck.

The Great White Hope (1970). Adapted by Howard Sackler from his play (1968). Directed by Martin Ritt. With James Earl Jones and Jane Alexander.

Hamlet (1948). Adapted by Laurence Olivier and Alan Dent from the play by William Shakespeare (1602). Directed by Laurence Olivier. With Laurence Olivier and Jean Simmons.

Hedda Gabler (1975). Directed and adapted by Trevor Nunn from the play by Henrik Ibsen (1890). With Glenda Jackson and Patrick Stewart.

Henry V (1989). Directed and adapted by Kenneth Branagh from the play by William Shakespeare (1599). With Kenneth Branagh and Derek Jacobi.

His Girl Friday (1940). Adapted by Charles Lederer from the play *The Front Page,* by Ben Hecht and Charles MacArthur (1928). Directed by Howard Hawks. With Cary Grant and Rosalind Russell.

Hurlyburly (1998). Adapted by David Rabe from his play (1984). Directed by Anthony Drazan. With Sean Penn and Kevin Spacey.

The Iceman Cometh (1973). Adapted by Thomas Quinn Curtiss from the play by Eugene O'Neill (1946). Directed by John Frankenheimer. With Lee Marvin and Robert Ryan.

The Importance of Being Earnest (2002). Directed and adapted by Oliver Parker from the play by Oscar Wilde (1894). With Colin Firth and Reese Witherspoon.

Inherit the Wind (1960). Adapted by Nathan E. Douglas and Harold Jacob Smith from the play by Jerome Lawrence and Robert E. Lee (1955). Directed by Stanley Kramer. With Spencer Tracy and Fredric March.

The Inspector General (1949). Adapted by Philip Rapp and Harry Kurnitz from the play by Nikolai Gogol (1836). Directed by Henry Koster. With Danny Kaye and Elsa Lanchester.

Jesus of Montreal (1989). Written by Denys Arcand and including a passion play. Directed by Denys Arcand. With Robert Lepage and Marie-Christine Barrault.

Julius Caesar (1953). Directed and adapted by Joseph L. Mankiewicz from the play by William Shakespeare (1599). With Marlon Brando and James Mason.

King Lear (1971). Directed and adapted by Peter Brook from the play by William Shakespeare (1605). With Paul Scofield and Irene Worth.

The Little Foxes (1941). Adapted by Lillian Hellman from her play (1939). Directed by William Wyler. With Bette Davis and Herbert Marshall.

Little Murders (1972). Adapted by Jules Feiffer from his play (1967). Directed by Alan Arkin. With Elliot Gould and Donald Sutherland.

Long Day's Journey Into Night (1962). From the play by Eugene O'Neill (1956). Directed by Sidney Lumet. With Katharine Hepburn and Ralph Richardson.

Look Back in Anger (1959). Adapted by Nigel Kneale from the play by John Osborne (1956). Directed by Tony Richardson. With Richard Burton and Claire Bloom.

Macbeth (1971). Adapted by Kenneth Tynan from the play by William Shakespeare (1606). Directed by Roman Polanski. With Jon Finch and Francesca Annis.

The Madness of King George (1994). Adapted by Alan Bennett from his play *The Madness of George III* (1991). Directed by Nicholas Hytner. With Nigel Hawthorne and Helen Mirren.

Major Barbara (1941). Adapted by George Bernard Shaw from his play (1905). Directed by Gabriel Pascal. With Wendy Hiller and Rex Harrison.

A Man for All Seasons (1966). Adapted by Robert Bolt from his play (1960). Directed by Fred Zinnemann. With Paul Scofield and Wendy Hiller.

The Man Who Came to Dinner (1941). Adapted by Julius and Philip Epstein from the play by George S. Kaufman and Moss Hart (1939). Directed by William Keighley. With Bette Davis and Monty Woolley.

Marat/Sade (1967). Directed and adapted by Peter Brook from the play by Peter Weiss (1964); English version by Geoffrey Skelton and verse adaptation by Adrian Mitchell. With Patrick Magee and Glenda Jackson.

M. Butterfly (1993). Adapted by David Henry Hwang from his play (1988). Directed by David Cronenberg. With Jeremy Irons and John Lone.

A Midsummer Night's Dream (1935). Adapted by Charles Kenyon and Mary McCall from the play by William Shakespeare (1595). Directed by Max Reinhardt and William Dieterle. With James Cagney and Olivia de Havilland.

Miss Julie (1950). Adapted by Alf Sjöberg from the play by August Strindberg (1888). Directed by Alf Sjöberg. With Anita Bjork and Ulf Palme.

Much Ado about Nothing (1993). Directed and adapted by Kenneth Branagh from the play by William Shakespeare (1600). With Robert Sean Leonard and Emma Thompson.

'night, Mother (1986). Adapted by Marsha Norman from her play (1982). Directed by Tom Moore. With Sissy Spacek and Anne Bancroft.

The Night of the Iguana (1964). Adapted by Anthony Veiller and John Huston from the play by Tennessee Williams (1961). Directed by John Huston. With Richard Burton and Deborah Kerr.

Noises Off (1992). Adapted by Marty Kaplan from the play by Michael Frayn (1982). Directed by Peter Bogdanovich. With Carol Burnett and Michael Caine.

The Odd Couple (1968). Adapted by Neil Simon from his play (1965). Directed by Gene Saks. With Jack Lemmon and Walter Matthau.

Oedipus Rex (1967). Directed and adapted by Pier Paolo Pasolini from the play by Sophocles (ca. 430 B.C.). With Franco Citti and Silvana Mangano.

Oleanna (1995). Directed and adapted by David Mamet from his play (1992). With William H. Macy and Debra Eisenstadt.

Othello (1965). Adapted from John Dexter's National Theatre production of the play by William Shakespeare (1604). Directed by Stuart Burge. With Laurence Olivier and Frank Finlay.

Our Town (1940). Adapted by Thornton Wilder, Frank Craven, and Harry Chandlee from the play by Thornton Wilder (1938). Directed by Sam Wood. With William Holden and Martha Scott.

The Philadelphia Story (1940). Adapted by Donald Ogden Stewart from the play by Philip Barry (1938). Directed by George Cukor. With Cary Grant and Katharine Hepburn.

The Piano Lesson (1994). Adapted by August Wilson from his play (1987). Directed by Lloyd Richards. With Charles Dutton and Alfre Woodard.

Plenty (1985). Adapted by David Hare from his play (1978). Directed by Fred Schepisi. With Meryl Streep and Tracey Ullman.

Prospero's Books (1991). Directed and adapted by Peter Greenaway from the play *The Tempest*, by William Shakespeare (1611). With John Gielgud and Isabelle Pasco.

Pygmalion (1938). Adapted by W. P. Lipscomb and Cecil Lewis from the play by George Bernard Shaw (1913). Directed by Anthony Asquith and Leslie Howard. With Leslie Howard and Wendy Hiller.

A Raisin in the Sun (1961). Adapted by Lorrraine Hansberry from her play (1959). Directed by Daniel Petrie. With Sidney Poitier and Ruby Dee.

Richard III (1995). Adapted by Richard Loncraine and Ian McKellen from the play by William Shakespeare (1592). Directed by Richard Loncraine. With Ian McKellen and Annette Benning.

La Ronde (1950). Adapted by Jacques Natanson and Max Ophüls from the play *Reigen*, by Arthur Schnitzler (1920). Directed by Max Ophüls. With Simone Signoret and Anton Walbrook.

The Ruling Class (1972). Adapted by Peter Barnes from his play (1968). Directed by Peter Medak. With Peter O'Toole and Alastair Sim.

Six Degrees of Separation (1994). Adapted by John Guare from his play (1990). Directed by Fred Schepisi. With Stockard Channing and Will Smith.

A Soldier's Story (1984). Adapted by Charles Fuller from his play *A Soldier's Play* (1982). Directed by Norman Jewison. With Howard E. Rollins, Jr., and Adolph Caesar.

A Streetcar Named Desire (1951). Adapted by Tennessee Williams from his play (1947). Directed by Elia Kazan. With Marlon Brando and Vivien Leigh.

Suddenly, Last Summer (1959). Adapted by Gore Vidal and Tennessee Williams from the play by Tennessee Williams (1958). Directed by Joseph L. Mankiewicz. With Elizabeth Taylor and Montgomery Clift.

Swimming to Cambodia (1987). Adapted by Spalding Gray from his theatrical monologue (1985). Directed by Jonathan Demme. With Spalding Gray.

Talk Radio (1988). Adapted by Eric Bogosian and Oliver Stone from the play by Eric Bogosian (1985). Directed by Oliver Stone. With Eric Bogosian and Alec Baldwin.

The Taming of the Shrew (1966). Adapted by Suso Cecci D'Amico, Paul Dehn, and Franco Zeffirelli from the play by William Shakespeare (1593–1594). Directed by Franco Zeffirelli. With Elizabeth Taylor and Richard Burton.

The Threepenny Opera (1931). Adapted by Leo Lania, Bela Balasz, and Ladislas Vajda from the play by Bertolt Brecht (1928). Directed by G. W. Pabst. With Lotte Lenya and Rudolph Forster.

Titus Andronicus (1999). Adapted by Julie Taymor from the play by William Shakespeare (1594). Directed by Julie Taymor. With Anthony Hopkins and Jessica Lange.

Twelfth Night (1996). Directed and adapted by Trevor Nunn from the play by William Shakespeare (1601). With Helena Bonham Carter and Ben Kingsley.

Vanya on 42nd Street (1994). Adapted by David Mamet from the play *Uncle Vanya* by Anton Chekhov (1897). Directed by Louis Malle. With Wallace Shawn and Julianne Moore.

West Side Story (1961). Adapted by Ernest Lehman from the musical play by Arthur Laurents (1957), based partly on *Romeo and Juliet* (1595–1596) by William Shakespeare; lyrics by

Stephen Sondheim and score by Leonard Bernstein. Directed by Robert Wise and Jerome Robbins. With Natalie Wood and Richard Beymer.

Who's Afraid of Virginia Woolf? (1966). Adapted by Ernest Lehman from the play by Edward Albee (1962). Directed by Mike Nichols. With Elizabeth Taylor and Richard Burton.

William Shakespeare's Romeo + Juliet (1996). Adapted by Craig Pearce and Baz Luhrmann from the play *Romeo and Juliet* by William Shakespeare (1595–1596). Directed by Baz Luhrmann. With Leonardo DiCaprio and Claire Danes.

The Women (1939). Adapted by Anita Loos and Jane Murlin from the play by Clare Boothe (1936). Directed by George Cukor. With Joan Crawford and Rosalind Russell.

Woyzeck (1979). Directed and adapted by Werner Herzog from the play by Georg Büchner (1836). With Klaus Kinski and Eva Mattes.

You Can't Take It with You (1938). Adapted by Robert Riskin from the play by George S. Kaufman and Moss Hart (1936). Directed by Frank Capra. With Jean Arthur and James Stewart.

Contributors

Lindsay Anderson (1923–1994) was a film director known for such pictures as *O Lucky Man!* (1973) and *Glory! Glory!* (1989). He also worked as a theater director and actor.

Antonin Artaud (1896–1948) was an actor, playwright, and theorist who struggled with mental illness throughout his career, but nonetheless became one of the most influential theater figures of the twentieth century. He proposed a "theater of cruelty," which would purge the audience of its own violent tendencies through aggressive theatrical effects and extreme dramatic visions. He is the author of *The Theater and Its Double* (1938; trans. 1958), a collection of his essays on theater published in 1938, and his most prominent play is *The Spurt of Blood* (1925).

Sarah Bay-Cheng is assistant professor of English and theater at Colgate University. She is the author of *Mama Dada* (2003), a study of Gertrude Stein's plays through the lenses of film, queer, and avant-garde theories.

André Bazin (1918–1958), French film critic and theorist, co-founded *Cahiers du cinéma,* one of the first magazines devoted entirely to film criticism. As a critic, he popularized the *auteur* theory and wrote about a wide range of films, including the American western and *film noir,* Italian neorealism, and the French New Wave.

Eric Bentley has been a writer, director, translator, and teacher. Perhaps best known as the first American translator of Bertolt Brecht's plays, Bentley is also the author of numerous influential critical works, most notably *The Life of the Drama* (1964) and *The Playwright as Thinker* (1946).

Ingmar Bergman is considered to be one of the greatest directors in film history. He has also been an influential theater director and a writer for television, cinema, and theater. His films include *Wild Strawberries* (1957), *The Seventh Seal* (1957), *Persona* (1966), *Scenes From a Marriage* (1973), and *Fanny and Alexander* (1982).

Roger Blin (1907–1984), French actor and theater director, was the first to stage Beckett's *Waiting for Godot* (in 1952), among other avant-garde plays. As an actor he appeared in numerous films throughout his career, including *Orpheus* (1949), *The Hunchback of Notre Dame* (1956), and *The Adolescent* (1979).

Leo Braudy is the Leo S. Bing Professor of Film at the University of Southern California. He has written a number of books, including *World in a Frame: What We See in Films* (1976) and *The Frenzy of Renown: Fame and Its History* (1986), and he is one of the editors of *Film Theory and Criticism,* now in its fifth edition.

Bertolt Brecht (1898–1956) was a dramatist, director, screenwriter, and theater theorist. Among his best-known plays are *The Threepenny Opera* (1928) and *Mother Courage and Her Children* (1941); his theoretical writings are collected in *Brecht on Theater,* translated by John Willett.

Peter Brook made his directorial debut in 1942 at the Torch Theatre in London with Marlowe's *Doctor Faustus.* Among his best-known directorial efforts are *A Midsummer Night's Dream* (1970 on stage) and *The Mahabharata* (1985 on stage; 1989 on screen), *King Lear* (1962 on stage; 1971 on screen), and *Marat/Sade* (1964 on stage; 1966 on screen). Brook is the author of numerous books on theater practice and theory, including *The Empty Space* (1968).

Judi Dench is a member of the Royal Shakespeare Company and also of the Royal National Theatre. Dench has appeared in many films, but she is probably best known to younger audiences for her portrayal of Queen Elizabeth in *Shakespeare in Love* (1998), for which she received the Oscar for best supporting actress.

Sergei Eisenstein (1898–1948) promoted the theory of a "montage of attractions," first in the theater and then in his work as a film editor and director. Eisenstein's theoretical writings on cinema include *Film Form* (1949) and *Film Sense* (1942). Among his best-known films are *Strike* (1924) and *Battleship Potemkin* (1925).

Miloš Forman is best known for his directing in America of movies like *One Flew over the Cuckoo's Nest* (1975), *Amadeus* (1984), and *Man on the Moon* (1999). After studying at the Prague Film Facility in his native Czechoslovakia, he made such widely regarded films as *Loves of a Blonde* (1965) and *The Firemen's Ball* (1967) before moving to Hollywood (where he has won two Oscars for best director).

After a short career in the theater as a playwright and actor, *D. W. Griffith* (1875–1948) acted in films for the Edison company before beginning to direct for the American Biograph Company. Among his most influential films are the *The Birth of a Nation* (1915) and *Way Down East* (1920).

Tom Gunning is professor of art history at the University of Chicago, and he earned his Ph.D. from New York University's Department of Cinema Studies. One of the foremost historians and theorists of early cinema, Gunning has published *D. W. Griffith and the Origins of American Narrative Film* (1991) and *The Films of Fritz Lang* (2000).

Peter Hall is the founder of the Royal Shakespeare Company. He has received many honors, including multiple Tony Awards. Among his stage productions are *Amadeus* (1980; restaged 1999) and *The Tempest* (1988), and he has directed *A Midsummer Night's Dream* (1968) for the screen.

Peter Handke, best known in the world of cinema for his screenplay of *Wings of Desire* (1988), wrote several important avant-garde works for the stage, including *Kaspar* (1968), *The Ride across Lake Constance* (1971), and *Offending the Audience* (1966). He has also directed several films, including *The Absence* (1995) and *The Left-Handed Woman* (1978, from Handke's own novel).

Stanley Kauffmann has been the film critic for *The New Republic* for more than four decades. In addition to writing theater criticism for such publications as *The New York Times* and *Saturday Review,* he taught at the Yale School of Drama from 1967 to 1986.

Elia Kazan is well known for his directing on both stage and screen. On Broadway, he directed the original productions of *The Skin of Our Teeth* (1942), *A Streetcar Named Desire* (1947), *Death of a Salesman* (1949), and *Cat on a Hot Tin Roof* (1955). Among his most successful films are *Gentleman's Agreement* (1947) and *On the Waterfront* (1954)—both of which won Academy Awards for best direction—as well as *A Streetcar Named Desire* (1951) and *East of*

Eden (1955). In 1999 the Academy of Motion Picture Arts and Sciences awarded him a lifetime achievement award for his contributions to cinema.

Siegfried Kracauer (1889–1966), a well-known German author and cultural critic, was forced to flee to the United States during World War II. His books include *From Caligari to Hitler: A Psychological History of the German Film* and *The Mass Ornament: Weimar Essays,* as well as the influential *Theory of Film.*

Richard Loncraine worked as a set designer, toy maker, and actor before turning to directing films. His first feature production was *Flame* (1975), and a number of other pictures followed, including *The Missionary* (1981) and *Richard III* (1995), starring Ian McKellen.

Baz Luhrmann has directed the aggressively updated and stylized films *Shakespeare's Romeo + Juliet* (1996) and *Moulin Rouge* (2001). He studied at the National Institute of Dramatic Art in Australia before directing his first stage production, *Strictly Ballroom,* in 1986, a cinematic version of which was released in 1992. In 2002, he directed *La Boheme* on Broadway.

David Mamet is an award-winning playwright, screenwriter, and film director. Among his most celebrated plays are *American Buffalo* (1977), *Glengarry Glen Ross* (1983, which earned him a Pulitzer Prize), and *Oleanna* (1992). His other screenplays include *The Postman Always Rings Twice* (1981), *The Verdict* (1982), *The Untouchables* (1987), and *Wag the Dog* (1997).

Keiko I. McDonald is a professor of Japanese literature and film at the University of Pittsburgh. She received her Ph.D. from the University of Oregon, and her many published writings include *From Book to Screen* (2000), *Japanese Classical Theater in Films* (1994), and *Cinema East* (1983).

Vsevolod Meyerhold (1874–1940) was a prominent actor and director on the Russian stage. He trained actors in the "biomechanical" technique, a reaction against the bias toward psychological realism in Stanislavsky's method.

Trevor Nunn became the youngest-ever artistic director of the Royal Shakespeare Company in 1968 (serving in that role until 1986). Outside the RSC, he has directed the Tony Award–winning *Nicholas Nickleby* (1979–80), *Les Misérables* (1985), *Cats* (1982), *Starlight Express* (1984), and *Sunset Boulevard* (1994), among other productions. Nunn has directed two films from plays: *Hedda* (1975), from Ibsen's *Hedda Gabler,* and Shakespeare's *Twelfth Night or What You Will* (1996).

Oliver Parker has worked primarily as a director for British film and television, although he also acts and writes. He can be seen performing in such movies as *Shepherd on the Rock* (1993) and *An Ideal Husband* (1999), the latter of which (originally a play by Oscar Wilde) he also directed. Among his other credits as a film director are Shakespeare's *Othello* (1995) and Wilde's *The Importance of Being Earnest* (2002).

Harold Pinter's numerous plays also include *The Birthday Party* (1957), *The Homecoming* (1965), *Betrayal* (1978), *Old Times* (1981), and *Moonlight* (1994). He wrote the screenplays for *The Servant* (1963), *The French Lieutenant's Woman* (1981), *The Handmaid's Tale* (1990), and *The Comfort of Strangers* (1990).

Roman Polanski worked as a stage and radio actor before studying at the Lodz Film School in Poland, where he began directing. Among his many film-directing credits are *Rosemary's Baby* (1969), *Macbeth* (1971), *Chinatown* (1974), and *The Pianist* (2002). Now living in France, he continues to act in movies and to make them.

Martin Rubin is the former film program director of the New York Cultural Center and the author of *Thrillers* (1999) as well as *Showstoppers* (1993). He has taught as the State University of New York at Purchase and the University of California, Santa Barbara.

Susan Sontag is best known as an author of essays and novels, but she has also worked as a film director and a playwright. Among her novels is *In America,* winner of the 2000 National Book Award for Fiction; her films are *Duet for Cannibals* (1969) and *Brother Carl* (1971).

Born in Nigeria, *Wole Soyinka* earned his B.A. from the University of Leeds in England and has taught at Cambridge and Yale, among other universities. In 1986, he received the Nobel Prize for Literature. Soyinka has written numerous works for the stage, including *The Lion and the Jewel* (1959) and *Death and the King's Horseman* (1975).

Julie Taymor is a director as well as a set and costume designer for both the stage and the screen. Among her works are the theatrical adaptations of *The Lion King* (1997) and *The Green Bird* (2000), as well as the film *Frida* (2002) and versions of Shakespeare's *Titus Andronicus* for both the stage and the screen (*Titus,* 1999).

A. Nicholas Vardac was an early film scholar and documentary filmmaker. While working for the U.S. Department of the Interior as a film producer, he created a number of documentaries that earned him awards, including one for *Japan Today, 1946.*

Sam Waterston studied at Yale and the Sorbonne in Paris before beginning his successful acting career. In 1994, he was nominated for a Tony Award for his portrayal of Lincoln in *Abe Lincoln in Illinois.* His film credits include *The*

Great Gatsby (1974) and *The Killing Fields* (1984). He currently stars as assistant district attorney Jack McCoy on the television series *Law and Order*.

Orson Welles directed and produced the infamous radio broadcast of "The War of the Worlds" with "The Mercury Theater on the Air" in 1938, and three years later he made his first film, *Citizen Kane* (1941), followed by such noteworthy movies as *The Magnificent Ambersons* (1942), *The Lady from Shanghai* (1948), *Touch of Evil* (1958), and Welles's Shakespearean "trilogy" composed of *Macbeth* (1948), *Othello* (1952), and *Chimes at Midnight* (1966).

Franco Zeffirelli was educated as an architect at the University of Florence before beginning his career as a set designer and stage director. After working on a number of well-known Italian theatrical productions, including Luchino Visconti's staging of Tennessee Williams's *A Streetcar Named Desire*, Zeffirelli began directing for the cinema. Among his films are Shakespeare's *The Taming of the Shrew* (1967) and *Romeo and Juliet* (1968).

Index

Abraham, F. Murray, 263, 266
Accident (Pinter's screenplay), 194, 197, 203
acrobatics: as spectacle, 243
acting: British vs. American approach, 386; for film and stage, 323–332; in silent films, 354; subtext, 387; teachers, 366–367; in theater vs. films, 12, 97–98, 158–159
actions: individual significance, 191
actor: persona and charisma, 160; presence, 126; relationship with theater audience, 212
actors, amateur, 10
actors, in film: director's work with, 232–233, 305, 343, 349; professional vs. non-professional, 331–332
Actors Studio, 335, 336–338, 341, 357, 365, 384
adaptation: plays to film, 1–2, 99

Aeschylus, 2
African cinema, 215–216
L'Age d'Or (Buñuel), 150
Akropolis (Grotowski), 159
Albee, Edward, 14, 336; *The Goat or Who Is Sylvia?*, 14
Allen, Dede, 350
Allen, Paul, 294
Allen, Woody: *Interiors*, 362
Altman, Rick, 47
Amadeus (Forman's film version), 257–66
Amarcord (Fellini), 296
Amédée or How to Get Rid of It (Ionesco), 168
America America (Kazan), 349–350
amusement parks, 52
Anderson, Joseph, 82, 92
Anderson, Robert, 335
Andersson, Bibi, 158
Angels in America (Kushner), 14